Ezra Pound's Japan

Ezra Pound's Japan

Andrew Houwen

BLOOMSBURY ACADEMIC
LONDON • NEW YORK • OXFORD • NEW DELHI • SYDNEY

BLOOMSBURY ACADEMIC
Bloomsbury Publishing Plc
50 Bedford Square, London, WC1B 3DP, UK
1385 Broadway, New York, NY 10018, USA
29 Earlsfort Terrace, Dublin 2, Ireland

BLOOMSBURY, BLOOMSBURY ACADEMIC and the Diana logo are trademarks of
Bloomsbury Publishing Plc

First published in Great Britain 2021
This paperback edition published 2022

Copyright © Andrew Houwen, 2021

Andrew Houwen has asserted his right under the Copyright, Designs and
Patents Act, 1988, to be identified as Author of this work.

For legal purposes the Acknowledgements on p. ix constitute an extension
of this copyright page.

Cover design: Namkwan Cho

All rights reserved. No part of this publication may be reproduced or transmitted
in any form or by any means, electronic or mechanical, including photocopying,
recording, or any information storage or retrieval system, without prior
permission in writing from the publishers.

Bloomsbury Publishing Plc does not have any control over, or responsibility for, any
third-party websites referred to or in this book. All internet addresses given in this
book were correct at the time of going to press. The author and publisher regret any
inconvenience caused if addresses have changed or sites have ceased to exist,
but can accept no responsibility for any such changes.

A catalogue record for this book is available from the British Library.

A catalog record for this book is available from the Library of Congress.

ISBN: HB: 978-1-3501-7430-6
PB: 978-1-3502-1680-8
ePDF: 978-1-3501-7431-3
eBook: 978-1-3501-7432-0

Typeset by Deanta Global Publishing Services, Chennai, India

To find out more about our authors and books visit www.bloomsbury.com and
sign up for our newsletters.

To David Ewick, to whom any study of Pound and Japan owes more than anyone else.

Contents

Acknowledgements ix
Note on the text x
List of abbreviations xi

1 Ezra Pound's Japan   1

Part One Pound and *hokku*

2 Herbert Spencer's 'minor image', Masaoka Shiki and the
   Meiji reinvention of haiku   23
3 Symphonies in white: Basil Hall Chamberlain and the
   introduction of '*hokku*' into English   41
4 Pound's '"Metro" hokku'   60

Part Two Pound and nō

5 'Nobody thought nō would rise again': Umewaka Minoru
   and the Meiji revival of nō   81
6 Ernest Fenollosa's 'single image' and the introduction of nō
   into English   97
7 'One of the great arts of the world': Pound's first nō translations 117
8 'Growing together': Pound's Japanese friends, nō and the
   genesis of *The Cantos*   136
9 'The closest parallel to my thought': Pound's nō plays and
   accomplishments   154

Part Three Nō and *The Cantos*

10 'Grow with the pines of Ise': Pound's early cantos and nō   175
11 'A treasure like nothing we have in the Occident': Pound's
   wartime cantos and nō   196
12 'The light sings eternal': Nō's place in the *Paradiso* of Pound's
   later cantos   217

Bibliography 239
Index of Published Works by Pound 252
Index of Names 254

Acknowledgements

This project began during a two-year Japan Society for the Promotion of Science (JSPS) fellowship at Tokyo Woman's Christian University (TWCU). I am grateful to the JSPS, TWCU, and, in particular, the unfailing patience, kindness, and dedication of my fellowship mentor, Eiichi Hara. I came to TWCU to study with David Ewick, undoubtedly the world's leading expert on the relationships between Anglophone poetry and Japan; he has been extremely generous in his lending of countless, often rare, books related to this book's theme, and I have benefited greatly from his knowledgeable conversation and everything that he has done for the study of Pound and Japan. The librarians at TWCU, the Bodleian Japanese Library, the Beinecke Rare Books and Manuscripts Library, the Museum of Modern Japanese Literature, the National Diet Library, and the Museum of Modern Art, Kanagawa and Hayama have always been invaluable in their assistance. I am also indebted to the many fruitful discussions with the co-presenters at the Ezra Pound International Conferences and those of the Ezra Pound Society of Japan. Finally, I would like to thank my wife, Gladys, for her love and support throughout the writing of this book.

Note on the text

Unless otherwise acknowledged, all translations from non-English texts are my own. Japanese names are presented in Japanese order, with the surname appearing first, unless they have published in English with Western name order. Writers and artists with a *gō* (artistic sobriquet), such as Hokusai, are always referred by this after the first mention and listed according to their *gō* in the Index.

Abbreviations

Published Works

17-27	Ezra Pound, *A Draft of the Cantos 17-27* (London: John Rodker, 1928).
CCP	Carroll F. Terrell, *A Companion to* The Cantos *of Ezra Pound*, 2nd edn (Berkeley: University of California Press, 1993).
DF	Ezra Pound, *Drafts and Fragments* (New York: New Directions, 1968).
ECJA	*Epochs of Chinese and Japanese Art: An Outline History of East Asiatic Design*, 2 vols (New York: Frederick A. Stokes, 1912).
EFF	*The Ernest F. Fenollosa Papers: The Houghton Library, Harvard University*, ed. Akiko Murakata, 3 vols (Tokyo: Museum Press, 1987).
EPJ	*Ezra Pound & Japan: Letters & Essays*, ed. Sanehide Kodama (Redding Ridge: Black Swan, 1987).
GCNTJ	*A Guide to Ezra Pound and Ernest Fenollosa's* Classic Noh Theater *of Japan*, ed. Akiko Miyake et al. (Orono: National Poetry Foundation, 1994).
GK	Ezra Pound, *Guide to Kulchur* (Norfolk: New Directions, 1938).
L	*The Letters of Ezra Pound, 1907-1941*, ed. D. D. Paige (London: Faber & Faber, 1951).
L/ACH	*Ezra Pound's Letters to Alice Corbin Henderson*, ed. Ira Nadel (Austin: University of Texas Press, 1993).
L/HP	*Ezra Pound to His Parents: Letters 1895-1929*, ed. A. David Moody, Joanna Moody and Mary de Rachewiltz (Oxford: Oxford University Press, 2010).

L/JQ	*The Selected Letters of Ezra Pound to John Quinn*, ed. Timothy Materer (Durham: Duke University Press, 1991).
L/MA	*Pound/The Little Review: The Letters of Ezra Pound to Margaret Anderson*, ed. Thomas L. Scott et al. (New York: New Directions, 1988).
NA	Ernest Fenollosa and Ezra Pound (eds), *'Noh' or Accomplishment: A Study of the Classical Stage of Japan* (London: Macmillan, 1916).
PC	Ezra Pound, *The Pisan Cantos of Ezra Pound* (Norfolk: New Directions, 1948).
PE	Hugh Kenner, *The Pound Era* (Berkeley: University of California Press, 1971).
PMN	Ezra Pound, *Plays Modelled on the Noh (1916)*, ed. Donald C. Gallup (Toledo: The Friends of the University of Toledo Libraries, 1987).
SC	James Longenbach, *Stone Cottage: Pound, Yeats & Modernism* (Oxford: Oxford University Press, 1988).
SRD	Ezra Pound, *Section: Rock-drill de los cantares* (New York: New Directions, 1956).
SZ	Shiki, *Shiki zenshū*, ed. Masaoka Chūsaburō, 22 vols (Tokyo: Kōdansha, 1975–8).
T	Ezra Pound, *The Translations of Ezra Pound* (Norfolk: New Directions, 1953).
TDLC	Ezra Pound, *Thrones 96-109 de los cantares* (New York: New Directions, 1959).
UMN	Umewaka Minoru, *Nikki*, ed. Umewaka Rokurō and Torigoe Bunzō, 7 vols (Tokyo: Yagi shoten, 2003).
VR	Helen Carr, *The Verse Revolutionaries: Ezra Pound, H. D. & the Imagists* (London: Jonathan Cape, 2009).
WT	Ezra Pound, *Women of Trachis*, Hudson Review 6, no. 4 (Winter 1954): 487–523.
XVI	Ezra Pound, *A Draft of XVI Cantos for the Beginning of a Poem of Some Length* (Paris: Three Mountains Press, 1925).

XXX	Ezra Pound, *A Draft of XXX Cantos* (Paris: Hours Press, 1930).
YT	Ōwada Takeki (ed.), *Yōkyoku tsūkai*, 2nd edn, 8 vols (Tokyo: Hakubunkan, 1896).

Archives

EPP	Ezra Pound Papers, YCAL MSS 43, Yale Collection of American Literature, Beinecke Rare Book and Manuscript Library, Yale University. References to *EPP* are followed by folder number.
MFBTK	Materials Formerly Belonging to Tamijuro Kume. The Museum of Modern Art, Kamakura & Hayama. References to *MFBTK* are followed by folder number.

1

Ezra Pound's Japan

'Of your country', a 25-year-old Ezra Pound wrote on 2 September 1911 to a Japanese poet, Yone Noguchi (1875–1947), 'I know almost nothing – surely if the east & the west are ever to understand each other that understanding must come slowly & come first through the arts'.¹ 'Almost', not 'nothing', because as a student in Philadelphia he had read James McNeill Whistler's conclusion to his 'Ten O'Clock Lecture', in which he claims that 'the story of the beautiful is already complete [. . .] with the birds, upon the fan of Hokusai – at the foot of Fusi-yama [sic]'.² In the five years following his letter to Noguchi, Pound embarked on an exploration of Japanese literature that helped to shape him as a poet during a crucial formative phase of his career. Noguchi had sent Pound along with his introductory letter of 16 July that year a copy of his latest volume, *The Pilgrimage*, which included six 'Hokku'.³ The year after their correspondence began, Pound submitted to *Poetry* 'In a Station of the Metro', which he described to its editor, Harriet Monroe, as his '"Metro" hokku'.⁴ It served as an example of the 'Imagiste' movement he had started that summer, which famously demanded that poets avoid 'mixing an abstraction with the concrete', 'Use no superfluous word', and employ 'the natural object' as 'the adequate symbol':

> The apparition   of these faces   in the crowd:
> Petals   on a wet, black   bough.⁵

This poem's role in Pound's poetic development is emphasized by Pound himself soon after its appearance in *Poetry*: in 'How I Began', published on 6 June 1913 in *T. P.'s Weekly*, he discussed it as one of his most important poems and imagined

---

1. Ezra Pound, letter to Yone Noguchi (2 September 1911), in *EPJ*, 4.
2. James McNeill Whistler, *The Gentle Art of Making Enemies*, 2nd edn (New York: G. F. Putnam's Sons, 1892), 159; Jo Brantley Berryman, 'Ezra Pound and James McNeill Whistler: Modernism and Conceptual Art', in Roxana Preda (ed.), *Ezra Pound and the Arts* (Edinburgh: Edinburgh University Press, 2019), 163.
3. Yone Noguchi, *The Pilgrimage*, 2nd edn, vol. 2 (London: Elkin Mathews, 1909), 137–42.
4. Pound, letter to Harriet Monroe (30 March 1913), in *L*, 53.
5. Pound, 'A Few Don'ts by an Imagiste', *Poetry* 1, no. 6 (March 1913): 201 and 206; Pound, 'In a Station of the Metro', *Poetry* 2, no. 1 (April 1913): 12.

Japan as a 'very old, very quiet civilization' in which 'some one might understand the significance' of his '"Metro" hokku'.⁶ The idea of 'Japan' thus began to take root in Pound as a contrast with a West that seemed to him indifferent to someone 'homesick / After mine own kind that know, and feel / And have some breath for beauty and the arts', as he puts it in his poem 'In Durance', composed before his departure for Europe in 1908.⁷

The poem's importance within Pound's oeuvre was further underscored in his 'Vorticism' essay of September 1914, named after the movement he had founded with Henri Gaudier-Brzeska and Wyndham Lewis that year. In his emphasis on avoiding the decay of 'images' into 'figures of speech', Pound used the Japanese '*hokku*' as an example of 'the language of exploration', that is, for the arresting new metaphor.⁸ 'The Japanese have had this sense of exploration' and have 'evolved' the '*hokku*'; Pound then cites his translation of one by Arakida Moritake (1473–1549):

> The fallen blossom flies back to its branch:
>   A butterfly.⁹

This is followed with a '*hokku*' by a 'Japanese naval officer' before Pound presents 'In a Station of the Metro'.¹⁰ Pound conceives of these as a 'one-image poem', which is 'a form of super-position, that is to say, it is one idea set on top of the other'.¹¹ This method of 'superposition' he likens to Whistler's 'arrangement in colour'. The '*hokku*' was thus, according to Pound's own account, a vital model for both the Imagist and Vorticist schools he founded in London.

The importance of *hokku* for Pound's Imagist and Vorticist movements has been acknowledged from the outset in critical studies of Pound. Fellow Imagist F. S. Flint, who had translated two '*haikai*' in 1908, implies in his 1915 'History of Imagism' that Pound's interest in Japanese forms stemmed from their writing of 'dozens' of '*tanka* and *haikai*' for the Thursday meetings of the 1909 group of poets that included Flint, T. E. Hulme, and Pound, and later gave rise to the Imagists.¹² 'In a Station of the Metro', in particular, gained widespread exposure in popular anthologies such as Louis Untermeyer's *Modern American Poetry: An Introduction*, which went through six editions from 1919 to the Second World War

---

[6] Pound, 'How I Began', *T. P.'s Weekly* (6 June 1913): 707.
[7] Pound, 'In Durance', in *Personae* (London: Elkin Mathews, 1909), 41.
[8] Pound, 'Vorticism', *The Fortnightly Review* n. s. 102, no. 573 (1 September 1914): 466.
[9] Ibid., 466–7 and 467.
[10] Ibid., 466–7.
[11] Ibid., 467.
[12] Flint, 'The History of Imagism', *The Egoist* 5, no. 11 (1 May 1915): 71.

and was even included in the US Army's *Education Manual* in 1942, while Pound was broadcasting on Rome Radio.[13] When critical attention shifted to Pound's work following the award of the Bollingen Prize in 1948 for his *Pisan Cantos*, *hokku*'s role in Pound's development was given prominence: Stanley Coffman's *Imagism; A Chapter in the History of American Poetry*, published in 1951, saw 'In a Station of the Metro' as the 'defining' poem of Imagism and identified 'the *hokku*' as 'the model' for it.[14] Hugh Kenner's *The Poetry of Ezra Pound* of the same year went further, claiming not only that Pound 'experimented' with 'the Japanese *hokku* [. . .] extensively', but that 'The *Pisan Cantos* are full of *hokku*'.[15] As David Ewick observes, Kenner's provocative claim about the importance of *hokku* for Pound throughout his career has been repeated in countless subsequent retellings of Pound's engagement with Japanese literature.[16]

J. B. Harmer's account of Pound's interest in *hokku*, in *Victory in Limbo: Imagism 1908-1917*, first proposed that Pound's source may have been Basil Hall Chamberlain because of their shared use of a two-line form rather than the three now conventional in English translations.[17] This claim is repeated in Helen Carr's *The Verse Revolutionaries: Ezra Pound, H. D. & The Imagists* of 2009. In the same year as Carr's publication, however, Yoshinobu Hakutani's *Haiku and Modernist Poetics* argued that Pound's use of the term '*hokku*' makes it 'most likely' that Pound's interest in it had been instigated by Noguchi.[18] Kiuchi Toru goes further, contending that 'none other than Noguchi' was Pound's inspiration.[19] Regarding the subject matter for 'In a Station of the Metro', Rupert Arrowsmith speculates that Pound may have read an English translation by Arthur Waley and Inada Hogitarō accompanying a Hokusai *nishiki-e* at the British Museum, of a *waka* by the ninth-century poet Ono no Komachi:

> While I have been sauntering through
> > the world, looking upon its vanities, lo!
> My flower has faded and the time of the long rains come.[20]

---

[13] Pound, 'In a Station of the Metro', in Louis Untermeyer (ed.), *Modern American Poetry: An Introduction* (New York: Harcourt, Brace and Howe, 1919), 137; Pound, 'In a Station of the Metro', in United States Armed Forces Institute, *Education Manual 131* (Washington, DC: War Department, 1942), 345.

[14] Stanley Coffman, *Imagism: A Chapter in the History of American Poetry* (Norman: University of Oklahoma Press, 1951), 149.

[15] Hugh Kenner, *The Poetry of Ezra Pound* (Norfolk: New Directions, 1951), 63.

[16] Ewick, 'Imagism Status Rerum and A Note on Haiku', *Make It New* 2, no. 1 (2015): 52.

[17] J. B. Harmer, *Victory in Limbo: Imagism 1908-1917* (London: Secker & Warburg, 1975), 133.

[18] Yoshinobu Hakutani, *Haiku and Modernist Poetics* (Basingstoke: Palgrave Macmillan, 2009), 73.

[19] Kiuchi Toru, 'Noguchi Yonejirō – haiku wo sekai ni hirometa hito' ('Noguchi Yonejirō – The Person Who Spread Haiku Around the World'), *Kadokawa haiku* 66, no. 10 (September 2016): 118.

[20] Rupert Richard Arrowsmith, *Modernism and the Museum: Asian, African and Pacific Art and the London Avant-Garde* (Oxford: Oxford University Press, 2011), 122.

Arrowsmith suggests that '"In a Station of the Metro" offers in its closing line an image strikingly similar to this contrast between the pale, fallen *hanami* petals and rain-wet cherry wood'.[21] This image arises from Waley's and Inada's translation rather than the Hokusai print: although the latter shows an elderly woman and a man sweeping blossoms, it depicts a dry spring day.

What no account of Pound's interest in *hokku* has as yet attempted, however, is a detailed examination of the Meiji-era (1868–1912) Japanese contexts that enabled Pound's discovery of '*hokku*' in the first place, which Chapter 2 does. Just as Pound's encounter with Noguchi introduced him to this poetic form, a then 21-year-old student, Masaoka Shiki (1867–1902), came across Herbert Spencer's *The Philosophy of Style*, which would play a pivotal role in Shiki's reforms of 'haiku', the term Shiki popularized. These reforms led to its rise to literary respectability in Japan. In 1889, Shiki wrote in his notebook how Spencer's 'minor image', in which something is communicated through a suggestive visual detail, resembled Bashō's famous 'old pond' *hokku*.[22] Shiki's 1892 English essay on 'Baseo [*sic*] as a Poet' also demonstrates his reading of *The Philosophy of Style*: it argues that 'if the rule that best is the simplest holds good in rhetoric, our Japanese "hotsku" [. . .] must be best of literature [*sic*]'.[23] Spencer proposes that 'the more simple and the better arranged' language is, 'the greater will be the effect produced', adding Polonius's aphorism in *Hamlet* that 'brevity is the soul of wit'.[24] Shiki realized that the *hokku* could be considered as the 'best of literature' according to Spencer's ideas because, when read as an independent poem, it most conforms to Spencer's principles of concretion (the 'minor image') and concision ('brevity'). While many traditions were being swept away by Western 'modernity', Shiki was thus able to argue for *hokku*'s preservation on Western terms.

Shiki's understanding of *hokku* also developed an emphasis on the use of juxtaposition that likewise echoes passages in *The Philosophy of Style*. Spencer had written that 'The opposition of two thoughts that are the reverse of each other in some prominent trait, insures an impressive effect', such as the 'visual antithesis' of black and white: 'a patch of black on a white ground looks blacker', he explains, 'than elsewhere'.[25] In his 1892–3 series of essays on *hokku*, *Dassai shoōku haiwa* ('Talks from the Otter's Den'), Shiki explains how the *kireji* ('cutting-word', an expression marking a division between the two parts of a

---

[21] Ibid.
[22] Shiki, *Fudemakase* ('Scribblings'), ed. Kanai Keiko et al. (Tokyo: Iwanami Shoten, 2003), 108–9.
[23] *SZ*, 16.
[24] Spencer, *The Philosophy of Style* (New York: Appleton & Co., 1872), 10–11.
[25] Ibid., 44–5.

hokku) 'stands between the main element [*shu*] and supporting element [*kyaku*] of the *hokku*'.[26] The use of contrast can be seen in many of Shiki's *hokku*, such as this one, composed in 1891:

> *fuyugare ya inaka musume no utsukushiki*
> winter desolation – the country girl's beauty[27]

The *kireji* '*ya*' marks a contrast or comparison. Here, the 'winter desolation' and the girl's youth (implied in '*musume*', literally 'daughter') and 'beauty' reinforce one another through a Spencerian 'antithesis'. It is through such an antithesis of the *hokku*'s main and supporting elements that, in Shiki's view, the *hokku*'s 'unity' is achieved. In the same series of articles, he first began using the term 'haiku' for an independent 'starting verse' ('*hokku*') of a *haikai renga* ('comic linked verse sequence'). He argued that *haikai renga*, unlike independent 'haiku', are not 'literature' (*bungaku*) because they have 'no unity'.[28] It was their arrangement of a main and supporting element, he felt, that gave them unity. His later encounter with the painter Nakamura Fusetsu (1866–1943) confirmed his belief in the importance of an aesthetics of structural unity.

Shiki thus brought about a revision of the *hokku*'s status in Japan. Before these reforms, it was considered 'common' (*zoku*), not 'refined' (*ga*) poetry.[29] This view resulted in its peripheral status in its earliest translations into English, as Chapter 3 explains. The first, W. G. Aston's three '*hokku*' in 1877, were described by their translator as not even 'deserv[ing] the name of poetry' and lacking even 'a quasi-classical character'.[30] For similar reasons, Chamberlain's 1880 anthology, *The Classical Poetry of the Japanese*, did not include a single one. The turning point came in 1898, when the popular writer Lafcadio Hearn included two chapters on 'hokku' in *Exotics and Retrospectives*, in which the first English version of Bashō's 'old pond' *hokku* appeared.[31] Hearn's source, his Imperial University student Ōtani Masanobu, had taken the 'hokku' from an anthology by a Shiki disciple, Mizuochi Roseki (1872–1919). After Hearn's publication, Aston and Chamberlain both began writing much more about this form: Aston now dedicated an entire chapter to them in *A History of Japanese Literature* in 1899; and in 1902, Chamberlain published a 119-page essay on

---

[26] SZ, 205.
[27] Shiki, *Kushū* ('Collection of Ku'), ed. Takahama Kyoshi (Tokyo: Iwanami Shoten, 2013), 16.
[28] Ibid., 258.
[29] Gabō Sanjin, 'Jo' ('Preface'), in Takenouchi Gengenichi (ed.), *Haika kijin dan* ('Conversations on Outstanding Haikai Writers') (Osaka, 1816), n. p.
[30] W. G. Aston, *A Grammar of the Japanese Written Language*, 2nd edn (Yokohama: Lane, Crawford, 1877), 208.
[31] Lafcadio Hearn, *Exotics and Retrospectives* (Boston: Little, Brown & Co., 1898).

'Bashō and the Japanese Poetical Epigram', which used the term '*Haiku*' for the first time in English as an alternative to '*Hokku*' and acknowledged Shiki as an important influence.[32] He claims that 'it is intensely modern' and resembles 'the work of the Western water-colorist of to-day'.[33] Extending the painterly analogy, he compares one of Yamazaki Sōkan's (1465–1553) '*Hokku*' to Whistler's paintings, describing it as a 'delicate symphony in white'.[34] Pound's reception of '*hokku*' was thus not only made possible by Shiki's revival of this form; its resultant reception in English also foreshadowed his association of it with a Whistlerian visual aesthetics in 'Vorticism'.

Hakutani's and Kiuchi's view that Noguchi must have been Pound's source for his interest in *hokku* because of their shared use of the term '*hokku*', though, is contradicted by the fact that Aston, Hearn, Chamberlain, and numerous other English translators who had also used it rather than Flint's '*haikai*'. Moreover, as Chapter 3 demonstrates, Noguchi's 'Hokku' are always written with a five-seven-five syllable count in three lines rather than Pound's two; they also frequently contain the kinds of concrete–abstract combinations ('Heaven's gate') against which Pound's Imagist dicta strove.[35] Only two English translators – Chamberlain and F. V. Dickins – had presented '*hokku*' in two lines before 1912. Despite Harmer's claim to the contrary, Chamberlain did translate the Moritake '*hokku*' Pound includes in 'Vorticism'.[36] In 'Bashō and the Japanese Poetical Epigram', Chamberlain's version reads:

> Fall'n flow'r returning to the branch, —
> Behold! it is a butterfly.[37]

This anticipates Pound's use of punctuation and lineation to foreground the comparison and contrast between the poem's two elements, the 'flow'r'/'blossom' and the 'butterfly', an approach also evident in Pound's '"Metro" hokku'. Chamberlain's painterly analogy for '*hokku*' also resembles Pound's in 'How I Began' and 'Vorticism'. '*Hokku*' thus came to function as an important model for Pound's Vorticist poetics of concretion, concision, 'superposition', and the 'one-image poem'. This model had been made available by changes in Japanese Meiji-era poetry, especially Shiki's emphasis on Spencer's tenets of the 'minor

[32] Basil Hall Chamberlain, 'Bashō and the Japanese Poetical Epigram', *The Transactions of the Asiatic Society of Japan* 30 (1902): 243 and 303.
[33] Ibid., 246–7.
[34] Ibid., 265.
[35] Noguchi, *The Pilgrimage*, vol. 2, 140.
[36] Harmer, *Victory in Limbo*, 133.
[37] Chamberlain, 'Bashō', 312.

image', 'brevity', and 'antithesis' and on 'unity'. The development of Pound's *hokku*-inspired poetics took place in the context of these global shifts.

Hokku were, of course, not the only Japanese model for Pound's poetics. At the end of his 'Vorticism' essay, he explains:

> I am often asked whether there can be a long imagiste or vorticist poem. The Japanese, who evolved the hokku, evolved also the Noh plays. In the best 'Noh' the whole play may consist of one image. I mean it is gathered about one image. Its unity consists in one image, enforced by movement and music. I see nothing against a long vorticist poem.[38]

Since the end of 1913, Pound had been translating Japanese nō plays. On 29 September 1913, Pound dined with Mary McNeil Fenollosa, widow of the Japanologist Ernest Fenollosa; Mary told Pound that she wished to give to him Ernest's nō notes and translations for him to edit and publish.[39] Pound received the first of these before staying as W. B. Yeats's secretary at Stone Cottage that winter, where he set about editing them. *Nishikigi* was published in *Poetry* in May 1914 and *Kinuta* and *Hagoromo* in the October 1914 *Quarterly Review*. Pound's first reaction was enthusiastic: he told Monroe when submitting *Nishikigi* that the nō were 'beautiful' and that his versions ranked 'as re-creation' rather than 'translation'; he introduced nō in the *Quarterly Review* as 'one of the greatest and least-known arts in the world'.[40] When 'Vorticism' appeared, Pound was translating the nō that appeared in *The Drama* in May 1915: *Sotoba Komachi, Kayoi Komachi, Suma Genji, Kumasaka, Shojo, Tamura* and *Tsunemasa*. Pound identified in these what he saw as the 'one-image' structure of *hokku*: nō has 'Unity of Image. At least, the better plays are all built into the intensification of a single Image', such as the 'red maple leaves and snow flurry in *Nishikigi*' and 'the pines in *Takasago*'.[41]

Pound's suggestion in 'Vorticism' that nō showed a way towards writing a 'long imagiste or vorticist poem' eventually played an important part in the genesis of *The Cantos* in the summer of 1915. In addition to Fenollosa's nō notes and translations, Pound had also begun to receive assistance from several Japanese collaborators. In April 1915, Pound met the Japanese dancer Itō Michio, who, with his friends the painter Kume Tamijūrō and the poet and playwright Kōri Torahiko, performed nō for him and Yeats in June. Itō also danced some

---

[38] Ibid., 471.
[39] Pound, letter to Dorothy Shakespear (2 October 1913), in *L/DS*, 264.
[40] Pound, letter to Monroe (31 January 1914), in *L*, 69; Pound, 'The Classical Drama of Japan', *Quarterly Review* 221, no. 441 (October 1914): 450.
[41] *NA*, 224.

of Pound's nō translations with a series of *kembu* ('sword-dances') translated by Pound and 'Masirni Utchiyama' that autumn.[42] During his third winter at Stone Cottage, as Chapter 9 will show, Pound not only completed further nō translations – *Awoi no Uye*, *Kagekiyo* and *Kakitsubata* – but also wrote his own nō, *A Supper at Mademoiselle Rachel* and *Tristan*, and two kyōgen (comic interludes for nō), *The Protagonist* and *The Consolations of Matrimony*, the last of which he intended to have performed with Yeats's *At the Hawk's Well* in April 1916. In September 1916, Pound had *Certain Noble Plays of Japan*, which collected four of Pound's nō translations – *Nishikigi*, *Hagoromo*, *Kumasaka* and *Kagekiyo* – published with Yeats's sister Elizabeth's Cuala Press; and in January 1917, fifteen of Pound's nō translations with Fenollosa's notes and Pound's commentary appeared with Macmillan. When Pound heard that Macmillan had accepted it for publication, he told his father that it was 'quite a step onward'.[43] In the years 1911 to 1916, then, *hokku*, *kembu* and nō in particular played a crucial role in Pound's poetic development.

Whereas Pound's interest in '*hokku*' has been discussed at great length in Pound studies despite, as Ewick notes, his only mentioning the term eight times in print nō's importance for Pound has been neglected in much of Pound scholarship.[44] Ewick traces this tendency back to Kenner. *The Poetry of Ezra Pound* only contains one reference to nō.[45] Moreover, Kenner's introduction to *The Translations of Ezra Pound*, which includes all of Pound's previously published nō translations, is scathing about nō's importance for Pound. His nō translations are 'exotic, thin, appreciated rather than lived', which 'prevents the *Noh* sequence from standing, as *Cathay* does, with his finest original work'.[46] Kenner's conclusion thus repeats T. S. Eliot's view in *Ezra Pound His Metric and Poetry* that 'The Noh are not so important as the Chinese poems' and that '"Cathay" will, I believe, rank [. . .] among Pound's original work: the Noh will rank among his translations'.[47] Several reviewers of the *Translations*, in turn, replicated this position from Kenner's introduction. John Edwards supported this view by quoting a 3 April 1918 letter from Pound to one of his financial benefactors at that time, John Quinn, from D. D. Paige's *The Letters of Ezra Pound 1907-1941*, which had been published in 1951. Pound, Edwards claims, 'never really liked the *Nōh* [sic] plays himself, calling them "unsatisfactory" and "too

---

[42] Pound, 'Sword-Dance and Spear-Dance', *Future* 1, no. 2 (December 1916): 54.
[43] Pound, letter to Homer Pound (20 June 1916), in *L/HP*, 371.
[44] Ewick, 'Imagism Status Rerum', 51.
[45] Ibid., 52.
[46] Hugh Kenner, 'Introduction', in *T*, 13–14.
[47] T. S. Eliot, *Ezra Pound His Metric and Poetry* (New York: Knopf, 1917), 27.

damn soft".[48] Since the publication of this letter in particular, many subsequent commentators to this day have similarly concluded that nō 'came to mean very little to Pound' and that his nō translations 'stand apart from the central line of Pound's studies with language'.[49]

In the same year as Kenner's *The Poetry of Ezra Pound*, however, Coffman had already briefly pointed out that 'In the "Noh" drama, too, Pound discovered confirmation of his theory of the Image' in their 'Unity of Image', and felt that 'it paralleled the structure sought in an Imagist poem'.[50] Earl Miner's *The Japanese Tradition in British and American Literature* explores the matter in more detail, observing that 'The first notable aspect' of Pound's 'discovery of nō is the enthusiasm it generated in him' from 1913 to 1916, citing as support for this observation another Pound letter, that to Monroe of 1914 describing nō as 'the best piece of luck' for *Poetry* since its founding, and Pound's statement of the following year that nō was 'one of the great arts of the world'.[51] He also draws on Pound's 'Vorticism' essay to claim that Pound's 'efforts to understand and to translate nō contributed an important element to his poetic theory'.[52] Ronald Bush's *The Genesis of the Cantos* proposes that 'The Noh cycle' or 'Ban-Gumi', in which one play of each category (a 'congratulatory' play, a 'battle-piece', 'pieces for females', 'Noh of spirits', a 'moral' play, and another 'congratulatory' play at the end) is performed in succession, especially 'appealed to Pound'.[53] In *Stone Cottage: Pound, Yeats & Modernism*, James Longenbach emphasizes Pound's association of nō during his time at Stone Cottage with a 'cultural elite': nō, as Pound remarks in 1915, is 'for the few, for the nobles, for those trained to catch the allusion'.[54] This evidence has led Ewick to conclude that nō, not *Cathay*, was Pound's 'greatest enthusiasm from the autumn of 1913 through 1916'.[55]

Previous scholarship on Pound's 'discovery of nō' has not yet explored in detail the Meiji-era contexts of nō's revival and the relationship between Fenollosa's aesthetics and his interpretation of nō during that period. Thus far, they have taken on face value Fenollosa's narrative, published by Pound,

---

[48] John Edwards, 'Pound's Translations', *Poetry* 83, no. 4 (January 1954): 235.
[49] Ibid.
[50] Coffman, *Imagism*, 160.
[51] Miner, *The Japanese Tradition in British and American Literature* (Princeton: Princeton University Press, 1958), 135.
[52] Ibid., 140–1.
[53] Ronald Bush, *The Genesis of the Cantos* (Princeton: Princeton University Press, 1976), 105–6 and 109.
[54] *SC*, 44 and 92.
[55] Ewick, 'Ezra Pound and the Invention of Japan, I', *Eibei bungaku hyōron* 63 (2017): 18.

that it was Umewaka Minoru alone 'through whose efforts the *Noh* survived the revolution of 1868'.[56] Drawing extensively on Japanese-language primary texts and scholarship, Chapter 5 interrogates this account and ascribes nō's Meiji-era revival to Empress Dowager Eishō's patronage of nō from 1870 and statesman Iwakura Tomomi's financial support. It also investigates the reciprocal relationship between nō's veneration of imperial rule and its imperial patronage. Nō plays were performed to raise money for the Sino-Japanese and Russo-Japanese wars, composed to celebrate Japan's victories, and even sung by soldiers on the battlefield. This veneration of an imperial rule that patronizes 'recondite' art anticipates Pound's interest in nō's political as well as aesthetic implications. Pound's nō-inspired aesthetics of the 'Unity of Image' or 'single Image', meanwhile, as Chapter 6 explains, derives from Fenollosa's contention that an artwork should be built around a 'single idea' or, as he later put it, a 'single image'.[57] In Fenollosa's view, nō accords with such an aesthetics: in a lecture included in the notes Pound receives, he writes that 'The Beauty and Power of *No* is its concentration. Every element [. . .] unite[s] to produce a single clarified impression'.[58] Although Fenollosa attended lessons with Umewaka in 1883 and again from 1899 to 1901, this conception, as Chapter 6 argues, was primarily developed through Fenollosa's reading of G. W. F. Hegel's lectures on aesthetics.

The importance of the 'Unity of Image' for Pound's Vorticism has, as we have seen, been examined in numerous discussions of Pound's interest in Japanese literature. One of the possibilities that has not yet been sufficiently explored, though, is nō's role in the formation of the 'vortex' metaphor itself. As Carr's *The Verse Revolutionaries* claims, 'Pound [. . .] had of course produced the new name' of the 'Vorticist' movement before the appearance of *BLAST* on 20 June 1914.[59] Pound had sent his 're-creation' of the nō play *Nishikigi* to Monroe on 31 January, after which it was published in the May issue of *Poetry*. Its composition and publication thus occurred in precisely the time leading up to Pound's coining of the term 'Vorticism'. It was the first 'Noh of spirits' Pound translated. The spirits of two lovers lead a travelling

---

[56] NA, 278.
[57] Fenollosa, *Bijutsu shinsetsu* ('An Explanation of the Truth of Art'), trans. Ōmori Ichū (Tokyo: Ryūchikai, 1882), 22; Fenollosa, 'Imagination in Art: Introductory Remarks', *The Annual Report of the Boston Art Students' Association* 15 (June 1894): 5.
[58] Fenollosa, 'Lecture V. No', in Akiko Murakata (ed.), *The Ernest F. Fenollosa Papers: The Houghton Library, Harvard University*, vol. 3 (Tokyo: Museum Press, 1987), 280.
[59] VR, 657–8.

priest to the burial mound where they reside. When the priest wonders, 'Is this illusion?' the man replies:

> You should tell better than we
> How much is illusion –
> We have been in the whirl of
>   those who are fading.[60]

They then perform a dance in which their sleeves are like 'snow-whirls'.[61] This 'whirl', which Pound gives as the play's 'single Image', is that of the dead moving about the present. In his *BLAST* 'Vortex', Pound portrays the 'vortex' as the 'point of maximum energy'; it is 'All the past that is vital, [...] is pregnant in the vortex, NOW' and 'charging the PLACID, NON-ENERGIZED FUTURE'.[62] *Nishikigi*'s 'whirl', as Chapter 7 argues, specifically provides Pound with his conception of the 'vortex' as the past of the 'whirl' of the dead's apparitions 'pregnant in the vortex, NOW'.[63] As Pound would later put it in the preface to his own nō, *A Supper at Mademoiselle Rachel*, it was *Nishikigi* that presented him with 'the closest parallel to my own thought'.[64]

With the outbreak of the First World War came a significant shift in Pound's understanding of nō's 'Unity of Image', which has not as yet received the attention in Pound scholarship that it deserves. In his translation of *Hagoromo*, which had been completed before *Nishikigi*, the role of the emperor's rule in providing the harmonious prosperity depicted in the play is omitted on multiple occasions. By the end of 1914, though, Pound had translated another 'big wad of Jap [sic] plays'.[65] These eventually appeared in *The Drama* in May 1915.[66] Among them was *Tamura*, which commemorates the bodhisattva Kannon giving her blessing to Sakanoue no Tamuramaro's (758–811) military campaign against the 'evil spirits' of the 'pine moor of Anono [sic]' in Ise.[67] Pound's introduction to the play emphasizes its celebration of imperial conquest: 'This play is to be regarded as one of those dealing with the "pacification of the country and the driving out of evil spirits".'[68] This pacification is due to benevolent imperial rule: as the 'plum-trees were

---

[60] Fenollosa (trans.), *Nishikigi*, in *Poetry* 4, no. 2 (May 1914): 43.
[61] Ibid., 48.
[62] Pound, 'Vortex', *BLAST* 1 (20 June 1914): 153.
[63] Ibid., 154.
[64] *PMN*, 23.
[65] Pound, letter to Homer Pound (30 December 1914), in *L/HP*, 340.
[66] Pound, 'The Classical Stage of Japan: Ernest Fenollosa's Work on the Japanese "Noh"', *The Drama* 18 (May 1915): 199–247.
[67] Ibid., 244.
[68] Ibid., 241.

blossoming' in Ise, 'All the scene showed the favour of Kuanon and the virtue of the Emperor'.[69] Pound's translation of *Tamura* thus marks a turning point in his understanding of nō's political implications. *Tamura* reinforced his view of Japan as a 'very old, very quiet country' but now, crucially, he began to ascribe this 'quiet' to a harmony centred around the emperor's rule. Pound's characterization of nō as 'for the few, for the nobles' also appealed to his growing 'sense of a cultural elite'.[70] He now started to identify such an elite with the imperial patronage he also found in his reading of Fenollosa's *Epochs of Chinese and Japanese Art*, in which poets such as Li Bai were supported by the enlightened reign of Emperor Xuanzong (685–762).[71]

Just over a month after the death of his friend, Henri Gaudier-Brzeska, on the western front, Pound sent his version of the nō play *Takasago* to Alice Corbin Henderson, Monroe's assistant editor at *Poetry*. It combines his Vorticist aesthetics of the past 'charging' the present with his politicized 'Unity of Image'. This 'Unity' is expressed in the play's '*sense* of the past time in the present', which accords with Pound's view in *BLAST* of the 'vital' past 'pregnant in the vortex, NOW'.[72] This relationship of the past and the present is explicitly symbolized by the paired pine trees of Takasago, 'the old age of the emperor [*sic*] Manyoshu' and of Sumiyoshi, 'our own time of Engi', separated by 'mountains and rivers' but nonetheless bound together.[73] The '*sense* of the past time in the present' gives the play a temporal as well as spatial unity. An old married couple, later revealed as the spirits of the paired pines, are visited by a travelling priest as they rake the 'inexhaustible' pine needles of imperial, literary, and vegetal regeneration: 'The pine-needles', as the old man tells the priest in Pound's translation, are the 'inexhaustible words' of a literary tradition that is underpinned by imperial rule. As the old man explains, the pines are also 'a sign of the happier reign'.[74] The chorus then sings that 'The waves of the whole sea are quiet, / The whole country well governed', a passage which, Pound notes, was sung every new year in honour of the shōgun, after which the whole play is also performed.[75] *Takasago*, as Chapter 8 proposes, thus demonstrated a symbiosis of literature with military and imperial patronage that anticipates Pound's turn to fascism in the 1920s.

[69] Ibid., 243.
[70] *SC*, 44.
[71] *ECJA*, vol. 1, 118.
[72] *L/ACH*, 110.
[73] Ibid.
[74] Ibid.
[75] Ibid.; Pound, 'The Classical Stage of Japan', 205–6.

By this time, he had met several '"very much over-civilized" young men' from Japan whom Pound later credited with teaching him about nō in London. Pound's friendship with Itō has been widely known since the publication of Paige's edition of Pound's letters, in which Pound relates to Monroe how he is 'very fond of him [. . .] this man is a samurai'.[76] One further friend has not yet been identified, the 'Utchiyama Masirni' from whose notes Pound produced his 'Sword-Dances'.[77] Pound's typescript drafts for these give his name more correctly as 'Utchiyama Masami'.[78] Despite Longenbach's praise for these 'Sword-Dances' and their importance for Pound in commemorating his friends on the frontline, this book is the first to connect these with their *kanshi* originals.[79] It is also the first to claim that the model for the 'Plain, academic, manufactured orientals, / Talking of Emerson, and Hoffmanstahl [*sic*] and Cezanne' was not, as Christine Froula, Ewick and Carrie J. Preston speculate, Itō or Kume, but Kōri.[80] It will explore the contrast between 'samurai' like Itō, as Pound saw him, and Westernized 'orientals' like Kōri that motivated the earliest drafts of *The Cantos*, which were composed on the back of programmes for Pound's 'Sword-Dances': these constituted a critique of Western civilization in contrast with an imagined Eastern harmony. Chapter 9 will also explore Pound's own nō plays, especially in the light of Pound's claim in his preface to *A Supper at Mademoiselle Rachel* that *Nishikigi* presented him with 'the closest parallel to my own thought', discussing in detail both plays' contributions to the further development of Pound's Vorticist poetics.

On 6 February 1917, Pound sent a draft of the first 'Three Cantos' to Henderson for publication in *Poetry*. In an undated note in the corrections for these cantos, which appeared over three issues of *Poetry* from June to August, Pound indicates *Takasago*'s importance for *The Cantos* as a whole:

> The theme is roughly the theme of 'Takasago', which story I hope to incorporate more explicitly in a later part of the poem.[81]

---

[76] Pound, letter to Monroe (25 September 1915), in *L*, 108.
[77] Pound, 'Sword-Dance and Spear-Dance', 54; Pound, letter to Homer Pound (12 November 1915), in *L/HP*, 356–7.
[78] *EPP*, 4278.
[79] *SC*, 201–2. Tara Rodman claims the poems were 'translated from the Japanese'; however, as they were *kanshi*, they were actually written in classical Chinese. Tara Rodman, *Altered Belonging: The Transnational Modern Dance of Itō Michio* (PhD Thesis: Northwestern University, 2017), 74.
[80] *EPP*, 3099; Christine Froula, *To Write Paradise: Style and Error in Pound's Cantos* (New Haven: Yale University Press, 1984), 131; Ewick, 'Draft of Canto IV', in *Japonisme, Orientalism, Modernism*, online; Carrie J. Preston, *Learning to Kneel: Noh, Modernism, and Journeys in Teaching* (New York: Columbia University Press, 2016), 48.
[81] Pound, 'Note to Printer', quoted in Roxana Preda, 'Three Cantos I-III: Calendar of Composition', *The Cantos Project*, online.

As Pound acknowledges, there is no explicit reference to *Takasago* in these 'Three Cantos', but there are to three other nō plays. The first canto's speaker seeks inspiration to begin his poem: 'Whom shall I hang my shimmering garment on / Who wear my feathery mantle, *hagoromo*?' In *Hagoromo*, a celestial maiden's feather mantle is found by a fisherman, who agrees to return it so that she can fly back to heaven if she performs the 'dance of the rainbow-feathered garment'.[82] The speaker thus wishes his poem to take flight and find a way to heaven. This way is lighted by Kannon, who comes as a 'Bright flame upon the river', as in *Tamura*, where she first appears as a 'golden light floating on the Kotsu river'.[83] The second canto contrasts this search for a way to paradise with perseverance through desolation. It compares the Cid's 'fine' assent to his banishment to Kumasaka's ghost, who has 'come back to tell / the honor of the youth who'd slain him', Ushiwaka. In Canto IV, first published in 1919, *Takasago* is incorporated 'more explicitly'. Out of the ruins of Troy and the barbarity of Cabestanh, Vidal and Actaeon's deaths, 'the light' of regeneration 'pours':

> The pines at Takasago
> > grow with the pines of Isé![84]

The canto thus not only contrasts the violence of Cabestanh's, Vidal's and Actaeon's ends with *Takasago*'s regeneration; it also functions, in line with Pound's 1917 note, as the structural model for such a cross-cultural comparison across spatial and temporal distances.

Kume was arranging for Pound to move to Japan when he was killed in the Great Kantō Earthquake in 1923; after that, Pound lost touch with his Japanese friends.[85] In 1936, however, a Japanese poet, Kitasono Katué, began corresponding with him. This revived his admiration for Japan. Nō reflects, he writes in *Guide to Kulchur* (1938), 'a high civilization'.[86] After seeing the Japanese film *Atarashiki tsuchi* ('New Land') in 1939, Pound told Kitasono that 'I have <had strong> nostalgia for Japan' because of its nō scene.[87] 'ALL the Noh plays ought to be filmed', he demanded, because 'It is like no other music'.[88] Pound praised nō as 'a treasure like nothing in the Occident'.[89] Nō also reappeared in *The Cantos*. While Pound

---

[82] NA, 172.
[83] Pound, 'Three Cantos – I', *Poetry* 10, no. 3 (June 1917): 119–20; NA, 84.
[84] XVI, 15.
[85] Kume, letter to Pound (24 March 1923), in *EPJ*, 23.
[86] GK, 81.
[87] Pound, letter to Kitasono (3 March 1939), in *EPJ*, 73.
[88] Ibid.
[89] Pound, 'Tri-lingual System Proposed for World Communications: Noted Scholar of Noh Suggests Bilingual or Trilingual Edition of Hundred Best Books of Japanese Literature', *Japan Times and Mail* (15 May 1939): 4.

was incarcerated at Pisa, 'Kuanon of all delights' returns to console the speaker of Canto LXXIV.[90] Pound portrays the Japanese soldiers in the Philippines as 'remembering Kagekiyo', the warrior whose 'Bushido spirit' Pound had lauded on many occasions, and compares their honour in defeat with the bandit Kumasaka.[91] He imagines himself as 'Genji at Suma', the exiled lover in *Suma Genji* and, in Canto LXXVII, as Awoi, the wronged wife in *Awoi no Uye*.[92] In Canto LXXVI, he remembers Kume and Itō.[93] 'Greek rascality' is contrasted with 'Hagoromo' and 'Kumasaka' with 'vulgarity' in Canto LXXIX; 'Give back my cloak, *hagoromo*', the canto's speaker demands in Canto LXXX, wishing he could also return to 'the clouds of heaven'.[94] Pound also wrote two nō-inspired translations of Greek tragedies, *Elektra* (1949) and *Women of Trachis* (1954). At the end of *The Cantos*, too, 'Kuanon', the irises commemorating Ariwara no Narihira's love for Fujiwara no Takaiko in *Kakitsubata*, 'Awoi', and the poet Ono no Komachi, who laments her lost youth in *Sotoba Komachi*, all come back to him as he contemplates his life's end.[95]

The reason for critics like Kenner and Edwards arriving at the conclusion that nō 'came to mean very little to Pound' was that, while they had almost certainly read Pound's 1918 letter to Quinn criticizing it as 'too damn soft', they almost certainly had not read Pound's then unpublished letter expressing his 'nostalgia for Japan' after seeing nō or Pound's *Japan Times and Mail* articles. Miner's 1958 study called attention to 'The pines at *Takasago*' in Canto IV and to this motif's repetition in Canto XXIX.[96] Myles Slatin was the first to publish Pound's note explaining that *The Cantos* would be based 'on the theme of "Takasago"'.[97] Kenner cites it in *The Pound Era*, though he then claims that Pound 'never got round' to translating *Takasago*; Pound's translation was discovered in a donation to Princeton in 1991, however.[98] Carroll F. Terrell's *A Companion to* The Cantos *of Ezra Pound* (1980) observes the repetition of the *Takasago* theme in Canto XXI, in which the correspondence of the 'pines of Isé' and *Takasago* rhymes

---

[90] PC, 6.
[91] Ibid., 20.
[92] Ibid., 43.
[93] Ibid., 40 and 42.
[94] Ibid., 63 and 78.
[95] SRD, 66; DF, 8; ibid., 10.
[96] Miner, *The Japanese Tradition*, 150.
[97] Myles Slatin, 'A History of Pound's Cantos I-XVI, 1915-1925', *American Literature* 35 (March 1963): 186.
[98] PE, 283; Miner, 'Pound and Fenollosa Papers Relating to Nō', *Princeton University Library Chronicle* 53, no. 1 (Autumn 1991): 12–16.

with the swelling of 'the Nile with Inopos'.⁹⁹ *A Guide to Ezra Pound and Ernest Fenollosa's* The Classic Noh Theatre of Japan (1994), edited by Akiko Miyake, Sanehide Kodama and Nicholas Teele, does not mention the Princeton donation but does examine the parallels Pound draws between nō and Greek mythology in *The Cantos*, such as the shared themes of regeneration in *Takasago* and the Eleusinian mysteries in Canto XXI.¹⁰⁰ *Ezra Pound's Radio Operas: The BBC Experiments, 1931-1933* (2002) by Margaret Fisher, meanwhile, points out how Pound's opera *Le Testament*, first performed in 1924, made use of nō-like 'masks, wigs and stylized gestures', thus further suggesting Pound's continued interest in nō into the 1920s.¹⁰¹

Following Miner's introduction of the most important nō references in the *Pisan Cantos*, an increasing understanding of the role of nō plays in the later cantos has developed. Although Kenner paid relatively little attention to nō, he does suggest in *The Pound Era* that, 'Instead' of Pound translating *Takasago*, 'after 40 years its hymn to vegetal powers became the whole of *Rock-Drill*', the collection after the *Pisan Cantos*.¹⁰² The allusions to 'the moon's axe' in *Hagoromo* which is 'renewed' at 'Miwo', an influential precursor for Pound's famous dictum 'make it new', in Canto CVI; to the iris of *Kakitsubata* in Canto CX; and to *Awoi no Uye* and *Sotoba Komachi* in the prayer at the end of Canto CX to 'Awoi or Komachi, / the oval moon' and its implication of fertility, a recurrent theme in *The Cantos* which coincides with that of *Takasago*, are explored in Massimo Bacigalupo's *The Forméd Trace: The Later Poetry of Ezra Pound* (1980).¹⁰³ Another significant advance in the awareness of nō's importance for the later cantos is made in Peter Stoicheff's *The Hall of Mirrors: Drafts and Fragments and the End of Ezra Pound's Cantos*, which proposes that in Canto CX 'the belief' returns that 'respect and ritualistic prayer can transcend the pains of darkness, jealousy, self-recrimination, sin, and old age [. . .] not beneath the poem's foreseen paradisal culmination in the eternal light of the sun, but beneath the Noh moon that is its symbolic reversal'.¹⁰⁴ The feminine aspect Pound had once perceived and rejected in nō is what Pound ultimately returns to for consolation. More recently, Diego Pellecchia's 'Ezra Pound and the Politics of Noh Film' has analysed Pound's

---

[99] *CCP*, 84.
[100] *GCNTJ*, xxix–xxx.
[101] Margaret Fisher, *Ezra Pound's Radio Operas: The BBC Experiments, 1931-1933* (Cambridge, MA: MIT Press, 2002), 37.
[102] *PE*, 284.
[103] Massimo Bacigalupo, *The Forméd Trace: The Later Poetry of Ezra Pound* (New York: Columbia University Press, 1980), 468 and 480.
[104] Peter Stoicheff, *The Hall of Mirrors: Drafts and Fragments and the End of Ezra Pound's Cantos* (Ann Arbor: University of Michigan Press, 1995), 99.

viewing of nō films in 1939, especially *Atarashiki tsuchi*; and Christopher Bush's '"I Am All for the Triangle": The Geopolitical Aesthetic of Pound's Japan' points out the political implications of Pound's revived enthusiasm for nō during the Second World War.[105]

This book will draw extensively on drafts and different editions of *The Cantos* to explore in unprecedented depth the role that nō plays in it. Pound first inserts the 'more explicit' reference to *Takasago* in a draft for Canto IV dated after 21 February 1918. The mention of *Takasago* and *Tamura* ('The Pines of Takasago grow with the Pines of Isé!') is written in pencil between the canto's Actaeon and Vidal sections, thus acting as a focal point connecting sections together.[106] The 'pines of Isé' are, as Terrell notes, the 'pine-moor of Anono' where Kannon drives out the 'evil spirits'; the 'correction' made to render the 'pines' of 'Takasago' and 'Isé' singular in the 1975 edition of *The Cantos*, in the belief that Pound mistook 'Sumiyoshi' for 'Isé', is thus incorrect.[107] The reference to Kannon is clarified in the 'forked tips / flaming as if with lotus': in 'Three Cantos – I', Kannon foots a boat that's 'but a lotus petal' and brings, as in *Tamura*, spring's new growth.[108] The political aspect of both plays' praise of centralized rule is foregrounded in Canto XXI, which compares Lorenzo de' Medici's 'intelligent constructivity' with Thomas Jefferson.[109] The Roman Empire prospered because of the 'great Roman vortex' and 'centralization' and the '*renascimento*' emulated this, Pound claimed in 1915.[110] The comparison of Jefferson and de' Medici is followed by a concluding section celebrating the vegetal and sexual 'source' of such 'renewal' titled, in *A Draft of the Cantos 17-27*, 'Takasago and Ise'.[111] The canto thus appropriates *Takasago* and *Tamura*'s fusion of political and vegetal regeneration and demonstrates how Pound drew on nō's veneration of centralized political rule in combination with its 'Unity of Image'. These pines, 'melted in air' like the 'moon-nymph' at the end of *Hagoromo*, also appear as the closing image of Canto XXIX.[112] *Takasago* and *Tamura*'s pines thus function as a vital 'way to paradise' throughout *A Draft of XXX Cantos*.

---

[105] Diego Pellecchia, 'Ezra Pound and the Politics of Noh Film', *Philological Quarterly* 92/4 (Fall 2013): 499–516; Christopher Bush, '"I Am All for the Triangle": The Geopolitical Aesthetic of Pound's Japan', in Paul Stasi and Josephine Park (eds), *Ezra Pound in the Present: Essays on Pound's Contemporaneity* (London: Bloomsbury, 2016), 75–106.
[106] *EPP*, 3117.
[107] *CCP*, 13; Pound, *The Cantos* (New York: New Directions, 1975), 15.
[108] XVI, 15; Pound, 'Three Cantos – I', 119.
[109] Pound, letter to Isabel Weston Pound (1 November 1924), in *L/HP*, 547.
[110] Pound, 'The Renaissance – II', *Poetry* 5, no. 6 (March 1915): 286.
[111] *17-27*, 27.
[112] XXX, 140.

When Kitasono contacted Pound six years after the publication of *A Draft of XXX Cantos*, he soon rekindled Pound's enthusiasm for nō. Far from losing interest in nō after 1917, Pound began to value it in the strongest terms from 1937 onwards. Pellecchia dates the 'turning point in his engagement' with nō to April 1939, when Pound saw the *Aoi no ue* film in Washington DC, while Ewick detects its 're-emergence' in the mention of nō in *Guide to Kulchur* in 1938.[113] Pound had, however, already responded to hearing about Margaret Leona's adaptation of his *Suma Genji* on the BBC on 7 January 1937 with his proud assertion that 'some of the Beauty has been brought over to the occident'.[114] This view of nō also found its way into his article on 'Totalitarian Scholarship and the New Paideuma', published in the National Socialist *Germany and You* on 25 April 1937: Pound gives as examples of 'primal and valid donations of other races' his rendering of 'the poems of Li Po (Rihaku) and the great plays of Japan ("Kagekiyo", "Hagoromo", etc.) into English'.[115] The fusion of Pound's aesthetics and politics is further encapsulated in Pound's dictum in the *British Union Quarterly* that 'THE STATE SHOULD MOVE LIKE A DANCE'.[116] If there were a dance that then embodied this fusion for Pound, it was nō. The 'strong nostalgia' Pound felt for Japan came from seeing *Atarashiki tsuchi*; as well as discussing the film's use of nō, Chapter 11 examines the film's broader themes in connection with Pound's imagining of Japan, especially its connecting of vegetal and sexual regeneration with benevolent imperial rule. It also explores Pound's references to the spirit of 'bushido' Pound finds in nō, like *Kagekiyo* in his *Japan Times and Mail* articles and Rome Radio broadcasts. It will then analyse the references to nō in the *Pisan Cantos* in the context of this wartime resurgence of interest in nō.

During Pound's hospitalization at St. Elizabeths after the war, he embarked on the translation of Greek tragedies which were influenced by nō, as *Le Testament* had been in 1924. The unfinished *Elektra*'s stage directions, in which Elektra, at a crucial moment in the play, displays a '*Slowness of turning of head, as per Noh*', was inspired by his viewing of the *Aoi no ue* film.[117] Pound also hoped that Umewaka's descendants would add his *Women of Trachis* 'to their [nō] repertoire'.[118] Soon after these translations, Pound began composing further

---

[113] Pellecchia, 'Ezra Pound and the Politics of Noh Film', 503; Ewick, 'Ezra Pound and the Invention of Japan, I', 26.
[114] Pound, letter to Kitasono (29 January 1937), in *EPJ*, 36.
[115] Pound, 'Totalitarian Scholarship and the New Paideuma', *Germany and You* 7, no. 4/5 (25 April 1937): 96.
[116] Pound, 'The State Should Move Like a Dance', *British Union Quarterly* 11, no. 4 (October–December 1938): 44.
[117] Pound and Rudd Fleming (trans.), *Elektra*, ed. Richard Reid (Princeton: Princeton University Press, 1987), 48.
[118] *WT*, 487.

cantos. This book will be the first to explore in detail Kenner's claim that *Takasago* 'became the whole of *Rock-Drill*'. In Canto XC, the 'Beatific spirits welding together / as in one ash-tree in Ygdrasail. / Baucis, Philemon' resemble the old couple in *Takasago*; Furthermore, 'Kuanon', paired with *Takasago* in Cantos IV and XXI, also reappears in that canto to lift the speaker to the heavens; that *Takasago* is alluded to is suggested by the passage in which 'the trees rise / and there is a wide sward between them' in the speaker's vision of paradise.[119] This vision is again underpinned by the prosperity of imperial rule; nō provided Pound with the model for this politicized aesthetics of 'Unity'. Finally, Chapter 12 makes use of Japanese-language sources to shed further light on Pound's first attendance of a live nō performance at the Teatro Eliseo in Rome on 10 June 1970, some two years before his death. Pound met Umewaka's grandson and watched *Aoi no ue* and *Takasago*. Hori Masato, whose nō teacher had taken part in the tour, rightly concluded that Pound's 'love of nō lasted his whole life'.[120] Though he never reached it, Japan had become a home for which Pound always felt a 'strong nostalgia'.

---

[119] *SRD*, 65–6 and 68.
[120] Hori, 'Ezura Paundo to nōgaku' ('Ezra Pound and Nō'), *Tōzai gakujutsu kenkyūsho kiyō* 4 (March 1971): 8.

Part One

Pound and *hokku*

2

Herbert Spencer's 'minor image', Masaoka Shiki and the Meiji reinvention of haiku

In 1889, Masaoka Shiki, then a 21-year-old student at the Preparatory School of the Imperial University, now known as Tokyo University, wrote in his notebook about reading Herbert Spencer's *The Philosophy of Style*:

> When I read Spencer's essay on literary style, *Philosophy of Style*, this spring, as soon as I reached the part about expressing the whole through a *minor image*, that is, expressing it through a part – in other words, not to say something is sad but to show the sadness itself – being the best approach in literature, I struck the desk and was so happy that I knew the 'old pond' *ku*. Having understood this and thought about the *ku*, I saw that it didn't have a difficult meaning at all. It expresses the quietness of the place without so much as using the word 'quiet' or 'still'![1]

Shiki was to become the great reformer of traditional Japanese poetry, and that '*ku*' is now arguably the most famous haiku in the world, Matsuo Bashō's (1644–94) *furuike ya kawazu tobikomu mizu no oto* ('An old pond – a frog jumps in, the sound of water'), composed in 1686. At a time when in Japan so many cultural traditions were being overthrown during the Meiji period, Shiki realized that this traditional form also had great literary value when seen from a Western perspective, and could thus more convincingly be argued to be worth preserving. This moment of discovery would ultimately prove to be pivotal for Pound's reception and understanding of this poetic form, as this and the following two chapters seek to demonstrate.

Shiki read Spencer's essay in an English edition published in Tokyo in 1887.[2] By that time, seventeen translations of Spencer's works had appeared in the preceding twelve years. Spencer's writings – including *The Philosophy of Style* –

---

[1] Shiki, *Fudemakase*, 108–9. Shiki quotes 'minor image' in English.
[2] Spencer, *Philosophy of Style: An Essay* (Tokyo: Kimura & Sons, 1887).

were widely used in English lessons at the Imperial University, which Shiki attended from 1890 to 1892.³ Among those who promoted Spencer's thought in those years was the university's first professor of Political Economy and Philosophy, Ernest Fenollosa, who taught there from 1878 (a year after the university's foundation) to 1886. Fenollosa had been a Spencer enthusiast since his own student days at Harvard between 1870 and 1876, having joined the Herbert Spencer Club there.⁴ Of the forty-eight examination questions that Fenollosa set for his Political Philosophy and History of Philosophy classes at Tokyo University in 1878–9 and 1879–80, for example, one third explicitly mentioned Spencer.⁵ At the time Shiki wrote down his observations on *Philosophy of Style*, then, Spencer's influence on Meiji Japan was at its height.

The qualities that Shiki identified in what were then still called '*hokku*' or '*haikai*' following his reading of *The Philosophy of Style* bear close comparison with those Pound most appreciated about them. The Spencerian '*minor image*' employs a suggestive indirectness that anticipates Pound's well-known Imagist dictum, 'the natural object is always the *adequate* symbol'.⁶ In Bashō's '*ku*', for instance, the sound of the frog jumping into the water suggests, rather than explicitly states, the 'quietness' that Shiki interprets as its principal theme. Three years later, after Shiki had entered the Imperial University to study Japanese Literature, his second-year English essay, 'Baseo [*sic*] as a Poet', discussed another advantage of such '*hokku*'. The essay begins:

> If the rule that best is the simplest holds good in rhetoric, our Japanese 'hotsku' (pronounced 'hokku') must be best of literature at that point. Hotsku which is composed of 17 syllables, should perhaps be the shortest form of verses in the world.⁷

Behind this, too, lies *The Philosophy of Style*. Spencer argues that, 'as in a mechanical apparatus, the more simple and the better arranged' the 'parts' of a language, 'the greater will be the effect produced': the 'friction and inertia' of language as the 'vehicle of thought' should be reduced 'to the smallest possible amount'.⁸ The '*hokku*', Shiki then argues, could also be considered as the 'best of

---

³ Matsui Takako, *Shasei no henyō: Fontanēji kara Shiki, soshite Naoya e* ('The Development of *Shasei*: From Fontanesi to Shiki and Naoya') (Tokyo: Meiji Shoin, 2002), 138.
⁴ Van Wyck Brooks, *Fenollosa and His Circle: With Other Essays in Biography* (New York: E. P. Dutton & Co., 1962), 2.
⁵ Fenollosa, *Published Writings in English*, ed. Yamaguchi Seiichi, vol. 1 (Tokyo: Edition Synapse, 2009), n. p.
⁶ Pound, 'A Few Don'ts', 201.
⁷ *SZ*, vol. 4, 16.
⁸ Spencer, *The Philosophy of Style*, 10–11.

literature' on Spencer's terms because the 'friction and inertia' of language has been reduced to '17 syllables'. Pound, likewise, later demanded in his Imagist manifesto that poets should 'Use no superfluous word', thus also emphasizing concision.[9]

In its advocacy of concision, *The Philosophy of Style* also cites Polonius's saying in *Hamlet* that 'brevity is the soul of wit' and Hugh Blair's *Lectures on Rhetoric and Belles-Lettres*:

> We are told that 'brevity is the soul of wit'. We hear styles condemned as verbose or involved. Blair says that every needless part of the sentence 'interrupts the description and clogs the image'; and again, that 'long sentences fatigue the reader's attention'.[10]

In Spencer's first quotation from Blair, the connection between the principles of concretion and concision is first suggested. In Blair's view, language must transmit an 'image' as efficiently as possible. Spencer similarly considers 'thought' to be grounded in the particularity of sensory impressions – a 'stock of images' – rather than in abstractions:

> This superiority of specific expressions is clearly due to a saving of the effort required to translate words into thoughts. As we do not think in generals but in particulars – as, whenever any class of things is referred to, we represent it to ourselves by calling to mind individual members of it; it follows that when an abstract word is used, the hearer or reader has to choose from his stock of images, one or more, by which he may figure to himself the genus mentioned [. . .] if, by employing a specific term, an appropriate image can be at once suggested, an economy is achieved, and a more vivid impression produced.[11]

Abstraction, like verbosity, Spencer claims, results in inefficiency of linguistic communication, because the hearer or reader must convert it to a particular 'image' from his or her 'stock of images'. Both concision and concretion are therefore considered to increase language's efficiency in producing such 'images' in the reader's mind. Shiki would frequently employ his translation of Spencer's 'vivid impression' ('*inshō meiryō*') in his critical writings on haiku to indicate one of the qualities to which they must aspire.

Spencer goes on to explain how poetry can create such a 'vivid impression'. As one of the means by which 'economy of the recipient's mental energy' can

---

[9] Pound, 'A Few Don'ts', 201.
[10] Spencer, *The Philosophy of Style*, 10.
[11] Ibid., 16.

be achieved, he gives 'the choice and arrangement of the minor images, out of which some large thought is to be built up':

> To select from the sentiment, scene, or event described, those typical elements, which carry many others along with them; and so, by saying a few things but suggesting many, to abridge the description; is the secret of producing a vivid impression. An extract from Tennyson's 'Mariana' will well illustrate this:
>
>> All day within the dreamy house,
>> The door upon the hinges creaked,
>> The blue fly sung i' the pane; the mouse
>> Behind the mouldering wainscot shrieked,
>> Or from the crevice peered about.
>
> The several circumstances here specified bring with them many appropriate associations. Our attention is rarely drawn by the buzzing of a fly in the window, save when everything is still. While the inmates are moving about the house, mice usually keep silence; and it is only when extreme quietness reigns that they peep from their retreats. Hence each of the facts mentioned, presupposing numerous others, calls up these with more or less distinctness; and revives the feeling of dull solitude with which they are connected in our experience. Were all these facts detailed instead of suggested, the attention would be so frittered away that little impression of dreariness would be produced.[12]

In addition to simply selecting fewer words, the most effective concision entails the power of those few words to suggest, rather than explicitly detail, many further elements of the scene described. The selection of each detail is thus also geared towards maximum efficiency. Shiki discovered this in Bashō's *hokku*. He observed that, just as the mouse's shriek in 'Mariana' calls to mind the silence of the rest of the house, the frog's splash suggests the quietness of the old pond 'without using the word "quiet" or "still"'. In both cases the 'image' is therefore more efficiently and vividly produced.

The efficiency of suggestive concision similarly underpins Spencer's preference for metaphors over similes. Referring to Richard Whately's *Elements of Rhetoric*, he writes:

> The superiority of the Metaphor to the Simile is ascribed by Dr. Whately to the fact that 'all men are more gratified at catching the resemblance for themselves, than in having it pointed out to them'. But after what has been said, the great economy it achieves will seem the more probable cause.[13]

---

[12] Ibid., 34–5.
[13] Ibid., 30–1.

Further on in his notebook entry on the connection between Spencer's principles and Bashō's *hokku*, Shiki also draws on Spencer's view of metaphors and similes to argue for the *hokku*'s literary merits. He contrasts Bashō's poem with Shinkei's (1406–75) *chiru hana no oto kiku hodo no miyama kana* ('Deep in the mountains, it is as if you could hear the sound of a petal falling'). 'I do not know which of these two is better, but in Shinkei's *hokku* there is the phrase "*hodo no*" ["as if"] and in Bashō's such words are not used; is Bashō's not perhaps better in this respect?'[14] Shiki implicitly refers to Spencer's dicta: to use explicit terms of comparison such as 'like', 'as if', and '*hodo*' contradicts the principle of suggestive efficiency in producing the most 'vivid impression'. Whereas Shinkei explicitly states the relation between the mountains and the falling petal, Bashō merely suggests that between the old pond and the frog's splash. Later, Pound would comment in his article on 'Vorticism' that in '*hokku*' such comparisons are implicit; in giving one example, he adds the comparative 'like' to his translation of it for the sake of 'clarity' but states that this 'would not occur in the original'.[15]

Not only the suggestiveness, but also the method of juxtaposition in contrasting the pond's silence and the 'sound of water' in Bashō's '*ku*' accords with Spencer's belief in the effectiveness of what he calls 'antithesis': 'The opposition of two thoughts that are the reverse of each other in some prominent trait, insures an impressive effect.'[16] He offers as an example the 'visual antithesis' of black and white: 'a patch of black on a whiter ground looks blacker, and a patch of white on a black ground looks whiter, than elsewhere.'[17] For Spencer, 'Antithesis' is another means by which the 'image' can be more efficiently conveyed. Although Shiki does not explicitly discuss the use of such contrast until a few years later, his early '*hokku*' written at this time are frequently concerned with these kinds of opposition. He wrote the following one in 1891:

> *fuyugare ya inaka musume no utsukushiki*
> winter desolation – the country girl's beauty[18]

The *kireji* (or 'cutting-word') *ya*, also used in Bashō's *hokku*, marks a contrast or comparison between what precedes and follows it. The 'winter desolation' and the girl's youth and 'beauty' reinforce one another; it is through such a 'visual antithesis', then, that the qualities of each are more clearly delineated. Through his reading of Spencer, Shiki could observe how aspects of Bashō's *hokku* –

---

[14] Shiki, *Fudemakase*, 109.
[15] Pound, 'Vorticism', 467.
[16] Spencer, *The Philosophy of Style*, 44.
[17] Ibid., 45.
[18] Shiki, *Kushū*, 16.

concision, concretion, suggestiveness and juxtaposition – marked this poetic form out as not only adhering to an influential Western view of what makes for the 'best' writing but, potentially, as constituting its 'best' example. Such uses of contrast also foreshadow Pound's Vorticist poetics of 'arrangement' and 'superposition'.

Shiki's interest in *hokku* intensified while attending the Imperial University from 1890 to 1892. He embarked on an extensive historical survey of this form and wrote about his findings in *Dassai sho'oku haiwa* ('Haikai Conversations from the Otter's Den'), which was serially published in the newspaper *Nippon* between 28 June 1892 and 25 December 1893. Before Shiki, the *hokku*, or 'starting verse', was traditionally the opening verse of a *haikai renga* ('comic linked-verse sequence'), although many acquired sufficient fame to be inscribed independently on paintings or memorial stones. In response to someone suggesting that 'good taste in *haikai* lies in *haikai renga* and *hokku* are just one small part of these', Shiki argues that the former 'are not literature'.[19] Unlike *hokku*, *haikai renga* have 'no unity or harmony running through them'.[20] Shiki now advocated writing independent *hokku* as works of literature in their own right. In *Dassai sho'oku haiwa*, he began using the term 'haiku' consistently to describe independent *hokku* seen in this way. This revolutionized the manner in which this poetic form was viewed. Behind Shiki's approach, though, lay *The Philosophy of Style*: it is only when *hokku* are considered as independent works that they can constitute the most salient examples of Spencer's principle of concision. In his emphasis on 'unity' as a prerequisite for 'literature', Shiki also anticipated Pound's Vorticist poetics of the 'unity of Image' that he identified in '*hokku*'.

This 'unity or harmony' can be achieved in *hokku*, Shiki argued, through the use of features such as the *kireji* ('cutting word'). He was certainly not the first to theorize about it, but it was particularly important for his understanding of the form. The *kireji*, he writes in *Dassai sho'oku haiwa*, 'stands between the main element [*shu*] and the supporting element [*kyaku*] of the *hokku*'.[21] As an example, he offers an unattributed *hokku* about Sarashina, a place famous for moon-viewing:

sarashina ya tsuki wa yokeredo inaka nite
Sarashina – the moon is good, though it's in the countryside[22]

[19] *SZ*, vol. 4, 258.
[20] Ibid.
[21] Ibid., 205.
[22] Ibid.

Here, the *kireji* is '*ya*', originally an exclamation. 'I am not sure whether this "ya" should be read as an exclamation', Shiki writes, 'but in a haiku it is used to mark the boundary between its phrases. In this *ku*, Sarashina is the main element (*shu*). The *ya* in Bashō's "old pond" *ku* is the same.'[23] In Bashō's '*ku*', the 'old pond' (*furuike*) preceding the *ya* would therefore be the 'main element' and the sound of the water made by the frog the 'supporting element'. It is this ordered and integrated arrangement of the *shu* and *kyaku* elements that gives *hokku* their 'unity' in Shiki's view. The *kyaku* serves to reinforce the centrality of the *shu*. Such uses of the *kireji* later showed Shiki how *hokku* could adhere to Spencer's 'antithesis'.

Although Shiki had deepened his interest in *hokku*, he still wanted to become a novelist at this time. In the same year in which he noted down his discovery of the connection he found between *The Philosophy of Style* and Bashō's '*ku*', he also recorded his enthusiasm for contemporary Japanese novels. One he especially 'loved reading' and wished to emulate was Aeba Kōson (1855–1922): 'now I am leaning towards the Kōson school.'[24] Kōson was also seen as one of the leading critics on what was then still usually known as the *haikai* genre.[25] In 1893, the year after Shiki left the Imperial University to start working as a literary editor for *Nippon*, Kōson published an essay, *Haikai ron* ('On Haikai'), which would turn out to be influential in the form's later reception in English. It demonstrated how, just as Shiki was developing into a *haijin* (a writer of *haikai*, *hokku*, or haiku), the form was already beginning to attract greater critical attention among literary circles in Japan. Kōson outlines its history and considers its contemporary situation.

According to Kōson, *hokku* first became autonomous works in the fifteenth century. It was from the time of Sōgi (1421–1502) and Arakida Moritake (1473–1549), both priests at Ise Shrine, that '*hokku* (a *hokku* is the start of a linked-verse sequence) was not followed by an ensuing verse and was written on its own. This was the start of what is known to many as *haikai*.'[26] Independently written *hokku*, however, remained the exception rather than the norm until Shiki.[27] What Kōson considers Moritake's 'most skilful work' is then cited:

rakka e ni kaeru to mireba kochō kana
   a petal falling from a branch – when seeing it return, a butterfly[28]

---

[23] Ibid.
[24] Shiki, *Fudemakase*, 96.
[25] Yanagida Izumi, 'Meiji bungaku ni okeru haikai seishin' ('The Spirit of Haikai in Meiji Literature'), in *Zuihitsu: Meiji bungaku*, vol. 1 (Tokyo: Heibonsha, 2005), 163.
[26] Kōson, *Sōrinshi hyōshaku haikai ron hakkenden shohyōtōshū* ('Commentary on Sōrinshi, On Haikai, and Various Questions on the *Hakkenden*') (Tokyo: privately printed, 1893), 2.
[27] Sawai Taizō, *Muromachi monogatari to kohaikai: Muromachi no 'chi' no yukue* ('Muromachi Tales and Early Haikai: Where Muromachi's "Knowledge" Went') (Tokyo: Miyai Shoten, 2014), 260.
[28] Kōson, *Sōrinshi*, 3.

The term 'haikai' originally meant 'comic'. Kōson quotes Moritake's view, however, that 'haikai provide elegant taste; moreover, I do not wish for them to be merely ridiculous. While they are comic, they should provide for the taste of a person of refined manners.'[29] Although Kōson does not discuss this *hokku* further, its humorous intent depends upon its allusion to a passage in Dōgen's (1200–53) Zen essay collection *Shōbōgenzō*, in which the Zen monk Hōchi responds to another monk's question, 'What happens if an enlightened person has illusion?' by responding, 'A broken mirror does not reflect again; a flower does not return to its branch.'[30] In other words, once enlightenment is achieved, it cannot be undone. Moritake's *hokku*, in which its viewer has the illusion that he or she sees a leaf returning to its branch, lightheartedly reverses this solemn truth, thus putting into practice his notion of this poetic form as both 'comic' and appealing to the taste of a 'person of refined manners'.

In 1893, Yamazaki Kagotarō (dates unknown) also published *Haikaishi dan* ('A Discussion of Haikai's History'). Yamazaki goes into far more detail than Shiki or Kōson about the development of the form's terminology. 'What is generally called *haikai* by people today is very different from the *haikai* of the past', he observes. What is often meant by '*haikai*' by the time he was writing *Haikaishi dan*, he makes clear, 'is the *hokku* of *haikai renga*': the starting verse of a *haikai* linked-verse sequence.[31] There are thus at least two uses of '*haikai*': one refers to the comic bent of a new kind of *renga* that had emerged by the fifteenth century; the other indicates what independent *hokku* themselves were generally called in the Meiji period before Shiki's reforms. To avoid the confusion arising from the various uses of '*haikai*', Yamazaki advocates using 'haiku', as Shiki had begun to do in his *Nippon* articles by that time: 'It would be more appropriate to say haiku for what people today generally call *haikai*, although in this book I have followed the generally known term *haikai*.'[32] Thus, although Shiki appears to have anticipated Yamazaki's proposed reform by a matter of months, it is the latter who explicitly called for it. It is therefore likely that Shiki's change of terminology was part of a more widespread contemporary trend.

While Kōson emphasizes the need for a revival of '*haikai*' and Yamazaki argues for reforming its terminology, they also serve as examples of the lack of clarity about precisely how it should be revived, aside from a new name. It

---

[29] Ibid.
[30] Dōgen, *Shōbōgenzō zenyaku dokkai* ('Treasury of the True Dharma Eye Complete with Translation and Commentary'), ed. Masutani Fumio, vol. 3 (Tokyo: Kōdansha, 2004), 151.
[31] Yamazaki Kagotarō, *Haikaishi dan* ('A Discussion of Haikai's History') (Tokyo: Hakubunkan, 1893), 14–15.
[32] Ibid., 216.

was in such circumstances that Shiki began to propose his own solutions. On 11 February 1894, a sister paper to *Nippon*, *Shō Nippon* ('Little Nippon'), was founded, with Shiki as its editor.[33] Shiki needed an illustrator; in March, an artist Shiki knew, Asai Chū (1856–1907), introduced him to a protégé, Nakamura Fusetsu (1866–1943).[34] Shiki was impressed by the latter's work and published many of his illustrations, often accompanied by his own haiku. They frequently talked about painting and literature; Shiki later observed that there were 'many things I realised about the connections between what Fusetsu was saying and haiku'.[35] Shiki had shown an interest in Western-style painting from as early as 1890, when he saw Honda Kinkichirō's (1851–1921) *Hagoromo no tennyo* ('The Angel of *Hagoromo*'), based on the nō play *Hagoromo* ('The Feather-Mantle'). This also inspired Shiki's 1893 novel, *Tsuki no miyako* ('The Capital of the Moon').[36] Fusetsu and Shiki also visited art exhibitions together. On one such occasion, they looked at a pair of folding screens by Sesshū Tōyō (1420–1506). According to Shiki, Fusetsu 'explained in detail the painting's fine arrangement; it was this that gave it unity and made it flawless. [. . .] For the first time I realised what a painting's fine arrangement meant'.[37] It was a revelation that would play a crucial part in Shiki's perception of haiku's possibilities.

In Donald Keene's account of Shiki's meeting with Fusetsu, it is 'the truth of Western paintings' compared to their 'stylized' Japanese counterparts that inspired Shiki. The former are 'faithful to the objects they portrayed'; Keene then suggests that Shiki learnt '*shasei* realism' from Fusetsu: 'A *shasei* haiku describes not the poet's emotions on observing a certain scene, nor the memories the scene brings back, but what he has just observed.'[38] However, Shiki's moment of realization arrived when he and Fusetsu were looking at a fifteenth-century Japanese painting. Indeed, Keene encounters some difficulty in fitting Fusetsu's own paintings with his understanding of *shasei*: 'A person familiar only with Fusetsu's paintings of the gods and goddesses of Japan or of the wise men of ancient China is likely to have trouble discovering any trace of *shasei* in these works.'[39] It is true that Fusetsu's notion of *shasei* involves observation of natural detail; but this is only one aspect of it, and not the most important. What Fusetsu explained to Shiki was the 'fine

---

[33] Maeda Kyōji, *E no yō ni: Meiji bungaku to bijutsu* ('Like a Painting: Meiji Literature and Art') (Tokyo: Hakusuisha, 2014), 193.
[34] Wada Katsushi, *Shiki no isshō* (Mishima: Zōshin, 2003), 318.
[35] Shiki, *Bokujū itteki* ('A Drop of Ink') (Tokyo: Iwanami Shoten, 1994), 156.
[36] Maeda, *E no yō ni*, 186.
[37] Ibid., 157.
[38] Keene, *The Winter Sun Shines In: A Life of Masaoka Shiki* (New York: Columbia University Press, 2013), 96–7.
[39] Ibid.

arrangement', which 'gave it unity and made it flawless'. The 'unity' created by this 'fine arrangement' must have recalled for Shiki his earlier view of the independent *hokku*'s 'unity' that gave it its status as the 'best of literature'.

To understand what it was that Shiki realized about a painting's 'fine arrangement', Fusetsu's artistic upbringing should be considered. In 1887, he had joined the Jūikkai (later named the Fudōsha), a group of *yōga* ('Western-style') painters. It was there that he learnt about Western techniques such as perspective and pencil sketching.[40] Many of the artists in this group, including Asai and Koyama Shōtarō (1857–1916), had been taught at the Kōbu Bijutsu Gakkō ('School of Technical Fine Arts') by Antonio Fontanesi (1818–82), its first professor, who taught there between June 1876 and October 1878. Fontanesi had visited Paris in 1855, where he encountered the work of the Barbizon school, which included Jean-Baptiste Camille Corot and Théodore Rousseau; in 1861, three of Fontanesi's paintings were exhibited at the Salon de Paris.[41] He was, as Matsui Takako notes, 'the first systematic teacher of Western painting in Japan'.[42] His ideas had a profound effect on Japanese art in the Meiji period.[43]

To begin with, Fontanesi had his Japanese students 'sketch from life', a term rendered into Japanese as *shasei*.[44] Sketching from life is crucial, he told his students, and the artist must observe nature closely; but Fontanesi also taught that merely attempting to copy what is seen is not enough. In one of his lectures, he explained:

> Great paintings that copy a natural scene as it is are rare. If the composition – with many trees clumped together, perhaps – is ugly, the number of trees should be reduced in response.[45]

While the elements of the painting must be well observed, the reduction of such elements to the essential ones is crucial. Concision is one step towards effective composition. Another, Fontanesi says, is the insertion of a single focal point:

> When the central object is fixed as the aim of a painting – that is, the central thing is copied in closer detail – it is best if the objects to the left and right of it are less detailed. Great paintings both now and in the past do this.[46]

---

[40] Fusetsu, 'Meiji shonen no seiyōga' ('Western-Style Painting in the Early Meiji Years'), *Bijutsu shashin gahō* 1, no. 4 (April 1920): 81.
[41] Matsui, *Shasei no henyō*, 6.
[42] Ibid.
[43] Ibid., 3.
[44] Ibid., 11.
[45] Kumamoto Kenjirō, *Meiji shoki raichō Itaria bijutsuka no kenkyū* ('A Study of Italian Artists in Japan in the Early Meiji Period') (Tokyo: Sanseidō, 1940), 149.
[46] Ibid.

In Fontanesi's view, both the elimination of lines that may cause confusion and the insertion of a focal point ensure that the main lines of a painting can be more clearly seen. Nothing is chosen that is not essential to the painting's main subject matter. Fontanesi's approach thus emphasizes clarity and simplicity in artistic composition.

These ideas influenced Fusetsu via Asai and Koyama. Like Fontanesi, he advocates a central focus for a painting's composition. This is 'fundamental': 'if it is assumed that there is no main idea, the result is necessarily that the entire picture becomes tangled and chaotic.'[47] In relation to the use of light and dark, he states that 'a focal point should be chosen, and the strongest light should fall on it. Where the brightness of the light is strongest is called the light's gathering point.'[48] Fusetsu also emphasizes the interplay between the main and subsidiary elements of a painting:

> In a painting, there is the main element of its subject matter, and the supporting element that makes this emphasis all the more vivid. This supporting element is called the *kyaku*. In any case, this distinction between the main and supporting elements is necessary; if this distinction is blurred, the painting cannot be said to qualify as art.[49]

Fusetsu stresses the importance of the 'supporting element' (the *kyaku*) as much as that of the 'main element' (the *shu*). What Shiki discovered when standing in front of those Sesshū folding screens, then, may have been the similarity between Fusetsu's notion of 'fine arrangement' in painting and his own understanding of the 'unity and harmony' of haiku as also being constituted by the arrangement of a main (*shu*) and supporting (*kyaku*) element. It is their contrast, rather than the former alone, that gives the painting what he would consider to be its harmony of composition. The strength of light at the 'gathering point' is emphasized by a contrasting darkness. Both *shu* and *kyaku* play an equally pivotal part in directing attention towards the painting's 'main idea'.

On 1 August 1894, some five months after Shiki and Fusetsu first met, the Sino-Japanese War broke out. Shiki was too ill to serve in the Japanese army but wanted to accompany it as a *Nippon* war correspondent. On 6 March 1895, he arrived in Hiroshima to sail to China, but did not leave until 10 April. While

---

[47] Fusetsu, 'Shukaku' ('The Main and Supporting Elements'), in *Gadō ippan* ('A Part of the Way of Painting') (Tokyo: Hakubunkan, 1906), 57.
[48] Ibid.
[49] Ibid.

waiting for the ship to depart, he wrote to a friend about the importance of *shasei* for the composition of his own haiku:

> When I want to write a lot, I look carefully at all kinds of things (particularly landscapes) and sketch from life [*shasei shi*].[50]

By the time he landed at Jinzhou in north-eastern China on 15 April, an armistice had already been signed. Shiki was disappointed, but nevertheless wrote several haiku on the scenes of the war's aftermath:

> *nashi saku ya ikusa no ato no kuzure ie*
> pear tree blossoming – after the battle, the wrecked house[51]

Unlike some of his earlier haiku, such as that of the country girl written four years before, there is no statement of any abstract quality such as 'beauty' ('*utsukushiki*') here; Shiki picks out two visual elements and does not explicitly comment on their relationship. As well as its concretion, the haiku's arrangement is also carefully structured. The new life of the pear blossoms serves to emphasize the house's destruction through the use of contrast. Fusetsu's notions of *shasei* and 'fine arrangement' strengthened Shiki's focus on these attributes of the haiku.

Shiki further developed these notions in relation to haiku in *Haikai taiyō* ('An Outline of *Haikai*'), which was serialized in *Nippon* from 22 October to 31 December 1895. The emphasis on the detailed observation of natural objects in *shasei* finds its counterpart, as Keene notes, in Shiki's revised understanding of Bashō's 'old pond' *hokku*. In 'Baseo as a Poet', Shiki had written that 'the hidden principle' of this *ku* is that of 'the purified, sacred Jenshū [Zen] (a sect of Buddhism)' and that focusing on the frog's splash resulted in the disappearance in Bashō's mind of 'lusts, avarices, fame, and passions'.[52] Now, however, he claimed that 'though there are those who over-analyse' Bashō's *hokku* 'by suggesting that it expresses an ideal tranquillity, the path to Zen enlightenment, or some other such idea, it is a *ku* that just is what it is and had no idea or anything else' behind it. Rather than using the term *shasei*, though, Shiki here foregrounded *hokku* that were *ari no mama* ('as is'). He quotes several examples, including one by Nozawa Bonchō (1640–1714):

> *naganaga to kawa hitosuji ya yuki no hara*
> the long single line of a river – snowy plain[53]

---

[50] Shiki, letter to Murakami Shōtarō (21 March 1895), in *SZ*, vol. 18, 531.
[51] Shiki, *Kushū*, 130.
[52] *SZ*, vol. 4, 19.
[53] Ibid., 44.

These kinds of *hokku* 'do not seek *takumi* ["cleverness", "skill"]'. They 'just connect things as they are [*ari no mama*] with other things as they are'.⁵⁴ In contrast with early *hokku*, they present, in Shiki's view, natural objects 'as is', without any 'hidden principle'. Although Pound describes his intention in composing his own '"Metro" hokku' as seeking the 'equation' for an 'emotion' rather than presenting natural objects 'as is', there is a resemblance between Pound's use of the 'natural object' as the '*adequate* symbol' in it and Shiki's emphasis on 'sketching' natural detail.

In his promotion of this *ari no mama* approach, Shiki may also have been influenced by Ozaki Kōyō's (1868–1903) essay 'Haikai ari no mama', which was published in the literary magazine *Taiyō* ('The Sun') on 5 July 1895. Kōyō was, like Kōson, a novelist who also wrote haiku. Kōyō's conception of *ari no mama* haiku differs from Shiki's in its overt statement of emotion. Where it resembles Shiki's interpretation of Bashō's *hokku* is its lack of wordplay, its avoidance of the kind of elaborate metaphor used in Moritake's *hokku*, and its close observation of everyday experience. Kōyō's approach is particularly indebted to that of Uejima Onitsura (1661–1738). In his *Haikai meikasen* ('A Selection of Famous *Haikai* Writers'), published in 1897, Kōyō includes a preface by Tan Taigi (1709–71) that singles out Onitsura's 'expression of *aware* ["pity" or "pathos"]' and considers him no less than Bashō's equal, the 'east' to Bashō's 'west'.⁵⁵ Among the *hokku* Kōyō includes in his selection of Onitsura's poems is the following:

mata hitotsu hana ni tsureyuku inochi kana
going together with yet another petal – a life⁵⁶

The comparison of a human life to a scattering petal had been a literary cliché for centuries before Onitsura's *hokku*; nonetheless, as Chapters 3 and 4 propose, it is likely that Pound read this *hokku* in English translation; it may therefore even have inspired the similar comparison of human faces and petals made in Pound's '"Metro" hokku'.

Shiki, though, was highly critical of such cliché; he was especially scathing about *haikai* poetry written in the Tempō era (1830–44), which he considered 'hackneyed' ('*chimpu*').⁵⁷ One of the effects of cliché, as he later made clear in his discussion of the *waka* poet Tachibana no Akemi (1812–68), is that 'it prevents the scene vividly appearing before the eyes'.⁵⁸ This not only recalls

---

⁵⁴ Ibid.
⁵⁵ Kōyō, *Haikai meikasen* ('A Selection of Famous *Haikai* Writers') (Tokyo: Shunyōdō, 1897), 150–1.
⁵⁶ Ibid., 165.
⁵⁷ Shiki, *Haikai taiyō* (Tokyo: Iwanami Shoten, 2016), 57.
⁵⁸ Shiki, *Utayomi ni atauru sho* ('A Book for Uta Poets') (Tokyo: Iwanami Shoten, 2013), 121.

Spencer's warning not to 'clog the image' but also looks forward to T. E. Hulme's advocacy of the original poetic 'image' that 'arrests your mind all the time with a picture'.[59] To encourage this approach, Shiki advises would-be *haijin* to go outside: 'to look for beautiful scenes in nature with the aim of copying reality is most appropriate for haiku.'[60] If going to the countryside is impossible, 'a half-day walk in the suburbs' or 'an after-dinner walk in Ueno or along the banks of the Sumida River', where one would have heard nō chanting at the house of the nō actor Umewaka Minoru or seen the setting for Bashō's 'old pond' *hokku*, 'is sufficient'.[61] As Maeda Kyōji points out, Fusetsu's *shasei*, in which he would make sketches without distinguishing between 'high' or 'low' subjects, served as an example for Shiki's haiku to depict subject matter beyond the scope afforded by previous literary convention and, thus, to give the form greater originality.[62] This originality would then result in 'the scene appearing more vividly before the eyes'; indeed, in the 'vivid impression' Spencer advocated.

Moritake's 'butterfly' *hokku* was also criticized for not adhering to Shiki's *ari no mama* approach. In an essay written in 1898, 'Furuike no ku no ben' ('A Discussion of the "Old Pond" Ku'), he contrasts the simplicity of Bashō's poem with a range of poetic techniques used by previous *haijin* such as Sōgi and Moritake. These include personification, metaphor, wordplay, and the use of old tales or common sayings. Among the four *hokku* he selects to illustrate this use of metaphor, he chooses two by Moritake. One is the 'butterfly' *hokku* cited earlier; the other reads:

karakasa ya tatae kagami no kesa no yuki
Tang umbrella – a mirror of this morning's snow[63]

Although the 'butterfly' *hokku* might seem, at first, to resemble a *hokku* that corresponds to Shiki's *ari no mama* approach, its use of metaphor marks it out in his eyes as radically different from, say, Bonchō's 'snow plain' *hokku*. Shiki's criticism of such kinds of metaphor is not aimed at the comparison of two elements as such – after all, his notion of 'fine arrangement' through the juxtaposition of the main and supporting elements is essential to his conception of haiku – but rather the depiction of those elements in a way that might lure a reader away from seeing each of them *ari no mama*, 'as they are'. From Shiki's

---

[59] T. E. Hulme, 'A Lecture on Modern Poetry', in Karen Csengeri (ed.), *The Collected Writings of T. E. Hulme*, (Oxford: Oxford University Press, 1994), 55.
[60] Shiki, *Haikai taiyō*, 58.
[61] Ibid.
[62] Maeda, *E no yō ni*, 233–4.
[63] Shiki, *Haikai taiyō*, 198.

perspective, the allusion to a famous Buddhist proverb in the 'butterfly' *hokku* and the visual discrepancy between the mirror and the umbrella in the one cited earlier result in the reader not perceiving the original objects with sufficient visual clarity.

Spencer's focus on concision, particularly the omission of the 'needless parts of the sentence' that are said to 'clog the image', is also taken up in Shiki's use of the term 'slackness' ('*tarumi*') to describe *hokku* that lack it. He explains this term by saying that 'tight' *hokku* are so carefully crafted that 'not one word can be removed'.[64] The words that cause the most slackening are particles, subject and topic markers, followed by adjectives and adverbs, and finally verbs. 'To give an example of 'slack *ku*', Shiki gives one by Narita Sōkyū (1761–1842), one of the Tempō-era poets whose 'hackneyed' *hokku* he had previously criticized:

> *monotaranu tsuki ya kareno wo teru bakari*
> faint moonlight – only shining on barren fields

> In this *ku*, only the moon and the barren field [the latter is a noun, not an adjective and a noun, in Japanese] are necessary elements. When saying 'faint moonlight – only shining on barren fields', the meaning of 'faint' is already implicit. [. . .] The meaning of 'only shining' is already implicit. Both are simply unnecessary. The meaning of this *ku* is nothing more than 'moon – barren fields' or 'barren fields – moon'.[65]

In Shiki's view, then, nouns are the least likely to cause slackening, although he cautions that 'if this argument is taken to its extreme, *ku* consisting only of nouns would be superior. A degree of slackness, however, is appropriate.'[66] While advocating concision, then, he also shows awareness of the problems that can arise if it is pursued too dogmatically. Pound's exhortation to 'Use no superfluous word' is similarly nuanced, allowing for the adjective that does 'reveal something'.[67]

Following Shiki's encounter with Fusetsu's conception of 'fine arrangement' and his discovery of its parallels with his own understanding of haiku, he proposed the as-yet-critically neglected Buson as one of the best models for haiku composition. In *Haikai taiyō*, he suggests that the *hokku* with the least 'slackness' were written not in Bashō's period but in the Anei (1772–81) and

---

[64] Ibid., 60.
[65] Ibid., 61–2.
[66] Ibid., 63.
[67] Pound, 'A Few Don'ts', 201.

Temmei (1781–9) eras – when Buson was at his peak.[68] Shiki's recognition of Buson as a major *haijin* culminated in his 1897 study *Haijin Buson*. He opens by provocatively suggesting that Buson might be considered Bashō's equal: 'Is Bashō without equal? I say that this is not the case.'[69] While Bashō was adulated beyond the reach of criticism, 'for a hundred years, Buson has been buried in the rubble, unable to spread his light'.[70] Shiki uses the term *kyakkan*, previously used by Yamazaki, to describe the quality he sees in many of Buson's *hokku*: this has usually been translated as 'objectivity', but consists in Japanese of two characters, which can be given as 'each' (*kyaku*) and 'view' or 'perspective' (*kan*). The effectivity of Buson's *kyakkan*, Shiki contends, is that it appeals more strongly to each reader's subjective perspective: employing a painterly analogy, he writes that 'to depict a part and allow the whole to be imagined appeals to the viewer's subjectivity'; not 'directly expressing emotion' but 'merely objectively depicting the thing that caused it' is what 'moves the viewer's emotions' most effectively.[71] Although Bashō has 'many haiku that express objective beauty when compared with earlier *waka* poems', he 'cannot reach Buson's objectivity'.[72]

In their apparent 'objectivity', Buson's *hokku* are considered to conform with the technique of the Spencerian 'minor image'. Shiki quotes some of Buson's *hokku* as examples of this approach, one of which reads:

> tsurikane ni tomarite nemuru kochō kana
> landing on the temple bell and falling asleep – a butterfly[73]

As is the case in the 'old pond' *hokku*, the quietness is evoked without using the word 'quiet'; this is reinforced by the *te*-suffix, which indicates that the butterfly's falling asleep occurs after the landing, thus emphasizing the length of time the bell remains silent. Shiki likens Buson's approach here to painting: 'it is like a painting giving only the outline, leaving it to the viewer to imagine the whole.'[74] His use of 'outline' (*rinkaku*) suggests that, as with Shiki's revelation when looking at the Sesshū screen with Fusetsu, it was not so much Western naturalist as traditional Far Eastern painting that served as the model for this painterly conception of Spencer's 'minor image'. If it is like a painting, it is one marked out with only a few monochrome brushstrokes; in Buson's 'butterfly' *hokku*,

---

[68] Shiki, *Haikai taiyō*, 63.
[69] Ibid., 103.
[70] Ibid.
[71] Ibid., 114.
[72] Ibid.
[73] Ibid.
[74] Ibid.

further visual details such as colour are left to the imagination. It is perhaps worth pointing out, in this context, that the only colour explicitly mentioned in Pound's '"Metro" hokku' is 'black', which forms a visual antithesis with the implied 'white' of the 'faces' and 'petals'.

The Philosophy of Style remained, then, one of the most fundamental influences on Shiki's understanding of haiku. Because of this, I am minded to agree with Maeda Kyōji's contention that Shiki's encounter with Fusetsu was 'not such a fundamental change' rather than with Matsui's claim that it was only after meeting Fusetsu that Shiki was able to 'depict a scene', 'make clear the focal point' and 'become aware of composition'.[75] Shiki's moment of revelation about the 'fine arrangement' of Sesshū's pair of screens, in which he realized that this arrangement consisted of a main (*shu*) and a supporting element (*kyaku*), was a confirmation of his earlier understanding about a haiku's composition, which he describes using the same terms and demonstrates in his early *hokku*. His promotion of Buson's 'objectivity' (*kyakkan*) is similarly anticipated by his understanding of the Spencerian 'minor image': Shiki argues that the 'silence' both Bashō's 'old pond' and Buson's 'butterfly' *hokku* is implied through the depiction of sensually apprehensible objects rather than explicitly stated, though Shiki goes into more depth in *Haijin Buson* about how such 'objectivity' appeals to the 'reader's subjectivity'.

Shiki's reading of *The Philosophy of Style* thus resulted in a profound change to how 'haiku', the term he popularized in Japan, came to be perceived, both in Japan and across the world. It was Shiki who promoted the idea that *haikai renga* were 'not literature' and that *hokku* should only be written independently. These independent hokku he then termed 'haiku', taking up Yamazaki's advocacy of this term to describe such *hokku* at around the same time. This allowed Shiki to claim that these *hokku*, now considered as poems in their own right, could be seen as the 'best of literature' by most closely adhering to Spencer's dictum that concision is essential to good writing. Shiki's contention that the best haiku have no 'hidden principle' emphasized how he saw it as seeking primarily to produce a Spencerian 'vivid impression'. In this, he departed significantly not only from the approach of earlier *haijin* such as Moritake, whose work he felt was characterized by elaborate wordplay and literary allusion, but even from earlier understandings of Bashō's *hokku*, including his own. He also established an association between haiku and painting, especially through the forgotten *hokku* of the painter Buson. Furthermore, his focus on the principles of concretion, concision, suggestive

---

[75] Maeda, *E no yō ni*, 219; Matsui, *Shasei no henyō*, 171–2.

indirection and juxtaposition, derived from *The Philosophy of Style*, affected the way haiku were understood in English translation and anticipated many of the similar dicta later advocated by Pound, as Chapter 4 proposes. When he finally died at the age of thirty-four on 19 September 1902, Shiki could hardly have imagined how influential his ideas about haiku would prove to be.

3

Symphonies in white
Basil Hall Chamberlain and the introduction of '*hokku*' into English

The first translations of *hokku* into English appeared in W. G. Aston's second edition of *A Grammar of the Japanese Written Language*, published in 1877. Aston had been appointed in 1864 as an interpreter at the British Legation in Edo.[1] In this capacity, he attended the Iwakura Mission's stay in the UK from August to December 1872.[2] That year, he also became a founding member of the Asiatic Society of Japan, along with other Japanologists such as Francis Brinkley and F. V. Dickins. Most attention in his chapter on 'Prosody', however, is devoted to the 'tanka', 'by far the commonest Japanese metre'.[3] 'Next to tanka', he adds, 'the commonest classical metre is *Naga-uta*' ('long poem'). Then follows the '*Sedôka*' and, finally, the '*Hokku*'. Aston comments that 'all poetry recognized as classical' is written in the first three of these forms.[4] 'The admirers of *Haikwai uta* claim for it a quasi-classical character, but it is objected with much reason that nothing which deserves the name of poetry can well be contained in the narrow compass of a verse of seventeen syllables.'[5] Not only is it given the least attention of these forms; Aston also considers it to be a lesser form than the other three. By the time Pound composed 'In a Station of the Metro', however, it had become the most prominent Japanese poetic form in the Anglophone world. This chapter will explore the causes of this reversal and outline the development of the '*hokku*' in English before the Imagists' encounter with it.

Among the three books on *hokku* in Aston's possession at his death was one whose introduction might have led Aston to his understanding of its position

---

[1] P. F. Kornicki, 'William George Aston (1841-1911)', in Hugh Cortazzi and Gordon Daniels (eds), *Britain and Japan 1859-1991* (London: Routledge, 1991), 64–5.
[2] Ibid., 65.
[3] Aston, *A Grammar*, 197.
[4] Ibid.
[5] Ibid., 208.

within Japanese poetry. The *Haikai kijin dan* ('Conversations on Outstanding *Haikai* Writers') is a *hokku* anthology compiled by Takenouchi Gengenichi (1742–1804); Aston's copy dates to 1816. One of the four introductions to this edition, attributed to Gabō Sanjin, begins by stating that 'Yamato-uta [tanka and other forms considered "classical"] are refined, haiku are common'.[6] In addition to demonstrating that Shiki was not the first to use the term 'haiku' but rather the first to use it consistently to distinguish it as an independent form, Gabō Sanjin's introduction also typifies how 'haiku' had been considered lower in status than 'classical' tanka. This view persisted into the 1890s: Yamazaki Kagotarō, who called for the use of 'haiku' to indicate independent *hokku* at around the same time as Shiki, concluded that 'in height of style', even the best *hokku* were 'inferior' to tanka.[7] This background throws into relief the audacity of Shiki's contention in *Haikai taiyō* that 'compared to other literature, the haiku form is not superior or inferior'.[8]

Aston includes three examples of '*Hokku*'. One of these, by the Bashō disciple Takarai Kikaku (1661–1707), indicates what were considered characteristics of good *hokku* before Shiki's reforms:

Yufudachi ya	Oh! if the summer-shower
Ta wo mi-meguri no	were only a god who
Kami naraba.	should make his rounds of
	visits to the rice-fields.[9]

Aston comments, 'The last verse is an acrostic on the word *yutaka*, "wealth" or "prosperity"'.[10] Such wordplay was common in *hokku*, not just in the early years of *haijin* such as Moritake, but also in the very *hokku* Shiki promoted as the outstanding examples of the approach he advocated. In his note on Bashō's 'old pond' *hokku* in 1889 – immediately preceding his account of reading *The Philosophy of Style* – he observed that it was an *oriku* ('acrostic verse'): the first syllables of each line spell out *fukami* ('depth').[11] The relative lack of attention to this aspect of Bashō's *hokku* since Shiki's reforms, both in Japan and abroad, is indicative of the relegation of features such as linguistic ingenuity and wordplay in favour of those Shiki wished to emphasize following his reforms: the depiction of natural detail 'as is', concision, concretion, suggestive indirection and

---

[6] *Haika kijin dan*, n. p.
[7] Yamazaki, *Haikaishi dan*, 66.
[8] Shiki, *Haikai taiyō*, 6.
[9] Aston, *A Grammar*, 208.
[10] Ibid.
[11] Shiki, *Fudemakase*, 108.

juxtaposition. Following the rise of *hokku*'s prominence in English and French translations in the wake of Shiki's reforms, these features were accentuated before Pound and other Imagist poets encountered this form.

Aston's claim that '*Hokku*' were less than 'quasi-classical' compared to other Japanese poetic forms was reinforced by Basil Hall Chamberlain's *The Classical Poetry of the Japanese* of 1880, which included neither a single example nor any discussion of the *haikai* genre. Chamberlain had arrived in Japan in 1873 and become a teacher of English at the Naval Academy.[12] In his view, the Japanese preference for the tanka, their 'favourite metre', over longer forms illustrates the tendency in Japanese poetry to 'consider brevity to be the soul of wit', the same *Hamlet* allusion Spencer uses.[13] Unlike Spencer, though, he considered this to result from a 'poverty of the intellectual constitution', in contrast with what he saw as the greater complexity of longer Western poetic forms.[14] By 1889, however, his opinion of 'brevity' in poetic composition appeared to have shifted with the publication of *A Handbook of Colloquial Japanese*. His emphasis on 'extreme shortness' as the 'chief positive characteristics of Japanese poetry' led him to a brief discussion of the 'hokku'.[15] Of the four examples he includes, he reserves most praise for Kaga no Chiyo's (1703–75) 'miniature ode', *Asagao ni tsurube torarete moraimizu*, which he translates: 'Having had my well-bucket taken away by the convolvuli – gift-water!' Chamberlain explains that 'As a poetess and a woman of taste', Chiyo 'could not bring herself to disturb the dainty blossoms' of the convolvuli twining around the rope of her well bucket and describes the *hokku* as 'a pretty little vignette, surely, and expressed in five words'.[16] Here, he lauds Chiyo's ability to express a 'pretty little vignette' in just 'five words'. His choice of 'vignette' to describe it also sets up an association of *hokku* with visual art that both Shiki and Pound were later to emphasize.

The reversal of *hokku*'s prominence in English translation came in the wake of Lafcadio Hearn's quotation and discussion of several examples in *Exotics and Retrospectives*, published in 1898, which included the first English translation of Bashō's 'old pond' *hokku*:

Old pond – frogs jumped in – sound of water.[17]

---

[12] Yuzo Ota, *Basil Hall Chamberlain: Portrait of a Japanologist* (Richmond: Japan Library, 1998), 203.
[13] Chamberlain, *The Classical Poetry of the Japanese* (London: Trübner, 1880), 12.
[14] Ibid., 18.
[15] Chamberlain, *A Handbook of Colloquial Japanese* (London: Trübner, 1889), 452.
[16] Ibid., 453.
[17] Hearn, *Exotics and Retrospectives*, 121. Hearn's prefatory note for the first edition is dated 15 February 1898; Chamberlain's for the third edition of *Things Japanese* is dated 5 March 1898.

Hearn had arrived in Japan in 1890, after which Chamberlain arranged his appointment as a schoolteacher in Shimane Prefecture that year. In contrast with Aston and Chamberlain's accounts of Japanese poetry, *hokku* achieve far more prominence in this book: two are used as chapter epigraphs, and they receive extensive coverage in the chapters entitled 'Frogs' and 'Cicadas', which discuss their depiction in Japanese poetry. Like Chamberlain, he associates 'hokku' with the visual arts: they create 'one complete sensation-picture' and 'are intended as tiny pictures – thumb-nail sketches'.[18] Since his appointment as Chair of English Language and Literature at the Imperial University in September 1896, Hearn had set his students monthly essay tasks. That of December 1897 was 'Poems on Cicadas and Frogs'.[19] One of his students, Ōtani Masanobu, included several translations of poems on frogs he had discovered for his monthly essay, including Bashō's aforementioned *hokku*; Hearn incorporated these into his 'Frogs' chapter. Nine further examples of *hokku* follow Bashō's, most of which Ōtani had discovered in a two-volume anthology edited by Mizuochi Roseki (1872–1919).[20] Hearn describes Roseki as a 'distinguished [. . .] young poet' living in Ōsaka.[21] Roseki was one of the principal disciples of Shiki.

According to Roseki's own account written on the occasion of Shiki's death, his interest in Shiki's new approach to haiku was first aroused by reading his *Dassai sho'oku haiwa* in *Nippon*, especially the discussion of Bashō's work.[22] In 1893, Roseki cofounded a literary magazine called *Ittenkō* ('One Spot of Red') in Ōsaka, but he describes his *hokku* at that time as 'immature Danrin-style' creations, referring to the pre-Bashō school that emphasized wordplay and elaborate metaphor.[23] He was 'terrifically moved' by Shiki's own haiku and resolved 'to study haiku seriously' and align himself with Shiki to form the '*Nippon* school'.[24] They began corresponding in the spring of 1894; another Shiki disciple, Takahama Kyoshi, claims that Roseki was the earliest convert to Shiki's ideas about haiku.[25] Following the publication of *Haijin Buson*, in which Shiki advocated Buson's importance and emphasized the visual 'objectivity' of his *hokku*, Roseki undertook further research on Buson and wrote haiku in

---

[18] Hearn, *Exotics and Retrospectives*, 121 and 124.
[19] Yone Noguchi, *Lafcadio Hearn in Japan* (London: Elkin Mathews, 1910), 109.
[20] Roseki, *Keichū kushū* ('Treasured Animal Haiku Collection'), vol. 2 (Ōsaka, 1897). Ōtani states that he discovered Roseki's anthology in Noguchi, *Lafcadio Hearn in Japan*, 109.
[21] Hearn, *Exotics and Retrospectives*, 121.
[22] Roseki, 'Hechimabutsu' ('Sponge Cucumber Buddha'), *Takarabune* 3, no. 1 (November 1902): 4.
[23] Ibid., 5.
[24] Ibid.
[25] Roseki, *Kushū* ('Selected Haiku'), ed. Tsubouchi Nenten (Tokyo: Furansudō, 2009), 89.

his style.[26] In 1896 and 1897, he published two anthologies of haiku on frogs; Shiki wrote the introduction to the first of these, describing how the idea for the anthologies sprang from Bashō's 'old pond' *hokku*.[27] Hearn's inclusion of what he still calls 'hokku' from Roseki's second anthology of frog-haiku thus indicates their resurgence in Japan, due in large part to Shiki's reforms. A few weeks after the publication of *Exotics and Retrospectives*, Chamberlain included a translation of Bashō's 'old pond' *hokku* in the third edition of *Things Japanese*.

The following year, Hearn extended his discussion of 'hokku' in a chapter on Japanese poetry in his next book, *In Ghostly Japan*. Unlike Aston's and Chamberlain's earlier accounts, 'hokku' dominate. He presents a conception of Japan as a land of poetry: 'Poetry in Japan is universal as the air. It is felt by everybody. It is read by everybody. It is composed by almost everybody [...] it is everywhere to be heard by the ear, *and seen by the eye!*'[28] This conception would prove to be popular in the Anglophone literary world; Pound would develop a strikingly similar view of Japan. Hearn also expands upon the comparison with painting that he had made in *Exotics and Retrospectives*:

> By the use of a few chosen words the composer of a short poem endeavors to do exactly what the painter endeavors to do with a few strokes of the brush – to evoke an image or a mood – to revive a sensation or an emotion. And the accomplishment of this purpose – by poet or by picture-maker – depends altogether upon capacity to *suggest*, and only to suggest.[29]

In their 'capacity to *suggest*', 'hokku' accord with the advice Hearn gave to his student to 'appeal to the reader's emotion' through the presentation of 'natural and simple incidents'. The visual concretion, concision and suggestive reticence emphasized in Shiki's haiku reforms are the characteristics Hearn identifies as the outstanding features of Japanese poetry.

Aston's *A History of Japanese Literature* of 1899 was the first major demonstration of haiku's increased prominence in English following Hearn's books. Whereas in 1877 he had not even accorded it even a 'quasi-classical status', Aston now dedicated an entire chapter to 'Haikai', which he presents as a synonym of the 'Hokku': 'In the sixteenth century a kind of poem known as Haikai, or Hokku [...] made its appearance.'[30] It is likely that Aston had

---

[26] Ibid., 89 and 92.
[27] Shiki, 'Keichū kushū jo' ('Preface to the Treasured Animal Haiku Collection'), in *Keichū kushū*, vol. 1 (Ōsaka, 1896), n. p.
[28] Hearn, *In Ghostly Japan* (Boston: Little, Brown & Co., 1899), 309.
[29] Ibid., 313.
[30] Aston, *A History of Japanese Literature* (London: William Heinemann, 1899), 289.

adopted the practice of also referring to the individual '*hokku*' of a '*haikai renga*' as a '*haikai*' before 1893. Aston's book contains the first English translation of Moritake's 'butterfly' *hokku*:

> *Thought I, the fallen flowers*
> *Are returning to their branch;*
> *But lo! they were butterflies.*[31]

The absence of further commentary means that its allusion to the *Shōbōgenzō* is not kept; in this new context, it merely appears as an observation of the visual similarity between a falling leaf and a butterfly rather than the comic reversal of a Buddhist teaching on enlightenment. This poem does not appear, however, in the three works concerning 'Haikai' in Aston's possession at the time of his death. As we have seen, Japanese essays of the 1890s on the history of *hokku* disagree on the importance of the poem: neither Yamazaki nor Kōyō mention it at all, and Shiki criticizes it for its elaborate use of metaphor. Kōson's *Haikai ron* stands out among these in not only including it but calling it Moritake's 'most skilful' *hokku*. It is possible that Chamberlain – who later acknowledges having read *Haikai ron* – may have shared his discovery of it with Aston.

Indeed, in the fourth edition of *Things Japanese*, published in 1902, Chamberlain included his own translation of Moritake's *hokku*:

> Out of [the tanka], at a later date, by the dropping of the second hemistich, grew the *Haikai* or *Hokku*, an ultra-Lilliputian class of poem having but seventeen syllables (5, 7, 5). Here are a couple of examples:
>
> | *Rakkwa eda ni* | |
> |---|---|
> | *Kaeru to mireba* | 'What I saw as a fallen blossom returning to |
> | *Kochō kana!* | the branch, lo! it was a butterfly.'[32] |

This is the also first time that he adds '*Haikai*' as a synonym of '*Hokku*', as Aston had done three years before. The increase in Chamberlain's estimation of this form, already evident in his revisions to the third edition, continues here: in his assessment of the merits of Japanese poetry in general, he includes Bashō as one of its greatest practitioners, not just of *hokku*: many of his 'are flashes of delicate fancy, atoms of perfect naturalistic description, specks of humour, truth or wisdom'.[33] Like Shiki, Chamberlain now recognized *hokku* as literature on a par with other forms of Japanese poetry.

---

[31] Ibid., 290; italics in original.
[32] Chamberlain, *Things Japanese*, 4th edn (London: Kegan Paul, Trench, Trübner & Co, 1902), 373.
[33] Ibid., 293.

Chamberlain's newly found enthusiasm for *hokku*, meanwhile, led to his lecture on 'Bashō and the Japanese Poetical Epigram', which was read at the Asiatic Society of Japan on 4 June 1902 and published in that year's issue of the society's journal. Whereas in *The Classical Poetry of the Japanese* Chamberlain had derided all Japanese poetry as inferior to that of the West and excluded *hokku* altogether, he now devoted a 119-page essay to the latter, which he introduces as having had 'a remarkable literary success'.[34] For the first time in an English-language publication, he gives '*Haiku*' as another 'native name' for what he translates as an 'epigram', the first of several indications of the influence of Shiki's reforms on the essay.[35] The difference between the '*Hokku*' as the 'initial stanza' of a tanka or a renga and the origin of the term '*Haikai*' out of the 'comic linked verses' known as '*Haikai no Renga*' is mapped out far more clearly than previous accounts.[36] Chamberlain also observes, as Yamazaki had, that '*Haikai*' later also came to be used to refer to an independent *hokku*.[37] His definition of '*Haiku*' as 'a cross between the two', however, is at odds with Yamazaki's more specific suggestion that independent *hokku* be distinguished from these by using the term 'haiku'.[38]

Nevertheless, his understanding of a *hokku* as an 'initial hemistich' of a longer poetic form allowed him to claim that the 'Japanese epigram' is 'essentially fragmentary': a 'second stave' (the two lines of seven Japanese syllables that conclude a tanka) or a longer linked-verse sequence 'is always there *in posse* if not in *esse*'.[39] As a result, an English translation should select a form 'which is calculated to produce on the English ear the impression of fragmentariness'.[40] For this reason, he opts not to use rhyme or a 'Greek or Latin hexameter' but a version that is 'as literal' as 'the disparity between English and Japanese idiom will allow', with an 'elementary metre and its suggestion of fragmentariness'.[41] The *hokku* he translates are given in unrhymed couplets that usually contain four stresses per line. Chamberlain himself is critical of this fragmentariness: he opposes the 'isolated and fragmentary' Japanese poem and the 'organic whole' of Western poems such as Tennyson's 'In Memoriam'.[42] If 'Japanese epigrams' are not an intact 'mirror reflecting the universe', they are 'thousands of fragments of

---

[34] Chamberlain, 'Bashō', 243.
[35] Ibid.
[36] Ibid., 260.
[37] Ibid., 260–1.
[38] Ibid., 261.
[39] Ibid.
[40] Ibid.
[41] Ibid., 253.
[42] Ibid., 307.

shattered glass, among which some of shattered crystal'.⁴³ This view contrasts with Shiki's argument that the 'haiku' is literature because, unlike *renga*, it possesses 'unity' and 'harmony'. The fragmentariness and lack of rhyme that Chamberlain disparaged, however, would later prove to be what many modernist poets prized and sought to emulate.

One of the aspects of 'Japanese epigrams' that Chamberlain did praise was its pictorial suggestiveness. As his brief note on this form in *A Handbook of Colloquial Japanese* and Hearn's publications had done, Chamberlain emphasizes the comparison between the 'Japanese epigram' and painting. Just as he had described Chiyo's *hokku* as a 'vignette', the 'Japanese epigram' is now portrayed as 'the tiniest of vignettes, a sketch in barest outline, the suggestion, not the description, of a scene or a circumstance'.⁴⁴ Where his view differs from before, however, is that he now considers it as 'modern' and comparable with Western painting as well:

> Across a distance of ten thousand miles and an interval of two centuries, the spirit of the seventeenth-century Japanese poet is identical with that which informs the work of the Western water-colourist of to-day. It is intensely modern, or at least imbued to the full with that love and knowledge of nature which we are accustomed to consider characteristic of modern times.⁴⁵

This represents a significant departure from his opinion of Japanese poetry expressed in 1880. Far from being inferior to Western poetry, it is so 'intensely modern' that it even anticipates the rise of the kind of landscape painting developed by the Barbizon school and the impressionists, who went out into 'nature' to sketch from life – the approach Fontanesi promoted to his Japanese students. Chamberlain's new estimation of the 'Japanese epigram' in this regard presents it not just as a historical curiosity, but as a poetic model suitable for 'modern times'.

Chamberlain extends this painterly analogy, comparing 'Japanese epigrams' not only with 'the Western water-colourist of to-day' but to the work of one of the greatest painters of the late nineteenth century, James McNeill Whistler. In Chamberlain's view, the 'prettiest' *hokku* is written by 'the father of epigrammatic poetry' and contemporary of Moritake, the Buddhist priest Yamazaki Sōkan (1465–1553):

---

⁴³ Ibid., 305.
⁴⁴ Ibid., 246.
⁴⁵ Ibid., 246–7.

> But for its voice, the heron were
> A line of snow, and nothing more.[46]

'How often', Chamberlain comments, 'has not this subject been treated by the Japanese painter, as a delicate symphony in white!'[47] Chamberlain's phrasing recalls the title of Whistler's *Symphony in White no. 1* (1862) and *Symphony in White no. 2* (1864), which Whistler named after the French poet Théophile Gautier's poem 'Symphonie en blanc majeur' to adhere to Gautier's advocacy of 'l'art pour l'art'. Both paintings are typified by an emphasis on composition over subject matter: as Ayako Ono observes, in *Symphony in White no. 2* 'the red of the lacquered bowl, the blue of the porcelain, the Japanese fan and the spray of azalea emphasise by contrast the white in the dress'.[48] Whistler was influenced in this manner of composition by Japanese *ukiyo-e* painting, especially that of Hiroshige. Chamberlain sees in the 'semi-Bohemian' Sōkan's *hokku* a similar focus on colour arrangements for their own sake rather than for any didactic purpose: just as the white of the girl's dresses in Whistler's paintings is reinforced by their white background, the snow's white in Sōkan's *hokku* accentuates that of the heron.[49]

Western painters aside, Chamberlain acknowledges 'the native commentators' on 'the Japanese epigram' – 'such men as Aeba Kōson, one of the leading littérateurs of the present day, and Shiki, and Kōyō Sanjin [a pen-name of Ozaki Kōyō]' – as the primary sources for his essay.[50] 'Not only have they compiled useful anthologies, and written books explaining the actual text of considerable numbers of famous epigrams', Chamberlain writes; 'some of their editions indicate the classic sources, both Japanese and Chinese, from which Bashō drew, and thus enable us to admire his erudition. One on Buson's epigrams gives the opinions of a whole circle of his admirers on most points.'[51] Included in the 1902 edition of the essay is a bibliography of the Japanese anthologies, editions and commentaries Chamberlain consulted. Of the twelve works listed, he picks out Kōson's *Haikai ron* as 'perhaps the best general view of the subject in a concise form'.[52] The two-volume Buson commentary edited by Shiki and two of his disciples, *Buson kushū kōgi* ('Talks on Buson's Collected *Hokku*') is

---

[46] Ibid., 265.
[47] Ibid.
[48] Ayako Ono, *Japonisme* (London: Routledge, 2003), 69.
[49] Chamberlain, 'Bashō', 265.
[50] Ibid., 303.
[51] Ibid.
[52] Ibid., 360.

also recommended.⁵³ Eleven of the fourteen works were published in or after 1893. In addition to the impact of one of Shiki's disciples, Roseki, on Hearn's popularization of the form, this demonstrates how the Western interest in *'hokku'* resulted from its remarkable revival in 1890s Japan. This was made possible by an extensive network of modern Japanese writers, editors, critics and publishers.

Kōson is Chamberlain's Japanese source for Moritake's 'butterfly' *hokku*. After having given it as one of two exemplary *'hokku'* in the 1902 edition of *Things Japanese*, Chamberlain now presented it in the two-line, four-stress couplet used throughout his translations in the essay:

Fall'n flow'r returning to the branch, —
Behold! it is a butterfly.⁵⁴

The first two words here are each contracted to single syllables in order to make them fit Chamberlain's four-stress line rule. Chamberlain uses both lineation and punctuation (a comma followed by an em dash) to emphasize the comparison between the image of the 'Fall'n flow'r' in the first line and that of the 'butterfly' in the second. The absence of explanation of the allusion to the Buddhist saying in the *Shōbōgenzō* and *Yashima* in both Kōson and Chamberlain also results in the English translation losing much of its earlier humorous effect and makes the *hokku* appear, instead, as a 'delicate fancy', an originally conceived metaphor for a fleeting moment of visual perception.

Chamberlain's reading of Kōyō's *Haikai meikasen* is also evident in his selections of *hokku* from Sampū, Jōsō, Izen and Onitsura, all of which also appear in Kōyō's anthology. Chamberlain accords an especially lengthy preface to Onitsura: 'he has a great reputation, some going so far as to assert that he unites the excellencies of all the schools. Bashō and he knew and respected each other, and Onitsura arrived independently at very much the conclusions as Bashō did.'⁵⁵ This view can be traced to *Haikai meikasen*, in which Taigi describes Bashō and Onitsura as the 'East and West, the left and right' of *hokku*'s 'golden age'.⁵⁶ Taigi's view of the 'depth' of Onitsura's *hokku* is likewise echoed in Chamberlain's opinion that Onitsura 'really penetrated below the surface of things to the *lacrimae rerum*'.⁵⁷ This quality is shown by three 'epigrams', which

---

⁵³ Ibid., 361.
⁵⁴ Ibid., 312.
⁵⁵ Ibid., 345.
⁵⁶ Kōyō (ed.), *Haikai meikasen*, 152.
⁵⁷ Ibid., 151; Chamberlain, 'Bashō', 345.

express how 'the world is a round of perpetual change, and all phenomena are evanescent'.[58] One reads:

> Together with one blossom more,
> Oh! life, thou goest on thy way.[59]

Again, the metaphorical comparison of the 'blossom' and 'life' is reinforced by the punctuation (in this case, a comma) and the lineation (with the metaphor's tenor and vehicle each appearing in one line). Moritake's 'butterfly' *hokku* and Onitsura's 'blossom' *hokku* indicate how Kōson and Kōyō's interest in *hokku* that involve the metaphorical comparison of two elements strongly influenced Chamberlain's selection and understanding of 'Japanese epigrams'.

Shiki dislikes such uses of metaphor; yet Chamberlain's essay is also strongly influenced by Shiki's criticism, as he explicitly acknowledges. This is nowhere more apparent than in the selection of thirteen *hokku* by Buson, whose literary reputation Shiki had brought from almost total obscurity to parity with Bashō. Chamberlain mentions Shiki's *Buson kushū kōgi* ('Lectures on Buson's Collected *Ku*'), which began to be published in book form in 1900. 'The greatest epigrammatist of the silver age (circa 1770-1780)', Chamberlain writes, 'was Buson'.[60] He emphasizes the painterly quality of Buson's *hokku*: their 'technique is unsurpassed: – he literally paints with words, and how few words!'[61] In Chamberlain's view, however, the visual clarity of Buson's *hokku* often accompanies semantic 'obscurity'.[62] Nowhere is this more obvious than in one which, Chamberlain notes, merits 'fourteen pages of discussion' in *Buson kushū kōgi*:

> Some water-fowl, and in the midst
> Of withered trees, two palanquins.[63]

Chamberlain lists some of the questions posed in Shiki's commentary: 'Was there any one in the palanquins?' (Meisetsu imagines there was; Shiki disagrees.[64]) 'Were they run-away lovers?' (Shiki proposes this.[65]) 'Were the bearers there, or had *they* run away?' (Shiki speculates on this.[66]) 'Whatever meaning it may

---

[58] Ibid., 346.
[59] Ibid.
[60] Ibid., 297.
[61] Ibid., 298.
[62] Ibid., 361.
[63] Ibid., 352.
[64] Shiki et al., *Buson kushū kōgi*, vol. 4 (Tokyo: Hototogisu, 1911), 69 and 73.
[65] Ibid., 70.
[66] Ibid., 74.

have', Kyoshi concludes, 'it goes without saying that its expression is skilful'.[67] In its very 'obscurity', it best embodies the quality of *kyakkan* ('objectivity') – the ability 'to depict a part and allow the whole to be imagined' – that Shiki had discovered in Buson's *hokku*. This fruitful 'obscurity' results from the absence of literary allusion compared with Moritake's 'butterfly' *hokku*. In its apparent non-metaphorical juxtaposition of visual objects, it also accords with Shiki's *ari no mama* approach.

The rise in the *hokku*'s status, both in Japan and the West, led to what has been considered the first one composed in English, by Yone Noguchi. Noguchi recalls that in September 1892 he visited the then seventy-year-old Hozumi Eiki (1822–1904), the most prominent Meiji *hokku* writer before Shiki, in Shiba Park, when Noguchi was a sixteen-year-old student at the nearby Keiō University.[68] The next year, he went to live in the United States; in April 1896, he befriended the poet Joaquin Miller, who encouraged his writing of English poetry.[69] This led to the publication of his English collections *Seen and Unseen: or, The Monologues of a Homeless Snail* and *The Voice of the Valley* (1897). It was only after Hearn's popularization of 'hokku', however, that he began writing his own. *The American Diary of a Japanese Girl*, written in the voice of 'Miss Morning Glory', was serialized in *Frank Leslie's Popular Monthly* before appearing as a book in 1902. The book version includes a farewell 'poem' of 'seventeen syllables' that 'Miss Morning Glory' writes before leaving America:

Sayonara no
Ureiya nokore
Mizu no neni!

Remain, oh, remain,
My grief of sayonara,
There in water sound![70]

In contrast with previous translations of 'hokku', Noguchi's English version adheres to a strict five-seven-five English syllable count: for this reason, he repeats 'remain' (*nokore* is only used once in the Japanese). The concluding line suggests its indebtedness to Bashō's 'old pond' *hokku* made famous for English readers in Hearn's *Exotics and Retrospectives*. Noguchi's biography of Hearn recalls that 'We Japanese have been regenerated by his sudden magic'; Hearn's

---

[67] Ibid., 82.
[68] Yone Noguchi, 'What Is a Hokku Poem?', *Rhythm* 4 (January 1913): 356.
[69] Noguchi, *The Story of Yone Noguchi as Told by Himself* (London: Chatto & Windus, 1914), 17.
[70] Noguchi, *The American Diary of a Japanese Girl* (New York: Frederick A. Stokes, 1902), 236.

promotion of 'hokku' was likely an important factor in Noguchi's adoption of this form in English.

In 1903, the art critic Sadakichi Hartmann touched on the '*haikai*' in his book on *Japanese Art*. Although Hartmann was half-Japanese, having been born in Nagasaki to a German father and a Japanese mother in 1867, he moved to Germany at a young age. From 1882 he lived in the United States, making regular visits to Europe to meet various well-known artists.[71] His viewpoint on Japanese poetry was arguably more Western than Japanese: he did not speak Japanese, and the bibliography of *Japanese Art* indicates its dependence on Western sources.[72] Among these are several of Chamberlain's works, including the second edition of *Things Japanese* and *The Transactions of the Asiatic Society of Japan*, in which Chamberlain's 'Bashō and the Japanese Poetical Epigram' appeared.[73] Like Chamberlain, Hartmann compares '*haikai*' with painting: the Tosa School of painting shares Japanese poetry's suggestiveness and its 'conciseness of expression', which 'has reached in the *haikai*, a stanza consisting of seventeen syllables, its extreme limit of brevity'.[74] Just as Chamberlain was critical of such brevity, Hartmann similarly finds that 'no great qualities can be claimed for these poetical forms', though 'it must be admitted that the Japanese poets have made the most of their slender resources'.[75]

In his article on 'The Japanese Conception of Poetry' published in the January 1904 issue of *The Reader*, however, Hartmann was far more positive about the potential benefits of the '*haikai*' for Western poetry. 'At a time when everything in Western literature tends towards brevity in expression', he begins, 'it may be interesting to examine a literature which, in its poetry at least, has always adhered to the principles of concision'.[76] The shift from perceiving '*haikai*' as a peripheral form to one of the most important during the 1890s is evident in Hartmann's view that 'The metrical forms most often encountered are those of the *tanka* and *haikai*'.[77] He shares Chamberlain's view of them as 'suggest[ing] a picture' over 'conveying the intricacies of speculative thought or a direct enunciation of ideas'.[78] This focus on Japanese poetry's visual aspect runs through the article: expanding upon Chamberlain's frequent description of '*Hokku*' as a 'vignette',

---

[71] Sadakichi Hartmann, *White Chrysanthemums: Literary Fragments and Pronouncements*, ed. George Knox and Harry W. Lawton (New York: Herder and Herder, 1971), 24.
[72] Hartmann, *Collected Poems, 1886-1944*, ed. Floyd Cheung (Stroud: Little Island Press, 2016), 7.
[73] Hartmann, *Japanese Art* (Boston: L. C. Page & Company, 1904), 280 and 281.
[74] Ibid., 54.
[75] Ibid.
[76] Hartmann, 'The Japanese Conception of Poetry', *The Reader* 3, no. 2 (January 1904): 185.
[77] Ibid.
[78] Ibid., 187.

Hartmann claims that the Japanese poet 'looks at the world with the eyes of an ideal realist, or rather of an impressionist. Life passes, like the views of a magic lantern, showing one beautiful landscape after another, each one containing sufficient material for an exquisite vignette.'[79] This aspect, promoted by Shiki and his disciples, is thus prioritized over other '*haikai*' tendencies such as the wordplay of Bashō's and Kikaku's acrostics.

According to Hartmann, the Japanese poet does not explicitly state the 'sentiment' he or she wishes to evoke. 'Frequently he does not even find it necessary to attach a sentiment to his word-pictures. He simply depicts a crow sitting on a withered branch,' he writes, referring to Bashō's well-known 'withered branch' *hokku*, 'and leaves it to the reader to add the poetic thought.'[80] Hartmann describes this method as using a 'single image' to depict an emotion or idea, a phrase that would later be of great importance to Pound's *hokku*-inspired Vorticist poetics, though it most likely derived from Fenollosa.[81] Unlike Chamberlain, though, he does not see this as demonstrating a 'poverty of the intellectual constitution', but rather as a better way of expressing emotions and ideas than their 'direct enunciation'.[82] Hartmann thus echoes Shiki's contention that Buson's 'objectivity', typified by the ambiguity of his 'water-fowl' *hokku*, allows him to 'appeal to the viewer's subjectivity' more effectively. Later in the article, however, Hartmann offers a different method of interpreting such ambiguity. Rather than suggesting it offers multiple interpretations, he claims that each 'image' hides a single, secret meaning: 'Every glimpse of nature is endowed with a symbol, a hidden meaning to all who know the hidden pass-word. In this graphic symbolism exists for the initiated the greatest charm of Japanese poetry.' The 'single image' method thus contains a contradiction between its meaning as open and plural on the one hand and hidden and singular on the other.

Although Hartmann concentrates on the visual aspect of *tanka* and *haikai*, he also examines its aural aspect. In his study of *The Classical Poetry of the Japanese* of 1880, Chamberlain had been critical of the absence of 'rhyme, tone, accent, quantity' and 'alliteration' in Japanese poetry, describing it as 'prosody reduced to its simplest expression'.[83] This criticism remained in his 1902 essay, despite his more positive perception of the '*Hokku*': 'the comparative weakness of the feeling for colour which characterises Japanese art' reappears in its poetry 'as

---

[79] Ibid.
[80] Ibid., 189.
[81] Ibid.
[82] Ibid.
[83] Chamberlain, *The Classical Poetry of the Japanese*, 4.

a want of feeling for rhyme and rhythm and stanzaic arrangement'.[84] The very features of Japanese poetry that Chamberlain deems weaknesses, however, Hartmann gives as its strengths. As Ewick notes, Hartmann argues that, because of the small number of vowel sounds in Japanese, and 'as there are no metrical rules', Japanese poetry 'is really nothing but a primitive application of *vers libre*'.[85] Hartmann was aware of more recent developments in French poetry since his visits to France from 1892 and thus understood the potential value of Japanese poetry as an example for such innovations.[86] He suggests, though, that 'Japanese poetry has never found an Edward FitzGerald' thus far because a 'poem interspersed with pivot-words', which he identifies as a 'peculiarity of the long poems' that is 'strictly prohibited to the *tanka* and *haikai* writers', is 'simply untranslatable'.[87] Hartmann's implication, then, is that '*tanka* and *haikai*' are the most 'translatable' forms; for this reason, as well as their accordance with what he considers the Western tendency towards brevity, it is these forms that he recommends as models for Western poets.

In the following issue of *The Reader*, that of February 1904, Noguchi also suggested Western poets adopt Japanese forms in 'A Proposal to American Poets'.[88] Noguchi's is more specifically limited to 'Hokku': 'Pray', he urges, 'try Japanese Hokku, my American poets'.[89] Like Chamberlain and Hartmann, he compares the 'Hokku' to a 'perfect picture'.[90] He also takes a step further than Hartmann's article by presenting four of his own English 'Hokku', in which he maintains a five-seven-five syllable count. The first reads:

> My girl's lengthy hair
> Swung o'er me from Heaven's gate:
> Lo, Evening's shadow![91]

This abounds in even more archaisms and awkward contractions than previous *hokku* translations: in addition to the archaic 'Lo', 'lengthy' is itself a forced lengthening of the more natural 'long' to fit the five-syllable count imposed on the opening line, while 'over' is shortened to make the second line seven

---

[84] Chamberlain, 'Bashō', 308.
[85] Hartmann, 'The Japanese Conception of Poetry', 186; Ewick, 'Sadakichi Hartmann, Japan, and English-Language Verse', in *Japonisme, Orientalism, Modernism*, online.
[86] Hartmann, *White Chrysanthemums*, 24–5.
[87] Hartmann, 'The Japanese Conception of Poetry', 186.
[88] Noguchi, 'A Proposal to American Poets', *The Reader* 3, no. 3 (February 1904): 248.
[89] Ibid.
[90] Ibid.
[91] Ibid.

syllables. Despite Noguchi's 'Hokku' avoiding rhyme, then, their adherence to a fixed syllabic pattern does not as readily lend itself to comparison with *vers libre*.

During these years, interest in 'hokku' also took root in France. Claude Eugène Maitre called attention to it in his review of Chamberlain's Bashō essay in 1903.[92] Drawing on Chamberlain's discussion of the form's terminology, Maitre suggests that the terms 'hokku' and 'haikai' present its 'deux caractères essentiels': 'hokku' ('hemistiches initiaux') conserves its 'caractère inachevé', 'haikai' ('poèmes comiques') that of its relative freedom of diction and subject matter compared to *tanka*.[93] Although he also notes the term 'haiku' as 'un compromis entre les deux autres', Maitre consistently adopts 'haikai'.[94] Like Chamberlain, Maitre considers 'haikai' to have experienced two great periods: that of Bashō and his disciples at around the turn of the eighteenth-century and the late eighteenth-century revival led by 'le samurai Yokoi Yayû, la poétesse Chiyo, le peintre Buson'.[95] Buson's status is here not as prominent as in Chamberlain's essay, but his inclusion is nevertheless a reflection of his reputation's sudden increase following Shiki's critical writing. Maitre also compares 'haikai' with Japanese painting, observing that both seek 'dans le spectateur ou le lecteur une sorte de collaborateur, un poète ou un peintre en puissance, dans lequel il suffit d'éveiller une émotion ou d'évoquer une image'.[96] He concludes that both seek 'moins un moyen d'*expression* qu'un moyen de *suggestion*', thus echoing Hearn's, Aston's, Chamberlain's and Hartmann's similar assertions.[97]

Paul-Louis Couchoud, a French doctor who travelled to Japan from 1904 to 1905, is more explicit in his reason for choosing 'haïkaï' rather than any other term in his series of articles 'Les haïkaï (Épigrammes poétiques du Japon)', published in *Les Lettres* from April to August 1906.[98] For Couchoud, 'haïkaï' signifies that which is '*comique, vulgaire, populaire*'; as a result, he associates it with 'l'École populaire, Ukyoe [sic], en peinture'.[99] He contrasts this with the 'uta' (now more commonly known as the *tanka*), which corresponds with 'la peinture classique de l'École Kano'. The 'uta' and the Kano school share 'noblesse d'inspiration', 'raffinement de forme', 'sujets traditionnels' and the same public: 'la cour de l'Empereur et du Régent, les princesses, les seigneurs lettrés, les

---

[92] Claude Eugène Maitre, 'Japon', *Bulletin de l'École française d'Extrême-Orient* 3, no. 1 (1903): 723–9.
[93] Ibid., 725.
[94] Ibid., 726.
[95] Ibid.
[96] Ibid., 729.
[97] Ibid.
[98] Paul-Louis Couchoud, 'Les haïkaï (Épigrammes poétiques du Japon)', *Les Lettres* 3 (April 1906): 189–98.
[99] Ibid., 190.

Symphonies in White 57

prélats esthètes.'[100] The 'haïkaï', meanwhile, is 'la poésie des gens qui ne portaient pas les deux sabres': that is, of those ranked below the samurai class.[101] 'Haïkaï' represent 'la peinture réaliste' in their freedom of high and low subject matter, but also because of their attention to visual detail: whereas the classical 'uta' requires 'l'education classique chinoise et japonaise', a 'haïkaï' can strike us even in translation because it is 'une vision qui s'addresse directement à notre oeuil'.[102] 'The abstrait', in this form, 'est eliminé'. The first example he gives of this is Sōkan's 'heron' *hokku* (despite his being a 'prélat esthète'); another is, ironically, the 'butterfly' *hokku* of another 'prélat esthète', Moritake:

> Un pétale tombé
> Remonte à sa branche:
> Ah! c'est un papillon![103]

As suggested in the previous chapter, however, it is precisely 'l'education classique chinoise et japonaise' that is required to understand this 'haïkaï': it alludes to the saying of a Chinese Zen monk that is discussed in a Japanese Zen text. For Couchoud, however, it is 'Un bref étonnement', 'la définition même du haïkaï'.[104] The surprise is that of a metaphor which appears new when translated into a different cultural context.

Because of his interest in how the 'haïkaï' conveys a vision that addresses itself directly to the eye, it is perhaps unsurprising that the most cited *haijin* in Couchoud's article is 'le peintre' Buson. Thirty-three 'haïkaï' by seventeen writers are quoted; of these, twelve are by Buson, with the next most frequently cited being Bashō with four.[105] One of the most striking examples he offers of the apparent visual directness of 'haïkaï' reads:

> Seule, dans la chambre
> Où il n'y a plus personne
> Une pivoine.[106]

Couchoud gives this as a straightforward evocation of how a Japanese person 'a parfois une fleur dans sa chambre, – iris, lys, ou pivoine'.[107] This 'haïkaï' does not appear in Chamberlain's essay or Maitre's review; it does, however, appear

[100] Ibid.
[101] Ibid.
[102] Ibid., 190–1.
[103] Ibid., 193.
[104] Ibid.
[105] Ibid., 189.
[106] Ibid., 196.
[107] Ibid.

in Shiki and his disciples' *Buson kushū kōgi*. Its obscurity is evident in the four commentators' disagreement about the location of the peony (which, unlike in Couchoud's translation, is not given in the original). Kawahigashi Hekigotō and Kyoshi suggest it is in a mansion's *tokonoma*; but Meisetsu and Shiki disagree, imagining it to be outside. Shiki observes that 'to imagine it is in a *tokonoma* is to guess about the Temmei era with Meiji examples'.[108] Whereas Meiji-era Japanese might indeed keep a peony in their room as Couchoud describes, in Buson's time this may not have been the case, Shiki cautions. What makes Buson's 'peony' *hokku* striking, then, is its ambiguity. There is nobody there in the *hokku* to explain its meaning except its reader. In this sense, it thematizes what Shiki saw as Buson's principle of 'objectivity'. Its appeal to each viewer's subjectivity facilitates its transplantation into different times and places such as Shiki's and Couchoud's.

In the same year as Couchoud's articles, the translator F. V. Dickins, who with Aston was a founding member of the Asiatic Society of Japan after having first arrived in Japan in 1863 as a naval surgeon, published his anthology of *Primitive & Medieval Japanese Texts*.[109] Twenty-seven translations of '*Hokku* or *haikai*' are included. All are acknowledged adaptations, of Chamberlain's translations in the latter's Bashō essay. In his versions of Japanese 'epigrams', Dickins preserves Chamberlain's two-line layout but alters the latter's versions by adding rhyme or half-rhyme. Hattori Ransetsu's 'leaf' *hokku*, for example, is presented thus by Chamberlain:

> A leaf whirls down, alackaday!
> A leaf whirls down upon the breeze.[110]

Dickins's adaptation, however, reads:

> A single leaf that flutters down,
> A single leaf the wind hath blown.[111]

Both translators thus render Ransetsu's *hokku* with two lines of tetrameter. Neither translation acknowledges the original pun on '*hito-ha*', which can mean both 'one leaf' and 'people', so that the repeated '*hito-ha chiru*' can be read as 'one leaf scatters' and 'people scatter'; indeed, as Chamberlain notes, it served as Ransetsu's 'death-poem'.[112] As with its first English translators not observing that

---

[108] Shiki et al., *Buson kushū kōgi*, vol. 4, 35.
[109] F. V. Dickins, *Primitive & Medieval Japanese Texts* (Oxford: Clarendon, 1906).
[110] Chamberlain, 'Bashō', 245.
[111] Dickins, *Primitive & Medieval Japanese Texts*, 310.
[112] Chamberlain, 'Bashō', 245.

Bashō's 'old pond' *hokku* is an acrostic, Chamberlain's and Dickins's translations of Ransetsu's *hokku* demonstrate once more how other aspects of this poetic form were accorded less attention than its purported emphasis on visual concretion.

This tendency was one of the outcomes of a dramatic shift in the translation of *hokku* into English. Whereas before 1898 its English translators had considered it as peripheral and even undeserving of the name of poetry, the publication of Hearn's *Exotics and Retrospectives* that year marked a pivotal moment in its reception. From then on, the scholars who had been dismissive of it thoroughly revised their estimations of it. The most telling example is Chamberlain's Bashō essay of 1902. This essay, in turn, influenced both Anglophone and Francophone commentators such as Hartmann, Dickins, Maitre and Couchoud. Between 1898 and 1906, it had quickly risen to become the most prominent form in Japanese poetry in both the Anglophone and Francophone worlds; it was this rise that made Pound's and other Anglophone modernist poets' encounter with *hokku* possible. This development was, in turn, caused by the Japanese revival of interest in *hokku* in the 1890s. Many of the *hokku* Hearn cites in *Exotics and Retrospectives* came from an anthology compiled by Roseki, a Shiki disciple. Chamberlain's Bashō essay drew on a wide range of recent Japanese critical literature on *hokku*, including Shiki and his followers' *Buson kushū kōgi*. In particular, Shiki's emphasis on what he saw as Buson's principle of 'objectivity', in which visual details suggest rather than state meaning and thus 'appeal to the viewer's subjectivity', runs through many translators' characterizations of *hokku* at this time. This was, however, merely the beginning of its influence in the West: in July 1908, a twenty-two-year-old poet who had read Couchoud's article was about to write his first book review for *The New Age*; his name was F. S. Flint.

4

Pound's '"Metro" hokku'

Flint was the first of the poets later referred to as the Imagists to introduce what he called 'haikai'. At the age of seventeen he began writing poetry as well as acquiring an interest in left-wing politics; after meeting David Eder's wife at a political rally on 29 July 1907, Eder arranged for Flint to have his poems published in A. R. Orage's left-leaning magazine *The New Age*. The second of these poems, 'Palinode', expresses Flint's desire to be liberated from poetic convention. It begins thus:

> I have grown tired of the old measures wherein I beat my song,
> And as the sounds on the hill-top where the winds and sea-birds throng,
> And the broad and mournful monody of the ever-singing sea,
> In heart-shaped rhythms my song henceforth must well from the soul of me.[1]

It consists, however, of three rhyming quatrains, thus giving the impression of the speaker trying but failing to break free from the 'old measures'. In his first book review for *The New Age*, which appeared on 11 July 1908, Flint discusses Kimura Shotarō and Charlotte Peake's *Sword and Blossom Songs*, an illustrated 'tanka' selection from the tenth-century *Kokinshū* anthology:

> It is a pity, however, that the translators did not choose some other measure than the heavy English rhymed quatrain. It is probable that nearly all the spontaneity of the Japanese tanka has thus been lost.[2]

In addition to reiterating Flint's distaste for the 'rhymed quatrain' against which the speaker of 'Palinode' unsuccessfully struggles, his conclusion suggests that he considered the original Japanese 'tanka' to be characterized by an opposing 'spontaneity'.

The reason for this may be discovered in his two translations of 'haikai', which he then cites as an example of how Japanese poetry could instead be 'translated

---

[1] F. S. Flint, 'Palinode', *The New Age* n. s. 2, no. 12 (18 January 1908): 232.
[2] Flint, 'Book of the Week: Recent Verse', *The New Age* n. s. 3, no. 11 (11 July 1908): 212.

into little dropping rhythms, unrhymed'.³ Both are from Couchoud's article, the source of Flint's use of the term 'haikai'. The first is Buson's 'peony' *hokku*, the second Moritake's 'butterfly' *hokku*:

> Alone in a room
> Deserted –
> A peony.⁴
>
> A fallen petal
> Flies back to its branch:
> Ah! a butterfly!⁵

Flint's versions closely follow Couchoud's, most evidently in the Moritake *hokku*, in which the punctuation is identical. Both Flint and Couchoud's translations thus share the absence of rhyme and metrical regularity found in French *vers libre*. Flint demonstrates his interest in this kind of poetry in his next *New Age* book review, in which he argues that 'A poet should listen to the individual rhythm within him before he turns, if ever, to the accepted form'.⁶ To support this argument, he cites Stéphane Mallarmé, one of the most well-known late-nineteenth-century practitioners of *vers libre*: 'In truth there is no prose; there is the alphabet, and then verses more or less compact, more or less diffuse. Each time there is effort after style there is versification.'⁷ Flint uses this to emphasize that 'Beauty, emotion, and supple rhythm', rather than 'grind[ing] an iambic barrel-organ', are 'the essentials of good poetry'.⁸ Couchoud's 'haikai' translations thus offered Flint, evidently unaware of the originals' formal regularity, a model for a poetry of 'individual rhythm'.

Flint also saw in 'haikai' the quality of suggestion similarly observed by Hearn, Aston, Chamberlain, Hartmann, Maitre and Couchoud. In his 1906 article, Couchoud only briefly touches on the ability of Japanese 'haïjin' to measure 'exactement le pouvoir suggestif de chaque mot'.⁹ In his first *New Age* book review, however, Flint expands on this: '"to them in poetry as in painting, the half-said thing is dearest" – the suggestion not the complete picture (one thinks of Stéphane Mallarmé).'¹⁰ Mallarmé's essay 'Crise de vers', published in *Divagations* in 1897, proposes that the poetic schools termed 'Décadente' or

---

3   Ibid., 213.
4   Ibid.
5   Ibid.
6   Flint, 'Book of the Week: Recent Verse', *The New Age* n. s. 3, no. 16 (15 August 1908): 312.
7   Ibid.
8   Ibid.
9   Couchoud, 'Les haïkaï', 197.
10 Flint, 'Book of the Week: Recent Verse' (11 July 1908): 212.

'Mystique' seek 'rien que la suggestion' by 'instituer une relation entre les images exacte', which creates an implied 'tiers aspect fusible'.[11] There is no benefit to be gained from the transposition of 'un fait de nature' unless it can emanate 'la notion pure'.[12] He offers the word 'fleur' as an example: 'Je dis: une fleur! et, hors de l'oubli où ma voix relègue aucun contour, eu tant que quelque chose d'autre que des calices sus, musicalement se lève, idée même et suave, l'absente de tous bouquets'.[13] This may have been the reason Flint chose Buson's 'peony' *hokku* to indicate such a quality of suggestion. Whereas Shiki considered this *hokku* to contain no 'hidden principle', Flint saw it through Mallarméan eyes as pointing towards 'la notion pure', the abstract idea which the words 'pivoine' and 'peony' serve to suggest; such poetry, as he put it in another *New Age* book review the following month, constitutes a 'concrete symbolism' which 'seeks to convey the inexpressible in a definite image'.[14]

Independently of Flint, T. E. Hulme was developing a similar poetics that would provide fertile ground for the transplantation of these Japanese forms. Like Flint, Hulme had read about the innovations of French *vers libre* poets in around 1905 or 1906.[15] In 'A Lecture on Modern Poetry', given at the London-based Poets' Club in November 1908, he noted the importance of the 'image' in such poetry over metrical regularity: in *vers libre*, 'The length of the line is long and short, oscillating with images used by the poet'.[16] Hulme's lecture advocated a poetry that 'appeals to the eye rather than the ear. It has to mould images'.[17] More specifically, 'two visual images form what one may call a visual chord' and 'unite to create an image that is different to both': in this Hulme also echoes Mallarmé's 'Crise de vers'.[18] Hulme saw the 'image' as central to poetic language: whereas poetry 'deals in images', prose uses 'images that have died and become figures of speech'; poetic language 'arrests your mind' with a 'picture'.[19] What Hulme does not yet touch on, though, is how what is conventional in one language can be 'poetic' when translated into another. Moritake's 'butterfly' *hokku*, for instance, which relies in Japanese on its readers' familiarity with a then well-known Buddhist saying, loses this conventionality in Couchoud's and

---

[11] Stéphane Mallarmé, 'Crise de vers' ('Crisis in Verse'), in *Divagations* (Paris: Bibliothèque Charpentier, 1897), 245.
[12] Ibid., 250.
[13] Ibid., 251.
[14] Flint, 'Book of the Week: Recent Verse', *The New Age* n. s. 3, no. 18 (29 August 1908): 353.
[15] Robert Ferguson, *The Short Sharp Life of T. E. Hulme* (London: Allen Lane, 2002), 47.
[16] Hulme, 'A Lecture on Modern Poetry', 52.
[17] Ibid., 56.
[18] Ibid., 54.
[19] Ibid., 55.

Flint's versions, thus 'arresting' the mind with a 'picture' much more noticeably in its new context. Its apparent suitability for a poetry that 'deals in images' resulted, moreover, from the emphasis on the visual aspect of *hokku* in their earliest English translations.

In his review of the Poets' Club anthology *Poems for Christmas MDCCCCVIII*, Flint picked out Hulme's poem 'Autumn' as one of only a handful of poems he found to be effective.[20] Flint's criticism of the Poets' Club 'rhymesters' in 'evening dress' listening to after-dinner speakers who 'lecture portentously' received a reply from Hulme, which was published in *The New Age*.[21] Hulme invited Flint to the forthcoming dinner. They began corresponding and met soon afterwards.[22] Flint and Hulme, together with Edward Storer, F. W. Tancred, Joseph Campbell and Florence Farr, started meeting at the Café Tour d'Eiffel on Thursdays from 25 March 1909.[23] Flint recalls that the group's shared dissatisfaction with the current state of English poetry led to their experimentation with a number of poetic forms, including 'the Japanese *tanka* and *haikai*', of which they 'wrote dozens of the latter as an amusement'.[24] 'In all of this', he adds, 'Hulme was ringleader'.[25] Moody argues that Flint's account of Hulme's importance and Pound's peripherality within the group at this time is an 'exaggeration'; in their enthusiasm for Japanese poetry, however, they preceded his by some three years.[26] Flint's interest in both these Japanese forms as demonstrated in his *Sword and Blossom Songs* review and his translations of Buson's and Moritake's *hokku* makes it most likely, as Carr has claimed, that Flint was the instigator of these experiments with Japanese forms.[27] It would appear, however, that nothing remains of the 'dozens' of '*haikai*' experiments from this period.

According to Flint, Pound joined this group on 22 April, although in Flint's recollection 'he could not be made' at this time 'to believe that there was any French poetry after Ronsard. He was very full of his troubadours.'[28] He had arrived in Europe the previous summer, looking to start his poetic career. If Pound participated in any of the experiments in writing '*tanka* and *haikai*' between his joining the group and its 'lingering death in its second winter' of

---

[20] Flint, 'Book of the Week: Recent Verse', *The New Age* n. s. 4, no. 16 (11 February 1909): 327.
[21] Ibid.; Hulme, 'Belated Romanticism', *The New Age* n. s. 4, no. 17 (18 February 1909): 350.
[22] Flint, 'Belated Romanticism', *The New Age* n. s. 4, no. 18 (25 February 1909): 371.
[23] Flint, 'The History of Imagism', 70.
[24] Ibid., 71.
[25] Ibid.
[26] Moody, *Ezra Pound: Poet: A Portrait of the Man & His Work*, vol. 1 (Oxford: Oxford University Press, 2007), 97.
[27] *VR*, 189.
[28] Flint, 'The History of Imagism', 71.

1910 to 1911, no evidence survives.[29] Soon after arriving in London, however, Pound was drawn to Japanese art. Elkin Mathews, who published Pound's first three poetry collections in England, introduced him to another poet he published, Laurence Binyon, then the assistant keeper of Prints and Drawings at the British Museum, in February 1909.[30] Although the Print Room, which he was able to visit on Binyon's introduction, contained 'thousands of *nishiki-e*', or 'brocade prints' by this time, Pound does not mention any interest in East Asian art in his correspondence or other writings until some three years later.[31] He did, however, record his attendance at two of Binyon's four lectures on the subject of 'Art and Thought in East and West: Parallels and Contrasts' in March 1909. Its comparisons between the 'Similar inspiration of both movements' in 'The Renaissance in Europe and Japan' and the role of 'Great patrons' such as 'de' Medici' and 'the Ashikaga Shoguns' suggested for Pound the importance of East Asian art.

Despite the 'lingering death' of Pound's regular meetings with Flint, Hulme and others by 1910, English-language interest in 'haikai' continued to build. At the end of 1910, Chamberlain's *Japanese Poetry* was published by John Murray.[32] It included his essay on 'Bashō and the Japanese Poetical Epigram'. On 16 July 1911, Pound was sent a book containing 'Hokku' when Noguchi, who had returned to Japan seven years earlier, sent him his 1908 collection *The Pilgrimage*, which included six 'Hokku'. One of these had also appeared in 'A Proposal to American Poets', although 'lengthy' had been changed to 'lengthened':

> My love's lengthened hair
> Swings o'er me from Heaven's gate:
> Lo, Evening's shadow![33]

All the 'Hokku' in *The Pilgrimage* are characterized by the same adherence to a five-seven-five syllable count, contractions ('o'er') to ensure this adherence, archaisms ('Lo'), and abstractions ('Heaven's gate'). Noguchi's fame from his previous stay in London evidently remained: Pound replied to him that he 'had, of course, heard' of him, but had 'neglected to read' his books, 'altho' they lie with my own in Mathews [sic] shop'.[34] This was Noguchi's biography of Hearn, published in 1910 by Mathews. 'Of your country', Pound adds, 'I know almost

---

[29] Ibid.
[30] Pound, letters to Isabel Weston Pound (6 and 9 February 1909), in *L/HP*, 157–8.
[31] Ibid., 110 and 112.
[32] Chamberlain, *Japanese Poetry* (London: John Murray, 1910).
[33] Noguchi, *The Pilgrimage*, vol. 2, 140.
[34] Pound, letter to Noguchi (2 September 1911), in *EPJ*, 4–5, 4.

nothing – surely if the east & west are ever to understand each other that understanding must come slowly & come first through the arts.'[35] He praised Noguchi's poems, which he told Dorothy Shakespear in August 'seem to be rather beautiful', although he does not include any 'Hokku' among the three poems he refers to in his letter.[36]

In July 1912, Noguchi responded to the recent spate of 'Hokku' translations by criticizing the term 'epigram' for 'Hokku'. Whereas the 'epigram' has, in his view, 'one object', which is 'to express something [. . .] before itself', Noguchi argues that the object of a 'Hokku' is 'a usefulness of uselessness, not what it expresses, but how it expresses itself spiritually'.[37] He goes on to criticize recent 'Hokku' translations in the clearest terms: 'We confess that we have shown, to speak rather bluntly, very little satisfaction with the translations of Professor Chamberlain and the late Mr. Aston.'[38] Noguchi is particularly scathing about 'Mr. Porter's defects' in William N. Porter's *A Year of Japanese Epigrams* published the previous year, especially regarding his addition of words he perceives not to be present in the originals and Porter's use of rhyme.[39] Instead of proposing alternative approaches to their translation, however, Noguchi concludes that 'To translate Hokku or any other Japanese poem into English rarely does justice to the original'; he 'gave up' his hope of doing so, he relates, when he wrote the 'Evening's shadow' *hokku* that had appeared in 'A Proposal to American Poets' and *The Pilgrimage*. Noguchi thus again advocates writing English 'Hokku' as he himself had done, rather than translating Japanese ones.

The following month, Harold Monro's *Poetry Review* devoted its entire issue to Flint's essay on 'Contemporary French Poetry'. Flint had already introduced Pound to contemporary French poets earlier in the year: on 21 February 1912, he informed his mother that Flint 'has put me on to some very good contemporary French stuff, – Remy de Gourmont, de Regnier [sic], etc'.[40] As Carr points out, Flint's article introduced Pound to the numerous schools of French poetry, such as 'le néo paganisme', 'l'unanimisme', 'l'abbaye', 'l'école de grâce', 'le paroxysme', 'l'impulsionnisme', 'le néo-Mallarmisme' and 'le Futurisme'.[41] As Pound later recalled, it was this article that led him to invent the name 'imagiste'.[42] Flint also describes how 'The symbolist poet attempts to give you an intuition of reality

---

[35] Ibid., 5.
[36] Pound, letter to Dorothy Shakespear (August 1911), in *L/DS*, 44.
[37] Noguchi, 'Hokku', *The Academy* (13 July 1912): 57.
[38] Ibid.
[39] Ibid., 57–8.
[40] Pound, letter to Isabel Weston Pound (21 February 1912), in *L/HP*, 274.
[41] *VR*, 480.
[42] *L/MA*, 155.

itself and of the forces, vague to us, behind it, by a series of images'.[43] Carr observes that Flint again advocates '*vers libre*' in this article; indeed, he does so particularly through the example of the 'impulsionnisme' school founded by Ernest Florian-Parmentier, who 'insists that rhythms should be subordinated to inspiration, obeying the emotive movement'.[44] But it also touches on the promotion of accentual over accentual-syllabic metre and assonant over full rhyme. Flint approvingly cites Robert de Souza's contention in *Du rhythme, en français* that French verse 'depends on accent and quantity', not the number of syllables; and he praises the symbolist view 'that rhyme should give place to assonance', arguing that assonance has 'an unexpectedness, nuances, and subtleties to which rhyme cannot attain'.[45] As an example he gives the assonant rhymes in 'Odelette IV' by Henri de Régnier, one of the two French poets Pound mentions to his mother.[46]

After returning from a walking tour of southern France in August 1912, Pound also continued to develop his appreciation for Japanese visual art. One approach lay through the paintings of Whistler inspired by Japanese prints at the American painter's Tate Gallery exhibition, which ran between 17 July and 31 October. On 25 September, he wrote to his father that he had sent '2 poems' to appear in the first issue of *Poetry*; one was 'To Whistler, American', 'On the loan exhibit of his paintings at the Tate Gallery'.[47] Both the blues and golds of 'In a Studio' and the colour contrasts of 'Brown and Gold – de Race' and 'Grenat et Or – Le Petit Cardinal', which Pound gives in the poem as works that are 'perfect as Dürer', are typical of Whistler's emphasis on formal arrangement over subject matter. Pound told Monroe that he was 'on the threshold of what I hope is an endeavor to carry into our American poetry the same sort of life and intensity' as Whistler's painting; he also mentioned in *The New Age* that among Whistler's exhibited works were those influenced by 'Japanese models'.[48] The impact these in particular had on him can be gleaned from his later assertion that 'From Whistler and the Japanese, or Chinese, the "world", that is to say, the fragment of the English-speaking world that spreads itself into print, learned to enjoy "arrangements" of colours and masses'.[49]

---

[43] Flint, 'Contemporary French Poetry', *The Poetry Review* 1, no. 8 (August 1912): 357.
[44] Ibid., 399.
[45] Ibid., 358 and 360.
[46] Henri de Régnier, 'Odelette IV', in *Jeux Rustiques et Divins* (Paris: Société du Mercure de France, 1897), 228–9.
[47] Pound, letter to Homer Pound (25 September 1912), in *L/HP*, 286; Pound, 'To Whistler, American', *Poetry* 1, no. 1 (October 1912): 7.
[48] Pound, 'Patria Mia: VIII', *The New Age* n. s. 9, no. 26 (24 October 1912): 612.
[49] Pound, 'Edward Wadsworth – Vorticist', *The Egoist* 1, no. 16 (15 August 1914): 306.

Pound's direct acquaintance with Japanese visual art also grew during these months. Two days after informing his father about having sent 'To Whistler, American' to *Poetry*, he returned to the Print Room where many Japanese prints were available; after that, he paid frequent visits until its closure a year later.[50] Arrowsmith believes that Pound may thus have seen a Hokusai *nishiki-e* illustration of the ninth-century poet Ono no Komachi's waka in the thirteenth-century *Ogura hyakunin isshu* ('Ogura One Hundred Poems by One Hundred Poets'), which had also been translated before 1912 by Dickins, Clay MacCauley and Porter. The Hokusai illustration is accompanied by an index card with a translation of the *waka*:

> While I have been sauntering through
>   the world, looking upon its vanities, lo!
> My flower has faded and the time of the long rains come.[51]

What this version does not fully demonstrate are the original's *kakekotoba* ('pivot-words'): the verb *furu*, though used only once, furnishes the translation both with 'sauntering' and the 'falling' implied in the 'long rains', though *furu* can also mean 'ageing'; *nagame*, meanwhile, can mean 'long rains' but also the index card's 'looking upon'.[52] Both *kakekotoba* help to emphasize the waka's comparison of fleeting human lives and natural phenomena. Hokusai's illustration also departs from the *waka*: although an elderly woman (presumably Komachi) and a man sweeping (unseen) blossoms appear, it depicts a dry spring day with cherry blossoms in full bloom. Hokusai may thus have interpreted *'nagame'* as only meaning 'looking upon'.

On 13 October 1912, Pound sent to Monroe 'Contemporania', a twelve-poem sequence that embodied his new approach. It appeared in the April *Poetry* issue.[53] In addition to its use of *vers libre* as promoted by Flint and Hulme, it avoids archaisms in favour of an 'ultra-modern' speech.[54] Guided by the speaker's desire in 'The Condolence' for a 'gathering of delicate forms' due to being 'bored with male stupidity', many of its poems depict 'delicate' women in the senses of 'alluring' and 'fragile'.[55] The woman in 'The Garden', for instance, is 'Like a skein of loose silk blown against a wall'; the comparison suggests a gracefulness but

---

[50] Arrowsmith, *Modernism and the Museum*, 116.
[51] Ibid., 121.
[52] Ibid., 107.
[53] Pound, letter to Monroe (13 October 1912), in *L*, 11.
[54] Ibid.
[55] Pound, 'The Condolence', *Poetry* 2, no. 1 (April 1913): 2.

also 'a sort of emotional anaemia'.[56] The sequence's final poem is 'In a Station of the Metro':

The apparition   of these faces   in the crowd:
Petals   on a wet, black   bough.[57]

In the context of the 'Contemporania' series, the 'faces' in the crowd are feminized: their depiction as fleeting petals implies the fragile beauty suggested by the 'loose skein of silk'. Mark Byron proposes that the spacing of the words indicates an intention 'to mimic the faces and petals that formed the poem's subject matter'; it is more probable, though, that the spacing foregrounds a three-stress metre that may not otherwise be as easily apparent due to the greater than usual number of unstressed syllables. Indeed, he told Monroe that 'In the "Metro" hokku, I was careful, I think, to indicate spaces between the rhythmic units': the units were thus 'rhythmic' rather than visually mimetic.[58] Pound may have been inspired in this regard by Flint's emphasis on accentual metre in 'Contemporary French Poetry'; Flint's promotion of assonant rhyme may also be detected in that of 'crowd' and 'bough'.

In *Haiku and Modernist Poetics*, Hakutani proposes that Noguchi's correspondence with Pound in 1911 makes him 'most likely' to be Pound's inspiration for the composition of 'In a Station of the Metro'.[59] Kiuchi Toru even claims that 'none other than Noguchi' was Pound's source.[60] Their basis for this claim, however, is that whereas 'Hulme and Flint studied *hokku* through French translators who used the terms *haiku* and *haikai*', both Noguchi and Pound 'consistently called it *hokku* in their writings'.[61] As we have seen, though, Aston, Chamberlain, Hearn, and Dickins also used the term '*hokku*'. Furthermore, Pound's poem is presented in two lines; the only English translators to have done the same until then were Chamberlain and Dickins. The lineation and punctuation of 'In a Station of the Metro' reinforce the juxtaposition of faces and petals: in this way, they embody Hulme's poetics of 'two visual images' that 'unite to create an image that is different to both'. Chamberlain's *hokku* translations present similar juxtapositions of two 'visual images'. This is evident, for instance, in his version of Moritake's 'butterfly' hokku:

---

[56] Pound, 'The Garden', ibid., 3.
[57] Pound, 'In a Station of the Metro', ibid., 12.
[58] Mark Byron, 'In a Station of the *Cantos*: Ezra Pound's "Seven Lakes" Canto and the *Shō-Shō Hakkei Tekagami*', *Literature and Aesthetics* 22, no. 2 (December 2012): 148; Pound, letter to Monroe (30 March 1913), in *L*, 53.
[59] Hakutani, *Haiku and Modernist Poetics*, 73.
[60] Kiuchi Toru, 'Noguchi Yonejirō', 118.
[61] Hakutani, *Haiku and Modernist Poetics*, 73.

Fall'n flow'r returning to the branch, –
Behold! it is a butterfly.[62]

Although Pound chooses a colon, as Flint does, to mark the division between the juxtaposed elements, his emphasis on there being two such elements through lineation and punctuation more closely resembles Chamberlain's and Dickins's than Noguchi's. Indeed, the 'Metro' poem's assonant rhyme suggests a possible influence from Chamberlain's version of Sōkan's 'heron' *hokku* or Dickins's rhymed and half-rhymed translations. Most importantly, perhaps, Pound acknowledges having read Dickins's *Primitive & Mediaeval Japanese Texts* in his introduction to the nō plays *Kinuta* and *Hagoromo* in October 1914.[63] He would thus have encountered Dickins's use of the term '*hokku*' and his two-line versions of Chamberlain's translations. Dickins is thus the most likely source for Pound's understanding of '*hokku*', a conclusion that has not yet been made in Pound studies despite the wealth of scholarship on the subject.

Drawing on Pound's possibly having read Komachi's *waka* on the index card of Hokusai's illustration, Arrowsmith claims that 'Pound's own short poem "In a Station of the Metro" offers in its closing line an image strikingly similar' to the Komachi *waka*'s 'contrast between the pale, fallen *hanami* petals and rain-wet cherry wood'.[64] It is plausible that Pound could have read this *waka*, although, as is the case with any other possible literary source for 'In a Station of the Metro', Pound does not explicitly mention it. Another potential Japanese origin for the 'petals' metaphor that has not yet been proposed appears in Chamberlain's *Japanese Poetry*. As discussed in the last chapter, Chamberlain's anthology abounds with *hokku* evoking the fragility and transience of human life, which they compare to falling leaves, drops of dew, and – most pertinently for Pound – scattering petals. Chamberlain's version of one of Onitsura's *hokku*, for example, reads:

Together with one blossom more,
Oh! life, thou goest on thy way.[65]

The comparison of human life to a falling 'blossom' resembles that of 'In a Station of the Metro'. Chamberlain's translation, moreover, also emphasizes the analogy through its punctuation and lineation. If Pound had read *Japanese Poetry*, this *hokku* would have stood out because of the greater length of Chamberlain's

---

[62] Chamberlain, *Japanese Poetry*, 212.
[63] Pound, 'The Classical Drama of Japan', 450.
[64] Arrowsmith, *Modernism and the Museum*, 122.
[65] Chamberlain, *Japanese Poetry*, 246.

commentary on it: it provides evidence for his view that Onitsura 'really penetrated below the surface of things to the *lacrimae rerum*'.[66] Although it lacks the 'long rains' of Komachi's *waka*, Onitsura's poem has the advantage that it is a *hokku*, the form to which Pound would later refer to describe his 'Metro' poem.

The date on which Pound sent 'Contemporania' to Monroe also contradicts Hakutani's claim that this poem was also partly inspired by Noguchi's January 1913 article, 'What is a Hokku Poem?'[67] It was, nevertheless, a possible influence on Pound's later understanding of *hokku*. In this article, Noguchi stresses the form's concision: 'how can you call it poetry if you cannot tell it by a few words? Therefore these sixteen [*sic*] syllables are just enough to our Japanese mind.'[68] He also foregrounds its avoidance of abstraction: 'the "hokku" poem itself is distinctly clear-cut like a diamond or star, never mystified by any cloud or mist like Truth or Beauty.'[69] Although this goes against the use of abstractions in his own 'hokku' cited in the article, it is apparent in his five 'hokku' translations (Noguchi had evidently changed his mind about translating them). His version of the Bashō 'withered branch' *hokku*, for instance, reads:

> On a withered twig,
> Lo, the crow is sitting there,
> Oh, this autumn eve![70]

As Pound had already composed 'In a Station of the Metro' by this time, these translations cannot have influenced it; but Pound's later estimation of its significance may have been affected by Noguchi's view of such 'hokku'. Noguchi suggests that Bashō's 'hokku' would be unappreciated by 'the West'; he contrasts it with the 'factories and smoke' of modernity, due to which 'the crows become scarce'.[71] Bashō's 'hokku' is presented as a way of thinking at odds with 'modern heterogeneous minds', who 'are beginning to turn somewhere else'.[72] This contrast between the products of modernity and the natural world is also evident in Pound's '"Metro" hokku', with its juxtaposition of the 'Station of the Metro' and the 'petals on a wet, black bough'.

The difference between Noguchi's and Pound's poetics is made clearer in the latter's 'A Few Don'ts by an Imagiste', which appeared in *Poetry* in March

---

[66] Ibid., 151; Chamberlain, 'Bashō', 345.
[67] Hakutani, *Haiku and Modernist Poetics*, 74.
[68] Noguchi, 'What Is a Hokku Poem?', 355.
[69] Ibid.
[70] Ibid., 359.
[71] Ibid.
[72] Ibid.

1913, the month before 'In a Station of the Metro'. Drawing among other sources on Hulme's notion of 'two visual images' that 'unite to create an image that is different to both', Pound had invented the term 'Imagisme' in the summer of 1912 under the influence of Flint's account of the various schools of contemporary French poetry. This Imagiste manifesto's famous exhortations to 'Go in fear of abstractions' and not to use 'an expression such as dim lands of *peace*' because it 'dulls the Image' by 'mixing an abstraction with the concrete' contradict Noguchi's frequent use of such expressions in his English 'Hokku', one of many possible examples being 'Heaven's gate' in the 'Hokku' quoted earlier.[73] Pound's demand, likewise, that poets 'Use no superfluous word, no adjective, which does not reveal something' is aimed at the habit of writers of fixed forms to 'put in what you want to say and then fill up the remaining vacuums with slush'.[74] In order to adhere to a strict five-seven-five syllable pattern in his English 'hokku', Noguchi often adds expressions ('Lo!') or contractions ('o'er') that arguably reveal only the need for such adherence at all costs. This requirement to fit the words to this syllable pattern also goes against Flint's 'Imagiste' tenet in the same issue of *Poetry* 'to compose in the sequence of the musical phrase, not in the sequence of the metronome'.[75] These tendencies in Noguchi's poetry were what Flint, Hulme and Pound were reacting against.

Two months after the appearance of 'In a Station of the Metro' in *Poetry*, Pound gave his first account of its composition as part of a series of writers' columns entitled 'How I Began' in *T. P.'s Weekly*. Unable to put his experience of getting out of a train at La Concorde and seeing 'a beautiful face, and then, turning suddenly, another and another' into words, 'only the other night it struck me that in Japan, where a work of art is not estimated by its acreage and where sixteen syllables are counted enough for a poem if you arrange and punctuate them properly, one might make a very little poem which would be translated as follows', he writes, before citing 'In a Station of the Metro' in a slightly different layout from that of its publication in *Poetry*:

> The apparition of these faces in the crowd:
> Petals on a wet, black bough.[76]

The effect of removing the 'clusters' of the *Poetry* version is that the poem no longer foregrounds a three-stress reading of each line. It is presented as if it

---

[73] Pound, 'A Few Don'ts', 201.
[74] Ibid., 201 and 206.
[75] Flint, 'Imagisme', *Poetry* 1, no. 6 (March 1913): 199.
[76] Pound, 'How I Began', 707.

were 'translated': this perhaps allowed for a greater freedom from expectations of metrical regularity. 'Haikai' had likewise provided Flint with the means to create *vers libre* in English some four years earlier. Pound's choice of 'Japan' as the model for this 'translation', 'where sixteen syllables are counted enough for a poem', recalls Noguchi's similarly erroneous statement in 'What is a Hokku Poem?' Kiuchi argues that this proves Pound had read this article, although he then mistakenly argues that Pound went on to write 'In a Station of the Metro' after having read it.[77] While it is not impossible that Pound made the same mistake independently of Noguchi, it seems likely that Noguchi's article influenced Pound's account of the composition of 'In a Station of the Metro', though not the composition itself.

If Pound had indeed read Noguchi's 'What is a Hokku Poem?' before writing 'How I Began', it may shed further light on the final sentence of his account: 'And there', he concludes after having cited 'In a Station of the Metro', 'or in some other very old, very quiet civilization, some one else might understand the significance'.[78] Pound's perception of Japan as a 'very old, very quiet civilization' calls to mind Noguchi's contrast between Japan, where a poem such as Bashō's 'crow' *hokku* can be appreciated due to the supposed absence of industrialization, and 'the West', where 'the crows become scarce' because of the 'factories and smoke' of modernity. Moreover, Pound perceives Japan as a country in which the 'significance' of a highly compressed and suggestive poetry would be understood. This impression of Japan as a 'very old, very quiet civilization' in which poetry was better appreciated, as opposed to the 'modern heterogeneous minds' who 'are beginning to turn somewhere else', had largely been created by Hearn. Pound suggests that Japan is only one of a number of such 'very old, very quiet' civilizations; but, judging from Pound's present tense, unlike ancient Greece and Rome or medieval Tuscany and Provence, he imagined it as still resisting Western modernity.

Another way in which previous translators influenced Pound's reception of *hokku* was in the analogy of this poetic form with painting. While describing how he struggled to put his 'beautiful experience' into words, Pound 'could get nothing but spots of colour. I remember thinking that if I had been a painter I might have started a wholly new school of painting.'[79] The transition from 'beautiful faces' to 'spots of colour' is a visual abstraction that allows for the ambiguity of the spots to resemble both faces and petals. This recalls the ambiguity of the 'spots

[77] Kiuchi Toru, 'Noguchi Yonejirō', 128.
[78] Pound, 'How I Began', 707.
[79] Ibid.

of colour' in Whistler's *Nocturne in Black and Gold: The Falling Rocket*. Pound knew this painting; although he noted that the 'nocturnes' were not at the Tate exhibition, Whistler was on his mind again when he wrote 'In a Station of the Metro'.[80] *Hokku* offered itself to him as a poetic form that seeks to reproduce such effects. Shiki was influential in marking it out as closely associated with painting. This influence can be seen in the first English commentaries on *hokku*: Hearn suggests that 'the composer of a short poem endeavors to do exactly what the painter endeavors to do with a few strokes of the brush'; Chamberlain sees the 'spirit' of the '*Hokku*' poet as 'identical with that which informs the work of the Western water-colourist of to-day' and compares Sōkan's 'heron' *hokku* with Whistler's symphonies in white; and Hartmann, Maitre, Couchoud and Flint make similar comparisons between *hokku* and painting.[81] Moritake's 'butterfly' *hokku* presents a strikingly similar blurring of detail in order to create the visual comparison between the leaf and the butterfly. This form thus presented an ideal way out for Pound's struggle to put those 'spots of colour' into an 'arrangement' of his own.

Pound continued to write what some have considered also to be '*hokku*'-like poems throughout 1913 into the early part of 1914. Poems such as 'Epitaph' (later 'Leucis'), which appeared in *The Smart Set* in December 1913 as part of the more lighthearted 'Xenia' series, are presented in two lines but written much more in the manner of the satirical two-line epigrams of Catullus: such poems do not contain the suggestive indirectness of 'In a Station of the Metro'.[82] In a special issue of *The Glebe* devoted to the 'Imagistes', he contributed three poems which draw on translations of Chinese poetry in Herbert Giles's *A History of Chinese Literature* of 1901. 'Fan-Piece for her Imperial Lord', for instance, one of Pound's five poems included in the issue as well as in the *Des Imagistes* anthology he edited the same year, draws upon Giles's longer version of Ban Jieyu's poem on a court lady losing the emperor's favour, condensing Giles's ten lines into three:

> O fan of white silk,
>   clear as frost on the grass-blade,
> You also are laid aside.[83]

---

[80] Pound, letter to Monroe (18 August 1912), in *SL*, 43.
[81] Hearn, *In Ghostly Japan*, 309.
[82] Pound, 'Epitaph', *The Smart Set* 41, no. 4 (December 1913): 47.
[83] Pound, 'Fan-Piece for Her Imperial Lord', *The Glebe* 1, no. 5 (February 1914): 45. Both this poem and 'Ts'ai Chih' (see in the following text) have their first and third lines capitalized, suggesting Pound may have intended them to consist of two lines, rather than three, but that the exigencies of printing required the otherwise long first lines to be presented as they are.

As with 'In a Station of the Metro', the metaphorical comparison is made without explicit statement of the underlying emotion: in the Metro poem, according to Pound's account of its composition, this had been what the 'beautiful faces' made him 'feel'; here, it is the lady's 'fear' (a word Giles includes in his version) of rejection.[84] Its form bears a partial resemblance to Noguchi's English 'Hokku', with the first two lines in five and seven syllables, though the last has seven.

The other Pound poem in *The Glebe* that employs a similar layout is 'Ts'ai Chih'. Unlike 'Fan-Piece for Her Imperial Lord', however, it has no basis in Giles's translations, nor any other until then, despite the proximity of its title to the name of the Han-dynasty poet 'Ts'ao Chih' (192–232):

> The petals fall in the fountain,
>   the orange-coloured rose leaves,
> Their ochre clings to the stone.[85]

Arrowsmith proposes that it is 'entirely constructed' and prompted by Allen Upward's faux-translations of Chinese in *Scented Leaves from a Chinese Jar*, which appeared in the same issue of *The Glebe*.[86] Arrowsmith is most probably correct; if Pound had indeed read Chamberlain's *Japanese Poetry*, however, he may have been partially inspired by Chamberlain's version of this *hokku* by the Bashō disciple Naitō Jōsō (1662–1704):

> Behold the leaf that sinks and clings
> Below the water to a rock![87]

As is the case with Moritake's 'butterfly' *hokku*, it is shorn of its contextual allusion and presented by Chamberlain simply as 'The observation of a tiny fact in nature'.[88] Chamberlain's source for the hokku, Kōyō's *Haikai meikasen*, remarks that it was written at a ceremony to mark the seventh anniversary of Bashō's passing (which thus dates it to 28 November 1700).[89] This context foregrounds the comparison between the falling of the leaf and Bashō's life.

Four months after the publication of the *Des Imagistes* anthology in February, Pound joined forces with a number of other artists including Wyndham Lewis to found the Vorticist movement, the name of which Pound had, like 'Imagisme',

---

[84] Pound, 'How I Began', 707; Herbert Giles, *A History of Chinese Literature* (London: William Heinemann, 1901), 101.
[85] Pound, 'Ts'ai Chih', *The Glebe* 1, no. 5 (February 1914): 46.
[86] Arrowsmith, *Modernism and the Museum*, 152.
[87] Chamberlain, *Japanese Poetry*, 233.
[88] Ibid.
[89] Kōyō, *Haikai meikasen*, 90.

invented. In his 'Vorticism' essay, published in the September 1914 issue of *The Fortnightly Review*, Pound sought to explain the group's approach. In Pound's view, Whistler acts as forerunner to their experiments. The article opens with Whistler's statement comparing the conveying of emotion 'by means of an arrangement of shapes, or planes, or colours' with that of music; Pound goes on to note that 'Whistler said somewhere in the *Gentle Art*: "The picture is interesting not because it is Trotty Veg [*sic*], but because it is an arrangement in colour." The minute you have admitted that, you let in [. . .] cubism and Kandinsky, and the lot of us'.[90] He then expands his account of the composition of 'In a Station of the Metro': the 'new school of painting' that he thinks of founding upon the 'emotion' of seeing the faces at La Concorde is now 'a "non-representative"' one, of 'painting that would speak only by arrangements in colour'.[91] In this light, the colour contrast within the poem between the darkness of the underground Metro station and the 'wet, black bough' on the one hand and the whiteness of the faces and petals on the other suggests that 'In a Station of the Metro' is a Whistlerian arrangement in black and white. It is 'From Whistler and the Japanese', Pound claimed in his article of the previous month on the Vorticist Edward Wadsworth, that 'the "world" [. . .] learned to enjoy "arrangements" of colours and masses'.[92]

By the arrangement of visual detail to constitute the non-visual 'Image', Pound also emphasized the importance, as Hulme had, of avoiding the decay of 'images' into 'figures of speech'; 'All poetic language', he also argues, 'is the language of exploration'; that is, exploration for the new metaphor that 'arrests your mind', to borrow Hulme's phrasing.[93] After offering the example of a child who uses 'the language of art' by asking to '*open* the light', Pound writes that 'The Japanese have had this sense of exploration. They have understood the beauty of this kind of knowing. A Chinaman said long ago that if a man can't say what he has to say in twelve lines he had better keep quiet. The Japanese have evolved the still shorter form of the *hokku*', before citing his version of the 'very well-known' Moritake 'butterfly' hokku:

> The fallen blossom flies back to its branch:
>   A butterfly.[94]

---

[90] Pound, 'Vorticism', 461 and 464.
[91] Ibid., 465.
[92] Pound, 'Edward Wadsworth – Vorticist', 306.
[93] Pound, 'Vorticism', 466.
[94] Ibid., 466–7.

He then adds a '*hokku*' apparently passed on to him by Victor Plarr of a 'Japanese naval officer':

> The footsteps of the cat upon the snow:
>   (are like) plum-blossoms.[95]

For Pound, then, the '*hokku*' is an original metaphor: it is an 'arrangement' of two comparable elements. Its ability to achieve this effect of originality, however, depends upon its appearance in translation: it can only do so when shorn of its allusions to its literary and religious contexts in Japanese. As the two previous chapters explain, Moritake's *hokku* refers to a passage from a medieval Zen text which it playfully reverses. A more educated reader of Moritake's *hokku* would not read it as merely a visual comparison. In much the same way, Pound's view of Japanese prints as 'arrangements in colour' rather than allusive works that refer to a network of antecedents, as Hokusai's *Hyakunin isshu* series does, is based on their removal from their Japanese contexts. In this way, translation – whether from literary texts or visual art – became an essential vehicle for Imagist and Vorticist poetry to achieve their aim of metaphorical originality.

Although Pound began to seek out different poetic models for a 'long imagiste or vorticist poem' from 1914, Pound looked back on the '*hokku*' as an important and instructive phase in his poetic development. Moreover, although he had previously contrasted the modern world with Japan as 'a very old, very quiet civilization' that would appreciate a *hokku*, he considered this form to be suitable for the composition of a 'modern poem'. In his article on the then recently deceased Remy de Gourmont (1858–1915) in *The Fortnightly Review* of 1 December 1915, Pound claimed that de Gourmont's prose sonnets 'are among the few successful endeavours to write poetry *of our time*' because of his 'personal, sweeping rhythm', 'wholly his own'.[96] Pound's phrasing recalls Flint's search for an 'individual rhythm' through *vers libre*. To make a 'modern poem', a 'natural tone of voice' to 'express or cause a deep feeling' is required: 'I am, let us say, in an omnibus with Michio Itow. He has just seen some Japanese armour and says it is like his grandfather's [. . .] he says: "When I first put on my grandfather's helmet, my grandmother cried . . . because I was so like what my grandfather was at eighteen."'[97] There, Pound writes, 'is material for an hokku'.[98] Reflecting more than twenty years later on the 1910s, he characterizes *hokku*

---

[95] Ibid., 467.
[96] Pound, 'Remy de Gourmont', *The Fortnightly Review* n. s. 98, no. 588 (1 December 1915): 1164.
[97] Ibid., 1165.
[98] Ibid.

as the 'contraposition' of 'two visual images' to create a 'metaphor', the 'third element' arising from them.[99] Citing Aristotle's aphorism that 'metaphor' is 'the hall-mark of genius', Pound claims that 'The hokku is the Jap's [sic] test' of such genius.[100] That Pound saw it as an important stage of his poetic development is evident in his statement that such 'metaphor starts TOWARD ideogram', the model for the poetics Pound had developed in the interim.[101]

This conception of the '*hokku*' persisted throughout Pound's life. His return to it in the 1940s had been prompted by his correspondence with the Japanese avant-garde poet Kitasono Katué (1902–78), who had founded the poetry magazine *VOU* in 1935. On 16 February 1941, he told Kitasono that 'I lived today a *hokku*, or at least it seems more suited to a Japanese context than to my heavier hand, so I offer it to the *VOU* club':

> Stage, a room on the hill among the olive trees
> the violinist playing the air of Mozart's 16th violin sonata/
> then a finch or some bird that escapes my ornithology tried to counterpoint. <all through in key>
>
> I suppose the subject is: War time.[102]

As with his earlier conceptions of the Whistlerian 'arrangement' and the 'superposition' of the 'one-image poem', Pound still sees the '*hokku*' as a comparison of two elements; here, it is the 'counterpoint' of the sonata and the bird's song. The fulcrum of the *hokku* is marked by a forward slash that further accentuates this structure. On 12 March, he sent Kitasono another:

> // Mediterranean March
>
> Black cat on the quince branch
>   mousing   blossoms[103]

This '*hokku*' resembles that of the 'Japanese naval officer' in 'Vorticism'. Like 'In a Station of the Metro', it also employs the colour contrast of black and pink-white. In the last letter to pass between them before the war cut off their correspondence, Kitasono informed Pound that 'I translated your Hokku "Mediterranean March"'.[104] Despite Pound's view that it these '*hokku*' were 'more

---

[99] Pound, 'D'Artagnan Twenty Years After', *The Criterion* 16, no. 5 (July 1937): 607.
[100] Ibid.
[101] Ibid.
[102] Pound, letter to Kitasono Katué (16 February 1941), in *EPJ*, 110.
[103] Pound, letter to Kitasono (12 March 1941), in ibid., 113.
[104] Kitasono, letter to Pound (28 May 1941), in ibid., 114.

suited to a Japanese context', and his earlier belief that such poems of his might only be understood in a 'very old, very quiet civilization' like Japan, Kitasono never published either in his *VOU* magazine. Japan was not the 'very quiet civilization' Pound had imagined.

Together with these later references to '*hokku*', Pound used this term only eight times in print or in correspondence, four of those appearing in 'Vorticism', as Ewick notes.[105] Both 'How I Began' and 'Vorticism' are, however, crucial accounts of his poetic development; in both, the '*hokku*' plays a pivotal role. It functions as an important model for his Imagist poetics of concision, concretion and 'arrangement' as well as for his Vorticist 'superposition'. This model's availability had been enabled by Shiki's reforms of the 1890s, which had drawn on this poetic form's apparent compatibility with Spencer's tenets of 'brevity', the 'minor image' and 'antithesis'. Shiki and many early English translators emphasized these qualities of '*hokku*'. Shiki's principle of 'unity' in a haiku's composition anticipated Hartmann's description of it as consisting of a 'single image' and Pound's understanding of it as a 'one-image poem'. Pound, however, based this understanding on '*hokku*' that contained metaphorical comparisons like Moritake's, which Shiki had derided for their apparent lack of originality and visual precision. The originality of such metaphors for Pound was generated by their translation into a different cultural context. It is fitting, though, that Pound always used the term '*hokku*': his '*hokku*' acted as a starting point from which he soon moved away towards longer forms. At the end of 'Vorticism', Pound writes:

> I am often asked whether there can be a long imagiste or vorticist poem. The Japanese, who evolved the hokku, evolved also the Noh plays. In the best 'Noh' the whole play may consist of one image. I mean it is gathered about one image. Its unity consists in one image, enforced by movement and music. I see nothing against a long vorticist poem.[106]

The '*hokku*' was vital to Pound between 1912 and 1914; 'Noh', as the rest of this book proposes, would be vital to him for the rest of his poetic career.

---

[105] Ewick, 'Imagism Status Rerum', 56.
[106] Pound, 'Vorticism', 471.

Part Two

Pound and nō

5

'Nobody thought nō would rise again'
Umewaka Minoru and the Meiji revival of nō

The fall of the shōgunate and the Meiji restoration of 1868 affected nō far more than *hokku* writers. Whereas the latter depended on *hokku*'s popularity, with their income often deriving from teaching amateur practitioners, nō had been an exclusively elite art form since the shōgun Ashikaga Yoshimitsu's (1358–1408) patronage of the earliest playwrights whose nō remain, Kanami Kiyotsugu (1333–84) and his son Zeami Motokiyo (1363–1443). With the exception of benefit performances of nō (*kanjin* nō), which were permitted once in every generation for the Kanze school, the most prominent of the five nō schools, their performances were restricted to the aristocratic and samurai classes.[1] During the Edo period, they almost entirely relied on financial support from the shōgunate. From 1593, under the shōgun Toyotomi Hideyoshi (1537–98), nō actors were provided with subsidies that were later fixed until the Meiji restoration.[2] Each daimyō was required to contribute one *koku* (enough rice to feed one person for a year) per ten thousand to them.[3] In 1866, 1,226 nō actors, musicians and related persons were being supported with 3,493 *koku* and additional land and money by the shōgunate.[4] They lived in what Furukawa Hisashi describes as 'extreme luxury': Katsuko, the wife of the nō actor Kanze Kiyotaka, then head of the Kanze school, recalled the 'boredom' of having 'nothing to do' from being allocated seven servants.[5] A nō musician, Ōkura Hanjirō, remembered that the Komparu School, another of the nō schools, owned a residence in Nara at that

---

[1] Ōwada Takeki, *Utai to nō* ('Utai and Nō') (Tokyo: Hakubunkan, 1900), 16.
[2] Furukawa Hisashi, *Meiji nōgakushi josetsu* ('An Introduction to the Meiji History of Nō') (Tokyo: Wanya Shoten, 1969), 6.
[3] Ibid., 5.
[4] Ibid.
[5] Ibid., 6; Kanze Katsuko, 'Kaikyūdan' ('Tales of Yesteryear'), *Nōgaku* 9, no. 8 (August 1911): 34–5.

time of a thousand *tsubo* (around 3,300 m²).⁶ The stability of this support helped to preserve nō throughout the Edo period.

Nō lay at the heart of the Tokugawa shōgunate's most important rituals. The most well-known of these was the *utaizome* ('first nō chanting'), a programme of nō plays that had been performed, according to Ōwada Takeki's 1900 account in *Utai to nō*, on the fourth day of the new year since the time of the Ashikaga shōgunate and the second day of the new year during Hideyoshi's reign. During the Edo period, it was held at the Great Hall of the shōgun's principal residence, Edo Castle, on the third day of the new year:

> On that day, in the first third of the Hour of the Rooster [between 5 and 5.40 pm], in the Great Hall of the Edo Castle's keep, the *sanke* [the three highest-ranking daimyō, relatives of the shōgun], the other daimyō, many nobles, those with at least ten thousand *koku*, and below them those of the rank that wear *hoi* robes and above attend. Everyone wears *noshime kamishimo* robes. When the shōgun offers the cup of sake, beginning with the heads of the Kanze, Hōshō, Komparu and Kita Schools (Kanze and Komparu every year, Hōshō and Kita every other year), the *waki* actors, the kyōgen actors, the musicians and the chorus each wear *suō* robes and *eboshi* hats and bow down on the verandah. Following the signal of the shōgun making three offerings with his cup, the head of the Kanze school, while remaining prostrate, performs the *shikai nami* passage [from the play *Takasago*] before the performance of the three plays *Oimatsu* ['The Aged Pine'], *Tōboku* ['The Northeastern Hall'] and *Takasago*.⁷

This programme particularly venerated the Tokugawa clan, originally named Matsudaira: the *matsu* ('pine') in their name was a commonly used symbol of the clan and features in *Oimatsu* and *Takasago*. The '*shikai nami*' refers to the passage sung by the chorus in *Takasago* in which 'the waves of the four seas [*shikai nami*] are quiet, and the land, too, is well governed'.⁸ The singing of this passage during the *utaizome* thus compared the rule of the Tokugawa shōgunate with that of Emperor Daigo (885–930) and, implicitly, the Ashikaga shōgunate in *Takasago*. It was only to be performed before the shōgun and at the Kasuga Shrine in Nara.⁹ Other ceremonies involving nō were the shōgun's official pronouncements and the promotions, successions, marriages and birthdays of nobles. The last nō performed for the accession of the shōgun, Tokugawa Iemochi, took place in

---

⁶ Ōkura Hanjirō, 'Komparu ryū no kokiroku' ('Ancient Records of the Komparu School'), *Nōgaku* 9, no. 12 (December 1911): 46.
⁷ Ōwada, *Utai to nō*, 13.
⁸ Ōwada Takeki (ed.), *Yōkyoku tsūkai* ('Nō with Commentary'), vol. 1 (Tokyo: Hakubunkan, 1892), 4.
⁹ Ibid.

1858 and also included *Takasago* in its programme of six plays.[10] In this way, nō pervaded the lives of the aristocratic and samurai classes and played a crucial role in expressing the shōgunate's power.

As a result, the resignation of the last shōgun, Tokugawa Yoshinobu, in 1868, had a dramatic impact on nō. During the violence of the Bōshin War, many nō theatres had already been lost: the Nishinotōin Katayama theatre, the Muromachi theatre and the Akezu Yamagawa theatre all suffered fire damage during the unrest in the capital of 1864.[11] In an attempt to avoid the rampaging armies, the aforementioned Komparu estate chained up its gates, and the actors fled to Nembutsu Temple with their most treasured possessions. The estate was destroyed, however, and the materials they had salvaged had to be sold.[12] After Yoshinobu's abdication, all nō actors' stipends, which had continued for over two and a half centuries, suddenly stopped. Kanze Kiyotaka followed Yoshinobu into exile in Suruga Province.[13] An edict was proclaimed banning the performance of nō, and Kiyotaka, among others, had to sell his nō robes; he had resolved, according to his wife, to burn himself to death with his nō masks if they also had to be sold.[14] His allowance had dropped from 256 *koku* to less than 2 *koku*.[15] Those who shifted their allegiances to the new régime hardly fared any better: Hōshō Kurō, head of the Hōshō School, tried and failed to set up as a trader; Matsumoto Kintarō wove bamboo umbrellas; and the Kanze actor Umewaka Minoru was forced into menial labour to support his family.[16] As Umewaka later recalled of this moment, 'nobody thought that nō would rise again'.[17]

Umewaka was one of several actors who nonetheless sought to keep nō alive in the years immediately following the Meiji restoration. Born Kujirai Kamejirō, he had been adopted into the Umewaka family, who had been nō actors for centuries: according to Umewaka's son Rokurō, the 'waka' ('young') in their family name (originally 'Umezu') had been granted by Emperor Go-Tsuchimikado to praise the nō performance of a sixteen-year-old ancestor in 1481.[18] Umewaka

---

[10] Furukawa, *Meiji nōgakushi*, 10.
[11] Ibid., 13.
[12] Ibid., 14.
[13] Kurata Yoshihiro, 'Meiji nōgakukai no hikari to kage' ('The Light and Darkness of the World of Meiji Nō'), *Nōgaku kenkyū* 25 (2000): 1.
[14] Kanze, 'Kaikyūdan', 38.
[15] Kurata, 'Meiji', 2.
[16] Matsumoto Kintarō, 'Ishingo no keireki dan' ('A Conservation on My Career After the Restoration'), *Nōgaku* 1, no. 7 (January 1903): 30; Kurata, 'Meiji', 10; Umewaka Minoru and Josui Ikiru, 'Ishin tōji no nōgaku' ('Nō at the Time of the Restoration'), *Nōgaku* 1, no. 1 (July 1902): 23.
[17] Ibid.
[18] Umewaka Rokurō, 'Bōfu no kushin' ('The Grief of My Father's Loss'), *Nōgaku* 7, no. 2 (February 1909): 48.

first performed nō in 1851 and acted in the nō programme commemorating the accession of the shōguns Tokugawa Iesada (1824–58) and Tokugawa Iemochi (1846–66).[19] In 1868, he used the Edo residence of the often-absent Nishio Tada'atsu (1850–1910), daimyō of Oki Domain, in Mukōjima (on the opposite bank of the Sumida River from his own house) to practice nō. By the following year, he had gathered a group of musicians together to practise nō in his own house and began to charge for performances.[20] Foreign dignitaries, meanwhile, were occasionally entertained with nō, such as the Duke of Edinburgh in 1869. Date Munenari, a prominent member of the new government, asked Hōshō Kurō and representatives of the other schools to perform nō for the visiting royal at Akasaka in Tokyo on 29 July.[21] The playwright Yoda Gakkai (1833–1909) records in his diary his attendance of a nō performance by the Kongō school in Tokyo on 11 April 1871.[22] Kanze Kiyotaka, Matsumoto Kintarō and others also gave a ten-day nō performance at Asama Shrine in Kai Province that year.[23] Umewaka, meanwhile, was already beginning to achieve commercial success: a programme held at his house in November 1871 had given him 'two years of subsidy in a single day'.[24] Nō had not entirely fallen with the shōgunate.

One of the audience members of a performance at Umewaka's house, noting the cramped space within which the actors had to perform, suggested constructing a more suitable nō stage there. Seven nō actors, including Umewaka and Kanze Tetsunojō, borrowed money from benefactors including the retired daimyō Nabeshima Naomasa (1815–71) and were thus able to pay the 500 yen to have a new nō stage constructed.[25] To pay off the loan, they performed a public nō programme for the theatre's opening in 1872; the first of these already raised a profit of 100 yen.[26] The following year, Umewaka invited Hōshō Kurō to collaborate on nō performances; in August 1873, the latter acted in a nō play at Umewaka's house.[27] By 1875, the seven nō actors were able to repay the loan to Nabeshima's estate and own the nō stage outright.[28] A more important and long-standing benefactor was Iwakura Tomomi (1825–83), an imperial courtier who led the Iwakura Mission to the West between 1871 and 1873.[29] As

[19] Ibid., 50.
[20] Umewaka and Josui, 'Ishin tōji no nōgaku', 23.
[21] Kurata, 'Meiji', 20; Furukawa, *Meiji nōgakushi*, 12.
[22] Ibid., 15.
[23] Ibid., 3.
[24] *UMN*, vol. 6, 335.
[25] Umewaka and Josui, 'Ishin tōji no nōgaku', 24.
[26] Ibid.
[27] Furukawa, *Meiji nōgakushi*, 21.
[28] Umewaka and Josui, 'Ishin tōji no nōgaku', 24–5.
[29] Sasaki Suguru, *Iwakura Tomomi* (Tokyo: Yoshikawa, 2006), 164–7.

the embassy's chronicler, the historian Kume Kunitake, later recalled, they were often entertained with opera.[30] Previously, he and the other ambassadors had paid little attention to nō, seeing it as something for 'warriors nostalgic for the end of the Tempō era [1830-44]', the last prosperous days of the shōgunate; after watching Western operas, however, they came to see its value in representing Japanese culture to foreign dignitaries.[31] Upon returning to Japan, Kume went to see nō at Umewaka's house but noted that audiences still only numbered fewer than thirty.[32]

Another proponent of nō after the Meiji Restoration was Emperor Meiji (1853–1912) himself. Nō was an art not just of the daimyō but also of the imperial court. Before his accession to the throne, nō formed a part of his broader cultural education.[33] It was performed, for instance, at the ceremony that made him the official heir to the throne in 1860.[34] Emperor Meiji suggested to the Empress Dowager, Eishō, to watch nō to alleviate her 'boredom' in 1870.[35] Following nō performances in the presence of the Emperor and Empress Dowager at the imperial palace in Kyōto in 1872 and at Iwakura's Tokyo residence in 1876, she had a nō theatre constructed in 1878 at her palace in Aoyama, patronized Kanze Kiyotaka, Kongō Tadaichi, Hōshō Kurō and Umewaka Minoru, and granted them 3,000 yen for costumes, with a further 80 yen for each performance over the next five years.[36] Iwakura, meanwhile, continued to invite foreign as well as imperial guests to his house to watch nō; the American former president Ulysses S. Grant told him after watching nō at his house on 8 July 1879 that he should 'treasure and preserve' this 'noble and elegant' art form.[37] The following year, Iwakura set up the Nōgakusha ('Nō Society') to co-ordinate its patronage by members of the nobility, many of whom included former daimyō such as Tokugawa Iesato (1863–1940), the head of the Tokugawa clan. In 1881, moreover, the Nōgakusha funded the construction of the Shiba Nō Theatre, the largest nō theatre in Japan.[38]

---

[30] Kume Kunitake, 'Nōgaku no kako to shōrai' ('Nō's Past and Future'), *Nōgaku* 9, no. 7 (July 1911): 1. On 6 March 1872, they attended Gaetano Donizetti's opera *Lucia di Lammermoor* at the National Theatre in Washington, DC; further opera performances were given for them in the UK, Russia, Denmark and Sweden. Kume, *The Iwakura Embassy 1871-3: A True Account of the Ambassador Extraordinary & Plenipotentiary's Journey of Observation Through the United States of America*, trans. Graham Healey and Chūshichi Tsuzuki, vol. 1 (Princeton: Princeton University Press, 2002), 212.
[31] Ibid., 2.
[32] Ibid.
[33] Keene, *Emperor of Japan: Meiji and His World* (Tokyo: Yushodo, 2004), 36.
[34] Ibid., 8 and 52.
[35] Kurata, 'Meiji', 17.
[36] Ibid.
[37] Ibid., 18; Keene, *Emperor of Japan*, 319.
[38] Ikenouchi Nobuyoshi, 'Shiba nōgakudō no yurai oyobi ryakureki' ('The Origins and a Brief History of the Shiba Nō Theatre'), *Nōgaku* 1, no. 2 (August 1902): 11.

Nō had thus recovered much of its earlier prestige within thirteen years of the restoration; it had done so through the perseverance of its actors and the patronage of the new Meiji nobility, including the imperial family.

During the 1880s, modern Japanese scholarship on nō also began to develop in the wake of nō's translation into English by Chamberlain. Konamakura Kiyonori's (1822–95) *Kabu ongaku ryakushi* ('A Brief History of Song, Dance and Music') was published in 1888 with an introduction by Chamberlain.[39] Four years after Konakamura's study, Ōwada Takeki's (1857–1910) *Yōkyoku tsūkai* ('Nō with Commentary') appeared. Ōwada had not just been a nō enthusiast since he began lecturing at Tokyo University in 1884; that year, he also began practising nō as an amateur in the Kanze school.[40] His diaries record his frequent attendance of nō plays, including many at Umewaka Minoru's house.[41] In one of his first publications, *Shijin no haru: shinchō shōka* ('The Poets' Spring: The New Wave of Poetry'), Ōwada criticized the writing of *kanshi* (Chinese-language poetry), which 'allowed no change' and had become *chimpu* ('hackneyed', the term Shiki later used).[42] To revive Japanese poetry, he advocated a combination of native Japanese poetry's 'spirit' and European 'freedom' and 'length' to express 'the emotions of the current generation': European poetry could serve as a model that 'does not seek to avoid human emotion'.[43] In his introduction to *Yōkyoku tsūkai*, Ōwada states that 'song and dance originated in human emotion'.[44] The 'purpose of art', Ōwada suggests, 'is to refine the emotions'; this quality, he claims, 'exists in nō'.[45] In the context of *Shijin no haru*, then, it appears that his interest in nō was motivated by his desire to revive Japanese literature through a return to forms that he believed possessed this quality.

Ōwada's description of nō's development suggests, as Konakamura does, that the 'first phase' of nō originated in *kagura* dance.[46] He also explains the term 'nō' as originating in an abbreviation for '*sarugaku no nō*' ('skilful *sarugaku*' or, simply, '*sarugaku* performance').[47] The first play that Ōwada includes in *Yōkyoku tsūkai* is *Takasago*, whose arrangement he attributes to Zeami. It is now thought

---

[39] Chamberlain, 'Preface', in Konakamura Kiyonori, *Kabu ongaku ryakushi* ('A Brief History of Song, Dance and Music'), vol. 1 (Tokyo: privately printed, 1888), n. p.
[40] Ōwada, 'Nikki bansui' ('Diary Excerpts'), *Nōgaku* 9, no. 4 (April 1911): 71.
[41] Ōwada, 'Nikki bansui', *Nōgaku* 9, no. 2 (February 1911), 80; Ōwada, 'Nikki bansui', *Nōgaku* 9, no. 5 (May 1911): 64.
[42] Ōwada, *Shijin no haru: shinchō shōka* ('The Poets' Spring: The New Wave of Songs') (Tokyo: Bunseidō, 1887), n. p.
[43] Ibid., 2–3.
[44] Ōwada, *Yōkyoku tsūkai*, vol. 1, 1.
[45] Ibid., 11.
[46] Ibid., 4.
[47] Ibid., 3.

to have been composed in 1423.⁴⁸ He states that 'it is first among all nō' and that 'its pines are the most prominent metaphor for the way of poetry and for celebrating imperial rule', adding that it was performed at the *utaizome* of the Tokugawa shōgunate, at which the lines describing how the 'waves of the four seas are quiet' under the emperor's rule are sung at the beginning.⁴⁹ In his 1902 commentary on the play in the magazine *Nōgaku*, Ōwada goes further by remarking that 'it goes without saying that it is the greatest congratulatory nō play'.⁵⁰ It opens with the *waki* (secondary actor), a priest at the Aso Shrine in Kyūshū named Tomonari, travelling to the capital and stopping at Takasago, where he encounters an old man and woman. The former sings of 'the Takasago pine' which did not yet exist when he was young; together with the old woman, he tells how 'the pine of life' is 'also a famous spot'.⁵¹ This is the first allusion within the play to a connection with imperial rule: the 'pine of life' was planted by Empress Jingū before her invasion of Korea in the third century.⁵² Ōwada does not mention this, however, merely repeating that the 'pine of life' is 'also a famous spot'.⁵³ Tomonari asks them which is the Takasago pine, to which the old man replies that it is 'the tree in whose shadow I am sweeping'. Indeed, the old man appears on stage carrying a rake and the old woman a broom to sweep the ever-falling pine needles.

The priest then poses the old man and woman the following question:

> The Takasago and Suminoe pines are called *aioi*. This place and Sumiyoshi are provinces apart. Why are they called *aioi*?⁵⁴

Ōwada explains that 'Suminoe' is 'an old name for Sumiyoshi', the site of the Sumiyoshi Shrine, which was dedicated to the Sumiyoshi sea deity. As Ueda Masa'aki notes, in the eighth-century *Kojiki* ('Records of Ancient Matters'), the Sumiyoshi sea deity initially consisted of three sea deities.⁵⁵ They functioned as protectors of ports and sea journeys; in the *Kojiki*, Empress Jingū is supposed to have asked them for protection before setting off with her ships bound for Korea.⁵⁶ The *Settsu fudoki*, a collection of Settsu Province folk tales, relates that

---

⁴⁸ Umehara Takeshi and Kanze Kiyokazu (eds), *Nō wo yomu* ('Reading Nō'), vol. 2 (Tokyo: Kadokawa gakugei shuppan, 2013), 251.
⁴⁹ *YT*, vol. 1, 1.
⁵⁰ Ōwada, 'Yōkyoku kōgi: Takasago' ('Lectures on Nō: Takasago'), *Nōgaku* 1, no. 1 (July 1902): 2.
⁵¹ *YT*, vol. 1, 2.
⁵² Royall Tyler, *Japanese Nō Dramas* (Harmondsworth: Penguin, 1992), 283.
⁵³ *YT*, vol. 1, 2.
⁵⁴ Ibid.
⁵⁵ Ueda Masa'aki, *Sumiyoshi to Munakata no kami* ('The Gods of Sumiyoshi and Munakata') (Tokyo: Chikuma Shobō, 1988), 4.
⁵⁶ Ibid., 15.

Empress Jingū named Suminoe Sumiyoshi because it was a 'good place to live' (*sumiyoshi*).⁵⁷ *Aioi*, meanwhile, puns on a variety of readings: Ōwada lists 相追 ('pursuing together') and 相老 ('growing old together') as possibilities, but indicates that 'two pines growing together is how it should be understood'.⁵⁸ *Ai* here means 'together' and *oi* 'growing', or 'living'. In his 1902 commentary, Ōwada adds that *Aioi* used to be the play's title; indeed, Zeami's fifteenth-century *Sarugaku dangi* ('Talks on *Sarugaku*'), discovered three years later, mentions this title.⁵⁹ Ōwada interprets the phrase as 'a metaphor for the auspiciousness of the emperor's reign': when considered as paired pines 'growing together' despite being provinces apart, it suggests a form of national unity (through *ai*, 'together') and prosperity (*oi*, 'growing').

The old man responds to Tomonari in the following way:

> As you say, the preface of the *Kokinshū* states that the pines of Takasago and Suminoe are thought to be like *aioi*. This old man is from Sumiyoshi in the province of Tsu. It is this old woman here who is from this place.⁶⁰

The old man directly quotes the passage in the preface to the tenth-century *Kokinshū* poetry anthology, written by Ki no Tsurayuki (868–946): 'The pines of Takasago and Suminoe are thought to be like *aioi*.'⁶¹ This conceit appears, however, to have arisen in *Takasago* itself. None of the waka in the *Kokinshū* that mention Takasago, Sumiyoshi or Suminoe suggests that the pines of Takasago and Suminoe are paired with each other. The anonymous waka no. 905 connects a 'little pine' at Sumiyoshi with the theme of longevity:

> It has been so long
> since I have laid eyes on it –
> how many ages
> has the little pine upon
> Suminoe's shore passed through?⁶²

The tenth-century poet Fujiwara no Okikaze's (dates unknown) *waka*, no. 909 in the *Kokinshū*, is sung by the old man as he and the old woman first arrive at centre stage:

---

⁵⁷ Ibid., 31.
⁵⁸ *YT*, vol. 1, 2.
⁵⁹ Ōwada, 'Yōkyoku kōgi: Takasago', 2.
⁶⁰ *YT*, vol. 1, 3.
⁶¹ Katagiri Yōichi and Takaoka Masao (eds), *Kokinshū zenhyōshaku* ('Collection of Poems Past and Present with Detailed Commentary'), vol. 1 (Tokyo: Yūbun shoin, 1976), 128.
⁶² Ibid., vol. 2, 740.

Whom do I know now?
Even though I am so old
that even the pine
of Takasago is not
a friend of mine from the past.[63]

In Okikaze's waka, the pine's age is hyperbolically contrasted with the speaker's in order to emphasize that the latter is even older. Ōwada makes no mention of this apparent discrepancy between the *Kokinshū*'s preface and Zeami's interpretation. He merely mentions that Tsurayuki edited the *Kokinshū* and that it was published 'by order of Emperor Daigo during the Engi era' (901–23).[64] This seemingly minor detail anticipates the play's emphasis on the importance of the connection between the flourishing of poetry and imperial rule.

The old man and old woman introduce the multiple significances of the *aioi* image to Tomonari. The first is the affection between a married couple, the old woman explains: when asked by the priest how an old couple can stay together despite such physical distance between them, she replies, 'though separated by ten thousand miles of mountains and rivers, the way of a couple's care that moves from each to the other is not long'.[65] The second significance is the relationship between the past and the present. The old couple explains:

Old Man	In the past, people said that it [*aioi*] is the sign of an auspicious reign.
Old Woman	Takasago is the previous reign of the *Manyōshū* in the distant past.
Old Man	Sumiyoshi is His Majesty, who lives in the present reign of Engi.[66]

The pairing of Takasago and Sumiyoshi thus also represents that of the imperial domain's past and present: through the initial metaphor of conjugal love, the play thus expresses the love that binds the nation's past and present together. The third significance of *aioi*, as the references to the *Manyōshū* and the *Kokinshū* already suggest, is poetry. The old woman adds that 'Pines mean unending leaves of speech': the Japanese for 'word' consists of the characters 'speech' and 'leaves', and pine needles are referred to as '*ha*' ('leaves').[67] The ever-falling 'leaves' of the pine stand for the continuous flourishing of poetry 'in the past and the present', which, as the old couple sing in unison, 'praises the imperial reign'.[68] Poetry and

---

[63] Ibid., 747.
[64] *YT*, vol. 1, 3.
[65] Ibid.
[66] Ibid., 3–4.
[67] Ibid., 4.
[68] Ibid.

imperial rule thus also 'grow together': the emperors provide the conditions for poetry to flourish and commission anthologies, while the poems thus produced sing the praises of the emperors' reigns.

After this, the 'four seas' passage traditionally sung by the head of the Kanze school before the shōgun at the *utaizome* appears. In the play, the chorus sings:

> The waves of the four
> seas are quiet, and
> the land, too, is well governed.
> The wind of the tides
> makes no sound among the boughs
> during His Majesty's reign.
> Together, the *aioi* pines
> are thus auspicious.
> Truly, looking up at them,
> are not words inadequate
> to describe this reign?
> The common people can live
> and be prosperous.
> For His Majesty's blessings
> being at peace.[69]

The Chinese emperor assumed the title of ruler of 'all under heaven'; other states were required to pay tribute. This universality of an emperor's rule is also apparent in the passage where Japan is mentioned by a poetic name, Shikishima. The chorus sings that the pines' 'leaves of speech' become 'seeds that polish the heart'; as a result, all living things will 'come under the shadow of Shikishima'.[70] While *Takasago* seeks to depict Japan's national unity by means of the paired pines of Takasago and Sumiyoshi, its depiction of imperial rule also approximates the universalism of its Chinese model. Moreover, the fact that it alludes to a Chinese model also indicates the play's trans-national conception of imperial rule.

This connection between the Japanese and Chinese imperial model is made more explicit in the play's reference to the first emperor of China, Shi Huangdi ('First Emperor', 259–210 BC), who unified the country in 220 BC. The chorus tells of how he came to venerate the pine above all other trees:

> This pine is the greatest of the ten thousand trees. It is dressed like eighteen dukes. It produces green during a thousand autumns and its age does not show.

---

[69] Ibid.
[70] Ibid.

It is a tree that even received the title of Marquis from the First Emperor. In other lands and in this realm it is praised by ten thousand peoples.[71]

Ōwada comments that the pine's description as 'eighteen dukes' refers to the constituent parts of the Chinese character for 'pine' (松): the left-hand radical (木, which itself means 'tree') is fancifully separated into 十 ('ten') and 八 ('eight'), which together can mean 'eighteen', while the right-hand element by itself (公) signifies 'duke' or 'prince'.[72] He adds that the text 'makes use of an historical event. After the Qin First Emperor sheltered under a pine tree, he bestowed upon it the title of fifth-rank grandee. *Shaku* ["Marquis"] is a noble rank'.[73] This event is recorded in the Chinese historian Sima Qian's *Historical Records*: in the year following his unification of China, Shi Huangdi was descending from Mount Tai after having performed sacrifices to heaven, earth, and 'the mountains and rivers' when 'there was a violent onset of rain' and 'he rested under a tree, which was consequently enfeoffed as fifth-rank grandee'.[74] The play's allusion to this account reinforces its comparison of the evergreen pine and the longevity and stability of imperial rule.

At the end of the play's first part, the old man and woman reveal that they are the spirits of the pines of Sumiyoshi and Takasago. In the second part, Tomonari travels by boat to Sumiyoshi, where he encounters the Sumiyoshi deity mentioned earlier. Usually, in *kami* ('god') nō such as this, the *shite* (main actor) of the first part (in this case, the old man) is shown to be the spirit of the *nochijite* (the *shite* of the second part), so that the old man is also presented not just as the Sumiyoshi pine's spirit, but also as the Sumiyoshi deity (who is thus also associated with the pine's spirit). The deity begins by reciting the lines supposedly spoken by an emperor to him:

> It has been so long
> since I have laid eyes on it.
> How many ages
> has the little pine upon
> Sumiyoshi's shore passed through?[75]

---

[71] Ibid., 5.
[72] Ibid.
[73] Ibid.
[74] Sima Qian, *The First Emperor: Selections from the* Historical Records, ed. and trans. Raymond Dawson (Oxford: Oxford University Press, 2007), 65.
[75] YT, vol. 1, 7; Suzuki Hideo (ed.), *Ise monogatari hyōkai* ('*The Tales of Ise* with Critical Commentary') (Tokyo: Chikuma Shobō, 2013), 363.

As Ōwada notes, this alludes to a *waka* in the *Ise monogatari* ('The Tales of Ise'), which explains that 'the emperor once visited Sumiyoshi'.⁷⁶ This *waka* itself alludes to the anonymous *waka* in the *Kokinshū* cited earlier. In the *Ise monogatari*, though, and in *Takasago*, the Sumiyoshi deity responds:

> You may not know it –
> our bond is harmonious.
> The shrine's pristine zone
> since many ages ago
> has given you its blessings.⁷⁷

The Sumiyoshi deity's 'may not know' (*shiranami*) puns on 'white waves' (*shiranami*); the implication is that the deity, as the guardian of sea voyages, has protected the emperor since time immemorial. Ōwada comments that 'blessings' here also implies 'protection of the imperial line'.⁷⁸ The play's allusion to this passage reinforces the intimate connection between the gods and the emperor, who is their descendant. The emperor is able to ensure that the 'waves of the four seas are quiet' in a literal as well as figurative sense through his bond with the Sumiyoshi deity.

In *Takasago*, however, the final two lines of the deity's response are altered and expanded. The Sumiyoshi deity sings:

> The shrine's pristine zone
> since ages past has performed
> plays for the *kami*.
> Set in order the rhythm
> of the night's *tsuzumi* drums.
> Priests of the shrine, soothe his heart.⁷⁹

The replacement of the line in which the Sumiyoshi deity, through his protection mediated by the 'shrine's pristine zone', gives his 'blessings' and, according to Ōwada, 'protection' to the emperor and the imperial line with one demanding the performance of *kagura* implies that the latter is the ritual by which these blessings are to be imparted. As Konakamura and Ōwada observe, nō is rooted in the *kagura* dances performed for the Shintō *kami*. Hardacre notes that during the Kamakura and Muromachi periods, 'the priests of the Kasuga Shrine were

---

[76] Ibid.
[77] Ibid.
[78] *YT*, vol. 1, 7.
[79] Ibid.

well known for performing *kagura* and Noh'.⁸⁰ *Takasago*'s author, Zeami, would have been familiar with *kagura* as his Yuzaki troupe was attached to Kagusa Shrine, where it was required to perform *sarugaku* at Shintō festivals that also included *kagura*.⁸¹ The Sumiyoshi deity himself then performs the 'god-dance' (*kamimai*) to carry out this ritual. *Takasago* thus not only takes as its subject matter the connection between the *kami* and the imperial line and the former's protection of the latter; it itself enacts the ritual that imparts the *kami*'s continued protection of the emperor's rule over Japan.

The Sumiyoshi deity's role is not limited to this function, however. In the first part, the season during which the 'waves of the four seas are quiet' is spring. Immediately before the chorus chants this line, the old man and Tomonari sing that 'The spring, too, is mild'.⁸² Following the Sumiyoshi deity's command to 'soothe his heart' through the performance of *kagura*, the chorus recites the first two lines of a *waka* by Urabe no Kanenao, after which the deity continues:

> The seas of the west.
> From out of the waves
> of Aokigahara,
> he rises up and appears,
> the god of the pine.
> O spring, it has come!
> Lingering snow melts away
> from Asaka shore.⁸³

The 'god of the pine' relates the creation of the Sumiyoshi deity according to the *Kojiki* and the *Nihon shoki*. After the male of the primordial pair, Izanagi, purifies himself in a stream of Aokigahara, the drops of water turn into the Sumiyoshi sea deities.⁸⁴ The Sumiyoshi Shrine celebrates the spring planting festival (*onda*).⁸⁵ It is said to have begun with Empress Jingū appointing *ueme* ('planting girls') to plant the first seeds to make them grow.⁸⁶ Until the Meiji era, the *ueme* were courtesans; presumably, their apparent fertility was felt to ensure that of the crops.⁸⁷ A 'Sumiyoshi dance' involving female *kagura*

---

⁸⁰ Helen Hardacre, *Shinto: A History* (Oxford: Oxford University Press, 2016), 183.
⁸¹ Erika de Poorter, *Zeami's Talks on Sarugaku* (Amsterdam: J. C. Giebens, 1986), 23.
⁸² *YT*, vol. 1, 4.
⁸³ *YT*, vol. 1, 7.
⁸⁴ Okimori Takuya et al. (eds), *Kojiki: shinkō* ('The *Kojiki*: A New Edition') (Tokyo: Ōfū, 2015), 33.
⁸⁵ Ueda, *Sumiyoshi to Munakata no kami*, 215.
⁸⁶ Ibid.
⁸⁷ Ibid.

dancers and *ueme* is still performed as part of the ritual.⁸⁸ Indeed, in *Takasago* the Sumiyoshi deity sings that there are 'many dancing girls' performing the ritual in his honour.⁸⁹ *Sarugaku* and *dengaku* also used to be performed at these ceremonies.⁹⁰ The play thus also implicitly connects the Sumiyoshi deity with causing the growth of crops in the spring. The affection that binds the old man and old woman can therefore also be considered as an emblem of fertility.

Nō actors and supporters made use of this praise of imperial rule in plays such as *Takasago* to demonstrate nō's support for the Meiji empire, particularly during the First Sino-Japanese and Russo-Japanese Wars. On 3 November 1894, four months into the First Sino-Japanese War, a three-day nō programme was held to raise money for the war effort, which generated a thousand yen.⁹¹ On the front line, when a certain Lieutenant Nagasawa of the 22nd Matsuyama regiment realized that the enemy was approaching, he commanded his soldiers to pause and, remembering the nō chants he had learned back in Matsuyama, sang them to calm his men's hearts. As a result, Nagasawa's soldiers were encouraged to engage in battle and put the enemy troops to flight.⁹² The imperial family also wished to express nō's 'martial spirit': at a party held at the house of Prince Sadanaru on 8 December 1896, a year and a half after the Japanese victory, Umewaka Minoru sang Emperor Meiji's war song, 'Seikan no eki' ('The Battle of Seonghwan'), while Hōshō Kurō performed Empress Dowager Eishō's nō play *Heijō* ('Pyongyang'), both of which celebrated Japan's victory.⁹³ The First Sino-Japanese War thus proved that nō was no longer considered, as Kume Kunitake had thought, something for 'warriors nostalgic for the end of the Tempō era'; for soldiers and the imperial family alike, it now served as an important expression of Meiji Japan's modern military strength.

It is therefore not surprising that nō's importance was again emphasized in relation to the Russo-Japanese War. This is especially evident in the anonymous editorials published in the magazine *Nōgaku*. One considers nō to be 'necessary for the nation' because 'it is martial music', 'awakens *Yamatodamashii*' ('Japanese spirit'), 'encourages the veneration of the emperor and love of the country',

---

⁸⁸ Ibid., 216.
⁸⁹ *YT*, vol. 1, 7.
⁹⁰ Ueda, *Sumiyoshi to Munakata no kami*, 217.
⁹¹ Furukawa, *Meiji nōgakushi*, 33.
⁹² 'Sensō to nōgaku' ('War and Nō'), *Nōgaku* 2, no. 3 (March 1904): 2.
⁹³ *UMN*, vol. 6, 438.

and 'prays for the protection of the gods'.[94] It notes that 'since ages past, nō has always been used during war'.[95] For instance, it describes how, after Tokugawa Ieyasu's defeat at the battle of Mikatagahara in 1573, he asked the nō actor Kanze Kokusetsu (1566–1626) to perform the 'waves of the four seas' passage from *Takasago*, which served as a 'good luck charm' for him and ultimately led to 'the pacification of all under heaven' under Ieyasu's leadership.[96] As in the previous war, a special nō programme to raise money for the war was performed in Kyoto on 27 March 1904.[97] *Nōgaku* also advertised the publication of Ōwada's *Gunka* ('War Songs'): these were, the magazine noted, 'imbued with the martial sense of nō'.[98] They describe how the war was fought 'for the sake of world peace' and for 'His Majesty the Emperor' so that 'the nation's light can shine over the globe'.[99] As the *Nōgaku* editorials and Umewaka and Hōshō's performances celebrating Japan's victories also suggest, nō's depiction as an art form that explicitly supported the imperial war effort was thus fervently encouraged by the nō establishment.

Their support of imperial rule was reciprocated by the imperial family's financial assistance after the Meiji restoration, most notably that of the Empress Dowager Eishō between 1876 and her death in 1897. Together with the construction of the Shiba Nō Theatre in 1881, her patronage was arguably the most momentous development for nō in the Meiji period. There was thus only a space of eight years from the sudden cessation of the shōgunate's support and the start of Eishō's, leading commentators such as Kurata Yoshihiro to suggest that the transition from the Edo to the Meiji period was one of 'continuation' rather than revival.[100] After Eishō's death, however, nō's financial situation returned to one of relative instability. While the *Nōgaku* editorials emphasized nō's ability to awaken 'veneration of the emperor and love of the country' during the Russo-Japanese War, they also criticized the lack of national funding. Whereas Eishō had supported nō financially, built a nō theatre in her palace, and attended many performances, 'the state' did not 'care about' nō's financial predicament; actors were once again predominantly 'funded by pupils and teaching fees'.[101] Nevertheless, the editorial thus also reveals another radical change for nō during the Meiji period: it had developed from the small turnouts of the early 1870s

[94] 'Sensō to nōgaku', 2.
[95] Ibid.
[96] Ibid.
[97] *UMN*, vol. 7, 104.
[98] Advertisement for Ōwada, *Gunka* ('War Songs'), *Nōgaku* 2, no. 5 (May 1904): 68.
[99] Ōwada, *Seiro gunka* ('War Songs for the Suppression of Russia') (Tokyo: Ikueisha, 1904), 2, 8 and 10.
[100] Kurata, 'Meiji', 15.
[101] 'Enzetsu' ('Speech'), *Nōgaku* 2, no. 2 (February 1904): 2.

into large, packed theatres. A constant stream of pupils now came in and out of Umewaka's house for nō lessons, part of the 'general fashion' for nō that had taken root by then.[102] Nō's traditional message of support and praise for imperial rule thus reached the largest audience in its history. Following the opening of Japan to trade in the Meiji period, for the first time it also spread across the world.

---

[102] Josui, 'Ishin tōji no nōgaku', 21; 'Enzetsu', 2.

6

Ernest Fenollosa's 'single image' and the introduction of nō into English

Whereas the translation of *hokku* into English mostly took place after Shiki's 1890s reforms, English-language interest in nō was present from the beginning of the Meiji era. This resulted from the use of nō as entertainment for the visits of foreign dignitaries. Indeed, the first description in English of a nō performance arose out of such an event. The diplomat Ernest Satow, a consular interpreter who had arrived in Japan in 1862, recorded his attendance of the nō play *Hachinoki* ('The Potted Trees') at the Kongō school's Iigura theatre in December 1868. Satow's account, however, was not published until 1921.[1] Algernon Mitford, a secretary to the British Legation in Tokyo at the time, was among those who accompanied Prince Alfred, the Duke of Edinburgh, at the nō programme performed by Hōshō Kurō and other prominent nō actors for the prince's state visit on 29 July 1869.[2] Mitford introduces nō in his *Tales of Old Japan*, published two years after the event, as 'a classical opera, called Nô, which is performed on stages specially built for the purpose in the palaces of the principal nobles'.[3] It was in one of these, the 'Yashiki' (noble residence) of 'the Prince of Kishū' (present-day Wakayama Prefecture) in Akasaka, that the performance took place.[4] Mitford ascribes its origins to a Shintō myth. Like Konakamura, he traces it back to 'the entertainments by which the Sun Goddess', the legendary ancestor of the Japanese imperial line, 'was lured out of the cave in which she had hidden'.[5] The 'pious intention' of 'the Nô' is still 'to pray for the prosperity of the country' and is highly regarded by 'the nobles of the Court, the Daimios, and the military class'.[6]

---

[1] Ernest Satow, *A Diplomat in Japan* (London: Seeley, Service & Co., 1921), 396–7.
[2] Kurata, 'Meiji', 20; Furukawa, *Meiji nōgakushi*, 12.
[3] Algernon Mitford, *Tales of Old Japan* (London: Macmillan, 1871), 156.
[4] Ibid., 157.
[5] Ibid., 156.
[6] Ibid.

Mitford proceeds to outline the plots of the four nō plays he attended with Prince Alfred. The first of these is Zeami's *Yumiyawata* ('The Bow of Hachiman'), translated by Mitford as *Hachiman of the Bow*. Like *Takasago*, it praises the peace that arises from the emperor's benevolent rule with a marine metaphor: 'The peace which prevails in the land is likened to a calm at sea. The Emperor is the ship, and his subjects the water.'[7] Indeed, as in *Takasago*, the *waki* more specifically states that now 'it is a time when the waves of the four seas are calm'.[8] After *Tsunemasa*, *Hagoromo* (which Mitford translates as '*The Suit of Feathers*'), a 'very pretty conceit', is summarized.[9] He is critical of the manner of its performance. 'The performers wear hideous wigs and masks, not unlike those of ancient Greece'; the 'beauty of the poetry' is 'marred by the want of scenery and by the grotesque dresses and make-up. In the *Suit of Feathers*, for instance, the fairy wears a hideous mask and a wig of scarlet elf locks [. . .] and the heavenly dance is a series of whirls, stamps and jumps, accompanied by unearthly yells and shrieks.'[10] Mitford is thus critical of nō's apparent anti-mimesis.

The first full translation of a nō play into English, however, was of *Takasago*. It appeared as an appendix to Dickins's *Chiushingura; or, The Loyal League: A Japanese Romance* in 1875 as 'The Ballad of Takasago'.[11] Dickins presents his version as 'a free imitation', organizing the play into rhymed quatrains. When the priest Tomonari asks the old couple how they can 'together dwell' while living 'so far apart', the old woman, or 'Spirit of Sumiyoshi', responds:

> Thou say'st not wisely, Sir, methinks;
> > From many a distant source
> Down rush the mountain-streams to join
> > In the river's mightier course.
>
> And so, by love or fate, two souls
> > Together drawn, make one,
> Although ten thousand leagues may seem
> > To bar their union.[12]

In the aforementioned first stanza, Dickins adds significantly to the phrase (*san zen ban ri*, 'ten thousand miles of mountains and rivers') for the distance that

---

[7] Ibid., 158.
[8] Zeami, 'Yumiyawata', in *YT*, vol. 5, 75.
[9] Mitford, *Tales of Old Japan*, 160.
[10] Ibid., 164.
[11] Dickins, *Chiushingura; or, The Loyal League: A Japanese Romance* (Yokohama: The Japan Gazette, 1875), 43–56.
[12] Ibid., 46–7.

separates the old couple: the 'streams' that 'rush' down 'From many a distant source' to the river are invented. The Japanese metaphor of 'the way' being 'short' that their 'care travels along', as I would interpret it, is discarded in favour of the more conventional 'souls' that are 'Together drawn' by 'love or fate'. Dickins's likely motivation for taking such liberties was to convey to a nineteenth-century Anglophone readership that these lines consist of traditional verse that adheres to its own formal constraints.

Chamberlain's 1876 introduction to his first translation of a nō play into English in *Cornhill Magazine* – his first literary publication – takes a different view from Mitford of nō's apparent anti-mimesis. The location he gives of the nō performances he hears in 'Jigura' is likely the Kongō school's Iigura theatre.[13] Whereas Mitford criticizes the 'dresses' as 'grotesque', Chamberlain finds them 'gorgeous in the extreme'.[14] Furthermore, the lack of stage scenery is not to be attributed to an absence of means: 'scenery [. . .] is allowed no place on the *Nō* stages, though carried to such perfection at the regular theatres of Japan'.[15] It is the result, rather, of a 'true sense of the fitness of things' and of the actors' fidelity 'to the old traditions of their art'.[16] Where such scenery is introduced, 'the spectator cannot help feeling that the spell is in a manner broken – so completely an ideal performance is but marred by the adoption of any of the adventitious aids of the melodramatic stage'.[17] Chamberlain thus praises nō as an 'ideal' (as opposed to a mimetic) art form, thus anticipating the views of later Anglophone commentators on nō. In *The Classical Poetry of the Japanese*, he includes his translations of *The Robe of Feathers* (*Hagoromo*), *The Death Stone* (*Sesshōseki*), *Life is a Dream* (*Kantan*), and *Nakamitsu*.

Nō's appeal as an 'ideal' rather than a mimetic art form soon also attracted the attention of Tokyo University's American professor of Philosophy and Political Economy at the time, Ernest Fenollosa (1853–1908). Fenollosa attended Harvard University from 1870 to 1876, gaining a BA in Philosophy in 1874 before carrying out postgraduate work.[18] It was during his last two years there that he became interested in Hegelian philosophy. In what remains to date the most recent and comprehensive biography of Fenollosa, Yamaguchi Seiichi claims that this interest came about through English translations of and articles

[13] Chamberlain, 'The Death-Stone: A Lyric Drama from the Japanese', *Cornhill Magazine* 34 (July–December 1876): 479.
[14] Ibid., 481.
[15] Ibid.
[16] Ibid.
[17] Ibid.
[18] Yamaguchi Seiichi, *Fenorosa: Nihon bunka no senyō ni sasageta isshō* ('Fenollosa: A Life Devoted to the Advocacy of Japanese Culture'), vol. 1 (Tokyo: Sanseidō, 1982), 26 and 28.

on his philosophy that appeared in *The Journal of Speculative Philosophy*.[19] Indeed, its first issues contain an English translation of Charles Bénard's (1807–98) paraphrase of Hegel's *Aesthetik* that would prove highly influential for Fenollosa's own aesthetics. In Bénard's paraphrase of Hegel's view, 'imitation' is not the purpose of art: 'Now of what use', Bénard has Hegel ask, 'to reproduce that which nature already offers to our view?'[20] He dismisses this conception of art's purpose as 'puerile talk'.[21] Art is not, and should not aspire to be, an inferior copy of nature; instead, 'the images which it places under our eyes are more ideal, more transparent, and also more durable than the mobile and fugitive existences of the real world.'[22] Art ought not to look to imitation, expression, or even moral instruction as its goals; 'it is the sense of the Beautiful to which it is addressed.'[23] This beauty is 'the unity, the realized harmony of the two principles of existence, of the idea and the form.'[24]

The principle of unity is not only apparent in Hegel's conception of beauty as the unity of idea and form; it is also evident in his understanding of how beauty arises from the composed unity of formal elements. 'Unity is an essential characteristic' of the 'Beautiful in nature': for instance, 'in the mineral, beauty consists in the arrangement or disposition of the parts, it is the force which resides in them, and which reveals itself in this unity'.[25] The 'bodies' of the 'solar system', likewise, 'co-ordinate themselves into a whole, the parts of which are independent, although attached to a common centre, the sun. Beauty of this order strikes us by the regularity of the movements of the celestial bodies.'[26] Beauty is thus created by a harmonious relation of constituent parts ordered around a dominant central focal point. The same principle operates for Hegel in beautiful painting. When 'arranging the different parts of a picture, the ordering and grouping of figures, and the distribution of objects', the painting should 'cause them to contribute to the total effect'.[27] The figures, in particular, 'should form a perfect whole in themselves'; without this unity, 'they are insignificant'.[28] Hegel's example of this is 'the "Transfiguration" of Raphael', in

---

[19] Ibid., 30.
[20] Charles Bénard, 'Analytical and Critical Essay upon the Aesthetics of Hegel', trans. J. A. Martling, *The Journal of Speculative Philosophy* 1 (1867): 39.
[21] Ibid.
[22] Ibid., 37.
[23] Ibid., 40.
[24] Ibid., 41.
[25] Ibid., 43.
[26] Ibid.
[27] Bénard, 'Benard's [sic] Essay on Hegel's Aesthetics', trans. Martling, *The Journal of Speculative Philosophy* 2 (1868): 45.
[28] Ibid., 44.

which the transfigured Jesus appears at the apex of the painting, the focal point of the painting's light, flanked by the prophets Moses and Elijah.[29] This formal unity had been conventional in European painting since Raphael and parallels Fontanesi's emphasis in the composition of painting on a central point upon which the light falls most strongly.

After his postgraduate studies at Harvard, Fenollosa enrolled in the Boston Museum of Fine Arts' Massachusetts Normal Art School in January 1877, where he was taught among others by John La Farge (1835–1910).[30] Lawrence Chisolm suggests that Fenollosa's 'abiding enthusiasm' for landscape painting was inspired by the Barbizon school, whose works had been exhibited at the Boston Museum of Fine Arts in 1875–6.[31] He might thus have been introduced to similar ideas about composition in painting to those expressed by Fontanesi. Soon after beginning art school, however, he was presented with a life-changing opportunity. Tokyo University, founded that year, needed a politics professor and asked the zoologist Edward Sylvester Morse, who had worked at Harvard and had been in Japan since June 1877 carrying out research, to recommend someone. Morse asked the Harvard professor of art Charles Eliot Norton, whose lectures on art history Fenollosa had attended as a postgraduate, for his opinion and was advised to recommend Fenollosa for the position.[32] On 12 July 1878, the twenty-five-year-old Fenollosa set sail for Japan, arriving on 9 August in time to begin his appointment as professor of philosophy and political economics at the start of the new academic year.[33] In addition to Spencer, Hegel featured prominently in the student examination questions he set for 1878–9 and 1879–80.[34]

During these two years, Fenollosa avidly collected Japanese paintings. He soon befriended a fellow Harvard graduate, Kaneko Kentarō (1853–1942), who had been selected to study abroad by the former daimyō of Chikuzen Province, Kuroda Nagahiro (1811–87), and departed for America on the same ship as the Iwakura Embassy. Kaneko recalled that he would visit Fenollosa every week during these first two years; in his living quarters, Fenollosa was 'surrounded by hanging *kakemono*'.[35] He would often buy these in the area around Kōtokuji, a

---

[29] Ibid., 45.
[30] Yamaguchi, *Fenorosa*, vol. 1, 31.
[31] Lawrence Chisolm, *Fenollosa: The Far East and American Culture* (New Haven: Yale University Press, 1963), 29–30.
[32] Ibid., 35.
[33] Yamaguchi, *Fenorosa*, 30 and 40.
[34] Fenollosa, *Published Writings in English*, n. p.
[35] Kaneko Kentarō, 'Ware to Fenorosa' ('Fenollosa and Me'), *Kōyūkai gappō* 19, no. 6 (November 1920): 165.

temple in Tokyo.[36] When Fenollosa asked Kaneko about where to find paintings, in the absence of art galleries or exhibitions in Japan at that time, Kaneko introduced him to the former daimyō who had sent him to study abroad. Kuroda was well known as an art connoisseur and was also a painter himself. Fenollosa was shown paintings by Sesshū, Shūbun and the Tosa School, as well as some Chinese ones from the Song and Yuan dynasties; Kaneko describes Fenollosa's reaction to these as 'like being struck by electricity'.[37] From then on, he stopped buying the popular works available around Kōtokuji and began to research the kind of paintings then mostly in the private possession of Japanese nobles and the former military élite. Fenollosa thus shifted towards an enthusiasm for art patronized by the aristocracy; his later interest in nō partly stems from this development.

His appreciation of Japanese painting inspired his lecture, 'An Explanation of the Truth in Art', which he gave at the Ryūchikai ('Dragon Pond Society'), a society consisting of politicians and art dealers, on 14 May 1882 at the Museum of Education in Ueno Park.[38] Published in November that year by the Ryūchikai, it marks a pivotal moment in modern Japanese art. In his view, 'The peak of beauty in Chinese art occurred in the Tang and Song dynasties. Now it has turned away and lost its energy. Japanese art was also magnificently beautiful some centuries ago but is now in decline'; his lecture's purpose, he says, is 'to argue for the urgent revival of this particular art in Japan'.[39] Such traditional modes of Japanese painting were then considered to be under threat with the adoption of Western techniques at institutions such as the recently established School of Technical Fine Arts, where Fontanesi had taught between 1876 and 1878. In his lecture, however, Fenollosa warns that *yōga*'s apparently superior 'imitation of natural objects' is not what constitutes great art.[40] 'Art', he claims, 'does not reside in sketching from life'; his Japanese translator gives 'sketching from life' as *shasei*, the term that would later become so important for Shiki. His criticism of imitation as the purpose of art suggests the influence of Hegel's *Aesthetik*, in particular the argument that it would be meaningless merely 'to reproduce that which nature already offers to our view'.[41] Art need not be mimetic: 'music

---

[36] Ibid.
[37] Ibid.
[38] Fenollosa, *Bijutsu shinsetsu*, n. p. The English original is no longer extant; all quotations are my retranslation of the lecture's Japanese translation.
[39] Ibid., 7.
[40] Ibid.
[41] Ibid.

does not copy nature but is considered art'; painting, likewise, contains dragons, angels and other subject matter not found in nature.[42]

Like Hegel's *Aesthetik*, Fenollosa argues that art resides in the 'idea' rather than in 'imitation': more specifically, the 'idea of the content and the idea of the form ultimately fuse' into the 'single idea' ('*tan'itsu no myōsō*') of the work of art.[43] Fenollosa's lecture also employs, as Hegel does, the notion of 'unity' to describe the relationship between a painting's elements. Echoing Walter Pater's famous assertion five years before that '*All art constantly aspires to the condition of music*', Fenollosa suggests that, 'regarding form, the harmony of painting's line, colour, and shading resembles that of music'.[44] To arrive at the 'unity' ('*tōitsu*') required by good painting, a 'gathering point' (*shūgō*) is needed: 'the gathering point is the main element [*shu*] and the other parts the supporting elements [*kyaku*].'[45] 'If this gathering point is absent', Fenollosa concludes, 'the idea of the art work cannot be expressed.'[46] Fenollosa's lecture thus anticipates Shiki's interest in painting as being composed of precisely these elements and his subsequent adoption of these terms to describe the arrangement of haiku. Fenollosa argues that *yōga* oil painting 'completely goes against the unity of subject' when compared to the 'white space' employed by *Nihonga* (traditional Japanese painting), which focuses the viewer's attention on the painting's main element.[47] His criticism of 'imitation' as the purpose of art and his emphasis on 'unity' of line, shading, colour and subject in painting would later profoundly influence his understanding of nō.

Fenollosa's introduction to nō may have arisen via the visit to Japan of Ulysses S. Grant discussed in Chapter 5. On 11 July 1879, three days after Grant had attended a nō performance at Iwakura Tomomi's residence in which he had told Iwakura to 'treasure and preserve' this 'noble and elegant' art form, Grant received a visit from Fenollosa and his wife, Lizzie. According to Fenollosa, 'Grant [. . .] said that he preferred Japanese music to Western orchestras.'[48] Grant was almost certainly speaking to him about the nō performance he had seen. It was Morse, however, who gave Fenollosa his first opportunity to sing nō. Morse first

---

[42] Ibid., 9.
[43] Ibid., 22.
[44] Walter Pater, 'The School of Giorgone', *The Fortnightly Review* 28 (1877): 528; Fenollosa, *Bijutsu shinsetsu*, 24.
[45] Ibid., 25.
[46] Ibid.
[47] Ibid., 31.
[48] Kurata, 'Meiji', 18; Yamaguchi, *Fenorosa*, 68.

visited Umewaka Minoru for nō singing lessons on 27 January 1883.[49,50] After several lessons, Morse reflected that 'As their pictorial art was incomprehensible to us at the outset, and yet on further acquaintance and study we discovered in it transcendental merit, so it seemed to me that a study of Japanese music might reveal merits we little suspected. For that reason I studied Utai [nō singing].'[51] His regular attendance of nō singing lessons with Umewaka, confirmed by Umewaka's diaries, testifies to his open-mindedness about this art form.

On 20 February, Fenollosa came on Morse's recommendation for his own first nō singing lesson with Umewaka.[52] During his first lesson, Fenollosa sang lines with Umewaka from the nō play *Kantan* ('Handan').[53] Almost all Fenollosa's nō lessons took place on Wednesdays, as there were no lessons at the university on that day.[54] From the second lesson onwards, it was Umewaka who went to visit Fenollosa.[55] On 7 March, Umewaka records in his diary that Fenollosa practised singing the *shikai nami* passage from *Takasago*.[56] These lessons continued every week with only one exception until 27 June (thirteen in all). Yamaguchi proposes that the reason for their discontinuation was the arrival in Japan of Isabella Stewart Gardner, a prominent Boston socialite and art collector, on 18 June.[57] Gardner wrote to a friend back in Boston on 30 July about the warmth of the welcome she had received from the Fenollosas while in Japan.[58] Nevertheless, when Gardner left, Fenollosa did not return to his nō lessons and would not do so until some fifteen years later. This contradicts the accounts of English-language biographies of Fenollosa, which claim that Fenollosa studied nō for 'twenty years' after 1882 (not 1883), as Van Wyck Brooks does, or that he did not begin studying nō until 1898, as Chisolm suggests.[59]

Nō's excellence as literature received more extensive treatment in Aston's *A History of Japanese Literature*. Aston opens his discussion of nō by comparing the 'Tanka' of the Kamakura and Muromachi periods unfavourably with the 'far greater interest' of 'the poetic art' of 'the Nō or lyrical drama'.[60] Nō's foremost

---

[49] *UMN*, vol. 4, 6.
[50] Edward S. Morse, *Japan Day by Day*, vol. 2 (Boston: Houghton Mifflin, 1917), 401.
[51] Ibid., 408.
[52] *UMN*, vol. 4, 8.
[53] Ibid.
[54] Yamaguchi, *Fenorosa*, vol. 1, 186.
[55] Ibid.; *UMN*, 9.
[56] Ibid., 10.
[57] Yamaguchi, *Fenorosa*, vol. 1, 186; Louise Hall Tharp, *Mrs. Jack: A Biography of Isabella Stewart Gardner* (Boston: Little, Brown and Company, 1965), 90.
[58] Yamaguchi, *Fenorosa*, vol. 1, 186.
[59] Brooks, *Fenollosa and His Circle*, 34; Chisolm, *Fenollosa*, 137.
[60] Aston, *A History of Japanese Literature*, 197.

quality, according to Aston, is its value as poetry. 'As dramas', he argues, 'the Nō have little value'; but their 'poetic ore' is 'richer' even than the classic anthologies of the *Manyōshū* and the *Kokinshū*.[61] A further development in Aston's presentation of nō is his emphasis on its sociopolitical contexts and motivations. Drawing on Ōwada's *Yōkyoku tsūkai*, he avoids Chamberlain's erroneous contention that Ashikaga Yoshimasa was the first shōgun to patronize nō in the fifteenth century: it was Ashikaga Yoshimitsu, rather, who first did so in the late fourteenth century.[62] 'From this time forward', Aston notes, 'the Nō were under the special patronage of the Shōguns.'[63] Ōwada is also the likely source for Aston's understanding that 'Hideyoshi [. . .] was very fond of the Nō, and is said to have taken part in them as an actor', and that 'in the Yedo period the Shōguns gave great attention to Nō performances. They were a ceremony of state.'[64] Aston does not just discuss their political patronage, but also their political motivation: like Mitford, he observes that in many plays 'a patriotic or martial enthusiasm is the inspiring motive'.[65] Aston thus observes how nō served to praise the imperial and military rule that supported it.

The foremost example of this political function of nō can be found, Aston claims, in *Takasago*, of which he provides a 'partial translation'.[66] He is unequivocal about its importance within the nō canon:

> It is the best known, and is considered the finest of all the Nō. Its popularity was testified to no longer ago than last year (1897) by the launching, from the yard of Messrs. Armstrong & Co. at Newcastle, of a cruiser for the Japanese navy bearing the name of *Takasago*.[67]

Aston thus also connects the play's praise of imperial rule with the present-day strength of Japan's military, which had been demonstrated in the First Sino-Japanese War five years before Aston's book. His connection of nō with Japanese military strength resembles those made in the nō fundraising performances for the war effort, the account in *Nōgaku* of Lieutenant Nagasawa singing nō in the battlefield to calm his men's hearts, and Umewaka's performance of Emperor Meiji's war song 'Seikan no eki' and Empress Dowager Eishō's nō play *Heijō*, as mentioned in Chapter 5. Aston thus observes how the strength of the Japanese

---

[61] Ibid., 203.
[62] Ibid., 199.
[63] Ibid.
[64] Ibid., 200.
[65] Ibid., 201.
[66] Ibid., 206.
[67] Ibid.

empire and military and nō's support of them were then intertwined. Aston presents it not as a mere relic of a distant feudal past, as Kume Kunitake had also first considered it before the Iwakura Embassy, but as an indication of the Meiji era's nationalism and 'martial spirit' that drove its rapid military modernization.

Unlike Chamberlain, his translation is 'freed from the temptation to introduce extraneous matter' found in 'a poetical version' such as Chamberlain's *The Robe of Feathers*; Aston attempts 'to bring in nothing of my own'.[68] He nonetheless seeks to indicate nō's alternation of prose and verse passages by using either prose or 'a rough and ready blank verse'.[69] His source for the translation is the 1896 edition of Ōwada's *Yōkyoku tsūkai*. Aston's translation thus avoids the liberties Dickins takes in his 'free imitation' of the play. When Tomonari asks the old couple how the 'fir-trees' of 'Takasago and Suminoye' can be 'called the fir-trees which "grow old together"' (Aston's version of the *aioi* phrase), the old woman responds:

> OLD WOMAN (*in verse*). What an odd speech! Though many a mile of mountain and river separate them, the way of a husband and wife whose hearts respond to one another with mutual care, is not far apart.[70]

The contrast with Dickins's archaism is particularly clear in the colloquialism of the first line quoted earlier. Aston's prose is careful in its translation of *tagai ni kayou kokorozukai no imose* as 'a husband and wife whose hearts respond to one another with mutual care'. 'The way' refers more persuasively to the original's metaphor of the '*michi*' ('way' or 'road'). Aston's version thus offers a clearer sense of the metaphors used in the Japanese original than Dickins's does.

The sections omitted from Aston's translation include the old woman's explanation that the Takasago pine stands for the past age of the *Manyōshū* anthology; that the pine tree is 'dressed like eighteen dukes'; and most of the second part, such as the chorus's statement that 'the way between the gods and the sovereign is short'.[71] Aston does, however, accord significant attention to the *shikai nami* passage of *Takasago*. Although he does not mention the role that this passage played in the *utaizome* performed at the Tokugawa shōguns' court, he precedes his version of it with the following note:

> (*Here the chorus strikes in with a canticle which is chanted as the indispensable accompaniment of every regular Japanese wedding, and is one of the best known passages in Japanese literature. Figures representing the two old folks under the*

---

[68] Ibid.
[69] Ibid.
[70] Ibid., 208.
[71] YT, 3, 5 and 7.

fir-tree with brooms in their hands are, on such occasions, set out on a sort of tray. This is a favourite subject of the Japanese artist.)[72]

The artists Aston mentions here might include Sumiyoshi Hirosada's (1793–1863) and Seisui Yōkō's (dates unknown) paintings of the play's old couple in the British Museum.[73] Unlike previous lines that are merely indicated as being written 'in verse', the *shikai nami* is given in loosely trimetric verse. This emphasis on the *shikai nami* passage serves to call greater attention to its message that the play's 'peace' is due to the age being 'Rich with the bounty / Of our sovereign lord'.[74] At the play's conclusion, the chorus sings that 'the song of ten thousand years' will 'Prolong our sovereign's life'.[75] Aston explains that this song is 'Equivalent to our "God save the Queen"', thus making it even clearer that *Takasago* was then thought of as a strongly nationalistic play.[76]

Aston returned home in 1889; Fenollosa did so one year later to take up a position as curator of Japanese Art at the Boston Museum of Fine Arts. Fenollosa further developed there his conception of the artwork's 'single idea' discussed in his Ryūchikai lecture. In an introductory lecture on 'Imagination in Art', he presents an updated formulation of his aesthetics:

> Without attempting a formal definition, I should say that, in art, imagination is the faculty of thinking and feeling in terms of a single image.[77]

Like the 'single idea' in his *Bijutsu shinsetsu*, the 'single image' differs from 'ordinary vision' in that it has 'persistence, congruity, natural limits, a kind of organization within itself', whereas in the latter 'the retina of the eye is filled with a crowd of points, masses of sensations, which do not bear any definite, permanent or significant relation to one another'.[78] Now, though, Fenollosa emphasizes the difference between 'thought' and 'images'. 'Thought' is 'an abstraction', 'like an algebraic equation in terms of x and y'.[79] It is, however, 'utterly inadequate to produce or suggest an image' because 'a thought implies general relations, but not a concrete image'.[80] Fenollosa criticizes the tendency towards this kind of 'thought' in modern schooling:

---

[72] Aston, *A History of Japanese Literature*, 209.
[73] William Anderson, *Descriptive Catalogue of the Collection of Japanese and Chinese Paintings at the British Museum* (London: Longmans, 1886), 152 and 319–20.
[74] Aston, *A History of Japanese Literature*, 209.
[75] Ibid., 211.
[76] Ibid.
[77] Fenollosa, 'Imagination in Art', 5.
[78] Ibid.
[79] Ibid., 8.
[80] Ibid., 6.

We have educated children too much to think, too little to see and feel wholes. No wonder a child frequently draws the bottom of a cylinder on one part of his paper, and its side on another. Such separation is just what abstract thought works. But the old masters of art in all its forms had not yet yielded to this tiresome pedantry of the intellect. They had the fresh, childlike power of seeing things in terms of pure images.[81]

What Fenollosa means with this kind of 'seeing' instead of 'thinking', then, is not merely what the 'retina of the eye' captures but, rather, the 'intuitive seizing upon the capacity for organization in one's raw material' as opposed to 'the cold weighing of the intellect'; this 'power of the imagination' is the Kantian 'faculty of Judgment'.[82] It is present in 'the great Greek sculptors', Italian Renaissance artists, and 'the Chinese and Japanese artists of the eighth, twelfth, and fifteenth centuries'.[83] Fenollosa's criticism of 'abstract thought' thus also echoes Spencer's in his *Philosophy of Style*.

In April 1896, however, Fenollosa returned to Japan after the scandal of his divorce from Lizzie and remarriage to Mary McNeil Scott, his former assistant at the museum.[84] Mary was perhaps the most important instigator of Fenollosa's revival of interest in nō. In a diary entry for 1 September 1896, she records having listened to 'the rich, plaintive murmur of a man's voice [. . .] singing ancient *No* songs. There is nothing exactly like this singing in the whole world.'[85] For her, it was 'more than music – it is poetry symbolized in sound'.[86] Okakura Kakuzō, a student of Fenollosa's at Tokyo University who had founded the Tokyo School of Fine Arts with him in 1887 and would later achieve fame with *Ideals of the East* (1903) and *The Book of Tea* (1904), visited them on 22 September and was equally enthusiastic about nō.[87] Mary wrote in her diary entry for that day that Okakura thought 'the rendition of *No* dramas offers a rich field'.[88] It was not until 17 October 1898, however, that the Fenollosas attended a nō play. After attending a programme of nō at the Shiba Nō Theatre that day, Mary noted in her diary that she was 'impressed' by the plays and found them 'beautiful'. 'E. & I determined to study Nō, and even to try to sing the songs.'[89] They would do so with the help, once more, of Umewaka's singing lessons and, this time, the

---

[81] Ibid., 8.
[82] Ibid., 9.
[83] Ibid., 8.
[84] Chisolm, *Fenollosa*, 119.
[85] *EFF*, vol. 3, 233.
[86] Ibid.
[87] Ibid.
[88] Ibid.
[89] Ibid., 234.

assistance of an English teacher at the Higher Normal School where Fenollosa had been teaching since April, Hirata Kiichi. On 29 October, Mary records in her diary that 'Mr. Hirata came to dinner, and after we went into E's study and he gave us some idea of the Nō for tomorrow'.[90] Evidently stimulated by Hirata's input as well as Mary and Okakura's enthusiasm, Fenollosa began his first 'No Notebook' that evening.[91]

Hirata, the Fenollosas and Osman Edwards attended a nō programme the following day at Umewaka's house.[92] In his diary, Umewaka records: 'Fenollosa came to watch today. It was the first time in many years that we had met.'[93] One of the plays Fenollosa saw that day was *Aoi no ue* ('Lady Aoi').[94] Hirata came to dinner at the Fenollosas' on 5, 9, 16 and 18 November to discuss and translate nō with them.[95] On 18 November, Umewaka arrived and gave Fenollosa singing lessons for the first time since 1883. Fenollosa wrote that Umewaka 'praised me, said everything was exactly right, and said that both he and Takeyo considered my progress wonderful; better than a Japanese could make. He said I was already advanced enough to sing in a Japanese company.'[96] Umewaka, though, gives no comment in his diary other than Fenollosa's arrival. Two days later, the Fenollosas again attended a nō programme, which included Zeami's *Kinuta* ('The Fulling Block').[97] Hirata again accompanied them and had come to Fenollosa's house beforehand to translate the plays.[98] Hirata was thus the one who produced the translations for Fenollosa, whose Japanese was almost non-existent, before they went to see a nō performance.[99] The importance of Hirata's role has been noted in Japanese-language scholarship since Yano Hōjin's claim that, 'Strictly speaking, it is more correct to call [Hirata] Tokuboku [Hirata's pen-name] the co-translator' of the nō translations, as he gave 'a great amount of assistance' to Fenollosa.

On 25 November, Umewaka records that his son Takeyo visited Fenollosa for the latter's second nō singing lesson, with Hirata again attending to interpret, and that Fenollosa 'sang the *kuse* of *Hagoromo* that he had practised years ago'.[100] Between then and 7 December, Hirata 'finished the translation of "Hajitomi"'

---

[90] Ibid.
[91] Ibid.
[92] Ibid.; *UMN*, vol. 6, 136.
[93] Ibid.
[94] Ibid.
[95] *EFF*, vol. 3, 235.
[96] *NA*, 47.
[97] *EFF*, vol. 3, 235.
[98] Ibid.
[99] Yano Hōjin, *Eibungaku yawa* ('Evening Talks on English Literature') (Tokyo: Kenkyūsha, 1955), 64.
[100] *UMN*, vol. 6, 143.

('The Lattice Shutter'), which they saw with Hirata at Umewaka's house on 11 December, with Umewaka himself in the lead role. That day's programme had begun with *Kanawa* ('The Iron Crown'), a play later adapted by one of Pound's Japanese acquaintances, the playwright Kōri Torahiko; a synopsis of the nō play would also be included in '*Noh*' *or Accomplishment*.[101] On 21 December, Mary notes in her diary that 'Hirata was here, though not to dinner, and made a beginning on *Hagoromo*'.[102] Hirata and Fenollosa's dedication to its translation led to Mary complaining on Christmas Eve that she 'went to bed with E & Hirata still mumbling Nō in the next room. Not a very gay Christmas Eve'.[103] On 26 December, Hirata and Fenollosa visited Umewaka and offered him a box of eggs and fifteen yen for the new year and apologies for 'the mistake of 1883', presumably Fenollosa's discontinuation of his lessons. In return, Umewaka presented them with copies of 'Seikan no eki'.[104] On 15 January 1899, the Fenollosas attended a nō programme at Umewaka's house: *Tsurukame*, *Tamura* and *Hagoromo* were among the nō plays performed that day, with Umewaka's son Manzaburō in the lead role for *Hagoromo*.[105]

Soon after this performance, however, Fenollosa became ill with a fever that disrupted his nō singing lessons. Umewaka records no further lessons with Fenollosa in his diary than the six he had given until then; on 26 March Takeyo went to visit 'Fenollosa, who is unwell'.[106] Mary records their attendance of nō programmes on 11 June at the Shiba Nō Theatre, and on 19 November at the monthly performance held at Umewaka's home, when Umewaka acted in the lead role in *Kayoi Komachi* ('Visiting Komachi').[107] *Suma Genji* ('Genji at Suma') and *Tamura* were also performed that day. Evidence of Hirata's collaboration with Fenollosa reappears in Mary's diary entry for 24 November and intensifies from 7 February 1900 onwards.[108] Fenollosa could still not translate the plays without Hirata, as his letter to Hirata of 20 March indicates: 'please come here in the afternoon [of 21 March], if you can, to translate some of the piece for Sunday. I hope you will not lose interest in the subject of No.'[109] That Sunday marked the third day of a nō programme commemorating the Umewaka family ancestors.

---

[101] *EFF*, vol. 3, 236; *UMN*, vol. 6, 147.
[102] *EFF*, vol. 3, 236.
[103] Ibid., 237.
[104] Ibid.
[105] Ibid.
[106] *UMN*, vol. 6, 172.
[107] *EFF*, vol. 3, 238; *UMN*, vol. 6, 221.
[108] Fenollosa, letter to Hirata Kiichi (24 November 1899), in Furukawa, *Ōbeijin no nōgaku kenkyū* (Tokyo: Tokyo Woman's Christian University Academic Society, 1962), 177–8.
[109] Fenollosa, letter to Hirata (20 March 1900), in Furukawa, *Ōbeijin*, 179.

The programme, written down in Fenollosa's notebook, included performances of 'Seikan no eki' and Empress Dowager Eishō's *Heijō, Ashikari, Dōjōji, Chōryō* and *Shōjō*.[110] On 27 April, 2 May and 22 May, Hirata and Fenollosa came to interview Umewaka about nō; Umewaka told them about his role in the revival of nō after the fall of the shōgunate discussed in the previous chapter. Fenollosa continued working on nō translations with Hirata right up to his departure for America on 17 August 1900.[111]

During his ten-month stay in America before returning for the last time to Japan, Fenollosa's first publication resulting from his interest in nō of the preceding three years appeared in the *Journal of the American Oriental Society*.[112] Fenollosa claims that nō involves a 'concentration upon a single emotional theme'.[113] Its aim 'is never sensational or realistic, but to lift the beholder, through a refined appeal to several of his faculties, into a single state of intense and imaginative emotional impression'.[114] Its anti-realism accords with Fenollosa's belief in his Ryūchikai lecture that it would be meaningless 'to reproduce that which nature already offers to our view' and echoes Chamberlain's positive view of nō as an 'ideal' rather than a mimetic art. The 'concentration' of nō assists its ability to create 'a single state of intense and imaginative emotional impression':

> As pure art, this brevity, and the general simplicity are perhaps an advantage; for there is no distraction or strain of attention; every beauty is fully comprehended by the audience, the concentration upon a single emotional theme becomes transparent, as it were, and thus, as in the Greek drama, the intensity of effect depends rather upon quality than quantity.[115]

Nō thus also meets Fenollosa's criterion for achieving a 'single image' that is required of the highest art: according to his lecture on 'Imagination in Art', it is the 'artistic vision' that is able to remove that which 'tends to distort the image, or disturb its integrity' and create a 'single image'.[116] Nō, likewise, avoids any 'distraction or strain of attention' from its 'single emotional theme'. It possesses the congruity and the 'unity' that he finds in the best art. Fenollosa's emphasis on this 'unity' of nō as 'emotional' indicates that it is achieved not through 'the

---

[110] *UMN*, vol. 6, 247–50.
[111] *EFF*, vol. 3, 241.
[112] Fenollosa, 'Notes on the Japanese Lyric Drama', *Journal of the American Oriental Society* 22, no. 1 (1901): 129–57.
[113] Ibid., 130.
[114] Ibid.
[115] Ibid.
[116] Fenollosa, 'Imagination in Art', 5.

cold weighing of the intellect' and 'abstract thought' but through an emotional intuition. Fenollosa's enthusiasm for nō was thus generated by its apparent accordance with the aesthetics he had previously developed.

Fenollosa returned to Japan for the last time on 14 May to conclude his studies of nō and Chinese poetry. Five days after arriving, he attended the monthly performance at Umewaka's house.[117] He came again on 8 June, when *Takasago* was one of the first plays performed on the first day of the three-day annual commemoration performance in honour of Umewaka's ancestors.[118] A week later, Fenollosa arrived at Umewaka's with a photographer, who took pictures of Umewaka and his nō stage. The following day, Fenollosa attended another nō programme that included *Kakitsubata*, *Kagekiyo* and *Kumasaka*.[119] On 29 June, Umewaka records in his diary that he 'talked about *Takasago* from its opening to its ending'.[120] Umewaka wrote to Hirata on 4 July, telling him he looked forward to discussing *Nishikigi* with him and Fenollosa on 9 July; Umewaka also told them more about his experiences of nō's predicament during the Meiji restoration.[121] By the end of July, Fenollosa appears to have concluded his nō studies. On 31 July, he wrote to Hirata asking him, 'what I should pay you for a salary for your kind work for me in June and July'.[122] He was clearly in a rush before his anticipated return to America: 'Also your thought of a salary for August, during which I want you to work for me all your workable hours. Please don't fail me in this, for I am relying on you. Please finish the Nō book as soon as possible.'[123] The 'Nō book' is, as Murakata claims, likely Ōwada's *Utai to nō*, published the previous year. This last letter to Hirata before Fenollosa's final departure from Japan on 21 September further demonstrates his reliance on Hirata's translation and interpretation.

That same year, two important English-language books appeared that discussed nō. The first was *Japanese Plays and Playfellows* by Osman Edwards, who had visited Japan for half a year and attended a performance with the Fenollosas at Umewaka's house on 30 October 1898.[124] A more wide-ranging assessment of nō appeared in Francis Brinkley's eight-volume *Japan: Its History, Art and Literature*, published between 1901 and 1904. Brinkley had arrived in Japan in 1866 and was the editor of the *Japan Weekly Mail* from 1881 until his

---

[117] *EFF*, vol. 3, 242.
[118] *UMN*, vol. 6, 326.
[119] Ibid., 330.
[120] Ibid., 333.
[121] Ibid., 333–4; *EFF*, vol. 3, 243.
[122] Ibid.
[123] Ibid.
[124] Osman Edwards, *Japanese Plays and Playfellows* (London: John Lane, 1901).

death in 1912. He goes into much greater detail than his predecessors about nō's patronage by the Ashikaga shōguns, who are credited not only for their military and political strength in 'putting an end to the dual monarchy' but also for their 'magnificent patronage of the arts': their reign 'saw the birth of a great art movement', which included the construction of the Golden and Silver Pavilion, tea ceremony, the 'incense cult', landscape gardening, and 'Nô'.[125] Elaborating on the 'incense cult', Brinkley relates that, during this time, 'each *Shôgun*, on receipt of his patent from the Throne, should repair to the temple, and cut off a small portion of the incense for his own use'; this was performed by all the Ashikaga shōguns, 'and even the bluff soldier Oda Nobunaga did not neglect it'.[126] Only later, however, did 'the pastime of "listening to incense"' come into being.[127] Brinkley goes further than any previous Anglophone commentator in praising nō: 'It is, indeed, more than doubtful whether any other people ever developed such an expressive vocabulary or motion, such impressive eloquence of gesture' as nō, which possesses 'a character of noble dignity and profound intensity of sentiment'.[128] He thus accords it a high position not only within Japanese literature, as Chamberlain had done, but also within world literature.

Following his final return from Japan, Fenollosa gave several lecture series across America. One such series was given at the Freer Gallery of Art in Washington, DC, between 27 February and the end of March 1903.[129] The fifth of its seven lectures was simply titled '*No*' and offered a broader discussion of nō than his 1901 article.[130] His interviews with Umewaka, conducted both before and after his 1901 article, result in an account of nō's revival after the Meiji era that exaggerates Umewaka's role:

> For three years after 1868 performances entirely ceased. But Mr. Umewaka Minoru, who had been one of the soloists in the Shogun's central troupe, remembered it all in his heart and had many stage directions and texts in MSS. In 1871 he bought for a song an ex-daimio's stage, [and] set it up by the Banks of Sumida River in Tokio.[131]

---

[125] Francis Brinkley, *Japan: Its History, Art and Literature*, vol. 2 (Boston: J. B. Millet Company, 1901), 108; Brinkley, *Japan*, vol. 3, 28.
[126] Ibid., 1.
[127] Ibid.
[128] Ibid., 29.
[129] *EFF*, vol. 3, 272.
[130] Fenollosa, 'Lecture V. *No*', in ibid., vol. 3, 274–92.
[131] Ibid., 278.

As readers of Mitford's *Tales of Old Japan* later found out, however, nō performances did continue after 1868, such as the one attended by the Duke of Edinburgh in 1869. The Kongō school also performed nō at their Iigura theatre before the group of seven nō actors – of which Umewaka was only one – borrowed the money to set up the theatre adjoined to his house; rather than costing 'a song', it took four years to pay back the loan. Fenollosa thus creates a narrative of the strong but isolated individual's perseverance overcoming adversity that would later appeal to Pound.

The lecture repeats the claim in his 1901 article, though worded differently, that nō involves a 'concentration upon a single emotional theme': 'The Beauty and Power of *No* is its concentration. Every element – costume, motion, verse, and music – unite to produce a single clarified impression.'[132] This unity is achieved by 'carefully excluding all such obtrusive elements as realism and vulgar sensation demand'.[133] He now traces this back, however, to 'Shinto dance, the root of the Japanese drama', in which 'every posture of the whole body – head, trunk, hands, and feet' is made 'harmonious as line to the eye, and all the transitions from posture to posture, harmonious and graceful in time'.[134] Fenollosa then touches on how, under the shōgunate, nō therefore also functioned as a 'great moral force for the whole social order of the Samurai'.[135] Fenollosa thus briefly connects the aesthetic unity he discovers in nō with the political unity that it serves to praise, a feature that would be of crucial importance for Pound. He does not go on, however, to draw the parallel Aston does between nō's veneration of imperial rule and Meiji imperialism's 'social order'.

In the month Fenollosa returned to Japan for his final three-month stay, Dickins began work on *Primitive and Mediaeval Japanese Literature*.[136] Of all the plays, '*Takasago* is, perhaps, the freshest in tone and the least artificial in diction and phrasing.'[137] Further emphasizing its importance, he also claims that 'in remembrance, perhaps, of the *Takasago* [. . .] three small pine trees were placed [. . .] and a pine-tree was represented upon a curtain'.[138] At the book's conclusion, he includes a significantly altered version of *Takasago* from his 1875 'Ballad of

---

[132] Ibid., 280.
[133] Ibid., 286.
[134] Ibid., 280.
[135] Ibid., 286.
[136] Haruko Iwakami and Peter F. Kornicki (eds), *F. V. Dickins' Letters to Ernest M. Satow, Kumagasu Minakata and Others: A Collection of Transcriptions and Japanese Translations* (Tokyo: Edition Synapse, 2011), 232.
[137] Ibid., 395.
[138] Ibid.

Takasago', typified by the different rendition of the old woman's speech when asked how the couple can be paired while living so far apart:

> *Dame.* Not well considered, Sir, would I say your words are, for though thousands of leagues of land and water part them, yet between wedded folk whose thoughts and feelings ay commingle never long is affection's path.[139]

In order, presumably, to suggest the play's antiquity, numerous archaisms are employed, such as the final clause's 'ay' and syntactical inversion. The influence of Aston's and Brinkley's more literal approaches is also evident, however: Dickins now alternates prose and verse, as the original does; the metaphor in the Japanese of the '*michi*' between the couple is indicated; and the degree to which he invents additional details is significantly reduced. Dickins's translation further solidifies the primacy of *Takasago* in early English nō translations: of the seven English nō translations published until then, three are of *Takasago*.

The work on nō that Fenollosa envisaged writing after his return to America, however, never materialized in his lifetime. He continued to carry out research for *Epochs of Chinese and Japanese Art*. This research eventually took him to the British Museum in London. Since the purchase of William Anderson's collection of Japanese paintings in 1881, the museum had built up a renowned collection of Japanese art, particularly under the Keeper of Prints and Drawings, Sidney Colvin (1845–1927), and his successor, Laurence Binyon.[140] Fenollosa wrote to Binyon in September 1908, asking to visit its collections, and made his first visit on 12 September. Only nine days later, however, he died of a heart attack at the age of fifty-five.[141] Although he was unable to complete his book on nō, his notes and some fifty translations survived him. He was one of several Westerners to have taken enthusiastically to nō. Over the course of the Meiji era, their reaction shifted from Mitford's dismissal of its anti-mimesis to Chamberlain's praise of this very quality as an 'ideal' rather than a mimetic drama. Furthermore, Chamberlain positioned nō as among the greatest works of Japanese literature; Brinkley went further by suggesting its high value in world literature. It was Fenollosa's conviction that nō embodied his Hegel-inspired aesthetics of the 'single image', however, that would later most appeal to the future editor of his notes and translations. Fenollosa could not have known that this editor, Ezra

---

[139] Ibid., 404.
[140] John Hatcher, *Laurence Binyon: Poet, Scholar of East and West* (Oxford: Clarendon, 1995), 64.
[141] Chisolm, *Fenollosa*, 211; Yamaguchi, *Fenorosa*, vol. 2, 297.

Pound, was at that moment also in London, having arrived on 14 August from Venice 'with £3 knowing no one' and applied for a British Museum reader's ticket.[142] Of all the early English translators of nō, it was Fenollosa, through Pound, whose work would do most to promote nō in the West as one of the great art forms of the world.

---

[142] Ewick, 'Strange Attractors: Ezra Pound and the Invention of Japan, II', *Eibei bungaku hyōron* 64 (2018): 33.

7

'One of the great arts of the world'

Pound's first nō translations

On 8 October 1908, just over two weeks after Fenollosa's death, Pound finally acquired his British Museum reading card.[1] It was not until February the following year, however, that Pound records having met Binyon: on either 9 or 10 February 1909, he wrote to his mother that he had had a 'delightful couple of hours with Lawrence [sic] Binyon'.[2] The month after, Pound informed her that 'Binyon has sent me a ticket for his lectures on Oriental & European Art. The first one was intensely interesting.'[3] On 24 March, Pound told his father that he had 'just come from hearing Binyon lecture'.[4] 'Lectures on Oriental & European Art' consisted of a four-part series on 'Art and Thought in East and West', given on 10, 17, 24 and 31 March. Pound's correspondence suggests that he attended at least two of these. Although the lectures have not all survived, an advertisement was discovered by John Hatcher. Comparisons are made between Eastern and Western developments in art: for example, the second lecture is titled 'The Renaissance in Europe and Japan' and discusses the 'Great patrons of art: Lorenzo de' Medici; Maximilian; the Ashikaga Shoguns'.[5] Binyon's lectures first exposed Pound to a detailed discussion of individual Japanese artists and the importance of Japan's political leaders' patronage of the arts. Together with Fenollosa, Binyon's conception of Far Eastern art played an important part in Pound's understanding of nō when he began translating them, especially his notion of them as consisting of a 'single idea'; during 1914 Pound developed this aesthetics into a politicized veneration of centralized imperial rule.

---

[1] Arrowsmith, *Modernism and the Museum*, 108.
[2] Pound, letter to Isabel Weston Pound (9–10 February 1909), in *L/HP*, 157.
[3] Pound, letter to Isabel Weston Pound (15 March 1909), in ibid., 164.
[4] Pound, letter to Homer Pound (24 March 1909), in ibid.
[5] Hatcher, *Laurence Binyon*, 159.

The advertisement for Binyon's lectures parallels many of the themes discussed in Binyon's *Painting in the Far East* of 1908. The comparison of 'Lorenzo de' Medici; Maximilian; the Ashikaga shoguns', for instance, is discussed in its ninth chapter, 'The Ashikaga Period in Japan'.[6] Under the rule of the shōgun Ashikaga Yoshimitsu, Kanami and Zeami's patron, 'there was intimate communication with the empire of the continent'.[7] This resulted in a 'Chinese Renaissance in Japanese art', which 'coincided nearly in date with the Renaissance in Italian painting'.[8] The drawing of equivalences between Western and Eastern painters in the advertisement for Binyon's lecture series is also apparent throughout the chapter: Binyon feels that another painter inspired by the northern Song school, Sesshū – whom Fenollosa praised in his Ryūchikai lecture and whose folding screens made Shiki realize the 'fine arrangement' in painting and its analogy with that of haiku – would have been 'welcomed' as a 'peer' by 'Rembrandt himself'.[9] Binyon thus emphasizes, as Fenollosa had in *Bijutsu shinsetsu*, that Japanese painters of this era are as worthy of consideration as the greatest Western artists. He also draws attention to their patronage by the Ashikaga shōguns. Ashikaga Yoshimasa, Yoshimitsu's grandson, encouraged 'the pastime of "listening to incense"', as noted by Brinkley, and fostered an art of 'Austerity': in the tea ceremony he promoted, 'even the garden without must harmonise, and show no gaudy tone, no luxuriant detail'; its 'secret lay in the discovery that beauty has most power on the imagination when not completely revealed'.[10] This art of austerity and suggestion was to prove influential for Pound's poetics.

Binyon's conception of the aesthetics of Chinese and Japanese painting bears a striking resemblance to Fenollosa's. He acknowledges Fenollosa's 'wide, intimate, and first-hand knowledge' of Far Eastern art.[11] Like Fenollosa, he stresses the 'artistic principle of unity' in Chinese painting.[12] Binyon developed this Fenollosan conception of Far Eastern art into the central theme of *The Flight of the Dragon*, published in 1911. The 'strong synthetic power' in Chinese art exemplifies the 'related order of movements' that constitutes 'Rhythmic Vitality', for Binyon the essential element in a work of art.[13] 'But what is rhythm? [...] the most typical, as it is probably the oldest of the arts, is the Dance; not the dance

---

[6] Binyon, *Painting in the Far East* (London: Edward Arnold, 1908), 161.
[7] Ibid.
[8] Ibid.
[9] Ibid., 161 and 166.
[10] Ibid., 168–70.
[11] Ibid., vii.
[12] Ibid., 50.
[13] Binyon, *The Flight of the Dragon* (London: John Murray, 1911), 13–15.

of modern Europe, but the dance of old Greece, old China, or old Japan.'[14] As an example of this dance, he relates what Mitford, Chamberlain, Aston, Edwards and Brinkley give as the legendary origin of nō, the dance for the sun goddess Amaterasu to entice her out of a cave.[15] Binyon concludes that 'Every statue, every picture, is a series of ordered relations, controlled, as the body is controlled in the dance, by the will to express a single idea'.[16] Pound cited this passage in the July 1915 issue of *BLAST* as one of Binyon's great 'moments' of insight.[17] Binyon's understanding of a work of art's unity recalls Fenollosa's conceptions of the 'single idea', 'single image' and, with reference to nō, 'single emotional impression'.

Following her husband's death, Mary McNeil Fenollosa sought an editor for his notes on nō and Chinese poetry. On 29 September 1913, she dined with Pound and the Indian poet Sarojini Naidu at the latter's house in London.[18] According to Mary, Pound was 'enthusiastic' about Fenollosa, after which she promised to send him the manuscripts. Pound recalls in T. S. Eliot's *Ezra Pound: His Metric and Poetry* that she had sought him out because of 'certain poems in *Lustra*'.[19] These cannot be Pound's versions of Chinese poetry such as 'Fan-Piece for Her Imperial Lord' and 'Liu Ch'e', however, as these were first published in February 1914; they might therefore include 'In a Station of the Metro' as an indication of his ability to recreate Far Eastern literature. Pound looked forward to receiving Fenollosa's notes: on 5 December he wrote to his father that 'I am to have Prof. Fenollosa's valuable *mss.* to edit & finish a book on the Japanese drama & an anthology of Chinese poets. It is a very great opportunity.'[20] He also read Fenollosa's *Epochs of Chinese and Japanese Art*, which Mary had edited from her husband's notes on Far Eastern art and published in 1912.[21] Pound's first mention of 'Noh' adopts Mary's spelling in her introduction to *Epochs*; she advises him to use 'Nōh [sic], as some French writers do'.[22] By 16 December he was at work on the nō, writing to his then fiancée Dorothy that 'I have cribbed part of a Noh (dramatic eclogue) out of Fenollosa's notes' while at Stone Cottage, where he spent the winter of 1913–14 as W. B. Yeats's secretary.[23] The play was *Kinuta*,

---

[14] Ibid., 15–16.
[15] Ibid., 16. Mitford, *Tales of Old Japan*, 156; Chamberlain, *The Classical Poetry of the Japanese*, 213; Aston, *A History of Japanese Literature*, 197–8; Edwards, *Japanese Plays and Playfellows*, 40.
[16] Ibid., 16–17.
[17] Pound, 'Chronicles', *BLAST* 2 (July 1915): 86.
[18] Pound, letter to Dorothy Shakespear (2 October 1913), in *L/DS*, 264.
[19] Harmer, *Victory in Limbo*, 235.
[20] Pound, letter to Homer Pound (5 December 1913), in *L/HP*, 315.
[21] Ibid.
[22] Ibid.
[23] Pound, letter to Shakespear (16 December 1913), in *L/DS*, 287.

shortly followed by *Hagoromo*: these are the first two translations in Fenollosa's notebook as well as those Mary described respectively as her own favourite and that of 'the average Japanese Nōh lover'.[24]

Pound sent his translation of *Kinuta* to G. W. Prothero's *Quarterly Review* by 6 January 1914; he submitted his *Hagoromo* by mid-January.[25] Both plays finally appeared in the October issue prefaced by Pound's edited version of Fenollosa's 1903 lecture, 'Nō'. Pound introduces nō as 'one of the greatest and least-known arts in the world [. . .] generally called *Noh* (accomplishment)', thus borrowing the term's translation by Brinkley, whose *Japan: Its History, Arts and Literature* he cites as one of the previous English publications on nō along with Dickins.[26] After his version of Fenollosa's lecture, Pound includes his revisions of the Hirata and Fenollosa translations of *Kinuta* and *Hagoromo*. The latter is translated as 'The Feather-Mantle'. Its authorship remains uncertain; it is first mentioned in 1524.[27] It is said that *Hagoromo* was performed for centuries during the spring new year at the Zenkō Temple in modern-day Nagano Prefecture in order 'for the sun to rise'.[28] The title's *hagoromo* is a celestial maiden's (*tennin's*) feather mantle left behind on earth at Miho no Matsubara, a pinewood by the sea south of Mount Fuji, and discovered by a fisherman, Hakuryō.[29] She cannot return to heaven without it. He gives it back on the condition that she performs the 'Dance of the Rainbow Skirt and Feather Mantle', which she does before flying back up to heaven over Mount Fuji at the play's conclusion. This legend is first recorded in the Chinese fourth-century *Xuanzhongji* ('Mysterious Stories') and *Soushenji* ('Stories of Seeking the Gods') before appearing in Japan in the eighth-century *Ōmi fudoki* ('An Account of Ōmi Province'), *Tango fudoki* and now lost *Suruga fudoki*.[30]

After Hakuryō agrees to return the mantle in exchange for 'the dance of the *tennin*', he questions her sincerity when she asks for him to return it first.[31] In Pound's version, like all his nō translations written in a mixture of prose and free verse, she replies:

Doubt is fitting for mortals; with us there is no deceit.[32]

---

[24] Mary Fenollosa, letter to Pound (25 November 1913), in *EPJ*, 8.
[25] Pound, letter to Shakespear (6 January 1914), in *L/DS*, 293; Pound, letter to Shakespear (14 January 1914), in ibid., 302–3.
[26] Pound, 'The Classical Drama of Japan', 450.
[27] Umehara and Kanze (eds), *Nō wo yomu*, vol. 4, 310.
[28] 'Hagoromo sōdan' ('A Discussion of *Hagoromo*'), *Nōgaku* 1, no. 5 (November 1902): 19.
[29] In the nō play, 'Miho' has always been pronounced 'Mio'. I am grateful to Richard Emmert for this information.
[30] Zhao Jianhong, 'Chūnichi hagoromo setsuwa kō' ('A Consideration of the Chinese and Japanese Feather-Mantle Tales'), *Chūgokugaku ronshū* 40 (July 2005): 52–70.
[31] Pound, 'The Classical Drama of Japan', 475.
[32] Ibid.

Ashamed, Hakuryō returns the feather mantle, and she performs the 'dance of the rainbow-feathered garment'.³³ The sky to which the maiden intends to return is described as 'everlasting'; the comparison that follows in the play between the longevity of the heavens and that of the moon, however, is given a different slant in Pound's translation. Whereas Ōwada explains that the 'jewelled axe's construction' of the 'palace of the moon' signifies its stability and longevity, Pound sees the axe as performing an 'eternal renewing': 'the palace of the moon-god is being renewed with the jewelled axe, and this is always recurring.'³⁴ This is due to Hirata and Fenollosa's version. As Yoshida Sachiko notes, they translate *shuri* ('construction') as 'mending'; their version reads: 'But the state of the palace of the moon deity (is this that) its being mended with the jewelled axe being an event always occurring.'³⁵ For Pound, this passage would prove an influential precursor to his famous conception of 'making it new'. Pound compares the ordered movement of the moon's phases, represented by the celestial maidens' dance, with Trivia's (Diana's) nymphs in Canto XXIII of Dante's *Paradiso*: she is the moon and they the stars which Dante's speaker then likens to the 'sol' ('sun') of paradise.³⁶ With this comparison, Pound was following in the footsteps of Binyon's lectures on 'Art and Thought in East and West' and laying the groundwork for the network of cross-cultural subject rhymes in *The Cantos*.

As in Canto XXIII of the *Paradiso*, *Hagoromo* compares the ordered movement of the moon with that of the sun. In Pound's translation, as the maiden dances, the chorus sings:

> It is quiet along the shore. There is naught but a fence of jewels between the earth and the sky, and the gods within and without, beyond and beneath the stars, and the moon unclouded by her lord, and we who are born of the sun! This alone is between, here where the moon is unshadowed, here in Nippon, the sun's field.³⁷

When the earth is blessed by the sun and moon's movements in this way, it creates a peaceful plenty close to the calm order of the heavens. The proximity of heaven and earth is represented by the emperor, the descendant of the sun goddess Amaterasu: as Hirata and Fenollosa's notes explain, the gods bless the 'misuye' (*misue*, 'descendant'), which 'refers to Japanese Emperor [*sic*]'.³⁸ Pound alters this reference to 'we who are born of the sun', thus removing the comparison between

---

³³ Ibid.
³⁴ Ibid.
³⁵ NA, 191.
³⁶ Dante Alighieri, *The Paradiso*, trans. Philip Wicksteed (London: J. M. Dent, 1910), 282–3.
³⁷ Pound, 'The Classical Drama of Japan', 475.
³⁸ NA, 193.

the sun and moon's movements and imperial rule. A further imperial reference is omitted in the play's allusion to an anonymous *waka* from the *Shūishū* in which, in Hirata and Fenollosa's rendering, 'my Lord's [the emperor's] reign is surely a rock that will not lessen, however rubbed by heaven's feather mantle that comes so rarely worn'.[39] Pound leaves out the explicit comparison of the rock with 'my Lord's reign':

> Nor is this rock of earth over-much worn by the brushing of that feather-mantle, the feathery skirt of the stars – rarely, how rarely![40]

These decisions suggest that Pound was as this stage little interested in the connection the play makes between the celestial movements and imperial rule. His translation of this passage emphasizes the distance between 'the earth and the sky' rather than the imperial rule that binds heaven and earth together. Nonetheless, Pound's detection of *Hagoromo*'s parallels with Dante's *Paradiso*, especially its depiction of the sun and moon's life-giving light and ordered movements, presented him with another fragment of paradise and played an important part in inspiring his life-long interest in nō.

The third play Pound translated was Zeami's *Nishikigi* ('The Brocade Sticks'). As Mary Fenollosa informed Pound, it was one of the plays her late husband 'specially loved'; Fenollosa himself noted in his 1903 lecture that it is 'the most weird and delicately poetic piece' of those he had come across.[41] On 31 January 1914 Pound sent it to Monroe, who published it in *Poetry*'s May issue.[42] Pound's new-found enthusiasm for nō begins to find expression in this letter: he tells her that the play 'will give us some reason for existing' and that it 'is too beautiful to be encumbered with notes and long explanation' before concluding that 'this Japanese find is about the best bit of luck we've had since starting the magazine'.[43] Unlike the previous attempts of 'dull and ludicrous' scholars, Pound sees his work as possessing literary quality: 'I don't put the work under the general category of translation either. [. . .] This stuff ranks as re-creation.'[44] Only Fenollosa is acknowledged as a translator; this was at Pound's request because his 'name' was 'in such opprobrium', probably due to the recent scandal of Pound's fellow *Imagiste* Richard Aldington's blasphemous poem, 'Lesbia'.[45] In Pound's notes

---

[39] Ibid., 193–4.
[40] Pound, 'The Classical Drama of Japan', 476.
[41] Mary Fenollosa, letter to Pound (25 November 1913), in *EPJ*, 8; *EFF*, vol. 3, 289.
[42] Pound, letter to Harriet Monroe (31 January 1914), in *L*, 69.
[43] Ibid.
[44] Ibid.
[45] Ibid.

at the back of the issue in which it appears (despite Pound's intention not to publish any), the play is presented as centred upon a fundamental contrast: 'It is a flurry of snow against a red spray of maples.'[46] This is the first indication of Pound's receptivity to Fenollosa's contention in the 1903 lecture, '*Nō*', that a nō play consists of a 'single clarified impression'.

Nishikigi concerns a man and a woman whom a priest visits in the 'county of Kefu' in Michinoku, then Japan's northernmost province. The man makes *nishikigi*, which Pound translates as 'Love-wands, or Charm-sticks', and the woman weaves *hosonuno*, 'narrow cloth'. The earliest extant reference to these *nishikigi* appears in the Buddhist monk Nōin's (988–?) eleventh-century *waka*, 'While the brocade sticks were standing, they already had withered away – the narrow cloth of Kefu, there's no meeting at the breast'.[47] A detailed commentary on *nishikigi* and *hosonuno* is given in Minamoto no Toshiyori's (1055–1129) *Toshiyori zuinō* ('The Mind of Toshiyori') of 1113:

> In the province of Michinoku, when a man wishes to court a woman, he does not tell her but cuts a piece of firewood and places one stick in front of the door of her house. Once he has stood it there, if she wishes to meet him she takes it inside [. . .] if she does not wish to meet him, she does not take it inside.[48]

Regarding *hosonuno*, Toshiyori comments that 'the narrow cloth of Kefu is woven from birds' feathers in Michinoku Province'.[49] It was called 'narrow' because it 'only covered the back and did not come over the chest'.[50] Nōin's *waka* puns on this inability of 'meeting at the breast' by comparing it with the unrequited love suggested by the uncollected *nishikigi*. As Iei Michiko argues, however, these urban writers understood little of such remote customs: the 'beautifully decorated wood', 'cloth woven from birds' feathers' and even the 'county of Kefu' were almost certainly inventions.[51] The nō play arose from the accumulation of such *waka* imagery.[52]

Upon hearing from the man and woman the story of a man who had laid a thousand *nishikigi* in front of a woman's door without reply, after which both died without fulfilling their love, the priest is taken by them to the burial mound where the thousand *nishikigi* and the dead couple reside. The man then reveals

---

[46] 'Notes', in *Poetry* 4, no. 2 (May 1915): 71.
[47] Iei Michiko, 'Nishikizuka no kōsatsu' ('An Examination of Nishizuka'), *Artes Liberales* 44 (June 1989): 177.
[48] Ibid., 178.
[49] Ibid.
[50] Ibid.
[51] Ibid., 188.
[52] Fenollosa (trans.), *Nishikigi*, 48.

himself to be the ghost of the suitor and the woman as his beloved. Echoing the man's earlier questioning of whether the love he wishes for is 'more than a dream', the priest now wonders about what he sees, 'Is it illusion?'[53] The man replies:

> Our hearts have been in the dark of the falling snow,
> We have been astray in the flurry,
> You should tell better than we
> How much is illusion –
> We have been in the whirl of
>   those who are fading.[54]

Nishikigi is Pound's first encounter with a *mugen* nō, in which ghosts of the past haunt the present. The 'whirl' derives from Hirata and Fenollosa's version ('O how glorious are the sleeves of the dance which seem to sweep in whirls of snow!') of the original, in which the chorus also sings of how the sleeves of the dancing man 'make the snow turn'.[55] This 'whirl' of the snow 'flurry', which Pound gives as the core of the play, is that of the dead moving about the present. This had long been a crucial preoccupation for Pound, as shown in his 1908 poem 'Histrion': 'the souls of all men great / At times pass through us.'[56] As Ewick notes, this aspect of *Nishikigi* 'sparked Pound's understanding that the "ghosts patched with histories" of the nô provide a method for "reconstructing the past"' that Pound would use when translating *Takasago* and beginning *The Cantos* the following year.[57] Moreover, the focal point of the play for Pound – the 'whirl' of the 'snow-flurry' representing the dead – would even sooner make an important contribution to his new conception of the 'vortex'.

According to Helen Carr, the first public use of 'Vorticism' to denote an artistic movement came on 12 June 1914, when Christopher Nevinson, an aficionado of F. T. Marinetti's Futurism, shared a platform with Marinetti at the Doré Galleries to present their Futurist manifesto and used the term to describe what Pound had given separately in the 1 April 1914 issue of *The Egoist* as the contents of the forthcoming first issue of *BLAST*, edited by Pound and Lewis: 'Cubism, Futurism, Imagisme'.[58] Carr claims that 'Pound [. . .] had of course produced the new name'.[59] If so, he would have decided upon it before 20 June

---

[53] Ibid., 36 and 43.
[54] Ibid., 43.
[55] *NA*, 124; *YT*, vol. 5, 101.
[56] Pound, 'Histrion', *Evening Standard and St James's Gazette* (26 October 1908): 3.
[57] Ewick, 'Nishikigi', in *Japonisme, Orientalism, Modernism*, online.
[58] Advertisement for *BLAST*, *The Egoist* 1, no. 7 (1 April 1914): 140.
[59] *VR*, 657–8.

1914, when *BLAST* was introduced as a 'Review of the Great English Vortex'; the composition of *Nishikigi* in January and its publication in *Poetry* in May precede this date. In 'Vortex', published in the first *BLAST*, Pound portrays the 'vortex' as the 'point of maximum energy':

> All experience rushes into this vortex. All the energized past, all the past that is living and worthy to live. All MOMENTUM, which is the past bearing upon us, RACE, RACE-MEMORY, instinct charging the PLACID, NON-ENERGIZED FUTURE.
>
> The DESIGN of the future in the grip of the human vortex. All the past that is vital, all the past that is capable of living into the future, is pregnant in the vortex, NOW.[60]

The Latin root of 'vortex' is, of course, a 'whirl' or 'whirlpool'. Not only does this coincide with the 'whirl' of the 'snow-flurry' in *Nishikigi*; the 'whirl' in the nō play is that of the dead, the 'energized past [. . .] bearing upon us'. Although Pound used the more concisely quotable 'Whirl' of H. D.'s 'Oread' as an example of Vorticism in *BLAST*, it is *Nishikigi*, rather than 'Oread', that specifically provides Pound with his conception of the 'vortex' in its expression of the past as the 'whirl' of the dead's apparitions charging the 'future'.[61]

The other important aspect of the 'vortex' that Pound took from nō is their apparent use of a central focal point around which the play is structured, which serves as the 'maximum point of energy' charged by what moves around it. Let us look once more at the note Pound appended to the end of his essay 'Vorticism' in the 1 September 1914 issue of the *Fortnightly Review*:

> I am often asked whether there can be a long imagiste or vorticist poem. The Japanese, who evolved the hokku, evolved also the Noh plays. In the best 'Noh' the whole play may consist of one image. I mean it is gathered about one image. Its unity consists in one image, enforced by movement and music. I see nothing against a long vorticist poem.[62]

Pound would go on to make this point two more times the following year, giving examples of such 'one-image' nō. At this moment, however, Pound's comment in May that *Nishikigi* 'is a flurry of snow against red maples' remained his foremost example of the 'one-image' nō. Pound's use of contrast here suggests the continued influence of Whistlerian 'arrangement'; but the notion that nō

---

[60] Pound, 'Vortex', 153.
[61] Ibid., 154.
[62] Pound, 'Vorticism', 471.

plays focus on 'one image' was newly derived (and also applied to '*hokku*') from Fenollosa's contention in his 1903 lecture, '*No*', that the beauty of a nō play lies in its 'elements [. . .] unit[ing] to produce a single clarified impression'. Pound also uses the term 'image' similarly to Fenollosa's and Binyon's 'single idea' and the 'single image' in the former's essay on 'Imagination in Art': it is not 'ordinary vision' but an intuitive grasping of unity between the elements of an artwork. For this reason, in 'Vorticism' Pound gives Dante's *Paradiso* as 'the most wonderful *image*': not because it presents a single visual object, but because the 'form of sphere above sphere, the varying reaches of light, the minutiae of pearls upon foreheads' constitute, for Pound, its unity of design.[63]

Pound's interest in nō at this time led to an intensification of his editing of the nō from the autumn to the end of 1914. On 7 September, after informing his father about his 'article on "Vorticism"', Pound told him he was 'finishing up another batch of the Fenollosa notes & translations'.[64] This enthusiasm may have been further spurred by a publisher's 'offer for a book on Noh or on troubadours' in December, though Pound refused; this was probably the 'Yale Press' which had approached him about publishing a nō book before Macmillan.[65] That Pound had been working during this time on nō as well as on *Cathay* is made clear in another letter to his father, on 30 December, that '"The Drama" a Chicago ¼ly is printing a big wad of Jap [*sic*] plays (5 or 6) & notes. probably in May'.[66] Unlike the nō translations of the previous winter, which had been completed at Stone Cottage, the 'big wad of Jap plays' was likely edited at his home in Kensington before he left for Stone Cottage after Christmas.[67] When they appeared in *The Drama* in May 1915, they were prefaced by Pound's introductory essay. Pound notes that only one book on nō had been produced to date, by 'Prof. Marie C. Stopes', who had edited and translated *The Plays of Old Japan: The Nō* in 1913; he describes Fenollosa's life as 'the romance par excellence of modern scholarship' and his work as 'the basis of a new donation, for a new way of understanding "the East"'.[68] Moreover, Pound praises nō in even stronger terms than the Fenollosa essay he had edited in the *Quarterly Review*: 'The *Noh* is unquestionably one of the great arts of the world, and possibly the most recondite.'[69]

---

[63] Ibid., 465.
[64] Pound, letter to Homer Pound (7 September 1914), in *L/HP*, 332.
[65] Pound, letter to Isabel Weston Pound (24 December 1914), in ibid., 339; Pound, letter to John Quinn (19 April 1917), in *L/JQ*, 105.
[66] Pound, letter to Homer Pound (30 December 1914), in *L/HP*, 340.
[67] *SC*, 8.
[68] Pound, 'The Classical Stage of Japan', 199.
[69] Ibid., 201.

The reason Pound gives for the latter is that 'The art of the illusion, or this love of illusion in art, is at the root of *Noh*'; he gives the example, which he had read in the third volume of Brinkley's *Japan: Its Art, History and Literature* and possibly also in Binyon's *Painting in the Far East*, of the Ashikaga-period pastime of 'listening to incense', which involved not only distinguishing between fragrances but also to 'give to each one of them a beautiful and allusive name'.[70] In another instance of Pound's discovery of cross-cultural 'subject rhymes' anticipating those of *The Cantos*, he compares this practice to 'the art of polyphonic rhyme' in Provence; the exclusivity of such aristocratic pastimes as *kōdō* and nō appealed to his growing 'sense of a cultural elite', further encouraged by his first winter with Yeats at Stone Cottage.[71] Nō was, like *kōdō*, 'for the few, for the nobles, for those trained to catch the allusion'.[72] After citing Umewaka's account of his ancestry from the 1900 nō programme in commemoration of his ancestors, Pound commends his 'Pride of descent, pride of having served dynasties now extinct'.[73] He also cites Ōwada's account in *Utai to nō* of the *utaizome* ceremony, in which the five schools perform 'the waves of the four seas passage' from *Takasago* and three plays, including *Takasago*, for the shōgun every new year.[74] Pound thus extended his vision of Japan as a 'very old, very quiet civilization' that respected and fostered high art. His nō research encouraged him to identify such a respect for the arts with the kind of aristocratic patronage he had also been trying to cultivate. He began to see imperialism as the primary model for a society that valued the 'recondite' art which he, too, saw himself as creating.

The first two plays after Pound's introductory essay are Kanami's *Sotoba Komachi* ('Stupa Komachi') and *Kayoi Komachi* ('Visiting Komachi'). Pound's translation demonstrates his awareness of the wordplay frequently used in nō plays, as he already knew, for example, from *Nishikigi*'s pun on unrequited love being compared to *hosonuno* because 'there's no meeting at the breast'. In the Ōwada edition from which Hirata and Fenollosa's now lost version presumably derived, when the Buddhist monk acting in the *waki* role asks Komachi, whose spirit is disguised as an old woman, what her name is, she replies, 'Ah! I am ashamed to give my own name', before the chorus adds, 'As Ono said, "I'm an old woman from Ichiwarano where the susuki grasses grow"'.[75] These lines contain two puns on Komachi's name: in her reply, 'my own' reads *ono*, a homophone of

---

[70] Ibid.
[71] Ibid.; *SC*, 44.
[72] Pound, 'The Classical Stage of Japan', 201.
[73] Ibid., 204.
[74] Ibid., 205–6.
[75] *YT*, vol. 5, 175.

Komachi's surname; and in the chorus's line, 'Ono' puns on 'she herself' (*ono*). Ōwada's edition gives the latter with the character for 'own'/'herself' (己) and adds those of Komachi's surname (小野) alongside to indicate the pun. Pound's typescript draft shows his awareness of this: he writes by Ono's reply that 'Her name is Ono, meaning name, there's a pun'.[76] In the *Drama* version, Pound plays on the 'Ono no' of her name: the monk (rather than the chorus, as in Ōwada's edition) says that 'If you go down by Itchihara you can hear the wind in the Sujuki [*sic*] bushes as in the poem of Ono no Komachi's, "Ono, no I will not tell the wind my name is Ono"'.[77] Pound thus substitutes an English pun for the Japanese and, in doing so, also demonstrates a more profound understanding than during his first interest in '*hokku*' of the degree to which traditional Japanese poetry is both allusive and playful with language. Similar uses of such wordplay would later appear in Canto IV.

Like *Hagoromo*'s celestial maiden, Komachi is associated in *Kayoi Komachi* with the moon. When she disappears into the susuki grass after half revealing her name to the monk, she is accosted by the spirit of Shōshō, a suitor who had attempted to visit her for a hundred nights but had failed to do so on the final night and so could not win her love. It is from these visits, and his apparition now, that the play derives its title. In Ōwada's edition, Shōshō seeks to dissuade the monk from praying for Komachi, before he addresses her by saying: 'Though it would be sad to suffer along with you, if you were to take the way of Buddha, my suffering would become all the heavier, and I would sink into the Mitsuse River', the river of the dead.[78] Komachi replies that 'your heart is unknown to me; my heart's an unclouded moon'.[79] Pound's version strengthens the contrast between Shōshō and Komachi: Shōshō tells Komachi that 'It is a sad heart I have to see you looking up to Buddha, you who left me alone, as I was diving in the black rivers of hell', after which Komachi responds: 'O dear, you can speak for yourself, but my heart is clear as new moonlight.'[80] Through this addition of 'black', absent in Ōwada's edition of the play, Pound's version further emphasizes the opposition between the darkness of Shōshō's suffering and her own heart that follows Buddha's path. Such a contrast echoes that of the petal faces in the dark station in Pound's 'Metro' poem and anticipates the association of moonlight with the paradisal light in *The Cantos*, in which

---

[76] *GCNTJ*, 33–7.
[77] Pound, 'The Classical Stage of Japan', 215.
[78] *YT*, vol. 5, 175.
[79] Ibid., 176.
[80] Pound, 'The Classical Stage of Japan', 215 and 216.

Komachi would also reappear. At the play's conclusion, Komachi offers 'a cup of moonlight' to Shōshō, after which 'Both their sins vanished' and they 'became pupils of Buddha'.[81]

Following *Nishikigi*, another of the plays Pound gives later in this essay of such a 'single idea' or, as he puts it, 'unity of image', is *Suma Genji*. Pound believes that this play is 'very near to the original, or early form, of the God-dance' of Amaterasu mentioned earlier.[82] The story is based on the twelfth chapter of the eleventh-century *Genji monogatari* ('The Tale of Genji') by Murasaki Shikibu (*c.* 978–*c.* 1014), in which the novel's hero, Prince Hikaru Genji, is exiled to Suma after his affair with an imperial consort. In the *Genji monogatari*, Genji hears that it is a place 'where long ago people [of high station] lived, but now it is a lonely, distant village'.[83] While at Suma, Genji wears a 'bluish grey hunting robe'.[84] As the years pass, the blossoms of 'a young cherry tree' he planted begin 'to scatter', which makes Genji 'weep often about all manner of things', such as the cherries that must now be in 'full bloom' at the 'South Hall', the Hall for State Ceremonies.[85] Before his exile, when he had danced the *Seikaiha* ('Blue Sea Waves') at court, Genji was himself compared to a 'cherry flower'.[86] The nō play, composed by Zeami, is mentioned in Zeami's *Sarugaku dangi* of 1430. A priest, Fujiwara no Okinori, travels from Miyazaki in Hyūga Province to visit Ise. On his way, he visits Suma, where an old fisherman collecting brushwood explains to him that he is looking at Genji's cherry tree. The fisherman then reveals himself to be the spirit of Genji, who 'descends from the sky' of the *tosotsu* (the heavenly realm where the Buddha resided before his birth) and dances the *Seikaiha* to celebrate the cherries blossoming and spring's arrival.

As in *Kayoi Komachi*, Pound draws out the light symbolism in the play, emphasizing the root of Genji's epithet 'Hikaru', 'Genji the gleaming', as his 'brighter apparition' is revealed in the second half of the play and he dances the 'Sei-kei-ha [*sic*], the blue dance of the sea waves'.[87] The *tosotsu* is translated simply as 'heaven' when Genji dances and the chorus sings that 'There was a light from heaven, / There was a young man at the dance here; / Surely it was Genji

---

[81] Ibid., 218.
[82] Ibid., 223.
[83] Murasaki Shikibu, *Genji monogatari*, ed. Ishida Jōji and Shimizu Yoshiko, vol. 2 (Tokyo: Dai Nippon, 2014), 201.
[84] Ibid., 251.
[85] Ibid., 250.
[86] Ibid., 11.
[87] Ibid., 221.

Hakari [sic]'.⁸⁸ The play's 'unity of image' depends upon the emphasis on the 'blue-grey' colour of the waves:

> Blue-grey is the garb they wear here,
> Blue-grey he fluttered in Suma;
> His sleeves are like the grey sea-waves.⁸⁹

Pound's 'blue-grey' translates Zeami's *aonibi*, which in turn is taken directly from the *Genji monogatari*: *aonibi* is literally 'dull blue', a light blue.⁹⁰ Pound's emphasis on unity of colour can be observed in his repetition of 'Blue-grey', which is absent in Ōwada's version.

Kayoi Komachi is thus, like *Nishikigi*, a *mugen* ('dream') nō. The past's charging energy, as Pound put it in 'Vortex', is again emphasized in the continuation of Pound's essay that follows the two Komachi plays and *Suma Genji*. To appreciate nō, one must 'put himself in sympathy with the priest eager to see "even in a vision" the beauty lost in the years, "the shadow of the past in bright form"'.⁹¹ This bringing to light out of darkness also appears in his portrayal of nō's legendary origin in the dance for the sun goddess Amaterasu: 'The first legendary dance took place when the light-goddess hid herself in a cave and the other gods danced on a tub or something of that sort to attract her attention and lure her out of a cave.'⁹² All previous accounts mentioned earlier describe Amaterasu as the 'sun goddess'; Pound's alteration to 'light-goddess' reveals his interest in the correspondence between this legend and the light symbolism he finds in Dante's *Paradiso* but also in *Hagoromo* and *Kayoi Komachi*. Furthermore, Pound had at this point probably read Binyon's portrayal in *The Flight of the Dragon* of this dance for the 'Sun-Goddess'; he would discuss this work in the first *BLAST*. For Binyon, this legend is his example of the 'oldest of the arts', the dance of 'old Greece, old China, or old Japan'. It is this form of 'the Dance' that, for Binyon, constitutes the foremost instance of 'Rhythmic Vitality' and the 'will to express a single idea'. Pound's reference to this legend further highlights the connection between his understanding of nō and Binyon's Fenollosa-inspired aesthetics of the 'single idea'.

Pound also gives specific examples of the 'best "Noh"' that conform to what he defines as their 'unity of image'. He contends that many nō plays have 'a very severe construction of their own, a sort of musical construction which I shall

---

⁸⁸ Ibid., 222.
⁸⁹ Pound, 'The Classical Stage of Japan', 222.
⁹⁰ Murasaki, *Genji monogatari*, 251; *YT*, vol. 6, 65; Pound, 'The Classical Stage of Japan', 222.
⁹¹ Ibid., 223.
⁹² Ibid.

present in a future article in connection with the Takasago play, when I get that latter ready for the public'.[93] *Takasago* is also one of the examples Pound gives of what he saw as nō's 'unity of image':

> the *Noh* has its unity in emotion. It has also what we may call Unity of Image. At least, the better plays are all built into the intensification of a single Image: the red maple leaves and the snow flurry in *Nishikigi*, the pines in *Takasago*, the blue-grey waves and wave pattern in *Suma Genji*, the mantle of feathers in the play of that name, *Hagoromo*.[94]

In a footnote, Pound adds that 'This intensification of the Image, this manner of construction, is very interesting to me personally, as an Imagiste'.[95] These nō plays 'are also an answer to the question' of whether it is possible to 'do a long Imagiste poem, or even a long poem in *vers libre*'.[96] The absence of the term 'Vorticism' here suggests either that this article predates Pound's invention of the term, or that Pound continued to see imagism as a way of expressing this structural unity. After all, in his 'Vorticism' article, Pound sees nō as a model for a 'long imagiste or vorticist poem'. Although the 'Vortex' places a greater emphasis on the past's 'charging' energy, both the 'Image' and the 'Vortex' are now characterized by the employment of a central focal point supported by the work's constituent elements.

Pound then presents his version of *Kumasaka*; although it is not given as an example of nō's 'Unity of Image', it would nonetheless prove another inspiration for Pound's Vorticism in *Gaudier-Brzeska: A Memoir*. No Hirata and Fenollosa draft translation of it survives. The play concerns the slaying of a notorious bandit, Kumasaka no Chōhan, by a boy, Ushiwaka, who later becomes the famous warrior Minamoto no Yoshitsune. An early version appears in the anonymous fourteenth-century *Gikeiki* ('The Story of Yoshitsune'). Ushiwaka accompanies the merchants Kichiji and Kichiroku at the Kagami Inn, where they are attacked by bandits.[97] In this version, Kumasaka no Chōhan does not appear: there are two bandits, Yuri no Tarō and Fujisawa no Nyūdō.[98] At first, they pay no attention to Ushiwaka, assuming him to be a courtesan. The tale's conclusion portrays his slaying of Yuri and Fujisawa. Kumasaka does appear, however, in the nō play *Eboshiori* ('The Hatmaker'), first performed in 1432 and translated, though

---

[93] Ibid., 224.
[94] Ibid.
[95] Ibid.
[96] Ibid.
[97] *Gikeiki* ('The Story of Yoshitsune'), ed. Kajihara Masa'aki (Tokyo: Shōgakukan, 1999), 49.
[98] Ibid., 50.

not published, by Pound.[99] Kajihara Masa'aki suggests that this play fused Yuri and Fujisawa into the fictional Kumasaka.[100] The anonymous *Kumasaka*, whose first-recorded performance took place in 1516, tells the story from Kumasaka's perspective.[101] Buddhist salvation is its principal theme: Kumasaka's ghost, disguised as a Buddhist monk, asks for a visiting monk to pray for an unnamed person. At the end of the play, after he has told of his being slain by Ushiwaka, Kumasaka asks the monk to 'help' him to 'the afterworld'.[102]

Pound's version of *Kumasaka* demonstrates his continued interest in nō's presentation of the 'energized past' in the present, as he had found in *Nishikigi*. Kumasaka narrates the past events that led up to his battle with Ushiwaka: 'Now', he says of the merchant Yoshitsuge before the battle, 'he is come to the village of Ubasike [*sic*].'[103] Pound asks us to 'Note the change to present tense in this passage; the narrative passage, corresponding to the old ballad recitation, ends, and the pantomime representation [. . .] begins'.[104] Pound portrays the play's conclusion as 'the Homeric presentation of the combat between [Kumasaka] and the young boy, Ushiwaka. But note here the punctilio. Kumasaka's spirit returns to do justice to the glory of Ushiwaka and to tell of his own defeat.'[105] This is what makes this scene, in Pound's view, 'among the most famous passages of *Noh*'.[106] Kumasaka's admiration for Ushiwaka is evident in his description of the latter's 'keen eyes' that spotted Kumasaka's approach and his having 'stood unafraid' when Kumasaka and his men attacked.[107] Kumasaka is associated with the pine tree: this is where the priest first encounters him, Ushiwaka kills him, and his spirit resides. Pound's version connects this pine with its function on the back of the nō stage, which his essay, citing Fenollosa's notes, interprets as 'a congratulatory symbol of unchanging green and strength'.[108] Pound compares the pine's 'strength' with Kumasaka's dignity in defeat, a comparison he would employ in *Gaudier-Brzeska: A Memoir*.

After *Kumasaka*, Pound includes a fragmented version of *Shōjō* before presenting *Tamura*. The latter was to be, like *Hagoromo*, a highly influential nō play for Pound because of its depiction of 'Kuanon', the bodhisattva Kannon

---

[99] Umehara and Kanze (eds), *Nō wo yomu*, vol. 4, 98.
[100] *Gikeiki*, 50.
[101] Umehara and Kanze (eds), *Nō wo yomu*, vol. 4, 148.
[102] Kanze no Ujinobu, 'Kumasaka', in ibid., 104.
[103] Pound, 'The Classical Stage of Japan', 236.
[104] Ibid., 238.
[105] Ibid., 233.
[106] Ibid., 238.
[107] Ibid., 237.
[108] Ibid., 231.

introduced in Binyon's *The Flight of the Dragon* as 'the impersonation of Mercy and Loving-kindness'.[109] The first part of *Tamura* portrays a visiting priest encountering a boy sweeping the cherry blossoms at Kiyomizu Temple in the capital. The boy tells him about a monk, Kenshin, who 'vowed to pray to Kannon' and saw a 'golden light floating on the Kotsu River', a legend derived from the twelfth-century *Konjaku monogatarishū* ('Collection of Old Tales').[110] A man, Kannon in disguise, then asks him to build a temple and find a patron for it; this patron is the military leader Sakanoue no Tamuramaro (758–811), the first to be given the title of *seii taishōgun* ('Great Barbarian-Subduing Generalissimo') used by subsequent shōguns. As in *Hagoromo* and *Kayoi Komachi*, light fulfils a symbolic role in the play; this symbolism is much more strongly accentuated than in the *Konjaku monogatarishū*. The 'boy' sweeping the cherry blossoms at Kiyomizu Temple tells the visiting priest that 'the light of the goddess Kuanon' has made these flowers 'brighter than usual'.[111] He says that Kenshin wished to see the 'true light of Kuanon', though in Ōwada's edition he simply 'vowed to pray' to her.[112] Kuanon's light is also associated with the moon. 'Look!' the boy tells the visiting priest, 'the moon is lifting itself over Mt. Otora [*sic*], and lights the cherry flowers'.[113] Mount Otowa is the location of Kiyomizu Temple, founded, according to the play, by the command of Kannon herself; this moonlight thus also symbolizes Kannon's blessing.

In the second part, the boy reveals himself to be Tamuramaro's spirit and explains that 'I conquered the eastern wild men' and 'beat down their evil spirit'; this refers to the aboriginal people who, at the time of the play's ninth-century setting, still occupied northern and eastern Japan.[114] Pound's introduction of *Tamura* foregrounds its celebration of imperial conquest: 'This play is to be regarded as one of those dealing with the "pacification of the country and the driving out of evil spirits".[115] 'The Emperor', in this case Emperor Heizei (773–824), 'bade me beat down the evil spirits in Sajuka [Suzuka] in Ise, and to set the capital of that country in peace'.[116] Hanada Ryōun describes the original 'evil spirits' as an insurrection of 'bandits'.[117] Before setting off with his army, he prays

---

[109] Binyon, *The Flight of the Dragon*, 43.
[110] *YT*, vol. 1, 10.
[111] Ibid.
[112] Pound, 'The Classical Stage of Japan', 241–2.
[113] Ibid.
[114] Ibid., 243.
[115] Ibid., 241.
[116] Ibid.
[117] Hanada Ryōun, *Yōkyoku ni arawaretaru bukkyō* ('Buddhism Appearing in Nō') (Kyoto: Kōgyō shoin, 1938), 339.

to 'Kuanon' for her blessing. The play ascribes the harmony and prosperity of the springtime to the harmonious relationship between the emperor and the gods: as the 'plum-trees were blossoming' in Ise, 'All the scene showed the favour of Kuanon and the virtue of the Emperor'.[118] *Tamura* contrasts Kuanon's 'light', which she 'pours' on the 'banner' of Tamuramaro's troops, with the 'evil spirits' who 'rain their black clouds' on the 'pine-moor of Anono' in Ise, a similar contrast of light and darkness to *Kayoi Komachi*.[119] The light of Kannon's blessing is thus made to justify the imperial conquest and 'pacification of the country'. Whereas in Pound's translation of *Hagoromo* the emperor's role in creating the play's peaceful harmony was downplayed, Pound now expressly emphasizes the connection between the spreading of the 'light' of mercy and wisdom and that of imperial rule. *Tamura* thus marks a watershed moment in Pound's understanding of nō's political implications.

During this time, Pound worked on several other nō translations that were not completed or published. One of these was *Hajitomi* ('The Lattice Shutter'), attributed to Naitō Kawachinokami (dates unknown). Like *Suma Genji*, it is based on the fourth chapter, 'Yūgao' ('Evening Faces'), of the *Genji monogatari*, and tells the story of a woman Genji had first tried to see through the '*hajitomi*' of her residence and then visited for many nights before his later downfall for another affair with an imperial consort and subsequent exile to Suma. In the *Genji monogatari*, when he takes her to an abandoned residence one night, a ghostly woman appears, and Genji's lover is found dead. In 'Affirmations VI: The "Image" and the Japanese Classical Stage', an article intended to be published in his 'Affirmations' series in *The New Age*, Pound saw his 'following' translation of *Hajitomi* as an 'illustration' of his idea that 'The European thinks by ideas, the Jap [sic] by "images"'.[120] *Hajitomi* is 'a succession of images' rather than a 'definite statement' of some morality.[121] These express the 'simple devotion to spirits, or to beautiful legend', though 'the beautiful spirits' exist only within 'the consciousness of the protagonist'.[122] Pound appears to have developed his idea about Japanese thought from Fenollosa's essay on 'The Chinese Character as a Medium for Poetry', which sees Chinese characters as a system of writing that offers a 'vivid

---

[118] Pound, 'The Classical Stage of Japan', 241.
[119] Ibid., 244. 'Ano' is correct; as with 'Miwo-no' in *Hagoromo*, Pound confuses the Japanese possessive particle 'no' with the place name.
[120] Pound, 'Affirmations VI: The "Image" and the Classical Japanese Stage', *Princeton University Library Chronicle* 53, no. 1 (Autumn 1991): 18.
[121] Ibid., 20–1.
[122] Ibid., 22.

shorthand picture of the operations of nature'.[123] Pound imagines that Japanese is a language 'without syntax', giving an example from *Nishikigi*: 'you cannot dip in the same river, / beneath the same tree's shadow / without bonds in some other life' is, 'literally', 'one tree, one river's stream to dip, other life's relation'.[124] Though this is the result of Fenollosa's crib – the Japanese is syntactical – Pound's impression of Japanese as an asyntactical language of fragmented 'images' may have inspired his development of a radically paratactical poetry in *The Cantos*.

Pound's first nō translations composed in 1914 were thus highly influential for Pound's oeuvre to an extent that has not yet been fully realized. Both his emerging conception of nō plays' apparent 'Unity of Image', derived from Fenollosa's presentation of their consisting of a 'single clarified impression', and the 'whirl' of the past's ghosts in *Nishikigi* played a fundamental role in Pound's invention of Vorticism; *Kumasaka*'s association of its lead character's martial dignity with the strength of a pine tree would offer a further model for his Vorticist poetics in *Gaudier-Brzeska: A Memoir*. Pound's enthusiasm at this time for nō, 'unquestionably one of the great arts of the world', is clearly visible in his comparisons of nō plays with Homer and Dante. In the coming two years he would develop this enthusiasm further, not only with two book publications of nō translations but also with his own nō plays and the beginning of *The Cantos*. His nō translations would make an important contribution to many of the major themes of *The Cantos*, including the vision of paradise glimpsed in *Hagoromo*; the light symbolism through which this vision is expressed in *Hagoromo*, *Kayoi Komachi* and *Tamura*; and the association of such an idealized world of harmony and plenty with imperial rule in *Hagoromo* and *Tamura*. And yet he struggled with Hirata and Fenollosa's fragmentary notes: 'one struggled with one's ignorance', he recalled in 1962; 'One had the inside knowledge of Fenollosa's notes and the ignorance of a five-year-old child'.[125] According to Marie Stopes, Pound 'invited himself' to see her and asked her to collaborate with him on translating the nō plays, but as she found 'he knew nothing whatever about the subject', she refused.[126] Pound would have better luck with finding collaborators in April 1915 when he met a Japanese dancer at the Café Royal called Itō Michio.

---

[123] Fenollosa, 'The Chinese Written Character as a Medium for Poetry', *The Little Review* 6, no. 6 (October 1919): 57.
[124] Ibid., 18.
[125] Donald Hall, 'E. P.: An Interview', in George Plimpton (ed.), *Writers at Work: The Paris Review Interviews, Second Series* (New York: Viking, 1963), 49.
[126] Ishibashi Hiro, 'Marie C. Stopes to nō (2)' ('Marie C. Stopes and Nō (2)'), *Eigo seinen* 124, no. 4 (1 July 1978): 36.

8

'Growing together'

Pound's Japanese friends, nō and the genesis of *The Cantos*

On 6 April 1915, Pound wrote to his father that he had recently met 'a most interesting Jap [*sic*]' who was 'interested in dancing, & helpful & interested in "Noh" work'.¹ This was the dancer Itō Michio (1892–1961). Two months after entering the Tokyo School of Music in April 1912, Itō first appeared on stage in the chorus of the school's production of Heinrich Werkmeister's opera, *Buddha*; Itō recalls that this encouraged him to pursue opera singing.² The following month, he co-founded the dramatic society Toridesha ('Fortress Society'), who gave their first performance on 15 October 1912, of Nagata Mikihiko's *Maihime Daria* ('Dahlia the Dancing Girl') and a Japanese adaptation of Maurice Maeterlinck's *Intérieur* in Tsukiji.³ Itō soon left to study opera singing abroad, however: on 6 November he departed for Berlin, arriving on 28 December. Itō's own reminiscences of spending six months in Egypt and another six months in Paris on the way – where he supposedly befriended the composer Claude Débussy, modelled for the sculptor Auguste Rodin, and watched Vaslav Nijinski with the *Ballets Russes* – are treated with justified suspicion by Senda Koreya, Dorsey Kleitz and David Ewick.⁴ Nevertheless, his artistic education was predominantly Western. After arriving in Berlin, he was tutored by the opera singer Elisabeth Maria Lehmann and attended the Dalcroze School of Eurhythmics in Hellerau from 13 August 1913, where he turned towards

---

[1] Pound to Homer Pound (6 April 1915), in *L/HP*, 45.
[2] Fujita Fujio, *Itō Michio: sekai wo mau: taiyō no gekijō wo mezashite* ('Itō Michio: Dancing the World: Towards a Sun Theatre') (Tokyo: Musashino, 1992), 26.
[3] Senda Koreya, 'Atogaki – Yume to Genjitsu' ('Afterword – Dreams and Reality'), in Helen Caldwell, *Itō Michio: hito to geijutsu* ('Itō Michio: The Man and His Art'), trans. Nakagawa Einosuke (Tokyo: Hayakawa shobō, 1985), 161.
[4] Ibid., 169–70; Dorsey Kleitz, 'Michio Ito and the Modernist Vortex', *The Hemingway Review of Japan* 13 (June 2012): 50; Itō, *Reminiscences*, trans. and ed. Ewick and Kleitz (New York: Edwin Mellen, 2018), 2.

studying dance.⁵ With the outbreak of the First World War, however, Itō had to flee Germany for London, departing on 14 August 1914, just over a week before Japan declared war on Germany.

Upon his arrival in London, Itō had expected to enter the Dalcroze School there, but it was shut. Unable to continue his dance studies, he fell into poverty. He began frequenting the Café Royal, however, where he met several prominent writers, artists and patrons including Augustus John, Rodin and Ottoline Morrell, as well as his fellow countrymen, the artist Fujita Tsuguharu and the dramatist Kōri Torahiko.⁶ The Chilean artist Álvaro Guevara (1894–1951) introduced him to Morrell's 'Thursdays', social events at her 44 Bedford Square residence involving dramatic performances.⁷ Morrell asked him to dance to anything he liked. He chose a piece by Chopin, the same one he had danced to enter the Hellerau Dalcroze School.⁸ It was attended among others by Yeats and another aristocratic patron of the arts, Lady Maud 'Emerald' Cunard. Morrell found his performance 'marvellously beautiful', and Cunard asked him if he wanted to perform at a friend's house the following day.⁹ It was during this evening that Itō apparently spoke with the prime minister, Herbert Asquith, an encounter recalled in Canto LXXVII.¹⁰ By the time he began his dance performance series at the Coliseum Theatre on 10 May 1915, he was already billed as 'the famous dancer Michio Itow'.¹¹ Before meeting Pound, though, he had practically no experience of or interest in nō.¹² Itō was happy to help, however, and introduced two Japanese friends who knew much more about it. These friends had until recently been paid little attention to in English-language Pound studies; as this chapter seeks to show, however, this helped Pound with his understanding of nō when he also began composing *The Cantos*, which, as he later stated, was based 'roughly on the theme' of the nō play *Takasago*.

The first of these was the then twenty-four-year-old playwright and poet Kōri Torahiko (1890–1924).¹³ Ewick cites Kōri Shunpei's account that both of Kōri's adoptive parents were 'leading disciples of nō' and that when Kōri was a child, the head of the Kanze School at the time, Kanze Kiyokado (1867–1911), tried to

---

⁵ Fujita, *Itō Michio*, 34–5.
⁶ Ibid., 49–50.
⁷ Robert Garthorne-Hardy (ed.), *Ottoline: The Early Memoirs of Lady Ottoline Morrell* (London: Faber & Faber, 1963), 276 and 278.
⁸ Fujita, *Itō Michio*, 51.
⁹ Ibid.; Garthorne-Hardy (ed.), *Ottoline*, 278.
¹⁰ PC, 47.
¹¹ Caldwell, *Michio Ito: The Dancer and His Dances* (Berkeley: University of California Press, 1977), 37.
¹² Itō, *Reminiscences*, 29.
¹³ Sugiyama Seiju, *Kōri Torahiko: Sono yume to shōgai* ('Kōri Torahiko: His Dream and His Life') (Tokyo: Iwanami shoten, 1987), 158.

adopt him because of his nō singing abilities.[14] Yamauchi Hideo merely observes, however, that his mother, Tomi, was 'good at Kanze-style nō singing', by then a widespread upper-class pastime as Chapter 5 suggests, and that 'Torahiko's talent was recognised'.[15] In any case, many acquaintances remembered this talent after his death, as Ewick also observes. Tanaka Uson, for example, recalls that Kōri was 'proficient in nō' and that he had a 'beautiful voice' on the one or two occasions he had heard him sing nō.[16] From an early age, Kōri similarly excelled at languages: after entering the elite Gakushūin school in 1903, he was reading Byron and Shelley in the originals, as well as Maeterlinck's *Pelléas et Mélisande* in English translation.[17] While at Gakushūin, he joined the Shirakaba ('White Birch') literary society. His article on Richard Strauss's opera *Elektra* was included in the April 1910 founding issue of the group's magazine.[18] Further *Shirakaba* articles of his on *Elektra* and on Strauss's adaptation of Oscar Wilde's *Salome* demonstrate his interest in Western dramatic forms as well as nō.

Tanaka, a fellow *Shirakaba* member, claims that 'a combination of nō, opera, bowler hats, Hofmannsthal and Wilde' gives the 'flavour' of Kōri's own dramatic works.[19] His first major published play was *Kanawa* ('The Iron Crown'), which appeared in the February 1911 issue of *Subaru*; a revised edition appeared in *Shirakaba*'s March 1913 issue. It is an adaptation of the nō play of the same name, a fourth-category 'woman' play on the theme of a woman's jealousy. Kōri's adaptation is his own play, loosely inspired by nō and with a different structure, added scenes and a radically altered ending. Four months after the first publication of *Kanawa*, since when he had entered Tokyo Imperial University (as the Imperial University was renamed in 1897) to study English Literature, Kōri had another nō-based play published in *Subaru, Kiyohime moshiku wa Dōjōji* ('Kiyohime, or, Dōjōji'). In April 1912, a revised version, *Dōjōji*, appeared in *Mita bungaku*, Keiō University's literary journal, where Yone Noguchi was teaching. Like *Kanawa*, the nō play *Dōjōji* is a fourth-category 'woman' play about a woman's jealousy. Soon afterwards, however, Kōri moved to Europe, sailing from Kobe on 16 August 1913 and settling in Munich in November.[20] Like Itō, Kōri quickly had to leave Germany due to the outbreak of the First World War; he

---

[14] Ewick, 'Notes Toward a Cultural History of Japanese Modernism in Modernist Europe, 1910-1920: With Special Reference to Kōri Torahiko', *The Hemingway Review of Japan* 13 (June 2012): 22.
[15] Yamauchi Hideo, 'Ryakuden' ('Outline Biography'), in Kōri, *Zenshū* ('Collected Works'), vol. 1 (Tokyo: Sōgensha, 1936), 1.
[16] Ibid., 28.
[17] Nagayo Yoshirō, 'Omoide' ('Reminiscences'), in ibid., 9 and 10.
[18] Kayano Hatakazu, 'Erekutora kōgai' ('An Outline of *Elektra*'), *Shirakaba* 1, no. 1 (April 1910): 38–51.
[19] Tanaka, 'Kōri-kun wo omou', 28.
[20] Sugiyama, *Kōri Torahiko*, 143 and 148.

left on 18 August 1914 for London, just four days after Itō.[21] *Kiyohime moshiku wa Dōjōji* was introduced in *Subaru* as 'the second of three plays on obsession'; Kōri never completed a third, but his interest in nō plays featuring the *hannya* ('demonic woman') mask suggests that he may have been influential in shaping Pound's understanding of this kind of play, as shown by Pound's translation of the *hannya* play *Aoi no ue*, which Pound would recall several times in *The Cantos*; *Dōjōji* is, like *Kanawa*, summarized in *'Noh' or Accomplishment*.[22]

The novelist Minakami Takitarō, who arrived in London the following month, recalls Kōri frequenting the Japanese Formosa Oolong Tearoom with Itō in Piccadilly in September 1914; they were also both seen at the Café Royal.[23] Like Pound, Kōri often visited the British Museum Reading Room.[24] After a trip to Rome at the end of April 1915, Kōri came back to London in May to hear that Itō was asking for him.[25] Itō had returned from a two-week stay at Ottoline Morrell's Garsington Manor near Oxford soon after his series of performances at the Coliseum Theatre of 10–24 April.[26] After arriving back in London, Itō was approached by Pound at the Café Royal.[27] In Itō's words, Pound asked him: 'I want to edit and publish a book about Japanese Noh drama. Please research it and help me. Professor Fenollosa studied Noh under Umewaka Minoru for seven years, and Mrs. Fenollosa gave me all his manuscripts.'[28] Itō at first replied, 'I can't help you. I know nothing at all about Noh. Besides, I think it is the dullest thing in the world.'[29] Pound told him, though, 'I'm American. You know it better than I do because you can say it's the dullest thing in the world, so you can help me.'[30] Itō agreed and, according to Pound's letter to his father of 16 May, wrote 'to Japan for books about the Noh.'[31] He also asked Kōri and a Japanese painter then also in London, Kume Tamijūrō, to arrange a performance of nō for Pound and Yeats; the latter had taken an interest in Pound's earliest nō translations at Stone Cottage and witnessed Itō's performance at Morrell's London residence. Itō and Kōri were thus already well acquainted, having frequently met at the Formosa Oolong Tearoom and the Café Royal since soon after they arrived in London.

[21] Ibid., 151.
[22] Hatakazu, 'Kiyohime moshiku wa Dōjōji' ('Kiyohime, or Dōjōji'), *Subaru* 4, no. 6 (June 1911): 1; *NA*, 123.
[23] Minakami Takitarō, 'Rondon jidai no Kōri Torahiko' ('Kōri Torahiko's London Years'), in Kōri, *Zenshū*, vol. 3, 31.
[24] Ibid., 32–3.
[25] Sugiyama, *Kōri Torahiko*, 157.
[26] Itō, *Reminiscences*, 28.
[27] Ibid.
[28] Ibid.
[29] Ibid.
[30] Ibid.
[31] Pound, letter to Homer Pound (16 May 1915), in *L/HP*, 347.

Kume was thus the third of the three '"very much over-civilized" young men' whom Pound remembered as having taught him, along with 'Fenollosa's notes on the Noh', what he 'really kn[ew] about Japan'.[32] Kume was born on 2 April 1893, the son of the politician and architect for the Imperial Household Agency, Kume Taminosuke (1861–1931).[33] According to Tsunoda Shirō, when Kume was a child, his father built a residence in Yoyogi with a nō stage; through his father's encouragement, Kume learned to perform nō dances.[34] Pound later recalled hearing that Kume had 'taken the tennin part when he was, I remember, six years old' and, on another occasion, that this performance was given 'before the Emperor'.[35] Morita Norimasa goes even further, suggesting that Kume 'had been trained by the great *shite* Umewaka Minoru, and had danced for Ernest Fenollosa'.[36] There is, however, no record of Kume taking lessons or, indeed, performing for Fenollosa in Umewaka's own diaries. A photograph dated 24 October 1907 survives, however, of Kume performing nō in Yoyogi.[37] After graduating from Gakushūin high school, Kume went to study at St John's Wood Art School in London in 1914.[38] Like Pound and Kōri, Kume often went to the Café Royal. According to the artist Fujita Tsuguharu's account, Kume was a regular visitor, as Kōri was, to Hester Sainsbury's (and later Kōri's) residence at 71 Royal Hospital Road in Chelsea.[39] Itō, Kōri and Kume thus all knew each other from the Café Royal; Itō and Kōri also met at the Formosa Oolong Tearoom; and Kōri and Kume were possibly acquainted through their visits to the Sainsburys' as well.

Their performance for Pound and Yeats took place in July 1915. Pound later recalled Kume performing nō at Kume's studio.[40] Nishiwaki's retelling of Kōri's account also claims that, while Kōri sang, someone 'pretended to perform nō', which Ewick interprets as referring to Itō, and that 'Yeats was greatly inspired' by

---

[32] Pound, 'From Rapallo: An Ezra Pound Letter', *The Japan Times and Mail* (26 August 1940): 8.
[33] Tateo Imamura, 'Hemingway, Pound, and the Japanese Artist, Tamijuro Kume', *The Hemingway Review of Japan* 13 (June 2012): 43.
[34] Tsunoda Shirō, 'Paundo to Kume Tamijūrō no kōyū' ('The Friendship of Pound and Kume Tamijūrō'), in Fukuda Rikutarō and Yasukawa Akira (eds), *Ezura Paundo kenkyū* ('Ezra Pound Studies'), (Kyoto: Yamaguchi shoten, 1986), 11.
[35] Pound, 'Study of Noh Continues in West', *The Japan Times and Mail* (10 December 1939): 8; Pound, letter to Iwasaki Ryōzō (6 September 1957), in *EPJ*, 143.
[36] Norimasa Morita, 'The Toils of Kōri Torahiko', in Cortazzi (ed.), *Britain and Japan: Biographical Portraits*, 9 vols, vol. 7 (Folkestone: Global Oriental, 2010), 301.
[37] *MFBTK*, 1220028m.
[38] Imamura, 'Hemingway', 44.
[39] Tsunoda, 'Paundo to Kume', 11; Fujita Tsuguharu, 'Ko Kōri Torahiko kun' ('The Late Kōri Torahiko'), in Kōri, *Zenshū*, vol. 3, 128.
[40] Garthorne-Hardy (ed.), *Ottoline at Garsington* (London: Faber & Faber, 1974), 41; Itō, *Reminiscences*, 28; Pound, letter to Isabel Weston Pound (9 April 1916), in *L/HP*, 367.

the performance.⁴¹ Nishiwaki does not record Pound's reaction to it, however; only Itō mentions Pound's presence.⁴² Indeed, it is possible that this performance was the one Pound fondly recalled more than forty years later to Iwasaki Ryōzō, his Japanese translator: Kume 'danced the tennin part [...] and remembered it in London in 1917 or about then'. In a wartime *Japan Times and Mail* article, Pound describes Kume's *Hagoromo* dance, particularly 'the movements of the tennin's wings' at the play's conclusion, as 'the most beautiful movements I have seen on and off any stage'.⁴³ Pound also recalled that 'Tami Koumé had a satisfactory edtn. of the Noh plays'; this suggests that Itō may indeed have written 'to Japan for books about the Noh'.⁴⁴ Not only Itō, then, but also Kume and Kōri helped Pound to understand more profoundly the performance as well as the texts of nō, although the Japanese friend who probably knew most about nō, Kōri, appears least prominently in his recollections.

At the end of June, Pound wrote to his father that a 'Chap, named Waley, from [the British] Museum', had been 'in last night to see Fenollosa mss'.⁴⁵ Although Ewick claims these 'mss' were of Fenollosa's essay 'The Chinese Written Character as a Medium for Poetry', which had been sent to Henderson at *Poetry* in January 1915, it is more likely he had come to look at Fenollosa's nō manuscripts. Five years later, Waley published his own *The Nō Plays of Japan*, which included six of the plays in Pound's *'Noh' or Accomplishment*. As Ewick points out, though, Waley played an important and, until recently, overlooked role in assisting Pound with his nō translations. In the 'Note' at the start of *'Noh' or Accomplishment*, Pound expresses his 'very deep thanks to Mr. Arthur Waley, who has corrected a number of mistakes in the orthography of proper names from such Japanese texts as were available, and who has assisted me out of various impasses where my own ignorance would have left me'.⁴⁶ They would have met in the British Museum's Department of Prints and Drawings, where Waley had joined as Binyon's assistant in June 1913 and which, as Chapters 3 and 6 show, Pound often visited at that time.⁴⁷ Thus, although Pound had failed to get help for his nō translations from Stopes, he received that of three Japanese – two of whom were especially knowledgeable about nō – and an Englishman

---

⁴¹ Ibid.; Ewick, 'Notes', 23.
⁴² Itō, *Reminiscences*, 29.
⁴³ Pound, letter to Iwasaki Ryōzō (6 September 1957), in *EPJ*, 143; Pound, 'Study of Noh Continues in West', 8.
⁴⁴ Pound, letter to Kitasono Katué (2 March 1937), in *EPJ*, 39.
⁴⁵ Pound, letter to Homer Pound (30 June 1915), in *L/HP*, 351.
⁴⁶ *NA*, v; Ewick, 'A Little History of Ezra Pound and Arthur Waley' (Ezra Pound and Japan, Tokyo Woman's Christian University, 12 March 2018).
⁴⁷ Ewick, 'A Little History'.

who would become one of the most well-known English translators of Japanese literature.

One week later, on 7 July 1915, Pound sent to Henderson three more nō plays: *Takasago*, *Genjo* and *Chorio*. Despite Hugh Kenner's claim to the contrary, then, Pound did indeed get 'round to the *Takasago*'.[48] He particularly praises this play, which is 'so full of poetry that Harriet [Monroe] might like it'.[49] If there was any space following his own work in *Poetry*'s September issue, 'she might take *Takasago* [...] or she may not want it at all. In which case please pass it along to DRAMA'.[50] It appears that these were lost either on their way to Monroe or to *The Drama*, although *Genjo* and *Chorio* came out in *'Noh' or Accomplishment*. Pound had written in 'The Classical Stage of Japan', published in May, that nō plays have 'a very severe structure of their own, a sort of musical construction which I shall present in a future article in connection with the text of the Takasago play, when I get that latter ready for the public'; yet his *Takasago* never saw print in his lifetime.[51] Nevertheless, he accords it the most attention of the three plays in his letter to Henderson:

> This play TAKASAGO might be called the very core of the 'Noh'. Because of its flawless structure it is called 'Shin no issei', the 'Most Correct' and other Noh plays are held to vary from it as from a norm.[52]

Pound's positioning of *Takasago* as the foremost nō play corresponds with the claim in Ōwada's *Yōkyoku tsūkai* that 'it is first among all nō', Aston's view that it is 'the best known and considered to be the finest of all the Nō', and Dickins's remark in *Primitive and Mediaeval Japanese Literature*, which we know Pound read, that it is 'the freshest in tone and least artificial in diction'.[53] Pound is thus unambiguous in his view of *Takasago*'s centrality within the nō canon and in his own praise of its 'flawless structure'.

One of the ways in which *Takasago* demonstrates its 'flawless structure' and, as he had described it two months before in 'The Classical Stage of Japan', its 'Unity of Image', is its '*sense of the past time in the present*'.[54] The pairing of

---

[48] *PE*, 283–4. For an earlier examination of the impact Pound's translation of *Takasago* had on *The Cantos*, see Andrew Houwen, 'Ezra Pound's Early Cantos and His Translation of *Takasago*', *The Review of English Studies* 65, no. 269 (April 2014): 321–41.
[49] Pound, letter to Henderson (7 July 1915), in *L/ACH*, 109.
[50] Ibid.
[51] Pound, 'The Classical Stage of Japan', 224.
[52] Ibid., 110. As Carrie J. Preston observes, however, *Shin no issei* in fact refers to the music played for the entrance of divinities. Preston, *Learning to Kneel*, 263.
[53] Ōwada, *YT*, vol. 1, 1; Aston, *A History of Japanese Literature*, 206; Dickins, *Primitive and Mediaeval Japanese Literature*, 395.
[54] *L/ACH*, 110.

the two pine trees – Takasago, 'the old age of the emperor [sic] Manyoshu', and Suminoye, 'our own time of Engi' – gives Pound a clear demonstration of the *Nishikigi*'s Vorticism: the paired pines represent what he described in 'Vortex' as the 'energized past, all the past that is living' 'charging' the 'FUTURE' through the present moment ('NOW').[55] The 'inexhaustible' falling pine needles suggest, for Pound, the 'energy' of the past passing from the 'Manyoshu' to the present 'time of Engi'.[56] This constitutes an important example of what Peter Nicholls describes as the 'superimposition, or grafting' of the past onto the present that Nicholls considers influential for Pound.[57] The vital force of the past charging the present is explained by the old couple whom a wandering priest, Tomonari, meets at Takasago. Tomonari asks them:

> Why do they call the pines in Takasago and Suminoye 'Ai-oi?' the two places are very far distant, and the word means 'growing together'.[58]

In the play's text, there is no explanation of *aioi* as meaning 'growing together': Pound doubtless relies on Hirata and Fenollosa's notes, which in turn derive from Ōwada's commentary. Ōwada mentions that it can mean, as Chapter 4 notes, 'pursuing together' or 'growing old together'; its primary meaning, though, is 'two pines growing together'.[59] Not only, then, does Pound consider *Takasago* to be an example of his conception of 'Unity of Image'; its pairing of two pines 'growing together' presents him with a 'form of super-position', two elements fused 'together' through a vortex-like 'energy', the force that generates their 'growing'. For Pound, then, *Takasago* confirms his previously stated conviction that nō offers the best model for a 'long imagiste or vorticist poem'.

In Pound's translation, it is clear that he associates the paired pines of the 'past' and 'present' with the vital inheritance of literary tradition. The old man tells Tomonari, 'anyone can read in the preface of Kokin that "It seems the pine trees of Takasago and Suminoye grow together".'[60] Even if Pound did not know that 'Kokin' refers to the tenth-century *Kokinshū* anthology, it is evident from his use of the term 'preface' and the quotation from it that *aioi* is a literary allusion which shapes and gives life to the play. Furthermore, in Pound's version the old woman explicitly compares the falling pine needles to words: 'The pine-

---

[55] Ibid.; Pound, 'Vortex', 153.
[56] *L/ACH*, 112.
[57] Peter Nicholls, 'An Experiment with Time: Ezra Pound and the Example of Japanese Noh', *Modern Language Review* 90, no. 1 (January 1995): 6.
[58] *L/ACH*, 112.
[59] *YT*, vol. 1, 3.
[60] *L/ACH*, 112.

needles are inexhaustible words.'[61] This suggests the influence of Hirata and Fenollosa's translation rather than Ōwada's commentary. In Ōwada's edition, the old woman's line is not discussed in his notes but given simply as 'Pines are inexhaustible leaves of speech'; the play draws out the etymology of *kotoba* ('words') through the insertion of the possessive particle *no* (*koto no ha*), where *koto* means 'speech' and *ha* signifies 'leaves'. Without any Japanese, it is unlikely that Pound would have guessed that 'leaves of speech' means 'words'. In any case, the importance ascribed to a vital literary past accords with Pound's own respect for literary tradition. As he notes in 'Vorticism' when he contrasts Vorticism with Futurism, 'The vorticist has not this curious tic for destroying past glories.'[62] *Takasago*, more explicitly than any other of Pound's nō translations, foregrounds this importance of literary tradition.

This literary tradition grows together with the everlasting imperial reign. The old man explains to Tomonari:

As men have said in the old times, 'It's a sign of the happier reign.'[63]

Takasago's fusion of vegetal and literary vitality with imperial rule thus offers Pound an example of a Confucian model of government in which the relationship between the sovereign and his subjects is like that between a man and his wife. The old man is, after all, the *shite*, or 'main' actor, and the old woman the *tsure*, or 'accompanying' actor. The symbolism of the 'calm spring sea' described by Tomonari in the opening lines is explained in the 'waves of the four seas' passage sung by the chorus.

> The waves of the whole sea are quiet,
> The whole country well governed
> The wind does not even rustle through the branches,
> It is surely a happy reign.[64]

Not only do these lines express the play's connection of the sea's calm with the peace brought about by imperial rule; Pound was already also deeply aware of the political significance of this passage, as 'The Classical Stage of Japan' demonstrates; there, he cites at length this passage's recital at the New Year *utaizome* ceremony before the shōgun, after which the whole play is also performed. Like *Tamura*, *Takasago* offered Pound an example of the symbiosis

---

[61] Ibid., 113.
[62] Pound, 'Vorticism', 468.
[63] L/ACH, 113.
[64] Ibid.

of the patronage of high art and not just benevolent imperial rule, but also a strong military ruler, the shōgun. Uniquely, among the nō plays he translated, however, this symbiosis is *Takasago*'s central theme.

This imperial and military rule is symbolized as 'light'. Whereas at the start the 'waves are hidden in mist', the revelation of the pine trees' significance is accompanied with the appearance of light: the old man observes that 'The light is smooth on the water' just before the chorus sings the 'waves of the four seas' passage. This light imagery recalls several of Pound's earlier nō translations: in *Hagoromo*, the bodhisattva Seishi is given as the 'source of light', a Dantescan 'Great Power' giving life through the sun's and moon's light; Komachi's heart, freed from resentment, is 'clear as new moonlight'; and Pound relates the mythical origin of nō as a performance for the 'light-goddess', Amaterasu. With *Tamura*, though, Pound more specifically connects the symbolic use of light in nō and imperial rule: Kannon 'pours' her 'true light' on the 'banner' of Tamuramaro's army and defeats the 'evil spirits' of the 'pine-moor of Anono'. The association of light with imperial and military rule in *Takasago* thus parallels that of *Tamura*, a subject rhyme Pound would employ in Canto IV. Pound's *Takasago* also shows how this benevolent imperial rule is rooted in Chinese precedent: the pine tree's nobility is accorded by 'The <emperor> Shiko'; that is, the first Chinese emperor, Shi Huangdi. Like fascism, this model of imperial rule is both nationalistic and international; this seemingly contradictory characteristic also runs through Pound's later engagement with fascism.

One of the aspects of such a model that appealed to Pound was its apparent stability, as suggested by the 'quiet' of the sea's waves. While much of the West was involved in a war that had, as Pound had told Henderson in his previous letter to her, resulted in the death of his closest friend Henri Gaudier-Brzeska, this imagined contrast of a peaceful, unchanging East governed by benevolent imperial and military rulers confirmed for Pound his view of the East just before the war as a 'very old, very quiet civilization' where 'some one' might 'understand the significance' of his '"Metro" *hokku*'.[65] Such rule, as Fenollosa's *Epochs* also suggested to him, appeared to him as being closely intertwined with generous artistic patronage. This view would have been strengthened not only by the 'pine-needles' representing the eternally verdant tradition of past and present poetry but also by the chorus's repeated depiction of Japan as the 'isle of verses'.[66] Pound's view of Japan thus follows in a tradition of representations of the East

---

[65] Pound, 'How I Began', 707.
[66] L/ACH, 114.

as an artistic paradise that includes Percival Lowell, Hearn and Porter. The First World War rendered the creation of such an idyllic environment for the arts, supporting and supported by a form of benevolent imperial and military rule, suddenly much more urgent and attractive for Pound. His preoccupation with this contrast between a peaceful East under benevolent imperial and military rule and a West in turmoil can be seen in his earliest drafts for *The Cantos*, as the following two chapters will explore in greater detail.

Pound wrote to Henderson again just over one month later, on 9 August 1915, to inform her that he was now 'working on a long poem which will resemble the Divina Commedia in length but in no other manner'.[67] This is the first unambiguous reference to Pound's beginning what would become *The Cantos*. The drafts at this initial stage are highly fragmentary. One such fragment is particularly noteworthy because of its later inclusion in Canto IV, which alludes to *Takasago* and *Tamura*. The opening of this fragment, '1B' in Christine Froula's classification of ur-Canto draft fragments, is a reworking of Pound's description of 'what matters in art' as 'a sort of energy, something more or less like electricity, a force transfusing, welding, and unifying. A force rather like water when it spurts up through bright sand and sets it in swift motion':

> the crystal fluid
> That spurts up through the mind,
> whirling its brown bright sande
> How does it live. How does it spurt and start?[68]

A later version of this fragment immediately follows the description of the paired pines of 'Takasago' and 'Isé' in Canto IV: as Chapter 9 will discuss in greater detail, this 'energy' is also that of the paired pine trees of *Takasago* and those of the Ise 'pine-moor' in *Tamura* 'growing together', which results in the conjugal felicity of the married couple, the fertility of the natural world, the continuity of the poetic tradition, and the prosperity of imperial rule.

Further on in this fragment is an allusion to Catullus's 'LXI', a dramatic choral ode celebrating the marriage of Junia Aurunculeia and Manlius Torquatus that employs the refrain, 'o Hymen Hymenaee' ('O Hymen Hymeneal'), a reference to Hymen, the Roman god of marriage:

---

[67] Pound, letter to Henderson (9 August 1915), in ibid., 120.
[68] Froula, *To Write Paradise*, 66; Pound, 'The Serious Artist', *The New Freewoman* 1, no. 10 (1 November 1913): 194; *EPP*, 3099.

> Drayas<d> moved so ~~among the~~ <upon the> sylvan dew,
> Hymen Hymaenaues,⁶⁹

Pound would later fuse this marriage scene with that of *Takasago*'s old married couple in Canto IV. It also anticipates the recollection of Pound's romantic encounter with H. D., whom he frequently called 'Dryad', in both H. D.'s *HERmione* and Pound's Canto XXIX, as Emily Mitchell Wallace claims; in Canto XXIX, it is also paired with the pine trees of *Takasago*.⁷⁰ In *HERmione*, H. D. takes the pseudonym 'Her' and Pound 'George Lowndes'. Despite her parents' disapproval of their affair, Her and George meet in '*the forest primeval, the murmuring pines and the hemlocks*', as George puts it, quoting Longfellow's 'Evangeline'.⁷¹ As they face each other, Her watches the 'concentric circle of trees above her head. [. . .] Tree on tree on tree. TREE. I am the Tree of Life.'⁷² Pound thus equates Catullus's 'LXI' with his love for H. D. Pound's 'arrangements' of *Takasago* with the Catullan marital ode in Canto IV, and his encounter with H. D. in Canto XXIX thus demonstrates the play's resonance with his own memories of him and H. D. under the '*murmuring pines*'.

Pound further developed his conception of 'arrangement' in relation to Japan in *Gaudier-Brzeska: A Memoir*, which he mentioned planning on 13 July 1915 to Quinn and finished by mid-October.⁷³ As in his 'Vorticism' essay, Pound emphasizes Whistlerian 'arrangement' as his aesthetic model. Whistler was, Pound thought, 'the only man working in England in the "Eighties" who would have known' what he, Lewis and Gaudier were aiming at in Vorticism. 'Applying this same principle' as Whistler's 'Arrangement in Grey and Black' to 'the arrangement of planes we get the new sculpture', Pound explains.⁷⁴ He offers the following example of such 'arrangement':

> The pine-tree in mist upon the far hill looks like a fragment of Japanese armour.
> The beauty of this pine-tree in the mist is not caused by its resemblance to the plates of the armour.
> The armour, if it be beautiful at all, is not beautiful *because* of its resemblance to the pine in the mist.

---

[69] Ibid.
[70] Emily Mitchell Wallace, 'Interior of 166 Fernbrook Avenue and Other Matters' (Ezra Pound International Conference, Wyncote, PA, 22 June 2017).
[71] H. D., *HERmione* (New York: New Directions, 1981), 65.
[72] Ibid., 70.
[73] Pound, letter to John Quinn (13 July 1915), in *L/JQ, 1915-1924*, 29; Pound, letter to Homer Pound (*c.* 18 October 1915), in *L/HP*, 354.
[74] Pound, *Gaudier-Brzeska: A Memoir* (London: John Lane, 1916), 146.

> In either case the beauty, so far as it is beauty of form, is the result of 'planes in relation'.
> The tree and the armour are beautiful because their diverse planes overlie in a certain manner.[75]

Pound's choice of 'planes' here parallels the comparison he makes in his *Kumasaka* translation between the 'unchanging green and strength' of the pine tree with the armed bandit Kumasaka's dignity in defeat. Pound's association of the pine as the 'symbol of unchanging green and strength' with 'Japanese armour' also suggests the connection made in his *Tamura* and *Takasago* translations between the pine and the strength of military rule that brings about a stable prosperity.

Pound's turn towards a military as well as aesthetic conception of the Japanese literature he encountered is similarly evident in his 'Sword-Dance and Spear-Dance' translations. These were composed 'from the notes of Masirni [sic] Utchiyama', whose 'voice booming ominous from behind the curtain' also accompanied Itō's dances for the poems.[76] These performances took place in a 'studio' at 1 Holland Lane, Melbury Road, Kensington, on 27 October and 2 and 9 November and featured the 'sword-dances' '"Kogun Funto" (the exhausted warrior)', '"Kawana kajima" (the enemy, in the dawn)' and '"Honoji" (dance of the spear)' alongside nō dances from 'Komachi', 'Shojo' and 'Hennia'.[77] The 'sword-dance' poems have not been discussed in comparison with their originals in Anglophone scholarship. They are based on classical Chinese poems by Japanese poets. 'Song for a Foiled Vendetta' was originally 'Fushikian Kizan wo utsu no zu' ('Scene of Fushikian Attacking Kizan'), by the poet and historian Rai Sanyō (1780–1832); 'The Sole Survivor', by Nishi Dōsen (1836–1913) about the famous samurai Saigō Takamori (1828–77), is entitled 'Jisei' ('Death Poem'); 'In Enemies' Country Just After War', by the Confucian, Tsukida Mōsai (1807–66), was originally untitled; and 'Honogi' is 'Honnōji', also by Sanyō.[78] All are seven-character quatrains. In a climate of urgent military modernization, publications of these 'sword-dance' poems were particularly fashionable in Japan during the

---

[75] Ibid., 146–7.
[76] Pound, 'Sword-Dance and Spear-Dance', 54. In the typescript drafts of these poems, Uchiyama's name is more correctly given as 'Utchiyama Masami'. *EPP*, 4278. A writer only identified by his personal name, 'Masami', contributed a series of articles and tanka to the London-based *Nichiei shinshi* from 1917 to 1918.
[77] *EPP*, 3099.
[78] Tanaka Heiji (ed.), *Kembu no shishū* ('Sword-Dance Poems') (Kyoto: Kōyūsha, 1893), 8, 10 and 13; Itsumin Koji (ed.), *Kembushū* ('Sword-Dance Collection') (Tokyo: Shūmeisha, 1890), 7–8. Midori Takeishi is the first to speculate on the Japanese originals' titles. Midori Takeishi, *Japanese Elements in Michio Ito's Early Period (1915-1924): Meetings of East and West in the Collaborative Works*, ed. and rev. David Pacun (Tokyo: Gendaitosho, 2006), 27.

Meiji era. These must have been especially poignant for Pound following the death on the battlefield of Gaudier-Brzeska in June, about whom Pound was writing his *Gaudier-Brzeska: A Memoir* at the same time as the programme of these 'sword-dances' was being put on.

It was on the back of seven programmes for these 'sword-dances' and nō dances that the next, more extended drafts of the 'long poem' that was to become *The Cantos* was written. 'But whats [sic] all this to us? the modern world' begins the first page of what Froula classifies as 'MS Ur 1' of Canto IV, after which it gives an account of a soldier who had 'enlisted' to serve in the 'trenches'; this anticipates the depiction of Gaudier-Brzeska's death, 'the best man killed in France / struck by a prussian bullet at St Vaast'.[79] On the fourth page, on the back of the fourth Itō dance programme, Pound presents another aspect of the 'modern world':

> What you dig up, talking with Orientals.
> Plain, academic, manufactured orientals,
> Talking of Emerson, and Hoffmanstahl ~~and~~ Cezanne
>   and Neitzz<c>he [...][80]

The reference to 'Plain, academic, manufactured orientals' is not to 'Itow or Tami Koumé, as Froula, Ewick and Preston speculate, but to Kōri.[81] In a letter to John Quinn of 8 September 1915, Pound writes:

> Itow brought in what he swears to be the best modern Japanese dramatist (I should think he was their precious Granville Barker, Takahama [sic] Kori, and he swore by the gods that there was NOTHING doing in Tokyo, said the theatres were full of translations of Strindberg, Maeterlinck, Hauptmann etc. etc. all done to the last degree of rottenness.)[82]

Kōri had read Maeterlinck's work and published in *Shirakaba* a number of articles on Strauss's opera *Elektra*, whose libretto Hugo von Hofmannsthal wrote. As Tanaka notes, Hofmannsthal was an important influence on Kōri. *Shirakaba* also featured several articles on Cézanne and Nietzsche. Pound's description of Kōri as 'Granville Barker' evokes Kōri's Western dress sense. Whereas Pound felt Itō to possess the 'samurai' spirit of the 'sword-dance' poems, Kōri represented for him the 'rottenness' of what Pound adds at the end of this passage in its next draft ('MS Ur 2' of Canto IV): 'Japan turns european'.[83]

---

[79] *EPP*, 3099; Froula, *To Write Paradise*, 63.
[80] *EPP*, 3099.
[81] Froula, *To Write Paradise*, 131; Ewick, 'Draft of Canto IV', 48.
[82] Pound, letter to John Quinn (8 September 1915), in *L/JQ*, 49.
[83] Pound, letter to Homer Pound (25 September 1915), in *L/HP*, 353; *EPP*, 3100.

Pound's contrast of the 'samurai' Itō and the 'european' Kōri closely resembles the one made in MS Ur 1 between what he sees as the once supreme, but now supposedly fading, literary and political vitality of the East and a war-torn West. The following year, with the war still going, Pound even wrote to his mother that 'A Japanese invasion is the only thing that will civilize the West'.[84] Pound's interest in the East now developed, in the form of these first attempts at *The Cantos*, into a proposed remedy for the 'civilization' that had killed his close friend. In their emphasis on a synthesis of Western and Eastern civilization, these lines parallel the opening of Pound's version of Fenollosa's essay, 'The Chinese Written Character as a Medium for Poetry'.[85] Regarding the Chinese and the Japanese, Fenollosa urges the West 'not to batter down their forts or exploit their markets, but to study and come to sympathize with their humanity'; 'their history [. . .] parallels that of the ancient Mediterranean peoples. We need their best ideals to supplement our own – ideals enshrined in their art' and 'their literature'.[86] Pound's Chinese and Japanese translations show how profoundly he embraced Fenollosa's view of their cultures. In the 'parallels' he had already made between *Hagoromo* and Dante's *Paradiso* and *Kumasaka* and Homer, Pound's high estimation of nō's cultural importance recalls not only the literary and artistic comparisons of Binyon's 1909 'Art and Thought in East and West' lecture series but also the comparable value Fenollosa claims in 'The Chinese Written Character as a Medium for Poetry' for East Asian and 'ancient Mediterranean' culture.

Such cross-cultural parallels between nō and the pre-modern European literature Pound prized continue in the next, significantly extended eighty-two-page manuscript draft of what would become the 'Three Cantos' published in *Poetry* in June–August 1917. Pound wrote to his father on 18 December 1915 that he was then at work on this draft, which he would have 'typed out' and sent to him 'as a much belated Xmas'.[87] He searches in this draft for a model on which to base his own work, as he asks Browning, 'Will you be my Virgil'.[88] He continues:

> Whom shall I conjure up, who is
>   my Sordello,
> my pre-Daun Chaucer, pre-Bocaccio,
>   as you have done pre-Dante.

---

[84] Pound, letter to Isabel Weston Pound (15 November 1916), in *L/HP*, 384.
[85] Pound, letter to Henderson (c. January 1915), in *L/ACH*, 92–3.
[86] Fenollosa, 'The Chinese Written Character as a Medium for Poetry – I', *The Little Review* 6, no. 5 (September 1919): 62–3.
[87] Pound, letter to Homer Pound (18 December 1915), in *L/HP*, 360.
[88] *EPP*, 3103.

> whom shall I hang my shimmering
> > garment on,
> whom set to dazzle, the serious
> > future ages[89]

The typescript draft that follows this one makes clear the allusion of the 'shimmering garment': following this line, Pound inserts, in pencil, 'Who wear my feathery mantle (hagoromo)'.[90] Pound understood the heavenly maiden's dance of the feather mantle not only through Fenollosa and Hirata's translation but also through Kume's performance of it for him, 'the most beautiful movements I have seen on and off any stage'. Without her 'feather-mantle', the maiden in *Hagoromo* cannot return to paradise. As well as expressing Pound's search for poetic inspiration, this allusion to the maiden's feather mantle more specifically parallels Pound's desire, put most directly in 'MS Ur 2' on the back of the seventh Itō dance programme, to find a 'way to paradise' in these cantos.[91]

This 'way to paradise' is lighted by Kuanon. On page 28 of 'Three Cantos MS A', her light once more appears on the water:

> Sea-waves over curled, boats with
> > the gods upon them,
> The flame above the river, –
> > being Kuanon –
> Kuanon visible,
> > as she comes on the river
> footing a boat   That's but one
> > one lotus petal,
> with some four-spread
> > genius,
> > > leading along,
> one hand upraised for gladness,
> > saying Tis she
> his friend, the mighty goddess

The 'flame above the river, / being Kuanon' alludes to the 'golden light floating on the Kotsu River' seen by Kenshin that indicates the appearance of the 'mighty goddess', 'Kuanon', whose light 'pours' on the 'banner' of the shōgun's troops to drive out the 'evil spirits' in *Tamura*. The further descriptions of Kannon suggest

---

[89] Ibid.
[90] *EPP*, 3105.
[91] *EPP*, 3100.

an additional source. Her appearance on 'one lotus petal' suggests the 'wooden Kwannon' in the Kondō ('Golden Hall') of Hōryūji with its 'lotos throne of petals' described in Fenollosa's *Epochs*.[92] An illustration of it, as the 'Corean Standing Kwannon with a Vase', also appears in the *Epochs*, with one hand indeed 'upraised', the other holding a water jar.[93] Pound's association of Kannon with water here stems from his translation of *Tamura*, in which the 'pure water' of the river on which she appears 'blesses the land and its people'. This depiction of Kannon would remain in the *Poetry* and *Lustra* versions of the 'Three Cantos'. Kannon would remain 'his friend, the mighty goddess' throughout his life.

In keeping with the contrast in 'MS Ur 1' between such paradisal Eastern images and the barbarism of 'the modern world', Pound juxtaposes Kannon's appearance with scenes of heroic perseverance in the face of the desolation that occurs when the light of such deities is obscured. One such scene in the typescript draft mentioned to his father on 18 December is that of the Cid, Ruy Díaz. When the Cid comes to Burgos, he goes to the place where he expects to lodge there but finds the door is shut. A 'child' reads out to him the 'King's writ'; the 'grave, bearded' Cid, according to Pound's *The Spirit of Romance*, 'assent[s] with as fine a simplicity' as the child's speech and honourably obeys the order without protest.[94] The draft then presents another instance of such heroic honour towards a child:

> Or Kumasaka's ghost come back to tell
> The honour of the youth who had slain him.
> These are the tales of war told over and over[95]

Pound had noted the 'punctilio' of the 'Homeric' combat between Kumasaka and the 'young boy', Ushiwaka: 'Kumasaka's spirit returns to do justice to the glory of Ushiwaka and to tell of his own defeat.'[96] He evidently saw a correlation between Cid's honourable assent to the child's speech and acceptance of this setback and Kumasaka's retelling of how a child had slain him in battle. Moreover, the last line cited earlier indicates Pound's continuing development of *Takasago*-like correspondences across large distances of space and time, already evident in his comparisons of nō with Dante and Homer. This would, of course, become a defining characteristic of *The Cantos*.

---

[92] *ECJA*, vol. 1, 61.
[93] Ibid., between pages 50 and 51.
[94] Pound, *The Spirit of Romance* (London: J. M. Dent, 1910), 65.
[95] *EPP*, 3105.
[96] Pound, 'The Classical Stage of Japan', 233.

Through his encounter with Itō, and then with Kume, Kōri, Uchiyama and 'Minami', Pound's interest in Japanese literature – in nō and *kembu* – intensified. Itō, Kume and Kōri had performed nō for him and begun to assist him with his nō translations. With the assistance of these Japanese acquaintances, he translated more nō plays, such as *Takasago*, which he would later describe as giving 'roughly the theme' of *The Cantos*. *Takasago* also presented him with a further instance of his conception of 'Unity of Image', which is formed by the 'arrangement' of 'planes in relation'. This conception was also inspired by his translation of *Kumasaka*, which offered a new model for his Vorticist poetics in *Gaudier-Brzeska: A Memoir*. In his first drafts of *The Cantos*, nō presented Pound with a vision of paradisal calm and prosperity. In his translation of *Takasago*, the themes of conjugal love, the fertility of the natural world, literary tradition and the empire are all united in the 'single Image' of the 'inexhaustible' pine needles. This vision of the East, not merely an aesthetic but also a political one of unified military and imperial rule, offered a contrast with a Western 'civilization' whose barbarism had resulted in the death of Gaudier-Brzeska; it was for this reason that Pound lamented Japan's Westernization. Three days after writing to his father about 'Three Cantos A', Pound left for Stone Cottage to spend the winter there with Yeats one last time.[97] As well as completing further nō translations that would later resurface in *The Cantos*, Pound turned, as Yeats did, to writing nō of his own.

---

[97] Pound, letter to Homer Pound (18 December 1915), in *L/HP*, 360.

9

'The closest parallel to my thought'
Pound's nō plays and accomplishments

While Pound spent his final winter at Stone Cottage with Yeats in 1915–16, Itō continued to dance nō plays and 'sword-dances' based on Pound's translations. After the first of the three Melbury Road performances, Pound wrote to his father that 'Itow's dances are going finely, especially the Noh stuff and the sword-dances. He is going to try to give the play of Kumasaka, not exactly as the Noh actors would do, but as the Kiogen actors. It ought to be very interesting.'[1] Pound's version of *Kumasaka* may thus have been among the 'Dances from the Noh Dramas' Itō performed at a Margaret Morris Club 'recital' on Flood Street, Chelsea, along with 'Classical Japanese Dances' and a 'Japanese War Dance' on 13 January 1916.[2] Pound's attendance at recital, however, is not recorded; he was perhaps already at work in Stone Cottage with the composition of his own nō plays. Of the two pieces that can be categorized as attempts at nō, the first was written with a preface that noted, once more, how at this time nō constituted for him 'the closest parallel to my thought'; as this chapter seeks to argue, it further extends the development of his *Nishikigi*-inspired Vorticist poetics.[3] The second of these, like the Japanese 'sword-dances' Itō danced on Melbury Road in October 1915 and Flood Street in January 1916, draws on a wide range of structural and thematic features found in his nō translations to create a nō play that expresses, as the earliest drafts of *The Cantos* do, the emotional devastation for Pound of Gaudier-Brzeska's death at Neuville St Vaast.

In 1987, Donald C. Gallup edited and published a collection of four previously unpublished plays written by Pound. The first, *The Protagonist*, Gallup claims to have been 'modelled specifically on the Japanese *kyogen*, or comic interlude'.[4] As

---

[1] Pound, letter to Homer Pound (30 October 1915), in *L/HP*, 355.
[2] Takeishi, *Japanese Elements*, 29.
[3] *PMN*, 23.
[4] Ibid., ii.

Pound's letter to his father about Itō performing *Kumasaka* 'as the Kiogen actors' suggests, he was aware of the term. Kyōgen (lit. 'mad words') are comic plays in their own right performed as part of a nō programme. The Fenollosas, however, appear to have had little interest in them. In his 'No Notebook', Fenollosa notes down the names of the kyōgen he saw as part of the nō programmes he attended between 1898 and 1901, but he only collaborates with Hirata on translating one.[5] They are briefly referred to in Fenollosa's history of nō as 'farces', and 'the actors of Kiogen' are among those who take part in the *utaizome* ceremony whose description Pound included in his commentary on the nō plays printed in *The Drama* in May 1915.[6] Brinkley's discussion of nō, however, which Pound read, refers in more detail to kyōgen: it explains how the 'solemn and stately' nō had to be counterbalanced by 'lighter scenes' called '*Kyōgen*'.[7] Itō, Kōri and Kume would likely have known more about kyōgen: Itō even claims in his not always reliable *Reminiscences* that Kume 'had performed *kyōgen* with his brother when he was in primary school'.[8] It is therefore possible, though unlikely, that Pound knew much at all about kyōgen at this time.

Both *The Protagonist* and the second play in Gallup's edition, *The Consolations of Matrimony*, are pastiches of J. M. Synge's 1907 play, *The Playboy of the Western World*.[9] *The Protagonist* features thirteen characters, far more than the two or three in Japanese kyōgen, and centres on these characters speculating on what crime a prisoner, Toomey, may have committed: two boys suggest he might be a 'forger'; a girl that he is 'the one that drowned the small boy, in the canal'; one of the boys that it might be 'Murder'; and three young men think that he is a 'spy of the Kaiser'.[10] This closely parallels the speculation about what crime Christy Mahon had committed in *The Playboy of the Western World*: Michael proposes it is 'larceny'; Jimmy that 'he followed after a young woman on a lonesome night'; Philly that 'the land was grabbed from him'; Michael that it was 'bailiffs'; Jimmy that he might have 'married three wives' or 'went fighting for the Boers', before Christy finally reveals that he had killed his father.[11] Pound's ending comically reverses Synge's resolution by revealing Toomey's 'crime' as having passed out drunk outside a woman's home.[12] As Neil Alexander notes, the granting of

---

[5] See *EFF*, 235–43.
[6] Pound, 'The Classical Drama of Japan', 460; Pound, 'The Classical Stage of Japan', 205.
[7] *SC*, 212; Brinkley, *Japan*, vol. 3, 31.
[8] Itō, *Reminiscences*, 29.
[9] Neal Alexander, *Regional Modernisms* (Edinburgh: Edinburgh University Press, 2013), 85–6.
[10] *PMN*, 3–7.
[11] J. M. Synge, *The Playboy of the Western World: A Comedy in Three Acts* (Dublin: Maunsel and Company, 1911), 15–18.
[12] Ibid., 20; *PMN*, 11–12.

George Brannan's wish to be rid of his wife in *The Consolations of Matrimony* by her being abducted by an outsider from America, Tim Healan, corresponds with Michael's affair with Dan Burke's wife, Nora, in Synge's *In the Shadow of the Glen*; George's declaration that he will 'break the top' of Tim's 'head' likewise recalls how Christy murders his father in *The Playboy of the Western World*.[13] Besides their humorous bent, though, these two plays have little to do with Japanese kyōgen.

In February, Pound wrote to his father that Yeats

> has done a play of his own on the Noh model, and is preparing a new dramatic movement, plays which wont need a stage, and which wont need a thousand people for 150 nights to pay the expenses of production. His play and a brief skit of mine will be done in Lady Cunard's big room in, I suppose, April.[14]

The upper-class audience Pound and Yeats had in mind aligned with Pound's enthusiasm for nō's aristocratic exclusivity: nō was, as he put it in *The Drama* in May 1915, an art form 'for the few, for the nobles, for those trained to catch the allusion'.[15] This 'brief skit' was most likely *The Consolations of Matrimony*, as Pound would write to his father in April that 'Lady Cunard has sole copy of my dialogue play. Have written to her for a copy, to have a few made.'[16] It is the only dialogue play in *Plays Modelled on the Noh*. It was not performed along with *At the Hawk's Well*, however, in which Itō famously danced the lead part of the Hawk on 2 April at Lady Cunard's drawing room, followed by another performance two days later at Lady Islington's residence; as Pound writes to his father, it was instead to be performed 'next month at Claridges'.[17] There is as yet no evidence, though, that either *The Protagonist* or *The Consolations of Matrimony* were ever performed in Pound's lifetime.

One nō-related project that did come off, however, was Pound's idea of publishing an edition of his nō translations with Cuala Press, run by Yeats's sister Elizabeth. Pound wrote to his father that 'Yeats is going to do an introduction for three of my Jap. plays, which his sister's press is now printing'.[18] By the end of February, Pound told his mother that he had 'done some more Jap [sic] plays' and that '3 or 4 are to be done in a book with an introduction by W B.Y.'.[19] This

---

[13] Synge, *The Playboy of the Western World*, 21–2; Alexander, *Regional Modernisms*, 86.
[14] Pound, letter to Homer Pound (February 1916), in *L/HP*, 362.
[15] Pound, 'The Classical Stage of Japan', 201.
[16] Pound, letter to Homer Pound (7 April 1916), in *L/HP*, 366.
[17] Pound, letter to Homer Pound (7 April 1916), in ibid.
[18] Pound, letter to Homer Pound (February 1916), in ibid., 362.
[19] Pound, letter to Isabel Weston Pound (27 February 1916), in ibid., 364.

suggests that, in all probability, the three plays mentioned in the earlier letter were those that were eventually to appear in *Certain Noble Plays of Japan* which he had previously published – *Nishikigi*, *Hagoromo* and *Kumasaka* – and that the translation of *Kagekiyo*, which was to be the fourth of Pound's nō translations in the book, was composed in February and then decided upon as a suitable companion to the other three. When Pound and Yeats returned to London at the beginning of March, they worked on rehearsals for *At the Hawk's Well*.[20] On 13 March, Pound informed his friend and benefactor John Quinn that, during these rehearsals, he had 'some undefined managerial function which consists partly in watching W. B. rushing about a studio shouting "Now . . . NOW . . . Now"'.[21] Yeats recalls being impressed by Pound's performance as Cuchulain during one rehearsal when the professional actor who was to play that role, Henry Ainley, did not turn up.[22]

Pound's enthusiasm for his Japanese friends continued after the performances of *At the Hawk's Well*. On 7 April, Pound also wrote to his father:

> Itow still here and likely to stay. He is the hawk in Yeats' play. Koumé and Fugita, two very charming and high-up japs [sic] also contribute to one's enjoyment of life. Koumé of Daiymio [sic] family. His father has two Noh stages in the back yard etc. He is a fine chap, looks a little like a miniature of Bill Williams. Fugita, evidently son of a much used general judging from family photos. He is a satirist with no end of humour and great talent. Koumé did the Hagoromo. <vide my translation Quarterly Review> the tennin part, before the Mikado at the age of seven. The flying movements of the dance are most exquisite. They are a fine pair of humans.[23]

'Fugita' is the now-famous Japanese painter Fujita Tsuguharu (1886–1968), also known as Léonard Foujita. He had come to Paris to study painting at the outbreak of the First World War and moved to London in early 1915.[24] He stayed, as Kōri did from May 1915, at Hester Sainsbury's residence, 71 Royal Hospital Road, and mentions Kume and Itō frequently visiting them there.[25] Kume, meanwhile, was involved in studying 'some play [sic]', as he told Pound, with Itō at the studio of Edmund Dulac, who designed the masks for *At the Hawk's Well*; on 9 April,

---

[20] See *SC*, 209–19.
[21] Pound, letter to John Quinn (13 March 1916), in *L/JQ*, 68.
[22] W. B. Yeats, 'A People's Theatre: A Letter to Lady Gregory', *Irish Statesman* 1, no. 23 (29 November 1919): 572–3.
[23] Pound, letter to Homer Pound (7 April 1916), in *L/HP*, 366.
[24] Fujita, 'Ko Kōri Torahiko kun', 127.
[25] Ibid., 128.

Pound wrote to his mother that Kume was 'doing the Kumasaka dance-part for us this evening in his studio'.[26]

In the same letter, moreover, Pound wrote that he was 'doing some "Noh" of my own: don't know that they'll ever get finished'.[27] He thus explicitly connects the other two plays in Gallup's edition, *A Supper at Mademoiselle Rachel* and *Tristan*, with nō. No text of the former survives, only a typescript of Pound's preface. The text of what Pound intended to introduce was probably his own translation of a letter by the French poet and playwright Alfred de Musset to Caroline Jaubert of 29 May 1839 published in de Musset's *Oeuvres posthumes*.[28] In the preface, Pound writes that 'it is a Japanese play that gives me the closest parallel to my thought'.[29] This 'Japanese play' is *Nishikigi*, as Pound explains: 'Listen to my Japanese priest. He has come upon two ghosts in a field. Suddenly a grey cave shows a light. He sees bright figures within it. He sees there is a flicker of fire. Then he sees that the cave looks like a house, not a house of today'.[30] The priest then 'loses his scientific detachment, and only wants to see how the things happened':

> Let it be a dream, or a vision,
> Or what you will, I care not.
> Only show me the times over-past and snowed under:
> Now, soon, while the night lasts.[31]

The image of the 'times over-past and snowed under' ties into what Pound considered to be the 'single Image' of the nō play, the 'whirl' of the 'falling snow', that of the past's ghosts. As Chapter 7 argues, this 'single Image' of the 'whirl' of the dead informed Pound's conception of Vorticism, in which 'the energized past [. . .] charg[es] the PLACID, NON-ENERGIZED FUTURE' and 'is pregnant in the vortex, NOW'.[32] It is for this reason that *Nishikigi* still gave him 'the closest parallel to my thought'. *A Supper* demonstrates Pound's development of his nō-inspired Vorticist poetics.

In *A Supper*, Pound seeks a European equivalent of this Vorticist principle that he saw in nō. 'You tell me', Pound states in his preface, 'you do not want Japanese things, that these new plays must be European'.[33] Pound's 'Japanese emotion' can

---

[26] Pound, letter to Isabel Weston Pound (9 April 1916), in *L/HP*, 367.
[27] Ibid.
[28] *PMN*, 30.
[29] Ibid., 23.
[30] Ibid.
[31] Ibid., 23–4.
[32] Pound, 'Vortex', 153.
[33] *PMN*, 23.

equally be discovered, though, he tells his intended audience, 'if you went to the Tuileries and really saw Marie Antoinette' or 'If suddenly you saw by the Tiber you saw re-acted, re-arranged, re-presented the events and heard the exact speeches on the morning after the Duke of Candia was murdered?'[34] This sense of the reconstructed past 'pregnant in the vortex NOW' had already charged the genesis of *The Cantos*, as the previous chapter proposes. De Musset's letter relates his encounter with the actress Rachel Félix after her performance as Amédaïde in Voltaire's *Tancrède*. At her home, she reads to him from Jean Racine's *Phèdre*. Writing in the present tense – the past emerging in the present – de Musset describes how, as she read, 'Tout à coup ses yeux étincellent; – la génie de Racine éclaire son visage: – elle pâlit, elle rougit. – Jamais je ne vis rien de si beau, de si interessant'.[35] Rather than the more explicit manifestation of ghosts such as those of *Nishikigi*, this passage from de Musset's letter suggests the fertility of the literary tradition, the 'génie' of Racine 'energizing' Rachel's face.

This parallel is further developed in what is Pound's only surviving nō play of his own, *Tristan*. Gallup suggests that Pound's attendance of Wagner's *Tristan und Isolde* at the Aldwych Theatre on 19 June 1916 'may well have been the initial impulse' behind *Tristan*.[36] The story of Tristan and Yseult is present from Pound's earliest collections, however. In *The Spirit of Romance* of 1910, he remarks that 'The Tristan and Ysolt legend stands apart from the other romances. The original energy and beauty of its motif have survived even later versions'.[37] Furthermore, in his later review of an Aldwych performance of the opera, his impression of Wagner's version is negative: 'In the "Tristan", whatever one had felt in the first acts was a little worn away in the last act.'[38] The likely sources for *Tristan* are, instead, listed in his discussion of the legend in *The Spirit of Romance*. 'The early texts of Thomas and Béroul are reprinted by the Société des Anciens Textes Français.'[39] Mikhail Oshukov has already traced much of the evidence for Pound's use of Béroul's twelfth-century Old French version in *Tristan*.[40] In my own discussion of *Tristan*, I will instead focus upon the correspondences between *Tristan* and Pound's nō-inspired Vorticist poetics.

---

[34] Ibid.
[35] Alfred de Musset, *Oeuvres posthumes* (Paris: Charpentier, 1860), 117.
[36] Pound, *PMN*, ii.
[37] Pound, *The Spirit of Romance*, 82.
[38] William Atheling, 'Music: Le Mariage de Figaro', *The New Age* n. s. 4, no. 7 (6 December 1917): 114.
[39] Pound, *The Spirit of Romance*, 82.
[40] Mikhail Oshukov, *Representation of Otherness in Literary Avant-Garde of Early Twentieth Century: David Burliuk's and Ezra Pound's Japan* (PhD Thesis: University of Turku, 2017), 273–90.

Several of Pound's early poems make use of the Tristan legend, particularly of Ysolt, whom Pound often identifies with H. D.[41] In 'To Ysolt. for Pardon', which appears in Pound's first published collection, *A Lume Spento*, Pound first presents a contrast between the colour brought by the speaker's 'songs' – which are compared to 'red leaves of the Autumn whirled' and 'green bough-banners' – when they are 'fragranced of thyself' and the 'dust-grey ways' of the world.[42] In 'Praise of Ysolt', published in *Personae*, the speaker conventionally compares his love as 'a fire' with his song 'ablaze with her', and similarly likens her to 'the spring upon the bough'; these contrast, once more, with the 'dust' of the 'many roads' the speaker has travelled.[43] Such an opposition is expanded upon in 'Sestina for Ysolt', which appears in *Exultations*. Its repeated 'greyness' contrasts with the 'loveliness' of Ysolt's 'white hands' (a second Ysolt in the Bédier version is known as 'Iseut aux Blanches Mains'), whose 'eyes are like the stars'.[44] Pound employs such colour contrasts of 'greyness' and 'dust' with the 'fire', the 'spring upon the bough', the 'green bough-banners' and the 'red leaves of the Autumn whirled' in *Tristan* to represent the world as being either animated by vegetal and sexual regeneration or turned, in the absence of such regeneration, into a wasteland.

The latter element is introduced at the start of *Tristan*. The 'Prologue' asks the play's audience to 'Think you will see a castle of great stones':

> And a sea
> Harsh, grey as granite, stretches out beneath us,
> Shot, to the south, with waves like microcline
> Giving a bluish light between the grey.[45]

In addition to the 'greyness' of the 'Sestina for Ysolt', Pound's depiction of the sea resembles that of 'The Coming of War: Actaeon', composed in the winter of 1914–15 at Stone Cottage. It opens with 'An image of Lethe': 'A sea / Harsher than granite, / unstill, ever moving.'[46] In the poem, the 'Harsher than granite' sea more clearly suggests the devastation of the war and the slaughter of millions. The lives of the dead remain, however, ghost-like, in the 'Host of ancient people, / The silent cortège', who are, like the sea, 'Unstill, ever moving'; their appearance is preceded by the 'faint light / but golden' on the water, as is Kuanon's in *Tamura*.

---

[41] K. K. Ruthven, *Ezra Pound as Literary Critic* (London: Routledge, 2013), 50.
[42] Pound, 'To Ysolt. For Pardon', in *A Lume Spento and Other Early Poems* (New York: New Directions, 1965), 119.
[43] Pound, 'Praise of Ysolt', in *Personae* (London: Elkin Mathews, 1909), 28–30, 29 and 28.
[44] Ibid., 28; Joseph Bédier, *Le Roman du Tristan*, vol. 2 (Paris: Librairie de Firmin Didot, 1905), 354.
[45] *PMN*, 33.
[46] Pound, 'The Coming of War: Actaeon', *Poetry* 5, no. 6 (March 1915): 255.

In *Tristan*, too, the 'grey as granite' sea is tinged with 'bluish light', like Genji's appearance as he dances 'the blue dance of the sea waves' in *Suma Genji*. Like Tristan and Yseult, 'Genji the gleaming' is a famous lover, whose tragic exile at Suma does not diminish his 'light'; Tristan and Yseult, likewise, are banished by King Mark but escape to the forest of Marrois and live there happily together.

The 'Sculptor', who acts as the *waki* by visiting the play's location, the 'castle of great stones', explains to a local woman that he is French. As in nō such as *Nishikigi*, *Kayoi Komachi*, *Takasago* and *Suma Genji*, the woman later reveals herself to be the spirit of one of the principal characters. The 'Sculptor' is clearly based on Gaudier-Brzeska.[47] The shock for Pound of his death suggests the personal significance of this play to him. The 'Sculptor' has come, as Fujiwara no Okinori does in *Suma Genji* and the visiting monk at Kiyomizu Temple in *Tamura*, because 'There is a tree here'.[48] Unlike in *Suma Genji* and *Tamura*, however, he has come 'to see a quince tree', not a cherry tree.[49] The quince is associated with Aphrodite and thus with love and fertility.[50] This association of the quince tree, which blossoms at the end of the play, with love suggests its affinity to the blossoming cherry tree in *Suma Genji*; the cherry tree anticipates Genji's 'blue dance of the sea waves', which expresses his youthful, amorous virility. The tree's symbolism in *Suma Genji* fuses together sexual and vegetal regeneration, as *Takasago* does with the paired pine trees. Pound thus connects together Celtic, Greek and Japanese love myths and incorporates them into a dramatic structure shaped by nō.

The woman disappears; then there is 'a flash of sleeve in the doorway' and the Sculptor sees the 'apparition of Yseult – in mediaeval costume'. Whereas the Sculptor's language is modern and colloquial – he had been wondering, 'Where is that damn woman gone?' – the language of the past emerges into the present moment when a 'Voice', Tristan's, calls from inside the tower:

> pena d'amor
> Per Yseutz la blonda.[51]

Tristan's words are from the twelfth-century Provençal troubadour Bernart de Ventadorn's poem 'Tant ai mo cor ple de joya' ('I suffer greater torment in love'). Like many of the nō plays Pound had translated until then, Tristan's 'apparition'

---

[47] Oshukov, *Representation of Otherness*, 276.
[48] *PMN*, 33.
[49] Ibid.
[50] Ovid, *Heroïdes, with the Greek Translation of the Planudes*, ed. Arthur Palmer (Oxford: Clarendon, 1898), 152.
[51] *PMN*, 35.

(the term Pound also uses for Yseult) creates the '*sense* of the past in the present' Pound had identified in *Takasago*: just as the nō play inserts poems from the anthology of the play's imagined past (the *Manyōshū* collection) and present (the *Kokinshū* collection), symbolized respectively by the pines of Takasago and Sumiyoshi, *Tristan* places fragments of language from the past (Bernart de Ventadorn's lines) alongside that of its present moment. Pound's creation of a macaronic verse based on the example of nō thus parallels the multilingual parataxis of *The Cantos* that he was also developing at this time.

Tristan also develops Pound's 'Unity of Image' that he had identified in nō through the colour contrast used in his earlier Tristan poems.[52] The 'emerald ring' and 'opaque green stone' Yseult and Tristan, respectively, wear derives from Béroul's 'anel' of 'esmeraudes' given to Yseult and the 'anel' of 'jaspe vert' which Yseult offers Tristan.[53] Tristan compares Yseult's eyes to 'malachite gone transparent', thus echoing Béroul's description of her eyes as 'vers'.[54] By contrast, both Tristan and Yseult 'are in costumes gilt and brilliant on one side only, or else one side is covered by a grey cloak'; these resemble Yseult's clothing in Bédier's version as she faces execution for adultery, 'vêtue d'un étroit bliaut gris, où court un filet d'or'.[55] The Sculptor observes how Tristan and Yseult's apparitions 'flash and fade through each other'; they are, the stage directions explain, 'almost invisible when the grey side is toward the audience'. Yseult expresses how she is 'torn between two lives': Tristan and Yseult are both dead and alive, both past and present; the grey-green colour contrast that runs through the play illustrates this duality. Their love has faded – 'There was three years' craft in the cup', Tristan laments, thus recollecting Béroul's 'III. anz d'amistié' – but their apparitions live on in the many versions of their story; these re-emerge in the play's literary present, like those of Komachi, Genji and the lovers of *Nishikigi* and *Takasago*.[56]

The play's depiction of Tristan and Yseult's survival into the present is encapsulated in the blossoming of the quince tree at the end. In Bédier's version, on which Belloc's English rendering depends, Mark buries Tristan and Iseut together:

> Mais, pendant la nuit, de la tombe de Tristan jaillit une ronce verte et feuillue, aux forts rameaux, aux fleurs odorantes, qui, s'élevant par-dessus la chappelle, s'enfonça dans la tombe d'Iseut. Les gens du pays coupèrent la ronce: au

---

[52] Oshukov, *Representation of Otherness*, 281.
[53] *PMN*, 36; Béroul, *Roman de Tristan* (Paris: Librairie de Firmin Didot, 1903), 57 and 84.
[54] *PMN*, 36; Béroul, *Roman de Tristan*, 90.
[55] Bédier, *Le Roman de Tristan*, 131.
[56] *PMN*, 37; Béroul, *Roman de Tristan*, 67.

lendemain elle renaît, aussi verte, aussi fleurée, aussi vivace, et plonge encore au lit d'Iseut la Blonde.⁵⁷

Like *Takasago*, Bédier's version of the Tristan legend suggests a correspondence between vegetal, sexual and literary regeneration. Though the individual's life may be lost, the vital force persists, metamorphosing into vegetation, both in a more literal and in a figurative sense as the literary tradition's 'inexhaustible leaves of speech'. It is this vital force that is the 'bluish light between the grey' in the sea, the 'emerald' and 'jasper' of Tristan and Yseult's rings, the 'malachite' of Yseult's eyes, and the forest of 'Marrois'. The quince blossoms, just as the pine needles' 'unchanging green' continues to fall in *Takasago*, because of what Pound described in 'Vortex' as the 'energized past, all the past that is living' charging the present. Pound was thus able to recreate in *Tristan*, his own nō-like play, what he had identified in *Takasago* as the '*sense* of the past in the present'.

While he was composing his own nō, Pound had three further nō translations published from the Fenollosa notes during 1916: *Awoi no Uye* ('Aoi no ue', 'Lady Aoi') appeared in the *Quarterly Notebook*'s first issue in June, *Kakitsuhata* ('Kakitsubata') in *The Drama* in August, and *Kagekiyo* in the Cuala Press *Certain Noble Plays of Japan* in September. Like *Suma Genji* and *Hajitomi*, *Aoi no ue* is one of the many nō plays based on the *Genji monogatari*. Genji is married at the age of twelve to his cousin, the sixteen-year-old daughter of the minister of the Left; she is never named but is conventionally referred to as Aoi. Princess Rokujō is likewise unnamed; Rokujō refers, instead, to her residence (on the *rokujō*, or 'sixth avenue', of Kyoto). There is little affection between Genji and Aoi: their 'hearts' were 'distant'.⁵⁸ Genji embarks on a series of affairs with other women. Rokujō is introduced in the sixth chapter, 'Yūgao', as one of these lovers: as he makes off with the Yūgao lady, he thinks of the 'Rokujō lady' and 'how tangled the thoughts, how jealous, how painful' it must be for her.⁵⁹ After the Yūgao woman dies, as recalled in *Hajitomi*, at the Aoi ('Hollyhock') festival in late spring, Aoi's and Rokujō's carriages collide, causing much damage to the latter; Rokujō's 'jealousy' now knows 'no bounds'.⁶⁰ Aoi soon becomes possessed by a *mono no ke* ('spirit-being'); exorcisms are performed in an attempt to remove it.⁶¹ A voice then speaks through Aoi, which Genji finally recognizes as Rokujō's.

---

⁵⁷ Bédier, *Le Roman du Tristan*, 288.
⁵⁸ Murasaki, *Genji monogatari*, vol. 2, 22.
⁵⁹ Ibid., vol. 1, 148.
⁶⁰ Ibid., vol. 2, 70.
⁶¹ Ibid., 78.

Rokujō herself, however, is still alive and elsewhere as this scene takes place. Finally, Aoi dies, while Rokujō leaves Kyoto.

The nō play, whose author remains unknown, opens with a 'courtier of the Emperor' explaining that Aoi has been possessed by a *mono no ke*.[62] A Shintō *miko*, or female priestess, absent in the *Genji monogatari*, is called to summon the malign spirit and find out if it is that of a living or a dead person.[63] Rokujō then appears and asks, 'Can I, riding on the three carriages of the [Buddhist] Law, escape out of the gate of the burning house?' She regrets 'Yūgao's broken carriage', a reference to the broken-down carriage in which Genji visited Yūgao but also possibly suggesting the broken carriages of her retinue in the clash with Aoi's.[64] Extending the carriage metaphor, Rokujō laments how this 'floating world' is 'an ox-carriage' and *rinne* (the cycle of death and rebirth) 'the wheel of a carriage'.[65] To exorcise Rokujō's jealousy, the courtier summons a 'holy man' from Yokawa, a reference to Enryakuji on Mount Hiei, the stronghold of Tendai Buddhism; in the *Genji monogatari*, likewise, Enryakuji monks perform exorcism rites for Aoi. Unlike in the original, however, the holy man drives the jealousy out of Rokujō's spirit through prayer to the four Buddhist guardian kings and the Buddhist deity Fudō-Myō-ō, thus enabling her to achieve enlightenment.[66] *Aoi no ue* thus shows Rokujō's spirit as appearing in the play's own dramatic present moment, separate from that of the *Genji monogatari*; in this present, the Buddhist holy man can 'intervene' in the story and save Rokujō.

Both Ernest and Mary Fenollosa's notes taken at the performance of *Aoi no ue* at Umewaka's house on 30 October 1898 appear confused about whether Aoi or Rokujō 'becomes the type of envy', as Ernest's notes put it.[67] Whereas in the *Genji monogatari* Aoi is distant from Genji and her sickness is due to Rokujō's jealousy, not her own, Mary notes that Aoi 'loves her husband, but he is a butterfly that does not remain content with one flower. [. . .] So she becomes a type of jealousy (shitto = jealousy).'[68] Although Mary notes that the 'spirit' that 'haunts her' is 'in reality the ghost of the Princess Rokujo, who hates Genji', she expresses doubt about this explanation: 'I cannot help believing that our translator Hirata has made some mistakes in this.'[69] Of course, Rokujō loves Genji and is jealous of Aoi. Ernest's notes are similarly opaque: 'The scene opens at the death bed of Aoi.

---

[62] YT, vol. 6, 22.
[63] Ibid.
[64] Ibid., 23.
[65] Ibid.
[66] Ibid., 27.
[67] GCNTJ, 235.
[68] Ibid., 236.
[69] Ibid.

(Rokujo Miyasudokoro.)'[70] He thus makes it appear as if Rokujo is another name for Aoi. In the Hirata-Fenollosa translation, this blurring of identities persists: Rokujō's entrance is first ascribed to 'Awoi no Uye', which is then crossed out and replaced with 'Rokujō'.[71] The chorus's address to Rokujō is later mistakenly interpreted as being 'said to Awoi no Uye'.[72] As the Ōwada edition does, each new instance of speech or song by Rokujō is marked '*Shite*' rather than with the character's name. This would, in turn, cause much confusion for Pound.

In Pound's introduction to the play in the *Quarterly Notebook*, he acknowledges in the first line that 'The rough draft of this play by Fenollosa and Hirata presents various difficulties', which 'even Japanese skilled in the art' are 'diffident' in explaining.[73] According to Pound, 'Awoi' is 'jealous of the other and later co-wives of Genji. This jealousy reaches its climax and she goes off her head with it when her carriage is overturned and broken at the Kami [sic] festival.'[74] He therefore mistakenly attributes both Rokujō's jealousy and her indignation at her broken carriages to Aoi. This leads Pound to conclude that '"Princess Rokujo", the concrete figure on the stage, is a phantom or image of Awoi no Uye's own jealousy'.[75] For him, *Awoi no Uye* thus anticipates Ibsen's apparent declaration that 'life is a "combat with the phantoms of the mind"'.[76] Pound may have been thinking of Mrs Alving's conception of 'ghosts' in the first English translation of Ibsen's *Gengangere* ('Ghosts') as 'dead ideas, and lifeless old beliefs' that 'cling to us'.[77] The error arguably reveals a significant aspect of Pound's literary technique: *Tristan*'s depiction of Tristan and Isolde's love and the Sculptor's visit appears to be a similar projection of Pound's own emotional turmoil regarding his failed relationship with H. D. and his lost friendship with Gaudier-Brzeska.

The changes Pound makes to the Fenollosa-Hirata draft itself are similarly revealing. In the Hirata-Fenollosa draft the *shite* (originally Rokujō) first appears by telling that she has come out 'from the dwelling of fire', which the translators correctly interpret as referring to the 'carriages drawn by sheep, deer, & ox, in Hokekio [the *Lotus Sutra*]'.[78] In the *Lotus Sutra* a rich man entices his sons out of the burning house with treasures to save them, which is then

---

[70] Ibid., 235.
[71] Ibid., 231.
[72] Ibid., 232.
[73] Fenollosa and Pound (trans.), *Awoi no Uye*, *Quarterly Notebook* 1, no. 1 (June 1916): 9.
[74] Ibid.
[75] Ibid., 10.
[76] Ibid.
[77] Henrik Ibsen, *The Pillars of Society and Other Plays*, trans. Havelock Ellis (London: Walter Scott, 1888), 157.
[78] *GCNTJ*, 231.

explained as the 'expedient means' through which living beings are saved from the cycle of death and rebirth.[79] In Pound's revision, however, she comes 'from the gate of hell', thus bringing the play closer to Dante's *Inferno*; Pound had also drawn a parallel between *Hagoromo* and the *Paradiso*. To exorcise the 'hell' of Awoi's (originally Rokujō's) jealousy, the 'holy man' in the Fenollosa-Hirata draft takes 'juzu of red wood, having angles, and rubbing it thoroughly, thoroughly, made a single prayer'.[80] In Pound's version, though, the holy man 'took the beads of red wood, the square beads with hard corners, and whirling and striking, said prayer'.[81] By employing the verb 'whirling', Pound imparts a Vorticist energy to the 'holy man's' actions: through his *directio voluntatis*, the 'holy man' is able to intervene in the *Genji monogatari*'s past narrative, which reappears in the play's dramatic present moment.

Pound felt a similar 'considerable diffidence' about the third of the plays he translated before the end of February, *Kakitsuhata* (later corrected to *Kakitsubata*), which was published in *The Drama*'s August 1916 issue.[82] It is based on the life of the poet Ariwara no Narihira (825–80) as told in the anonymously compiled late-ninth-century *Ise monogatari* ('The Tales of Ise'), particularly its ninth section. Narihira decides to leave the capital, and his lover, to travel eastwards in search of a new place to live.[83] They stop at Yatsuhashi ('Eight Bridges') in the province of Mikawa (in present-day Aichi Prefecture), a famous spot for irises ('kakitsubata'). Someone asks Narihira to compose an acrostic waka with one syllable of 'kakitsubata' at the head of each of the five verses of the poem:

karakoromo	being accustomed
kitsutsu narenishi	to a wife who would wear such
tsuma shi areba	beautiful garments
harubaru kinuru	I ponder deeply about
tabi wo shi zo omou	coming on this long journey[84]

The 'wife', Narihira's lover, is thought to refer to Fujiwara no Takaiko (842–910), the 'Nijō ("Second Avenue") princess' who in 859 performed the Gosechi dance in the imperial palace and in 866 became consort to Emperor Seiwa (850–81).[85] In addition to the original's acrostic, which makes the poem, as Shiki said of

---

[79] Kumārajīva, *The Lotus Sutra*, trans. Burton Watson (New York: Columbia University Press, 1993), 56.
[80] GCNTJ, 233.
[81] Pound and Fenollosa (trans.), *Awoi no Uye*, 15.
[82] NA, 191; Fenollosa and Pound (trans.), 'Kakitsuhata', *The Drama* 23 (August 1916): 428–35.
[83] *Ise monogatari*, ed. Katagiri Yōichi and Tanaka Maki (Osaka: Izumi shoin, 2016), 8.
[84] Ibid., 9.
[85] Ibid.

Bashō's 'old pond' *hokku*, an '*oriku*', the poem contains numerous 'pivot words' (*kakekotoba*): *ki* can mean both 'to come' and 'to wear'; *tsuma* 'wife' and the 'hem' of a garment; and *harubaru* the stretching of cloth and the 'long' in 'long journey'.[86] The memory of his beloved thus weaves its way through his thoughts.[87]

The nō play, attributed to Komparu Zenchiku, opens with a monk going on a pilgrimage to the eastern provinces in late spring when he sees irises in bloom at Yatsuhashi.[88] He meets a woman who tells him the story of the *Ise monogatari*'s ninth section, then invites him to stay the night at her house.[89] When he enters, he sees a 'radiant' garment, which she explains is that of Takaiko, and the *sukibitai* (diaphanous headdress) of Narihira.[90] She then reveals that she is 'the spirit of the iris' and performs Takaiko's Gosechi dance wearing both items.[91] As she dances, she and the chorus relate that Narihira is a 'god of Yin and Yang' and a 'bodhisattva of song and dance'.[92] The play's weaving together of sexual, vegetal and literary fertility is expressed, as in *Takasago*, in its unpacking of the etymology for *kotoba* ('words') as 'leaves of speech' ('koto no ha'): it is through Narihira's 'waka' that his 'leaves of speech' live on; though his body is mortal, the *Ise monogatari* that contains his poems 'has no end'.[93] The identity of the 'spirit of the iris' seems ambiguous: Itō Masayoshi cites a medieval belief that it is Takaiko's 'form' (*katami*); Umehara and Kanze, meanwhile, maintain that neither Narihira nor Takaiko appear in the play.[94] The combination of Narihira's *sukibitai* and Takaiko's dress in the *shite*'s dance suggest, however, that the spirit fuses Narihira's and Takaiko's forms into one, just as Narihira's poem binds the two together.

This conception of the temporary body as the outer dress of the enduring spirit draws on Pound's profound interest in Ovid's *Metamorphoses*. Miyake claims that, for Pound, the spirit of the iris corresponds with the soul of Beatrice appearing when Dante sees a young lady in Dante's *Convivio*.[95] In the preface to the *Drama* version omitted from later editions of Pound's *Kakitsubata* translation, however, Pound compares the play's theme not to Dante but to Ovid. Narihira 'was in his day the incarnation of Apollo'.[96] After Narihira's departure from the capital, 'As

---

[86] Ibid.
[87] Ibid.
[88] *YT*, vol. 3, 171.
[89] Ibid., 173.
[90] Ibid.
[91] Ibid.
[92] Itō Masayoshi (ed.), *Yōkyokushū* ('Collected Nō'), vol. 1, 2nd edn (Tokyo: Shinchōsha, 2015), 422.
[93] *YT*, vol. 3, 174.
[94] Ibid.; Umehara and Kanze (eds), *Nō wo yomu*, vol. 3, 73.
[95] *GCNTJ*, xxxvi.
[96] Fenollosa and Pound (trans.), 'Kakitsuhata', 428.

Ovid after favour, and after affairs with ladies of the court, was exiled', he 'seems to have left the court and written poems *Ex Ponto*, poems of regret'.⁹⁷ Pound might have felt an affinity with Narihira in this sense, having become an exile after 'affairs with ladies' in Crawfordsville.⁹⁸ In Golding's translation of Ovid's *Metamorphoses* that Pound admired, Apollo explains to Daphne that 'By mee men learne to sundrie tunes to frame sweete ditties true', just as Narihira is the 'bodhisattva of song and dance'.⁹⁹ As Phoebus, meanwhile, Apollo is the sun, 'of all the worlde' the 'onely perfect light'.¹⁰⁰ In this, too, he resembles Narihira, who spreads the 'calm light' (*jakkō*) of the Buddhist paradise.¹⁰¹ Pound's translation further emphasizes the association of Narihira and Takaiko's love with light: to the local girl's description of Narihira's love for Takaiko Pound adds that 'She was his light in her youth'; the 'flaunt and flare' of 'the flowers Kakitsuhata / That flaunt and flare in their marsh' are likewise Pound's invention.¹⁰² The 'flare' of the irises is the light of Narihira and Takaiko's love flaring up in Narihira's and then the spirit of the irises' memory through his poem.

At the end of August, Pound wrote to his mother that Cuala's *Certain Noble Plays of Japan* was ready to be ordered; on 18 September, two days after its publication, Pound sent a copy to his father.¹⁰³ It was published in a limited edition of 350 copies in red-and-black lettering reminiscent of William Morris's Kelmscott Press. Like the aristocratic exclusivity of the performance of *At the Hawk's Well*, the book's peritext shows how Pound sought a readership for *Certain Noble Plays of Japan* of 'the few', 'the nobles', as his choice of title also suggests.¹⁰⁴ Yeats's introduction to the book reinforces this suggestion: not only does he describe in detail how 'Noh was made a necessary part of official ceremonies at Kioto, and young nobles and princes [. . .] were encouraged to witness and to perform' in an art form that 'created an image of nobility'; he also repeats Aston's claim in *A History of Japanese Literature* that 'Kwan-ami was a small daimio' when he writes that 'A small daimio or feudal lord [. . .] was the author [. . .] of many plays'.¹⁰⁵ Yeats again draws on Aston to connect nō not just

---

⁹⁷ Ibid.
⁹⁸ Moody, *Ezra Pound: Poet*, vol. 1, 60–1.
⁹⁹ Ovid, *Metamorphoses*, trans. Arthur Golding (London: De la More Press, 1904), 33.
¹⁰⁰ Ibid., 42.
¹⁰¹ *YT*, vol. 3, 174.
¹⁰² Fenollosa and Pound (trans.), 'Kakitsuhata', 431 and 433.
¹⁰³ Pound, letter to Isabel Weston Pound (31 August 1916), in *L/HP*, 377; Pound, letter to Homer Pound (19 September 1916), in ibid; for the date of the book's publication, see *The Letters of W. B. Yeats*, ed. Allan Wade (London: R. Hart-Davis, 1954), 612.
¹⁰⁴ Pound, 'The Classical Stage of Japan', 201.
¹⁰⁵ Fenollosa and Pound (eds), *Certain Noble Plays of Japan* (Dundrum: Cuala Press, 1916), x; Aston, *A History of Japanese Literature*, 199.

'The Closest Parallel to My Thought' 169

with medieval but also modern Japanese military power: 'in 1897 a battleship was named Takasago, after one of its most famous plays,' he writes.[106] Yeats's introduction clearly shows the political as well as aesthetic importance of nō for Pound and Yeats: both display their admiration for a military aristocracy that generously patronizes the arts.

Nō's connection with the Japanese military class is further indicated by the inclusion of *Kumasaka* alongside *Nishikigi* and *Hagoromo* in the book, but also by its fourth and final play, *Kagekiyo*, whose authorship also remains uncertain. Like Narihira in *Kakitsubata*, its principal character, the warrior Taira no Kagekiyo, is in exile: after having fought for the losing Heike side in the Gempei War of 1180–5 against Minamoto no Yoshitsune (who as a boy had slain Kumasaka in the play of that name), he was, according to Pound's version of the Hirata-Fenollosa translation, 'banished to Miyazaki in Hinga [Hyūga]', on the island of Kyūshū.[107] His daughter, Hitomaru, whom he had left in care in 'Tagami [Sagami] province', at the opposite end of Japan, comes on 'such a long journey, under rain, under wind' to find her father.[108] Kagekiyo is now blind, 'wear[ing] out the end of [his] years'.[109] When she arrives at his hut, at first he lets her pass, 'not telling my name'; 'this', he says, 'is the true love of a father' because, in his view, 'I thought this would put dishonour upon you'.[110] The villager explains to Kagekiyo that Hitomaru 'has heard of your old fame in Uashima [Yashima]', the battle for which Kagekiyo is well known through the fourteenth-century *Heike monogatari* ('Tale of the Heike').[111] He then relates his actions in the battle, the crux of the play.

For Pound at the time, *Kagekiyo*, and particularly its ending, stood out among his nō translations. In his own review of his nō translations in *The Little Review* in August 1917, he writes that 'I do not think the final passages of this play will greatly suffer from any comparison the reader will be able to make. If I had found nothing else in Fenollosa's notes I should have been well paid for the three years I have spent on them.'[112] The scene Kagekiyo relates in the play is his portrayal in the eleventh book of the *Heike monogatari*. In the *Heike monogatari*, Zeami's earlier nō play *Yashima*, and *Kagekiyo*, Kagekiyo attacks one of the warriors of the Minamoto clan at Yashima, Mionoya no Jūrō; tries to grab the neckpiece of

[106] *Certain Noble Plays of Japan*, x; Aston, *A History of Japanese Literature*, 206.
[107] Fenollosa and Pound (eds), *Certain Noble Plays of Japan*, 41.
[108] Ibid., 41 and 47.
[109] Ibid., 42.
[110] Ibid., 47.
[111] Ibid., 48.
[112] Pound, review of *Certain Noble Plays of Japan* and *'Noh' or Accomplishment*, *The Little Review* 4, no. 4 (August 1917): 9.

Mionoya's helmet; and successfully gets a hold on it before Mionoya escapes.[113] *Kagekiyo* adds a significant detail, however: as Mionoya escapes, each warrior praises the other's strength: 'How terrible, how heavy your arm!' Mionoya exclaims, while Kagekiyo replies, 'How tough the shaft of your neck is!' before they 'both laughed out over the battle, and went off each his own way'.[114] It is this moment Pound especially prizes: in *Kagekiyo*, he writes in his review, 'we find a truly Homeric laughter'.[115] It is a laughter that rises above conflict, as does that of the gods after the argument between Zeus and his wife Hera in the first book of the *Iliad*. This *humanitas* beyond conflict also underpins Pound's statement in the same review that 'One cannot consider Odysseus, or Hamlet, or Kagekiyo as foreigners, one can only consider them human'.[116] Such a rising to the nobler emotions clearly resonated with Pound, who, as we have seen, had suffered the grief of losing friends caused by the ongoing war.

Pound received an offer for a book of his nō translations from Macmillan on 19 June 1916; the following day, he wrote to his father that 'Getting placed with the Macmillan here, is quite a step onward'.[117] After receiving proofs by 18 August, Pound completed their revision by 19 September.[118] The title, 'Noh' or Accomplishment, draws on Brinkley's rendering of the word 'nō'.[119] After the photograph of Umewaka taken on 15 June 1901 at the front of the book, in the prefatory 'Note', Pound acknowledges that the 'vision and the plan are Fenollosa's', but also offers his 'very deep thanks to Mr. Arthur Waley, who has corrected a number of mistakes in the orthography of proper names'.[120] Waley's assistance is indeed evident in the numerous changes to proper Japanese names in 'Noh' or Accomplishment. These changes include the alteration in *Hagoromo* of Hakuryo disembarking in 'Subara' to 'Matsubara'; Pound's misreading of Fenollosa's handwriting for the priest in *Tamura*, 'Kenshu', is corrected to 'Kenshin'; 'Kuanon' is altered in *Tamura* to 'Kwannon'; and 'Kakitsuhata' to 'Kakitsubata'.[121] It is curious, however, to observe the shortcomings of Waley's help with *Suma Genji*,

---

[113] *Heike monogatari*, ed. Ichiko Teiji, vol. 2 (Tokyo: Shōgakukan, 1994), 361-2; Imai Shōnosuke et al. (eds), *Chūinbon Heike monogatari*, vol. 2 (Tokyo: Miyai shoten, 2011), 249-50; *YT*, vol. 2, 10; Ibid., 75.
[114] Fenollosa and Pound (eds), *Certain Noble Plays of Japan*, 49.
[115] Pound, review of *Certain Noble Plays of Japan* and *'Noh' or Accomplishment*, 9.
[116] Ibid.; Hugues Salel, *Les dix premiers livres de l'Iliade d'Homère, prince des poètes* (Paris: Jehan Loys, 1545), li. Pound recommends Salel's translation. Pound, 'Early Translators of Homer', *The Egoist* 5, no. 7 (August 1918): 97.
[117] Pound, letter to Homer Pound (20 June 1916), in *L/HP*, 371. Underline in the original.
[118] Pound, letter to Homer Pound (18 August 1916), in ibid., 376; Pound, letter to Homer Pound (19 September 1916), in ibid., 377.
[119] Brinkley, *Japan*, vol. 3, 251.
[120] *NA*, v.
[121] *NA*, 167, 84, 84-90, and 207-19.

as he would later become famous for his translation of the *Genji monogatari*. In the *Drama* version, Pound had confused chapters of the *Genji monogatari* for provinces, an error that remains in *'Noh' or Accomplishment*. Genji relates that 'I was chujo in Hahakigi province. I was chujo in the land of maple-feasting'.[122] These refer to *The Tale of Genji* chapters Waley would translate as 'The Broom Tree' and 'The Festival of Red Leaves'.[123] Genji's mentioning that he was known as 'Hikam [sic] Kimi' ('*hikaru kimi*', lit. 'Shining Lord') is also uncorrected.[124] Waley's role in the editing of *'Noh' or Accomplishment* thus suggests that his own Japanese was then still far from perfect.

Thanks to Waley's help, *'Noh' or Accomplishment* was finally published on 12 January 1917. Its publication marked Pound's own culminating accomplishment after three years of translating nō plays from Fenollosa's manuscripts. During those three years, Pound's nō translations had already had a profound impact on the development of his own poetry. His note at the end of his 'Vorticism' article in *The Fortnightly Review* is the first of three instances in which Pound proposes nō as the model for 'a long imagiste or vorticist poem' because it 'is gathered about one image'.[125] *Nishikigi* made an important contribution to his development of Vorticism; this was further developed in Pound's *Kumasaka*-inspired idea of 'planes in relation' expressed in *Gaudier-Brzeska*; and nō was an important catalyst for the genesis of *The Cantos*, begun just weeks after submitting his translation of *Takasago*, whose theme, he later wrote, would be 'roughly' that of *The Cantos* itself. His high estimation of nō during this period is undoubtable: 'The Noh is unquestionably one of the great arts of the world', he wrote in May 1915. He compared it on numerous occasions with the works of Homer, Ovid, and Dante, arguably the writers he most revered prior to his encounter with Fenollosa's manuscripts. He wrote his own nō in 1916 and published two books of his nō translations. Above all, after Gaudier-Brzeska's death, nō, particularly in *Takasago*, presented him with a vision of paradisal calm under benevolent imperial and military rule that contrasted with a West tearing itself apart. Though Pound's attitude towards nō dramatically shifted the following year, nō had nonetheless permanently altered his poetry and poetics, as the following chapters seek to argue.

---

[122] Ibid., 63.
[123] Murasaki, *The Tale of Genji*, trans. Waley (London: G. Allen & Unwin, 1925), 9.
[124] *NA*, 40.
[125] Pound, 'Vorticism', 471.

Part Three

Nō and *The Cantos*

10

'Grow with the pines of Ise'

Pound's early cantos and nō

On 4 January, eight days before the publication of *'Noh' or Accomplishment*, Pound sent his father 'the first 3 cantos of the long poem'.[1] On 6 February, he sent it to Harriet Monroe via Alice Corbin Henderson for publication in *Poetry*.[2] Henderson found the cantos 'very beautiful' and told Pound that she liked them 'tremendously'.[3] Monroe replied to Henderson that she 'took sick' after reading 'two or three pages'; but, on Henderson's insistence, she told Henderson on 9 April to print the three cantos over three issues, to which Pound agreed on 24 April.[4] The three cantos thus appeared in the June, July and August issues of *Poetry*. Furthermore, in an undated note to the *Poetry* printer that Pound must have written between then and their publication from June, Pound indicates in pencil the central importance of *Takasago* for the entire 'long poem':

> The theme is roughly the theme of 'Takasago', which story I hope to incorporate more explicitly in a later part of the poem.[5]

It is this note that Hugh Kenner cites in *The Pound Era* when he claims that although Pound 'never got round' to translating *Takasago*, 'when [Pound] sent the three Ur-Cantos to Miss Monroe he had said that his long poem's theme was ("roughly") *Takasago*'s theme: twin pines, to whose spirits distance is no barrier'.[6] We now know that Pound did translate *Takasago* and considered it to be at the 'very core' of Noh. This chapter will investigate the extent to which Pound's nō translations influenced the 'Three Cantos', but above all how the

---

[1] Pound, letter to Homer Pound (4 January 1917), in *L/HP*, 387.
[2] Preda, 'Three Cantos I-III'.
[3] Henderson, letter to Pound (17 February 1917), in *L/ACH*, 190.
[4] Monroe, letter to Henderson (19 March 1917), in ibid., 194; Monroe, letter to Henderson (9 April 1917), in ibid., 194–5; Pound, letter to Monroe (24 April 1917), in *L*, 110.
[5] Preda, 'Three Cantos I-III'.
[6] *PE*, 283–4.

'theme' of *Takasago* persisted as an important structural and thematic model, not just for Canto IV, but throughout the first thirty cantos.

Pound's 'more explicitly' in the note to the *Poetry* printer suggests that there may already be an implicit 'incorporation' of the theme of *Takasago* in the 'Three Cantos' published in *Poetry*. The first possible correspondence is to the 'spirit-Noh' in general, not just *Takasago*. As he had done in the draft of these cantos sent to his father on 18 December 1915, Pound considers as his model Browning's *Sordello*:

> Ghosts move about me
> Patched with histories. You had your business:
> To set out so much thought, so much emotion:
> To paint, more real than any dead Sordello,
> The half or third of your intensest life,
> And call that third *Sordello*?
> [...]
> Is't worth the evasion, what were the use
> Of setting figures up and breathing life upon them,
> Were't not *our* life, your life, my life, extended?[7]

The 'Ghosts' that 'move about me / Patched with histories' suggest a clear parallel with the ghosts and spirits that appear with their 'histories' in the 'spirit-Noh' plays. These lines also refer to *Sordello*: in the poem's opening, the speaker asks his interlocutor to 'view / The host I muster! Many a lighted face / Foul with no vestige of the grave's disgrace.'[8] However, it is *Takasago*'s theme of paired pine trees, 'Though the mountain and river lie between', that gives Pound the structural basis for such distant cross-cultural comparisons.

If there is indeed an implicit specific reference to *Takasago*, it may occur in the paradisal vision which first occurs in the manuscript draft Pound sent to his father on 18 December 1915 and would eventually appear in Canto III.[9] In the *Poetry* version, the speaker sets out his 'matter' in 'straight simple phrases':

>   Gods float in the azure air,
> Bright gods, and Tuscan, back before dew was shed,
> Is it a world like Puvis'?
>   Never so pale, my friend,
> 'Tis the first light – not half-light – Panisks

---

[7] Pound, 'Three Cantos – I', *Poetry* 10, no. 3 (June 1917): 114–15.
[8] Robert Browning, *Sordello* (London: Edward Moxon, 1840), 3.
[9] *EPP*, 3103.

And oak-girls and the Maenads
Have all the wood. Our olive Sirmio
Lies in its burnished mirror, and the Mounts Balde and Riva
Are alive with song, and the leaves are full of voices.
'Non è fuggito.'
          'It is not gone.' Metastasio
Is right. We have that world around us[10]

Though the landscape is 'Tuscan', the waves of Lake Garda are quiet like 'the whole sea' in *Takasago*, and 'the leaves are full of voices', those of the 'gods' in the trees. The 'leaves [. . .] full of voices' closely recall how, in *Takasago*, the 'pine-needles' are the 'inexhaustible words' of literary tradition scattering down the ages, their green 'eternal'.[11] The pine of Takasago representing the past age of the 'Manyoshu', reappearing in the play's present, alongside the one of Sumiyoshi representing 'our own time of Engi', corresponds with the suggestion Pound ascribes to Pietro Metastasio: 'that world' of the past's 'ghosts' is 'not gone' but 'around us', evergreen.

As discussed in Chapter 8, however, not just *Takasago* but also *Hagoromo*, *Tamura* and *Kumasaka* appear in the drafts that would eventually become the 'Three Cantos'. The references to all three nō plays are also explicitly referred to in the *Poetry* version. In the typescript version, to which I shall refer as 'Three Cantos A', after the manuscript Pound sent to his father on 18 December 1915, Pound inserts a more explicit allusion to *Hagoromo* in pencil:

Whom shall I conjure up, who<'>s my Sordello,
My pre-~~Dante~~ <Daun> Chaucer, pre-Boccacio?
    ~~and~~ <as> you have done pre-Dante.
Whom shall I hang my shimmering garment on
    <Who wear my feathery mantle (hagoromo)>[12]

In 'Three Cantos B', the third complete typescript draft of the 'Three Cantos', the parentheses are removed and 'hagoromo' is italicized; this is how it appears in *Poetry*.[13] In the context of the surrounding lines, the 'shimmering garment' in *Hagoromo* gives its wearer the ability to fly in the sense that the poem can take flight: the speaker seeks for someone ('my Sordello') to inspire the poem to begin. This allusion also fits, however, into Pound's stated intention of

---

[10] Pound, 'Three Cantos – I', 118.
[11] *L/ACH*, 113 and 115.
[12] *EPP*, 3105.
[13] *EPP*, 3109; Pound, 'Three Cantos – I', 117.

finding, as he writes on the back of one of the Itō dance programmes, a 'way to paradise': the heavenly maiden can only return to paradise with her *hagoromo*, her 'feather mantle'. The reference to *Hagoromo* not only suggests a seeking of poetic inspiration similar to Browning's 'pre-Dante' source for *Sordello* but also indicates the ultimate destination that the poem's speaker wishes to reach through the poem's composition.

The reference to 'Kuanon' also remains in the published *Poetry* version. As the note to the *Poetry* printer indicates, Monroe had suggested changing the spelling to 'Kwannon', the one Pound adopted, most probably on Waley's advice, in *'Noh' or Accomplishment*. As discussed in Chapter 8, the 'way to paradise' Pound's speaker seeks is lighted by the 'Kwannon' of *Tamura*:

> Fine screens depicted, sea waves curled high,
> Small boats with gods upon them,
> Bright flame upon the river! Kwannon
> Footing a boat that's but one lotus petal,
> With some proud four-spread genius
> Leading along, one hand upraised for gladness,
> Saying, "'Tis she, his friend, the mighty goddess! Paean!
> Sing hymns ye reeds,
>   and all ye roots and swans and herons be glad,
> Ye gardens of the nymphs put forth your flowers."[14]

The 'Bright flame upon the river' alludes to the 'golden light floating on the Kotsu river' in *Tamura* and her 'hand upraised for gladness' to the 'Corean Standing Kwannon with a Vase' in Fenollosa's *Epochs*. Her appearance as light on the water corresponds with the 'burnished mirror' and the 'Gods' of Lake Garda. Kannon's depiction also accords with that of Venus in Botticelli's *Nascita di Venere* later in 'Three Cantos – I'. Like Kannon, Botticelli's Venus is a goddess associated with the rebirth of spring: while Kannon blesses the 'roots and swans and herons' and, in Pound's translation of *Tamura*, is associated with the coming of the cherry blossoms, Botticelli 'Brings' Venus 'ashore on that great cockle-shell' and 'Spring and Aufidus fill the air / With their clear-outlined blossoms.'[15]

The second of the 'Three Cantos' contrasts the 'Bright flame upon the river' of these deities' appearances with heroic perseverance amidst desolation when their light is obscured, such as the 'Drear waste, great halls' of the 'Mantuan palace' that belonged to the Gonzaga family.[16] As discussed in Chapter 8, Pound

---

[14] Pound, 'Three Cantos – I', 119–20.
[15] Ibid., 121.
[16] Pound, 'Three Cantos – II', *Poetry* 10, no. 4 (July 1917): 180.

compares the ghost of Kumasaka's honour in praising the child Ushiwaka's superiority when they had fought, and Ushiwaka had killed him with the 'fine' assent of the Cid to the 'child' who reads out the 'King's writ' banishing him from the kingdom in the *Poema del Cid*. The *Poetry* version of 'Three Cantos – II' makes this comparison as an illustration of how 'These are the tales of war told over and over'. After the description of Cid and his men seeking 'the salt-sea victories', the *Poetry* version reads:

> Another gate?
>   And Kumasaka's ghost come back to tell
> The honor of the youth who'd slain him.
> Another gate.
>   The kernelled walls of Toro

The 'kernelled walls of Toro' refers to Lope de Vega's 1619 play *Las Almenas de Toro* ('The Battlements of Toro'), which features the Cid's exploits before his exile. The 'gate' thus reveals a crucial feature of *The Cantos*' architecture: it functions as the portal that allows for the *Takasago*-like correspondences between literary references across great distances of space and time.

Six days after Pound sent the typescript draft of the 'Three Cantos' for *Poetry*, however, he wrote to Quinn about his mixed feelings regarding nō, and Japanese literature more generally:

> China is fundamental, Japan is not, Japan is a special interest, like Provence or 12-13 century Italy (apart from Dante). I dont mean to say there arent interesting things in Fenollosa's Jap stuff. (Or fine things, like the end of Kagekiyo, which is, I think, 'Homeric'.) But China is solid. One can't go back of the Exile's Letter, or the Song of the Bowmen, or the North Gate.[17]

Pound may have seen China as 'fundamental' in the sense that nō was, to some extent, one of the many Chinese cultural imports into Japan. Pound would soon discuss this more explicitly, but he would have already read this view of Chinese cultural influence on Japan in Fenollosa's account of nō's Chinese origins:

> Now it happened that a form of secular drama had already arisen in China among the Mongols, and the germs of a comic Kamakura drama had been engrafted upon the Fujiwara Court dances in Japan. [. . .] Hence the invention of the *Japanese No drama* as the greatest product of the Ashikaga, under the supervision of Yoshimochi himself.[18]

---

[17] Pound, letter to Quinn (10 January 1917), in *L/JQ*, 94.
[18] *ECJA*, vol. 2, 66.

Pound would also have seen the allusions in nō to Chinese history, such as Shi Huangdi in *Takasago*. Another sense in which he was coming to see China as 'fundamental', though, was in qualitative terms. On the one hand, he repeats his assertion of the 'Homeric' qualities of *Kagekiyo*, which, given the importance Pound always placed on Homer's poetry, is high praise indeed; 'Provence' and '12-13 century Italy (apart from Dante)' were also highly influential for Pound throughout his poetic career. He also appears to say, though, that nothing is superior to Li Bai's 'Exile's Letter', Qu Yuan's 'Song of the Bowmen of Shu', or Li Bai's 'Lament of the Frontier Guard' in *Cathay*. Pound would later also outline the reasons for this judgement about the literary merits of Chinese poetry compared to nō in more detail.

In his August review of his own nō books, he contrasted nō with Chinese poetry in more explicit terms: 'This Japanese stuff has not the solidity, the body, of Rihaku (Li Po).'[19] This 'solidity', which echoes the 'solid' Pound used to describe 'China' in his letter to Quinn, is 'classical' rather than 'romantic': the 'delicacy' of the Japanese poet 'is not always a weakness', and Pound praises *Kagekiyo* not only as 'Homeric' but as a work that will not 'suffer by any comparison the reader will be able to make'.[20] 'Where a Chinese poet shows a sort of rugged endurance', however, 'the Japanese presents a fine point of punctilio. He is "romanticist" against the "classical" *and* poetic matter-of-factness of the Chinese writer.'[21] Pound's distinction recalls T. E. Hulme's 1911 lecture, 'Romanticism and Classicism', which contrasts 'hard' classicism with 'damp' romanticism.[22] Hulme advocates for the former, whose 'solidity' and 'rugged endurance' involves emotional restraint, and disparages the latter, which involves explicit expression of emotion or, as Hulme puts it, 'moaning or whining'.[23] Indeed, the tears of Shōshō in *Kayoi Komachi*, the couple in *Nishikigi*, the celestial maiden of *Hagoromo*, Kagekiyo and Rokujō suggest an art form rooted in open affective expression. As Peter Liebregts argues, Pound is far more ambivalent than Hulme in his view of these opposites; at this moment, though, at least in public, Pound adhered to Hulme's poetics of 'hard' classicism.[24]

Most likely motivated by his dislike of the more 'delicate' aspect he saw in nō in contrast with the 'solidity' of Li Bai's poetry, Pound wrote to Margaret

---

[19] Pound, review of *Certain Noble Plays of Japan* and *'Noh' or Accomplishment*, 8.
[20] Ibid.
[21] Ibid.
[22] Hulme, 'Romanticism and Classicism' (1911), in Herbert Read (ed.), *Speculation: Essays on Humanism and the Philosophy of Art* (London: Kegan Paul, Trench, Trübner, 1924), 126.
[23] Ibid.
[24] Peter Liebregts, *Ezra Pound and Neo-Platonism* (Teaneck: Fairleigh Dickinson University Press, 2004), 96.

Anderson on 24 May that he had 'revised and condensed my long poem, i.e. the first three cantos of it, between Saturday [19 May] 11:15 p.m. and Sunday [20 May] 8 a.m.' for reprinting in the Knopf edition of *Lustra*, which appeared in October.[25] Pound cut the allusion to the '*hagoromo*' in the *Lustra* version of the 'Three Cantos'. The explicit allusions to *Tamura* and *Kumasaka*, however, remain completely unaltered in the *Lustra* version, as do the more implicit references to *Takasago*, *Kakitsubata*, and the more general parallels with nō such as the 'Ghosts' that 'move about' the speaker, 'patched with histories'. It would thus be difficult to suggest, then, that Pound's estimation of nō at this stage was negative or even dismissive; indeed, there are more explicit references to nō plays than to Li Bai, despite the latter's apparent 'solidity', in these two versions of 'Three Cantos'.

In a long letter to Quinn on 3 April 1918, Pound was in a particularly uncompromising mood. Yeats's *Per Amica Silentia Lunae* does not 'hang together'; H. G. Wells 'disgust[s]' him; the opening of Henry James's *A Small Boy and Others* is 'disgusting'; and 'Noh' comes in for particular criticism:

> And I find 'Noh' unsatisfactory. I dare say its all that could be done with the material. I don't believe anyone else will come along a[nd] do a better book on 'Noh', save for encyclopedizing the subject. And I admit there are beautiful bits in it. But its all too damn soft.
> Like Pater, Fionna [*sic*] MacLeod, James Mathew Barrie, not good enough.
> I think I am justified in having spent the time I did on it; but not much more than that.[26]

The gendered association between effeminate men (Pater), men pretending to be women (MacLeod), and children's stories (Barrie) with being 'soft' and 'not good enough' suggests that Pound felt nō to be lacking in what he might have seen, along Hulme's lines, as the masculine virtues of 'rugged endurance'. It is noteworthy that the nō he does continue to praise, *Kagekiyo*, portrays 'the old Bushido spirit' of a male warrior's courage and how 'tough the shaft' of his neck is.[27] In the third version of 'Three Cantos', published in *The Future* in February and March 1918, not only the heavenly maiden of *Hagoromo* but 'Kwannon' also disappears, along with any explicit reference to nō. By 1918, it appeared as if Pound had severed all ties with nō.[28]

---

[25] Pound, letter to Margaret Anderson (24 May 1917), in *L/MA*, 54.
[26] Pound, letter to Quinn (3 April 1918), in *L/JQ*, 147.
[27] *NA*, 188.
[28] Pound, 'Three Cantos' (February and March 1918), republished in Bush, *The Genesis of the Cantos*, 301–9.

One important mention of nō the following year that has not as yet attracted attention, however, is Pound's reference to *Nishikigi* and *Hagoromo* in 'Pastiche: Regional – XVIII', published in *The New Age* on 20 November 1919. Pound emphasizes the importance of literature's political role. A deeper understanding of other cultures' literature can lead to peace. Pound offers the example of the relationship between Frederic II, Holy Roman Emperor (r. 1220–45) and 'Malek-Comel', Al-Kamil, Abbuyid Sultan of Egypt (r. 1218–38), at the time of signing the peace treaty of 18 February 1229, which resulted in ten years of peace: 'the fury of the Pope' and of 'the Mahomedan world' was provoked when 'two cultured men, Frederic II and Malek-Comel, without bloodshed meet, discuss geometry, and make a sensible agreement over Jerusalem'.[29] He compares such fury with the 'enthusiasm' in 'California [. . .] should the Americo-Japanese negotiations be entrusted to someone who had read "Nishikig" and "Hogoromo" [*sic*] instead of [. . .] an illiterate concessions-grabber'.[30] The reference to 'Americo-Japanese negotiations' may refer to Japan's failed demand for a racial equality clause to be included in the Treaty of Versailles due in part to American opposition. Pound, who saw the universal *humanitas* in Kagekiyo's courage in defeat rather than something 'foreign', knew that the Japanese were just as 'human' as any Westerner. Pound would later put his conclusion that 'Universal peace will never be maintained unless it be by a conspiracy of intelligent men' to the test when he offered to make peace for America with Japan following his arrest in the Second World War.[31]

Furthermore, of course, Pound had told Monroe *The Cantos*' theme was 'roughly the theme of "Takasago"'. In what would become Canto IV, Pound maintains the 'luminous detail' in 'MS Ur 1' of 'Sen-sei Pere Henri Jacques', who expresses its emphasis on a reconciliation between East and West by his talking 'with the sennin near the summit of Rok-ko'. The contrast between the 'modern world' that had killed Gaudier-Brzeska and Henri Jacques's seeking of reconciliation with the East is developed into one between a 'destructive' West and a 'paradiso' that draws extensively on Eastern allusions.[32] This 'paradiso' is not just Eastern, however: the manuscript fragments from 'MS Ur 1' Pound uses in his Canto IV drafts to depict a world of vegetal and sexual fertility include 'the crystal fluid / That spurts up through the mind, / whirling its brown

---

[29] Pound, 'Pastiche: Regional – XVIII', *The New Age* n. s. 26, no. 3 (20 November 1919): 48.
[30] Ibid.
[31] Ibid.
[32] Yoshida Sachiko, '*Hagoromo* to *The Cantos*: Paundo no Paradise no ichidanpen' ('*Hagoromo* and *The Cantos*: Pound's Fragment of Paradise'), in Rikutarō and Akira (eds), *Ezura Paundo kenkyū*, 170–1.

bright sand' and Aurunculeia's marriage in Catullus's 'LXI'. The contrasting images of destruction are changed from Gaudier-Brzeska and the 'modern world' to Provençal and Ovidian tales: on the reverse of a letter to Quinn dated 21 September 1917, a handwritten fragment of the tale of 'Cabestang' and 'The Lord of Polhonac' appears, a reference to Guillems de Cabestanh, who was cooked by Raymond of Rousillon and eaten by Raymond's wife and Cabestanh's lover, Soremonda; on the back of a 21 February 1918 letter from *The Future*, a manuscript fragment refers to the story found in Ovid's *Metamorphoses* of Itys, who is cooked by his mother, Procne, and fed to his father, Tereus.[33]

The first direct mention of *Takasago* in the drafts of what would become Canto IV occurs in what Froula gives as 'MS A'.[34] Its use in this draft suggests its importance as a structural device for the canto. At this stage, the canto acquires many of the oppositions that would survive into the published Canto IV versions: Actaeon, eaten by his own hounds after Diana turns him into a stag in Ovid's *Metamorphoses*, is compared with the Provençal troubadour Peire Vidal, who disguises himself as a wolf to woo Loba of Penautier and is also chased by his own hounds. This tale of violence and destruction is made to parallel the tales of Itys and Cabestanh. The mention of *Takasago* appears between the Actaeon and Vidal sections:

> stumbling, stumbling along, muttering, muttering Ovid:
> 'Pergusa, Pool of Gargaphia'
>   seeking Salmacis' pool
> 'She stood out above them all.'
>   <'The Pines of Takasago grow with the Pines of Isé'>
> ~~The Lord of Polhonac killed Cabestang in the hunt,~~
>   ~~Cooked his vitals, served up the stuff in a pie~~
> ~~His neighbors hanged him.~~[35]

This *Takasago* reference, which is maintained throughout the published editions in which Canto IV appears, is written in pencil in the transition between these two sections. It stands out from the preceding and ensuing sections by its sudden shift in subject matter. It is a focal point of transition in the canto, connecting sections together. This corresponds with the allusion's own subject matter, *Takasago*'s super-position of two entities across spatio-temporal distance. Just as the pine trees are paired despite their separation in time and space, Canto

---

[33] *EPP*, 3115.
[34] *EPP*, 3117.
[35] Ibid.

IV pairs the ancient Greek Actaeon and Itys with the Provençal of Vidal and Cabestanh.

This is not just a reference to *Takasago*, however: it is not the single pine of Takasago that grows with the pine of Sumiyoshi, as presented in *Takasago*; the 'Pines' of the play 'Takasago' suggest the paired pines that both appear at Takasago in the first part of the play. In Canto IV, they 'grow with the Pines of Isé'. According to Terrell, this refers to the 'pine-moor of Anono' in Ise where Tamuramaro conquers the 'evil spirits' with Kannon's 'light' pouring on his troops. Terrell claims, however, that 'Pound confuses Isé with Sumiyoshi in Settsu Province [. . .] the location of the legendary pine tree which forms a pair with the one growing at Takasago'.[36] In the editing of the Faber and New Directions editions of *The Cantos* after Pound's death, Pound's 'Pines' are replaced with 'pine' in both cases based on such an understanding.[37] This discounts on insufficient grounds the possibility of reading Pound's pairing of the 'Pines' of *Takasago* and *Tamura* as intentional, as Peter Makin argues.[38] Pound's translations of *Takasago* and *Tamura* both foreground the 'pacification of the country' through benevolent imperial rule. 'All the scene', the chorus in *Tamura* sings, 'showed the favour of and the virtue of the Emperor'; in *Takasago*, it chants, 'The waves of the whole sea are quiet, / The whole country well governed.' In both plays, this prosperity is connected with spring's arrival – in *Tamura*, plum and cherry blossoms, and in *Takasago* the 'calm spring sea' – and represented as light: in *Tamura*, Kannon appears as a 'light floating on the Kotsu river', then as the 'light' on the banners; in *Takasago*, likewise, the old man observes how 'The light is smooth on the water'. Both plays suggest the interconnection between vegetal regeneration and benevolent imperial rule. Pound thus pairs Kannon's divine love and the Sumiyoshi deity's virility.

This pairing of *Takasago* and the Kannon of *Tamura* is made clearer in the published versions of Canto IV, beginning with *The Fourth Canto*, forty copies of which were printed on 'japanese vellum' with John Rodker's Ovid Press on 4 October 1919.[39] The *Takasago* and *Tamura* passage in the Ovid Press version reads:

---

[36] *CCP*, 13. Terrell's claim that the 'Tree of the Visages' stems from 'a mistranslation of *seimei zyu* (生命樹), meaning "trees of life", a synonym for "pine trees" used in the Nō play *Takasago*' is also mistaken with regard to Ōwada's (or any other extant Japanese edition) of the play, which does not contain this term; neither does the English phrase appear in Pound's translation.

[37] Pound, *The Cantos* (London: Faber & Faber, 1975), 15. The 'Pines of Ise', however, remain in Canto XXI.

[38] Peter Makin, *Pound's Cantos* (Baltimore: Johns Hopkins University Press, 1985), 305–6.

[39] Bush, *The Genesis of the Cantos*, 198.

> Thus the light rains, thus pours, *e lo soleils plovil,*
> The liquid, and rushing crystal
> > whirls up the bright brown sand.
> Ply over ply, thin glitter of water;
> Brook film bearing white petals
> ('The pines of Takasago grow with pines of Ise')
> > 'Behold the Tree of the Visages.'
> The forked tips flaming as if with lotus,
> > Ply ovezr ply
> The shallow eddying fluid
> > beneath the knees of the gods.[40]

Pound's allusion to Daniel's Provençal combines with Kannon's 'Brook film bearing white petals' and 'forked tips flaming as if with lotus' in their shared emphasis on the 'light', which 'rains' and 'pours', just as Kannon's 'light' is a 'rain' that 'pours' in *Tamura*.[41] The 'rushing crystal' that 'whirls up the bright brown sand' recalls Pound's description of 'what matters in art' in 'The Serious Artist': 'a sort of energy [. . .] a force transfusing, welding, and unifying. A force rather like water when it spurts up through bright sand and sets it in swift motion.'[42] Together with this analogy, the pairing of *Takasago* and *Tamura* acts as a central metaphor for Pound's technique of Vorticist super-position. Canto IV can thus also be said to constitute the fruition of his multiple statements from 1914 onwards that nō provides the model for a 'long imagiste or vorticist poem'.

Following the publication of Canto IV as *The Fourth Canto* with Rodker's Ovid Press in October 1919, in the June 1920 issue of *The Dial*, and in *Poems 1918-1921*, it next appeared in the Three Mountains Press edition of *A Draft of XVI Cantos for the Beginning of a Poem of Some Length* in 1925. On 11 May 1923, Pound wrote to his mother that 'S Oiseau [the Paris-based American publisher William Bird] is preparing a de looks edtn. of Malatesta at 25 dollars a shot'; the illustrator Henry Strater was 'at work on special capitals'.[43] The following day, he wrote to Kate Buss, an American journalist with whom he had been maintaining a correspondence since 1916, that 'It is to be one of the real bits of printing; modern book to be jacked up to somewhere near level of mediaeval mss'.[44] Strater's 'sketches', which Pound had seen, were 'A1'.[45] He told her that the

---

[40] Pound, *The Fourth Canto* (Paris: Ovid Press, 1919), 3.
[41] *NA*, 90.
[42] Pound, 'The Serious Artist', 194.
[43] Pound, letter to Isabel Weston Pound (11 May 1923), in *L/HP*, 511.
[44] Pound, letter to Kate Buss (12 May 1923), in *L*, 187.
[45] Ibid.

book was 'Not for the Vulgus. There'll only be about 60 copies for sale.'[46] Pound thus continued to demonstrate his favouring of a poetry that was, like nō, 'for the few; for the nobles'. He completed revisions of all sixteen cantos by October.[47] Ninety copies were published in January 1925, including five on 'Imperial Japan paper' at the price of $100.[48]

Between the publication of *The Fourth Canto* and *A Draft of XVI Cantos*, Pound had moved from London to France at the end of 1920 to escape what he saw as the 'dead mentality' of England at that time, eventually settling in Paris.[49] From January 1922 to February 1923, Kume lived there too. In 1939, Pound recalled that it had been '16 years since I heard a note of Noh (Kumé and his friends sang it to me in Paris)'.[50] Pound later gave more details: 'a Tokugawa and some daimyo gave bits of *Noh* and *Kiogen* privately in [Kume's] studio in Paris.'[51] Indeed, in Kume's address book for 1921, there is an entry for a 'Tokugawa' in London and a 'Matsudaira', the Tokugawa shōguns' original clan name, in Paris.[52] In 1918, Pound had reported that Kume was to be married to 'the half-jap daughter of Capt. Brinkley'.[53] According to Tsunoda, it was in fact Kume's brother, Gonkurō, who married Hashimoto Aya, Brinkley's son John's niece.[54] John came to Paris and befriended Kume and Pound; on 11 July 1922, Pound held an exhibition at his Paris home of Kume's paintings, on the invitation of Pound, Kume, and 'Capt. J. Brinkley'.[55] One of Kume's now lost paintings, which Pound called 'Tami's Dream', hung on the walls of the Pound household until the Second World War.[56] The effect of his continued contact with Kume may be discerned in the use of nō-like 'masks, wigs and stylized gestures' in Pound's opera *Le Testament de Villon*, first performed in Paris in 1924.[57] Pound even had plans to move to Japan after Paris. He did not then 'know whether I go to Milan or Japan when my [...] lease here is up'.[58] Kume told Pound he would talk to 'some people of Gakushuin', his and Kōri's alma mater, 'to find you situation

---

[46] Ibid.
[47] Pound, letter to Isabel Weston Pound (6 June 1923), in *L/HP*, 513; Pound, letter to Homer Pound (24 August 1923), in ibid., 517; Pound, to Homer Pound (October 1923), in ibid., 519.
[48] *XVI*, 2.
[49] Moody, *Ezra Pound: Poet*, vol. 1, 407.
[50] Pound, letter to Kitasono Katué (3 March 1939), in *EPJ*, 73.
[51] Pound, letter to Iwasaki Ryōzō (6 September 1957), in ibid., 143.
[52] *MFBTK*, 1220036m.
[53] Pound, letter to Homer Pound (24 January 1918), in *L/HP*, 411.
[54] Tsunoda Shirō, 'Paundo to Kume', 12.
[55] *EPJ*, p. 22.
[56] Imamura, 'Hemingway', 42.
[57] Fisher, *Ezra Pound's Radio Operas*, 37.
[58] Pound, letter to Homer Pound (16 July 1922), in *L/HP*, 500.

[sic]'; but he died in the Great Kantō Earthquake of 1 September 1923.[59] 'Had Tami lived', Pound later reflected, 'I might have come to Tokio'.[60]

The connection Pound makes in Canto IV between regeneration and the nō plays *Takasago* and *Tamura* is more explicitly made in Canto XXI, which is arguably the next 'paradisal' canto after IV and XIII. Binyon had considered the 'parallels' between the Medici and the Ashikaga shōguns in the lecture series on 'Art and Thought in East and West' that Pound attended in 1909. Pound makes a similar cross-cultural comparison of Lorenzo de' Medici with Thomas Jefferson in Canto XXI. While travelling in Italy, Pound wrote to his father on 1 May 1924 to ask if he knew 'any thing about American Presidents'; 'Jefferson's letters I have read. He was probably the only civilized man who ever held down the job.'[61] At the end of the month, he reported that he had found 'one or two plums': 'Jefferson trying to get a gardner [sic] who cd. play the french horn', a detail of civilized behaviour that Pound was to include in Canto XXI.[62] Jefferson asks for a 'domestic band of musicians' from a country 'where music is cultivated and / Practised by every class of men' for 'reasonable wages', as long as the players possessed 'Sobriety and good / nature'.[63] By 25 October, he had begun incorporating this material into a canto: he informed his father that he was 'using a bit of Jefferson in the XX or thereabouts'.[64] He was now looking for another 'historic character who can be used as illustration of intelligent constructivity'.[65] He had found one by 11 February 1925, when he had begun 'reading for the Florentine canto'.[66] By 25 March, Pound had completed a typescript draft of 'seven cantos [...] up to Canto XXIII'.[67] Canto XXI was first published in *A Draft of the Cantos 17-27* in 1928 by Rodker in an edition of 101 copies, 5 of which were again printed on 'Imperial Japan paper, signed by the author'.[68]

Canto XXI compares the 'intelligent constructivity' of Lorenzo de' Medici with Thomas Jefferson; Pound would make a similar political comparison in *Jefferson and/or Mussolini* in 1935. Pound's parallel between de' Medici and Jefferson builds on his conviction, as stated in his 1915 sequence of essays, 'The Renaissance', that his Vorticist super-position could be applied politically as

---

[59] Kume, letter to Pound (24 March 1923), in *EPJ*, 23.
[60] Pound, letter to Kitasono (24 May 1936), in ibid., 28.
[61] Pound, letter to Homer Pound (1 May 1924), in *L/HP*, 528.
[62] Pound, letter to Homer Pound (28 May 1924), in ibid., 531.
[63] *17-27*, 26.
[64] Pound, letter to Homer Pound (25 October 1924), in ibid., 545.
[65] Pound, letter to Isabel Weston Pound (1 November 1924), in ibid., 547.
[66] Pound, letter to Homer Pound (11 February 1925), in ibid., 556.
[67] Pound, letter to Homer Pound (25 March 1925), in ibid., 561.
[68] *17-27*, 5.

well as aesthetically: the '*renascimento*' in Italy began with 'an appreciation of the great Roman vortex, an understanding of, and awakening to, the value of a capital, of centralization, in matters of knowledge and art'. Pound was convinced that if America adopted this model, it would experience 'an age of awakening which will overshadow the quattrocento'.[69] He evidently saw Jefferson as the closest American parallel with what he saw as the enlightened patrons of art, Malatesta and Lorenzo de' Medici. When such a 'vortex' of centralized power occurs, the culture regenerates. Both Jefferson and de' Medici are seen by Pound as 'outstanding personalities' able to spread 'Kungian order' around them. Like Jefferson, Lorenzo de' Medici patronizes the arts and thus brings enlightened peace and prosperity: he arranged for 'Ficino' to be 'taught the greek language'; 'begat [. . .] a University'; and 'made peace by his own talk in Naples'.[70] Both men are leaders who combine political strength with patronage of learning and the arts.

Together with the 'Kungian order' of de' Medici and Jefferson, 'Eleusinian energy' is required for cultural regeneration. The canto returns to the scenes depicting regeneration in Canto IV: we see again Actaeon's 'hounds on the green slope'; the 'black, soft water' of Diana's nymphs is 'still black in the shadow'; the 'hounds on the green slope' are the 'dogs' that 'leap on Actaeon'; and Danaë's tower reappears as the 'turris eburnea'.[71] As 'the gold fades in the gloom' with the passing of de' Medici's enlightened rule, the 'dry black of night' approaches:

> And after that hour, dry darkness
> Floating flame in the air, gonads in organdy,
> Dry flamelet, a petal borne in the wind.
> Gignetei kalon.[72]

The 'gonads in organdy' and 'Gignetei kalon' ('A beautiful thing is born') suggest the fertility rite with which the Eleusinian Mysteries are associated in Frazer's *Golden Bough*. Pound's poetry and prose show evidence of his having read Frazer's work from 1909.[73] He mentioned reading *The Golden Bough* to Margaret Anderson in May 1918 and would later describe Frazer as 'essential to contemporary clear thinking' in *How to Read*.[74] In Frazer's account of the

---

[69] Pound, 'The Renaissance – II', 286; Pound, 'The Renaissance – III', *Poetry* 6, no. 2 (May 1915): 88.
[70] *17-27*, 25–6.
[71] Ibid., 27.
[72] Ibid., 26.
[73] *VR*, 262.
[74] Pound, letter to Margaret Anderson (*c*. May 1918), in *L/MA*, 216; Pound, *How to Read* (London: Desmond Harmsworth, 1931), 39.

Eleusinian Mysteries, 'the union of the sky-god Zeus with the corn-goddess Demeter', performed 'to make the fields wave with yellow corn', was 'represented by the union of the hierophant with the priestess of Demeter, who acted the parts of god and goddess' at night, the 'torches having been extinguished'. 'After a time the hierophant reappeared, and in a blaze of light silently exhibited to the assembly a reaped ear of corn, the fruit of the divine marriage.'[75] The 'petal' in the canto is the new growth of spring brought about by such a divine marriage, and corresponds with the 'Brook film bearing white petals' in Canto IV; the 'Floating flame', too, recalls Kannon's 'Bright flame' in 'Three Cantos – I' and the 'branch tips flaming as if with lotus' in Canto IV. Frazer considers the Eleusinian Mysteries to be one of countless examples of ancient beliefs across many different cultures around the world in the 'imitative magic' of sexual regeneration resulting in vegetal regeneration.[76]

Frazer pays particular attention to the 'imitative magic' of fertility rituals 'to quicken the growth of trees' and the veneration of 'tree-spirits' that make crops grow (for which Frazer gives, among many others, Japan as an example, citing Aston's *Shinto*), give rain and bless women with offspring.[77] In its celebration of sexual and vegetal regeneration, *Takasago* thus bears comparison with the Eleusinian Mysteries. In *A Draft of the Cantos 17-27*, the entire Eleusinian section that concludes Canto XXI is included under the marginal note '*Takasago and Ise*'; Pound's pencilled instruction in the draft, 'ital. in marg', indicates this as his deliberate choice rather than Rodker's.[78] This conditions our reading of the following lines depicting the dawn after the 'night' of the Eleusinian Mysteries:

> Shore to the eastward, and altered,
> And the old man sweeping leaves.
>   'Damned to you Midas, Midas lacking a Pan!'
> And now in the valley,
> Valley under day's edge: *Takasago*
>   'Grow with the pines of Ise   *and*
> 'As the Nile swells with Inopos.   *Ise*
>   'As the Nile falls with Inopos.'[79]

In the light of this marginal note, the 'Shore to the eastward' is 'altered' to that of Takasago and, 'to the eastward' of Takasago, Sumiyoshi. The 'old man sweeping

---

[75] James Frazer, *The Golden Bough*, 3rd edn, vol. 2 (London: Macmillan, 1911), 120.
[76] Ibid., 97.
[77] Ibid., 21, 47 and 50.
[78] *17-27*, 27; *EPP*, 3198.
[79] Ibid.

leaves' is the 'old man' sweeping the 'pine-needles', the 'inexhaustible words' of the fertile literary tradition, who reveals himself to be the virile Sumiyoshi deity. The following line is not, of course, from *Takasago* but refers to the tale of Midas in the *Metamorphoses*. In relation to *Takasago*, though, it suggests that 'the country well governed' depends on sexual, vegetal and literary fertility; it does not merely depend on gold, as Jefferson and de' Medici had understood.

As in Canto IV, the 'pines of Ise' allude to Kannon's 'light' that 'rains' and 'pours' on the 'pine-moor of Anono' in Ise in *Tamura*. It is in Canto XXI that Pound first establishes the correspondence between Isis and Kannon that he would make in Canto CX in the form of 'Isis Kuanon'.[80] Just as the pines of Takasago and Sumiyoshi are said to be paired, in Callimachus's hymns to Artemis and Delos the River Inopos on the island of Delos is said to rise and fall with the Nile.[81] Frazer observes that 'the Egyptians held a festival of Isis when the Nile began to rise' as it is Isis 'who maketh the Nile to swell'.[82] Frazer also claims that Isis is connected with Demeter, the 'corn-goddess' of the Eleusinian Mysteries: Isis 'must surely have been a corn-goddess'; the Greeks 'identified her with Demeter'.[83] Not only does Pound find in *The Golden Bough*'s depiction of Isis a parallel for Kannon as a goddess of fertility; he could also have read there how, 'when men's minds were disquieted, when the fabric of empire itself, once deemed eternal, began to show ominous rents and fissures, the serene figure of Isis with her spiritual calm [. . .] should have roused in their breasts a rapture of devotion not unlike that which was paid in the Middle Ages to the Virgin Mary'.[84] It is thus perhaps for this reason, too, that Pound finds a parallel between Isis and Kannon: the latter, for Pound, is likewise a 'serene figure' of 'spiritual calm', whose 'arrows of wisdom' and 'bow of "Great Mercy"' cast out 'evil spirits' and, as Pound puts it in the *Poetry* and *Lustra* versions of 'Three Cantos – I', has 'one hand upraised for gladness' as she blesses the 'flowers' of the spring. Underpinning this regeneration, though, as in *Takasago* and *Tamura*, is the political order brought about by such 'outstanding personalities' as Jefferson and de' Medici.

Even before the publication of *A Draft of the Cantos 17-27* had been completed, Pound was at work on three more cantos to complete the first set of thirty. 'Am blocking in Cantos 28-30 but they wont affect the present volume', Pound wrote

---

[80] *SRD*, 66.
[81] H. W. Tytler (trans.), *The Works of Callimachus* (London: T. Davison, 1793), 94 and 134.
[82] Frazer, *The Golden Bough*, vol. 6, 33.
[83] Ibid., 117.
[84] Ibid., 118.

to his father on 7 September 1927.[85] Pound also explained to his father his 'main scheme' for *The Cantos*:

A.   A. Live man goes down into world of Dead
C.   B. the 'repeat in history'
B.   C. the 'magic moment' or moment of metamorphosis, bust thru from quotidien into 'divine or permanent world'. Gods etc.[86]

The journey of the 'Live man' who 'goes down into world of Dead' most obviously recalls Odysseus in Canto I and Dante in the *Divina Commedia*; but it also corresponds with the journey of the *waki* who goes down into the world of the dead in nō such as *Nishikigi, Kayoi Komachi, Suma Genji, Kumasaka, Tamura, Kagekiyo, Awoi no Uye, Kakitsubata* and *Takasago*. Canto XXI illustrates the 'repeat in history' of Jefferson and Lorenzo de' Medici, who are juxtaposed across vast spatial and temporal distances as examples of 'intelligent constructivity'. The 'bust thru from quotidien into "divine or permanent world"' is the live past, the life force that is permanent, charging the present with its energy, the 'Ghosts' that 'move about' the speaker of 'Three Cantos – I' and Canto II, 'patched with histories'. This occurs as a metamorphosis in nō such as *Takasago*, in which the old man and woman reveal themselves to be the spirits of the pines: the 'inexhaustible' pine needles in Pound's translation of it depict the life force that is permanently present.

Pound's continued interest in nō throughout the 1920s is shown not only in his use of the themes of *Takasago* and *Tamura* in particular in *The Cantos* but also in the enthusiasm of his proposal to Glenn Hughes and Yozan T. Iwasaki to publish a revised version of his nō translations. On 9 November 1927, he wrote to Hughes that he wondered 'if Iwasaki is trained in Noh or if you and he want to undertake revision of my redaction of Fenollosa's papers on the Noh'.[87] He was unable to do so himself because 'I had not the philological competence necessary for an ultimate version'.[88] He needed 'a Jap [*sic*] on the job [. . .] who knows Noh'.[89] As he later reflected, 'since Tami Koumé was killed in that earth quake I have had no one to explain the obscure passages or fill up the enormous gaps of my IGNORANCE' about nō.[90] Pound also clearly felt that there would be interest in a revised edition: 'If the work were copper-bottomed and guaranteed

---

[85]   Pound, letter to Homer Pound (7 September 1927), in *L/HP*, 636.
[86]   Pound, letter to Homer Pound (11 April 1927), in *L/HP*, 626.
[87]   Pound, letter to Glenn Hughes (9 November 1927), in *L*, 214.
[88]   Ibid.
[89]   Ibid.
[90]   Pound, letter to Kitasono (24 May 1936), in *EPJ*, 27–8.

complete in every detail, I don't think there ought to be difficulty in getting a good publisher or in making it the "standard work on the subject".[91] 'I shd. like to protect Fenollosa', Pound wrote, 'from sonzovbitches like – [. . .] who knows a little Nipponese' and had produced 'flatfooted renderings'.[92] Pound here probably refers to Waley, who, after assisting Pound with *'Noh' or Accomplishment*, had published *The Nō Plays of Japan*. Waley's versions frequently borrowed Pound's phrasing, such as Kagekiyo's praising 'how strong the shaft' of Mionoya's neck is, while criticizing Pound and Fenollosa's understanding of *Awoi no Uye*: 'There is nothing obscure or ambiguous' in the play, he writes, despite Pound's claim it 'presents various difficulties'.[93] Following Kume's death, Pound had no Japanese to assist him in revising his nō translations; nevertheless, his willingness to do so is clear.

The emphasis in Pound's 'main scheme' on recurrence is already shown in the repetitions of the Diana, Danaë, *Takasago* and *Tamura* motifs in Cantos IV and XXI; these recur once more in the paradisal vision of Canto XXIX. 'Cantos 28-30' were eventually published in the *Hound & Horn* in April 1930 and included that August in *A Draft of XXX Cantos* in an edition of 212 copies published by Nancy Cunard, who had taken over the Three Mountains Press and renamed it the Hours Press. Canto XXIX presents the culminating paradisal vision for *A Draft of XXX Cantos* as a whole. Its opening lines allude to Dante's *Paradiso*:

> Pearl, great sphere, and hollow,
> Mist over lake, full of sunlight[94]

Dante's heaven is described as 'l'eterna margerita' ('the eternal pearl') in Canto II of the *Paradiso*; in Canto IX of the *Paradiso*, it is a 'sfera' ('sphere') that 'scintilla, / come un raggio di sole in acqua mera' ('sparkles / as the sun's ray in pure water'). In Canto IX, Dante encounters Cunizza da Romano in the third sphere, that of the planet Venus, who tells him she 'quire folgo, / perchè mi vinse il lume d'estra stella' ('here I glow because the light of this star overcame me').[95] Cunizza appears in Canto XXIX as someone who has loved ('The light of this star o'ercame me'): first, she loves Sordello, 'who lay with her in Tarviso', then 'a soldier named Bonius'; later, she shows another form of love in freeing her father's 'serfs'.[96] Dante does not make clear why she is in heaven. Pound's

---

[91] Pound, letter to Hughes (9 November 1927), in *L*, 214.
[92] Ibid.
[93] Waley, *The Nō Plays of Japan* (London: George Allen & Unwin, 1921), 133 and 180.
[94] Ibid., 135.
[95] Dante, *The Paradiso*, 16–17 and 108–9.
[96] *XXX*, 135–6.

account of her emancipation of serfs suggests this act of love may have been the cause.

Just as Jefferson and Lorenzo de' Medici constitute a parallel of 'intelligent constructivity' in Canto XXI, Cunizza's love is 'rhymed' in the canto with that of a figure who bears a striking resemblance to H. D., as Emily Mitchell Wallace has argued.[97] In H. D.'s *HERmione*, completed in 1927, George Lowndes, a pseudonym for Pound, meets 'Hermione', that of H. D., in *'the forest primeval, the murmuring pines and the hemlocks'*. 'You have an octopus intelligence', George tells Hermione; 'Hermione let octopus-Hermione reach out and up and with a thousand eyes regard space and distance'.[98] When she is 'thrown flat on wood moss', George 'let light through to fall on her face'.[99] 'Under the sea, deep down in her deep-sea consciousness', Hermione 'was putting out premature feelers; octopus became potato in a cellar. George stepped through suddenly as through an open stuck-fast cellar window' before 'The kisses of George smudged out her clear geometric thinking'.[100] This affects our reading of the following lines in Canto XXIX:

> Wein, Weib, TAN AOIDAN
> Chiefest of these the second, the female
> Is an element, the female
> Is a chaos
> An octopus[101]

This passage not only corresponds with H. D.'s account of George and Hermione's encounter in the forest; George's letting light pour onto Hermione's face and her 'deap-sea consciousness' also recalls the sunlight on the lake at the start of the canto and Dante's description of his body entering paradise in Canto II of the *Paradiso* as 'com' acqua recepe / raggio di luce' ('as water doth receive a ray of light').[102] Cunizza and H. D.'s love contrasts with the sterility, the 'vain emptiness' of the 'ephebe' and the 'virgins' who 'return to their homes' unsatisfied.[103]

As in Canto XXI, the canto concludes on the recurrence of the Eleusinian motif that forms, as Leon Surette suggests, the 'imaginative heart' of *The*

---

[97] Wallace, 'Interior of 166 Fernbrook Avenue'.
[98] H. D., *HERmione*, 71.
[99] Ibid., 72.
[100] Ibid., 72–3.
[101] *XXX*, 138.
[102] Ibid., 139; Dante, *The Paradiso*, 16–17.
[103] *XXX*, 137.

194   *Ezra Pound's Japan*

Cantos.[104] 'Let us consider the osmosis of persons', the speaker proposes.[105] We see, as in Canto IV and Canto XXI, the 'Tower, ivory, the clear sky / Ivory rigid in sunlight', that of Danaë impregnated by Zeus; the 'Blossom cut on the wind' recalls 'Spring and Aufidus fill[ing] the air / With their clear-outlined blossoms' in 'Three Cantos – I', the 'brook-film bearing white petals' of Canto IV, and the 'petal borne in the wind' in Canto XXI; and the 'white hounds on the slope' are, again, the 'dogs' that 'leap on Actaeon' in Canto IV and the 'hounds on the green slope of Canto XXI.[106] The canto then ends:

> Pine by the black trunk of its shadow
> And on hill, black trunks of the shadow
> The trees melted in air.[107]

The pines of Takasago and Ise recur in Canto XXI along with these other images of sexual and vegetal regeneration; in this light, the 'Pine by the black trunk of its shadow' can be read as the pines of *Takasago* and *Tamura*. As in Canto IV and Canto XXI, the pines illustrate the canto's theme of sexual and vegetal regeneration; here, however, the union is completed through a final 'osmosis', 'The trees melted in air', just as Hermione's 'deep-sea consciousness' is 'smudged' by George's letting 'light pour on her face' and Dante's body merges into the 'sphere' of paradise like 'a ray of sunlight on pure water'. The melting of the trees 'in air' also echoes the celestial maiden's return to paradise in Pound's translation of *Hagoromo*: in the final lines, as she rises over Mount Fuji, the mountain 'melts into the upper mist. In this way she (the Tennin) is lost to sight'.[108]

In this way, the pines of Takasago and Ise provide the culminating paradisal vision not just for Canto XXIX, but for *A Draft of XXX Cantos* as a whole. Pound's suggestion to Monroe that 'The theme' of *The Cantos* would be 'roughly the theme of "Takasago"' thus applies to *A Draft of XXX Cantos*, which is constructed around this recurring vision of the 'divine and permanent world' of the 'gods'. The composition of *The Cantos* was begun by Pound's contrasting of a destructive West that had descended into a barbaric war that had killed Gaudier-Brzeska with the peaceful prosperity of Eastern benevolent imperial rule in which, as in *Takasago*, 'The waves of the whole sea are quiet, / The country well governed', and the pine needles of sexual, vegetal, and literary regeneration are

---

[104] Leon Surette, *A Light for Eleusis: A Study of Ezra Pound's Cantos* (Oxford: Clarendon Press, 1979), 67.
[105] *XXX*, 139.
[106] Ibid.
[107] Ibid., 140.
[108] *NA*, 176.

'inexhaustible'. From the 'MS A' draft of the 'Three Cantos' published in *Poetry* and *Lustra* onwards, the 'way to paradise' the earliest drafts of *The Cantos* sought is lighted by Kannon. Her presence in *The Cantos* remains clear through the recurrent references to the 'pines of Ise', where her 'light' conquers the 'evil spirits'. The correspondence of the pines in *Takasago* and *Tamura* parallels the 'equipoise' of 'Eleusinian energy' and 'Kungian order' Pound sought in *The Cantos*: the regeneration suggested by the 'inexhaustible' pine needles and the coming of the spring in *Takasago* and *Tamura* is paired with the order of imperial rule sustaining it in both plays. Despite Pound's criticism of nō as 'too damn soft' in 1918, the centrality of *Takasago* and *Tamura* in the 'Eleusinian' cantos in *A Draft of XXX Cantos* demonstrates that nō remained important to Pound throughout the 1920s. Furthermore, the political as well as aesthetic 'unity' that Pound had discovered in these plays anticipated what he later concluded the 1920s meant for him: 'the new synthesis, the totalitarian'.[109]

---

[109] *GK*, 95.

11

'A treasure like nothing we have in the Occident'

Pound's wartime cantos and nō

Following Itō's departure to America in 1916, Kume's death in 1923, and Pound's move to Rapallo the following year after his move to Japan fell through, Pound's contact with Japanese was cut off until 26 April 1936, when a Japanese poet, Kitasono Katué, wrote to him. Their correspondence would last some three decades. In Kitasono's first letter, he asked if Pound could 'make some ideas of our group', the *VOU* magazine Kitasono had founded in July 1935:

> For a long time, since Imagism movement, we have always expected you as a leader on new literature. Especially your profound appreciation in the Chinese literature and the Japanese literature has greatly pleased us.[1]

Pound's response to Kitasono's first letter demonstrates his continued enthusiasm for Japanese literature, especially nō. He lamented to Kitasono that 'since Tami Koumé was killed in that earth quake I have had no one to explain the obscure passages or fill up the enormous gaps of my IGNORANCE' about nō.[2] Pound goes on to state Japan's importance for him: 'Two things I should do before I die, and they are to contrive a better understanding between the U.S.A. and Japan, and between Italy and Japan.'[3] Kitasono's correspondence rekindled his curiosity about nō, as his sending to Kitasono on 29 January 1937 of an article on the first television performance of *Suma Genji*, based on Pound's translation, indicates. This chapter argues that the still widely held view that Pound's interest in nō ceased in 1917 is untrue; as the next chapter shows, this perception was based on the lack of widespread access in the 1950s to Pound's correspondence and

---

[1] Kitasono, letter to Pound (26 April 1936), in *EPJ*, 27.
[2] Pound, letter to Kitasono (24 May 1936), in ibid., 27–8.
[3] Ibid., 28.

Japanese publications. From 1936, Pound's enthusiasm for nō grew stronger than ever and would remain so for the rest of his life.

Pound's *Suma Genji* was first performed at the Players' Theatre in Covent Garden on 27 December 1936 as part of a variety programme directed by Peter Ridgeway; the music was by William Alwyn.[4] The television performance Pound informed Kitasono of, though, was broadcast from Alexandra Palace, the BBC's television transmission centre since 1935, on 7 January 1937. The *Morning Post* article of the following day was translated by Kitasono and appeared in the March 1937 issue of *VOU*; it found *Suma Genji* to be 'one of the most felicitous' performances of the programme.[5] The *waki*, the monk visiting Suma, was played by Leonard Sachs and, in a reversal of the exclusively male acting in traditional professional nō, the lead role of Genji by Margaret Leona, who also arranged the choreography.[6] According to a 26 January letter Leona had sent to Pound, the performance departed significantly from Japanese nō: the musical accompaniment consisted of a harp and a Western flute; Leona performed barefoot in a 'crepe' dress 'representing a kimono' with 'sleeves that reached down to the ground' to suggest the 'grey waves' pattern'; and the background consisted of a 'grey screen' showing 'the outline of snow-capped mountains and five branches of trees with blossoming flowers'.[7] Pound's enthusiasm for the performance is suggested by his proudly asserting that, 'at any rate, some of the Beauty has been brought over to the occident'.[8]

Pound's reawakened appreciation of nō is evident in his article, 'Totalitarian Scholarship and the New Paideuma', published in the National Socialist propaganda journal *Germany and You* on 25 April 1937. Pound asserts the 'need of a new methodology', that of 'the reintegration of the arts in totalitarian synthesis'.[9] This would consist not only of seeing the interrelations between different art forms but also of 'each nation' being able to 'give its valid part' to 'World Literature' and 'receive in turn the primal and valid donations of other races'.[10] Pound gives the example of his having 'helped to bring the Ta Hio [*sic*] and the poems of Li Po (Rihaku) and the great plays of Japan ("Kagekiyo",

---

[4] Adrian Wright, *The Innumerable Dance: The Life and Work of William Alwyn* (Woodbridge: Baydell Press, 2008), 74.
[5] Kitasono, 'Eikoku ni okeru "Suma Genji" no jōen' ('A Performance of *Suma Genji* in Britain'), *VOU* 17 (March 1937): 29.
[6] Ibid.
[7] Ibid., 29–30.
[8] Pound, letter to Kitasono (29 January 1937), in *EPJ*, 36.
[9] Pound, 'Totalitarian Scholarship', 95 and 96.
[10] Ibid., 96.

"Hagoromo", etc.), into English'.[11] The 'old Bushido spirit' Pound had found in *Kagekiyo* and the association of *Hagoromo* with benevolent imperial rule are brought together in Pound's article under the banner of his new artistic method of 'totalitarian synthesis'. They are not only chosen because of Japan's developing alliance with Italy and Germany, which was to be consolidated in the anti-Comintern pact later that year. Pound describes the fascist 'march on Rome' as the 'new phase' that 'followed the work of Wyndham Lewis and Gaudier-Brzeska'.[12] The nō plays themselves also portray, in *Kagekiyo*'s case, the courage of the 'men in action' in the 'march on Rome' that Pound thus explicitly saw as the 'new phase' of the Vorticist movement and, in *Hagoromo*'s case, the veneration of imperial rule that underpinned Pound's turn to fascism.

Pound's estimation of nō as among the 'primal and valid donations of other races' at this time extended to Japanese literature more generally. In his first letter to Kitasono, he had responded to Kitasono's explanation of *VOU* as having 'started from Dada and passed Surrealism' by claiming that 'if <some of> the Noh plays are not surrealist in the best sense, I shd. welcome a statement as to what they shd. be called'.[13] Pound and Kitasono evidently subscribed to a similar conception of modernity according to which different cultures and periods were considered as being at less or more developed stages of a universal model of what constitutes cultural progress; thus, in the example above, Pound sees nō as being as 'modern' as surrealism, as Bush points out.[14] As early as *The Spirit of Romance*, Pound had proposed that 'All ages are contemporaneous. It is B. C., let us say, in Morocco. The Middle Ages are in Russia. The future already stirs in the minds of a few.'[15] This way of thinking allows Pound to make cross-cultural comparisons and evaluate the 'donations' of 'races' as being 'primal and valid' or not. In his January 1938 introduction of poems by members of Kitasono's *VOU* magazine in Ronald Duncan's *Townsman*, this conception of modernity is also evident: 'it may be that from now on any man who wants to write English poetry will have to start reading Japanese.'[16] He concludes by remarking that 'nowhere in Europe is there any such vortex of poetic alertness. Tokio takes over, where Paris stopped.'[17] Pound's recalibrating of 'Tokio' as the new global 'vortex' of

---

[11] Ibid.
[12] Ibid., 95.
[13] Pound, letter to Kitasono (24 May 1936), in *EPJ*, 28.
[14] Bush, 'The Geopolitical Aesthetic', 97.
[15] Pound, *The Spirit of Romance*, vi.
[16] Pound, 'VOU Club', *Townsman* 1, no. 1 (January 1938): 4.
[17] Ibid.

'poetic alertness' is commendable in its movement away from Eurocentrism but nonetheless relies on a problematic universal model of cultural development.

In his other publications following the beginning of his correspondence with Kitasono, Pound continues to demonstrate his renewed interest in nō. In his *Guide to Kulchur*, published the year after *The Fifth Decad of Cantos*, he discusses nō in several instances. Before his discussion of nō, Pound returns to his allusion to Brinkley's account of 'listening to incense' in his 1915 *Drama* article on 'The Classical Stage of Japan'. The first of the 'ideogrammic' ways in which to define 'CIVILIZATION', according to Pound, is this 'pastime', which shows a 'high degree of civilization'.[18] The second is 'Noh': 'Fenollosa is said to have been the second European to be able to take part in Noh performance', Pound claims.[19] 'The whole civilization reflected in Noh', he concludes, 'is a high civilization'.[20] He gives as examples the nō plays *Kumasaka* and *Kagekiyo*. Of the former, he writes that 'The ghost of Kumasaka returns not from a grudge and not to gain anything; but to state clearly that the very young man who had killed him had not done so by a fluke or slip, but that he had outfenced him'.[21] Regarding *Kagekiyo*, Pound repeats his association of Kagekiyo with a 'Homeric robustness' that parallels the 'rugged endurance' he had discovered in Li Bai's poetry. Pound thus sought to portray nō as something not to be associated with an effeminate *Japonisme* – 'The Noh is not merely painting on silk or nuances *à la* Chas. Condor [sic]', the latter an artist influenced by Japanese painting as Whistler had been – but as one with the masculine virtues of 'the old Bushido spirit'.[22]

Pound's veneration of this 'old Bushido spirit' bears comparison with the arguments that had been made in Japan in favour of promoting nō as a vehicle for encouraging and reinforcing militaristic nationalism. As Chapter 5 shows, publications such as the magazine *Nōgaku* emphasized how soldiers were inspired by nō chants on the battlefield in the First Sino-Japanese War; Umewaka himself performed war songs and nō plays celebrating Japan's military victories; and it had been claimed that nō was 'martial music' imbued with *Yamatodamashii* ('Japanese spirit') that 'encourages the veneration of the emperor and love of the country'.[23] Pound had understood this connection between nō and an imperialism supported by strong military force in his translations of *Tamura* and *Takasago*; Yeats's earlier repetition of Aston's anecdote of the Japanese battleship

---

[18] *GK*, 80.
[19] Ibid., 81.
[20] Ibid.
[21] Ibid.
[22] *NA*, 188.
[23] 'Sensō to nōgaku', 2.

named after *Takasago* encapsulated his understanding of the relationship between nō and the modern 'Bushido spirit' that had led to Japan's more recent military victories. The historical context of Pound's praise of nō in *Guide to Kulchur* is no less significant: Italy had joined the anti-Comintern pact with Germany and Japan in November 1937.[24] His demand in the book for 'Tokio' to supply 'editions of the Odes, the *Ta Hio* and the four *Classics*, *Li Po* (Rihaku), and at least 400 pages of the post-Confucian great poets, and a few dozen Noh dramas' also indicates Pound's recognition of Japan as the inheritor and rightful possessor of the Chinese cultural tradition he admired.

Performances of Pound's nō continued after those of *Suma Genji*. In October 1938, Pound returned to London to arrange the disposal of Dorothy's mother Olivia's possessions following her death on 3 October. Noel Stock's biography mentions Pound's interest in putting on a 'Noh play':

> He [Pound] badly wanted to put on a Noh play performed in a theatre and to this end Ronald Duncan persuaded Ashley Dukes to lend them the Mercury Theatre. Benjamin Britten produced a musician who could play gongs and another of Duncan's friends, Henry Boys, suggested a female dancer named Surita Magito. One afternoon, with Duncan as audience, Pound recited one of his own translations while the girl danced.[25]

The Mercury Theatre at 2 Ladbroke Road, Notting Hill, was another prestigious venue for the performance: Eliot's *Murder in the Cathedral* and Auden's *The Ascent of F6* had been performed there in 1935 and 1937, respectively. Moody's more recent biography adds that 'In the sparse audience were Lewis and Eliot'.[26] Pound did not mention this performance in his letters to Kitasono, Lewis or Eliot, and it is as yet unclear which of Pound's nō plays was performed. Britten's letter to Duncan of 3 October, however, notes that an adaptation of a nō performance on which Pound collaborated with Britten and Duncan was already being planned before Olivia's death.[27] It is possible that Pound drew on Leona's adaptation of *Suma Genji*, which likewise featured a female actor in the lead role. It is clear, in any case, that the performance demonstrates the continued development of Pound's enthusiasm for nō following the start of his correspondence with Kitasono.

---

[24] Reto Hofmann, *The Fascist Effect: Japan and Italy, 1915-1952* (Ithaca: Cornell University Press, 2015), 111.
[25] Noel Stock, *The Life of Ezra Pound* (Harmondsworth: Penguin, 1974), 454.
[26] Moody, *Ezra Pound: Poet*, vol. 2, 302.
[27] Benjamin Britten, letter to Ronald Duncan (3 October 1938), in Donald Mitchell and Philip Reed (eds), *Letters from a Life: Selected Letters and Diaries of Benjamin Britten*, vol. 1 (London: Faber & Faber, 1991), 587.

Published soon after these dance performances of Pound's nō translations, another of his contributions to fascist periodicals further suggests the close connection between his aesthetics and his politics. In the October–December 1938 issue of Oswald Mosley's fascist magazine, the *British Union Quarterly*, he proposes that 'THE STATE SHOULD MOVE LIKE A DANCE'.[28] If there were any form of dance that embodied such a fusion of his aesthetics and politics at this time, it was nō. The Vorticist aesthetics of the 'Unity of Image' that Pound had identified in his translations of plays such as *Suma Genji* and *Takasago*, with the latter also explicitly emphasizing a political unity through the paired pines 'growing together' while 'the whole country' is 'well governed', merges with his fascist-inspired politics of a similarly idealized social coherence. As in Pound's translation of *Tamura*, however, this social harmony is enforced through military strength: just as Kannon's light 'pours' on the 'banners' of Tamuramaro's troops to dispel the 'evil spirits' on the 'pine-moor of Anono' in Ise, the fascist 'march on Rome', which Pound saw as the continuation of what Lewis and Gaudier had started, Italy's invasion of Abyssinia, and Japan's of China, including the Nanjing massacre, had already occurred by the time Pound's article appeared in Mosley's magazine. Pound had justified Italy's colonial invasion of Abyssinia on the grounds that 'Italy needs colonies to EMPLOY her sons [. . .] she damn well needs Abyssinia to INSURE economic independence'.[29]

During this time, Pound even revived his interest in moving to Japan, which Kume had been arranging before he was killed in the Great Kantō earthquake of 1923, as discussed in Chapter 10. Kitasono thanks Pound for a now-no-longer-extant letter dated 5 May 1938 in which Pound must have made enquiries about such a move: Kitasono advises that 'In Formosa the climate is not good and I cannot encourage you to become a professor there. I think Tokio Imperial University or Kyoto Imperial University is most suitable for you. I will watch to obtain such an opportunity.'[30] Perhaps the most significant turning point in Pound's estimation of nō occurs in his 3 March 1939 letter to Kitasono:

> I have <had strong> nostalgia for Japan, induced by the fragment of Noh in *Mitsuco*. If you can continue such films nothing in the West can resist. We shall expect you AT LAST to deliver us from Hollywood and unbounded cheapness.
>
> ALL the Noh plays ought to be filmed/or at any rate ALL the music shd/ be recorded on the *sound track*.

---

[28] Pound, 'The State Should Move Like a Dance', 44.
[29] Pound, letter to Odon Por (4 April 1936), in Tim Redman, *Ezra Pound and Italian Fascism* (Cambridge: Cambridge University Press, 2009), 168.
[30] Kitasono, letter to Pound (23 July 1938), in *EPJ*, 66–7.

> It must be 16 years since I heard a note of Noh (Kumé and his friends sang it to me in Paris) but the instant the Noh (all too little of it in that film) sounded I knew it.
> It is like no other music.[31]

Not only does Pound's letter indicate his 'nostalgia' for the nō Kume performed for him in London and Paris; it is when he sees '*Mitsuco*', rather than the entire film of *Aoi no ue* the following month in Washington, DC, as Pellecchia claims, that Pound's interest in nō significantly intensifies.[32] This was the first time that he saw nō being professionally performed by one of the nō schools.[33] At this point, he is far from considering nō to be 'unsatisfactory' or 'too damn soft', as he had felt in 1918 following the mixed reception of *'Noh' or Accomplishment*. Pound is now unequivocal in his praise of it as 'like no other music'. Pound would reiterate his demand for 'ALL the Noh plays' to be 'filmed' throughout the war in his *Japan Times* articles and radio broadcasts.

'*Mitsuco*' refers, as Pellecchia and Bush note, to the Japanese-German film *Atarashiki tsuchi* ('New Land'), first released in Japan on 4 February 1937. The title's 'new land' is Manchuria, which Japan had invaded on 18 September 1931 and subsequently colonized. The film's lead character, Yamato Teruo (whose surname, an archaic native Japanese name for Japan, suggests his association with *Yamatodamashii*, 'Japanese spirit') is torn between his feelings for his German friend Gerda Storm and his duty to marry his adoptive father's daughter, Mitsuko (played by a sixteen-year-old Hara Setsuko) when he returns to Japan with Gerda. When Gerda asks him if he wants to return to Europe, he replies to her in German, 'No, Gerda. I am Japanese and live for Japan.'[34] He explains that he was looking at Manchuria, where there is 'new land' ('neue Erde') that is 'richly abundant'; but first 'order and peace' ('Ordnung und Frieden') must be established, which is 'the mission of the Japanese people'. Teruo's patriotism is rekindled by his reacquaintance with a series of scenes that seek to represent Japanese culture. As he wrestles with his dilemma, his adoptive sister, Rieko, says to him that 'If you let the wind of Japan blow on you, you'll soon get better'; 'look', she tells him, 'the spring is so beautiful'. Cherry blossoms scatter on the river; lanterns light the blossoms at night; they listen to traditional music and dancing; they attend a performance of the nō play *Aoi no ue*; and he visits his teacher, a Buddhist monk, at the latter's temple.

---

[31] Ibid.
[32] Pellecchia, 'Ezra Pound and the Politics of Noh Film', 503.
[33] Ibid., 501; Bush, 'The Geopolitical Aesthetic', 97.
[34] *Atarashiki tsuchi* ('New Land'), dir. by Arnold Franck and Itami Mansaku (J. O. Studios, 1937).

'A Treasure Like Nothing We Have in the Occident' 203

The monk's words of advice are then spoken by an invisible narrator in German. 'It is necessary to learn the knowledge of the west', his teacher tells him. The 'thoughts' and 'feelings' of 'what your ancestors thought', 'gathered over thousands of years and encapsulated in the short word "Shinto"' (despite the monk being Buddhist and the various shots of Buddhist statues in the temple that appear as the German narrator tells Teruo the teacher's words), is that 'as an individual, you are not so important'. 'You are', he says to Teruo, 'but a link in the long chain of generations of your ancestors'. 'Your blood', he continues, 'is but a drop in the eternal stream of life'. The 'respect' you must show to 'your father' is 'a symbol of your love and gratitude for all of this', which for 'us' has 'the name "Japan"'. The scattered petals floating down the river in the earlier scene thus take on a significance similar to that of the 'brook film bearing white petals' in Canto IV: both represent the ever-recurring regeneration of the spring and the energizing life force bearing the petals of individual existence. In both, too, this regeneration is underpinned by benevolent imperial rule: in the case of *Takasago* and *Tamura*, sources for this image in Canto IV, it is the 'country well governed'; likewise, in *Atarashiki tsuchi*, it is the empire of Japan.

The metaphor of racial 'blood' is also evident in Teruo's comment to Rieko as they watch *Aoi no ue* (for which the film used the same footage of *Aoi no ue* Pound would later see in Washington, DC): when Rieko asks if he understands the play's archaic words, he replies that he does not 'understand them well. But I feel that the ancestral blood within me profoundly comprehends it.'[35] The play's exorcism scene that they watch as they speak ties into the film's theme of 'exorcising' Teruo's earlier attachment to Western thought, which had vied with his 'Japanese spirit'. At the film's conclusion, Teruo and Mitsuko marry and move to the 'new land' of Manchuria. As Teruo tills this new land in his Komatsu tractor, protected by a Japanese soldier standing guard, Mitsuko carries their newborn baby in the field and Teruo lays it down on the soil.[36] The film thus connects the fertility of the 'new land' with that of the couple and the Japanese empire in a manner comparable with *Takasago*, whose paired pines represent sexual as well as vegetal and political regeneration. Pound's praise of nō is motivated by the parallels he detected between its politicized aesthetics and his own turn towards 'the new synthesis, the totalitarian'.

In the same letter, Pound also told Kitasono that 'There is a mention of Japan at the edge of my Cantos'.[37] This was Canto LVIII, part of Pound's 'China

---

[35] Ibid., 45:30–45:37.
[36] Ibid., 1:42:55–1:45:17.
[37] Pound, letter to Kitasono (3 March 1939), in *EPJ*, 72.

Cantos', which drew extensively on the eighteenth-century Jesuit Joseph Anne-Marie de Moyriac de Mailla's *Histoire générale de la Chine*, a translation of the *Tongjian gangmu* ('Outline of the Comprehensive Mirror'), attributed to the neo-Confucian philosopher Zhu Xi (1130–1200). The canto opens with 'Sinbu' (de Mailla's transcription of the legendary founding Emperor Jimmu), who 'put order in Sun land, Nippon, in the beginning of all things'.[38] 'Sun land, Nippon' is not in de Mailla but recalls Pound's *Hagoromo* translation, in which the gods bless 'Nippon, the sun's field'.[39] 'Sinbu' and the imperial dynasty are descendants, like nō, of 'Ten Seo DAISIN', the sun goddess or, in Pound's rendering in *'Noh' or Accomplishment*, the 'light-goddess', Amaterasu.[40] 'Shogun Joritomo', Minamoto no Yoritomo (1147–89), who fought with the Genji against the Heike of Kagekiyo, is another Poundian 'outstanding personality', as he 'put an end to internal wars' and brought about the cultural prosperity that later allowed nō to flourish. That the shōgunate 'drove the Xtians out of Japan / till there were none of that sect on the island' because of 'the hauteur of Portagoose prelates', an event absent in de Mailla but recorded in Brinkley's *Japan* and Fenollosa's *Epochs*, would have met with Pound's approval: in 1938 he had told Kitasono that Christianity and Buddhism 'do not lead to clear thinking', a view reiterated throughout *The Cantos*.[41] Pound's revived interest led him to asking Kitasono for 'a "Tong Kien Kang Mou" of Japan'; he had found M. J. Klaproth's translation of the *Nipon* [sic] *Dai itsi ran*', Hayashi Gahō's (1618–88) seven-volume *Nihon ōdai ichiran* ('A Chronicle of Japan's Rulers') of 1652 but expressed disappointment that it is 'mere chronicle'.[42] Indeed, though detailed, its description of events is terse, without the *Tongjian gangmu*'s analytical depth. If Pound had found a translated history like de Mailla's, the China Cantos could have been combined with, or followed by, 'Japan Cantos'. As the *Pisan Cantos* would demonstrate, the composition of *The Cantos* depended on the circumstances of contemporary politics and the availability of materials.

On 27 March 1939, shortly before his departure to America on 13 April to receive an honorary doctorate from his alma mater, Hamilton College, Pound sent his first two 'brief notes for the *Japan Times*', for which he had begun to write through the intervention of Kitasono, who arranged for Pound to write for

---

[38] Pound, *The Cantos*, 316; Joseph Anne-Marie de Moyriac de Mailla, *Histoire générale de la Chine, ou Annales de cet empire*, 13 vols, vol. 10 (Paris: Pierres et Clousier, 1779), 356.
[39] *NA*, 174.
[40] de Mailla, *Histoire*, vol. 10, 356; *NA*, 58.
[41] Brinkley, *Japan*, vol. 3, 103; *ECJA*, vol. 2, 114; Pound, *The Cantos*, 316; Kitasono, letter to Pound (23 July 1938), in *EPJ*, 68.
[42] Pound, letter to Kitasono (3 March 1939), in ibid., 73.

the *Japan Times and Mail* with its editor, Mōri Yasotarō (1882–1959). These were published on 15 May and 5 June. As Pound had told Kitasono in his letter earlier in March, he writes in his first article:

> The whole of the Noh could be filmed, or at any rate the best Noh music could be registered on sound-track. Your film Mitsuko filled me with nostalgia. It is 15 years since Tami Koumé's friends sang me fragments of Noh in Paris but the instant I heard that all too brief reproduction here in Rapallo (in a small village cinema) I knew whence it came. You have there a treasure like nothing in the Occident. We have our masterwork: Mozart, Purcell, Janequin, Dowland.[43]

Whereas in 1918 he had found nō to be 'unsatisfactory' and 'too damn soft', his enthusiasm for it was now undeniable and expressed in the strongest terms: it is 'a treasure like nothing in the Occident', on a par with Pound's favourite Western composers. In his attempt further to promote nō's importance in the west, Pound was putting into action his 'Totalitarian Scholarship', through which the 'primal and valid donations of other races' are transmitted to each other.

Soon after reaching America, Pound visited the Library of Congress on 22 April, where he 'persuaded the curator of the Japanese collection of the National Archives', Shio Sakanishi, 'to put on for him a film with authentic soundtrack of the Noh play *Awoi no Uye*', a part of which he had seen in *Atarashiki tsuchi*.[44] Although, according to Moody, Pound returned to Italy on 17 June, Sakanishi remembers meeting Pound only once, 'close to the end of September', after Pound had rung her up to suggest having dinner at her house.[45] 'Pound's interest had not waned in the slightest', she recalls; Pound even read her a passage from *Nishikigi*.[46] In his third *Japan Times and Mail* article, 'Study of Noh Continues in West', Pound again enthused about nō in the strongest terms, remembering that Kume's dancing of the 'movement of the tennin's wings' in *Hagoromo* 'are the most beautiful movements I have seen on or off any stage'. He also reports having seen, 'by the kindness of Dr. Shio Sakanishi [...] "Aoi no Uye" [*sic*] on the screen with the sound of the singing and the crescendo of excitement as the hero rubs his rosary with the ever faster rattling of beads against beads.'[47] The film showing *Aoi no ue* was produced in 1935 by the Japanese 'Board of

---

[43] Pound, 'Tri-lingual System', 4.
[44] Moody, *Ezra Pound: Poet*, vol. 2, 302; *EPJ*, 225.
[45] Sakanishi Shio, 'Manukarezaru kyaku: Ezura Paundo (ichi)' ('An Uninvited Guest: Ezra Pound (One)'), *Eigo bungaku sekai* 7, no. 8 (November 1972): 2; Sakanishi, 'Manukarezaru kyaku: Ezura Paundo (ni)' ('An Uninvited Guest: Ezra Pound (Two)'), *Eigo bungaku sekai* 7, no. 9 (December 1972): 12.
[46] Ibid., 11.
[47] Pound, 'Study of Noh Continues in West', 8.

Tourist Industry' and filmed with a specially created stage at the PCL film studio. It was entitled *The Classical Noh Drama of Japan*, thus adopting the spelling Pound had popularized. It was acted by the Komparu and Hōshō schools, with Sakurama Kintarō playing Rokujō and Hōshō Arata the 'holy man'. It does not show the entire play, instead lasting only just over thirty minutes, of which the first six minutes introduce 'Noh' more generally, with the scene of the 'holy man' 'whirling and striking' at Rokujō appearing first. This concluding scene of the play is then shown in full without subtitles or further commentary.

In his *Japan Times and Mail* contributions, Pound repeatedly connected nō with the contemporary political situation in the lead-up to the Tripartite Pact between Germany, Italy and Japan, which was signed on 27 September 1940. In his 4 March 1940 article, he stresses Japan's importance in relation to Chinese culture, repeating the conventional Japanese view at the time used to justify the invasion of China: Japan and China are 'different'.[48] 'As regards the Chinese elements in Japanese art and culture', Pound continued, 'Japan continued to preserve some of the best Chinese skills and customs when China had fallen into her decadence.'[49] This is a somewhat different emphasis from his 1917 assertion that 'China is fundamental, Japan is not'. As an example of Japan's difference, Pound offers *Kumasaka*, which 'is basicly [sic] Japanese. [. . .] The gist of what three or more races have meant by chivalry, Ritterschaft and bushido finds concentrated expression in that Noh drama.'[50] The contemporary political implications of 'Ritterschaft and bushido' for Germany and Japan hardly need mentioning. Pound similarly links the 'Homeric' *Kagekiyo* not only to the 'classic epos' of 'Greece' but now also to that of the 'nordics', of which the Nazis, as is well known, made much in their racial propaganda.[51] Pound's emphasis on *Kumasaka* and *Kagekiyo* as the more 'masculine' plays of 'bushido' remains from when he first translated them; what had changed since then was his recalibration of their virility as models of courage for totalitarian states at war.

Despite Moody's claim that Pound's 'communications' continued in Japan until September 1940, Pound's last article for the *Japan Times* (under the title *Japan Times and Advertiser*) in fact appeared on 14 December 1940.[52] Moreover, his 'Itarii tsūshin' ('Letters from Italy') were published in *VOU* and *Shin gijutsu*

---

[48] Pound, 'Ezra Pound Asks Scholars Here to Solve Issues', *Japan Times and Mail* (4 March 1940): 6.
[49] Ibid.
[50] Ibid.
[51] Ibid.
[52] Moody, *Ezra Pound: Poet*, vol. 3, 13; Pound, 'Usury and Humanity Do Battle While China Is Heavily Engaged', *Japan Times and Advertiser* (14 December 1940): 4.

('New Technique'), its changed title, until March 1941.[53] Pound's last letter to Kitasono is dated 12 April 1941; he was not to write to Kitasono again in person until after his release from St Elizabeth's Hospital. Even after war broke out between Japan and the Allies on 7 December 1941, he continued his radio broadcasts until 25 July 1943, the day after Mussolini was deposed. Nō also appears in these. In 'March Arrivals', broadcast in March 1941, Pound proposed what he had also done in a letter to Kitasono that month: 'I should quite plainly propose to give Guam to the Japanese in return for one set of color and sound films of the 300 best Noh dramas.'[54] Again, the focus of his praise of nō is 'Kumasaka and Kagekiyo', which he urges is the 'point' up to which the 'American citizen' must be 'educated'.[55] In his 29 January 1942 broadcast, he criticizes the BBC's apparent characterization of Japanese as 'jackals': 'Anybody who has read the plays entitled Kumasaka and Kagekiyo, would have AVOIDED [. . .] the sort of fetid imbecility I heard a few nights ago from the British Broadcasting Company.'[56] For Pound, the Guam proposal was, as he confirmed, no joke: he was convinced that a deeper respect and understanding for other cultures could foster the peace depicted in such nō as *Hagoromo* and *Takasago*.[57]

This political importance that Pound always placed on literature was equally evident in his interaction with three Japanese in December 1943 and after his arrest by the Allies on 3 May 1945 for his radio broadcasts.[58] That earlier meeting was with 'three Japanese, envoys from their Embassy', with whom Pound had 'a genial discussion'; when under Allied arrest, he remarked that this meeting demonstrated 'the perception of a diplomacy based on humanity' which offered 'an avenue of approach NOT closed by the horrors of jungle warfare'.[59] Such a view recalls Pound's comparison in his 20 November 1919 article in *The New Age*, 'Pastiche: Regional – XVIII', between the enlightened conversation of 'two cultured men', 'Frederic II and Malek-Comel', despite the war between their states and the absence of 'someone who had read "Nishikig" and "Hogoromo"' [sic] conducting 'the Americo-Japanese negotiations'.[60] 'Universal peace will never be maintained', Pound's article concludes, 'unless it be by a conspiracy of intelligent

---

[53] Pound, 'Itarii tsūshin' ('Letter from Italy'), *Shin gijutsu* 32 (March 1941): 22–4.
[54] Pound, 'March Arrivals', in Leonard W. Doob (ed.), *'Ezra Pound Speaking': Radio Speeches of World War II* (Westport: Greenwood Press, 1978), 384.
[55] Ibid.
[56] Pound, 'On Resuming', in Doob (ed.), *'Ezra Pound Speaking'*, 26.
[57] Pound, 'March Arrivals', 384.
[58] Moody, *Ezra Pound: Poet*, vol. 3, 72 and 100.
[59] Ibid., 72.
[60] Pound, 'Pastiche: Regional – XVIII', 48.

men'.[61] When brought to the US Counter Intelligence Center in Genoa, Pound sought to put this conviction into practice: he asked staff to cable President Truman to ask that he negotiate for America with the Japanese to achieve peace; 'he would appeal not to the Japanese militarists, but to the ancient culture of Japan.'[62] His appeal, as he predicted in 1919, fell on deaf ears, and on 24 May he was sent to Pisa.[63] By 20 September, nearly four months into his incarceration, he wrote to Dorothy that he had 'enough cantos for a volume', which consisted of 'a Decad 74/83', the *Pisan Cantos*.[64] In his cage, exposed to the elements and facing possible execution, nō played a crucial role in his attempt to come to terms with defeat.

The first passage in which, as Ewick rightly claims, the 'return of the "compound tense" of the nō' occurs in the *Pisan Cantos* is not, as Ursula Shioji suggests, in line 428 but in line 78 of the first of the *Pisan Cantos*, Canto LXXIV.[65] Out of the 'tragedy of the dream in the peasant's bent shoulders', Pound's paradisal vision re-emerges.[66] This passage, which is repeated in Canto LXXVI, appears in the canto's first extant typescript draft:

> paraclete or the verbum perfectum: sinceritas
> from the death cells in sight of Mt. Taishan @ Pisa
>   as Fujiyama at Gardone
>   when the cat walked the top bar of the railing
>   and the water was still on the West side
>   flowing toward the Villa Catullo
>   where with sound ever moving
>   in diminutive poluphloisboios
>   in the stillness outlasting all wars
>   'La Donna' said Nicoletti
>   'la donna,
>   la donna!'[67]

Pound recalls 'Fujiyama' when thinking of 'Gardone' by Lake Garda, where, as related in 'Three Cantos – I', he saw 'Gods float in the azure air'. Later in the canto, Pound also remembers the line from 'Three Cantos – I', '"ghosts move

---

[61] Ibid.
[62] Moody, *Ezra Pound: Poet*, vol. 3, 105.
[63] Ibid., 116.
[64] Ibid., 127.
[65] Ewick, 'Strange Attractors', 20; Ursula Shioji, *Ezra Pound's Pisan Cantos and the Noh* (Frankfurt am Main: Peter Lang, 1998), 91.
[66] *PC*, 3.
[67] Ibid., 5.

about me" "patched with histories".[68] If the *Pisan Cantos* has a central theme, it is that of the nō-like ghosts patched with histories moving about the speaker. As in 'Three Cantos – I', Gardone is associated with the celestial maiden of *Hagoromo*, who at the conclusion of Pound's translation of the play flies up into the sky as 'Fuji is blotted out little by little' and 'melts into the upper mist'.[69] This is the very scene whose dance movements Pound had described just six years before as 'the most beautiful movements I have seen on or off any stage'. 'Fujiyama' thus refers here to the *Hagoromo* maiden. This passage also echoes the maiden's paradisal 'sinceritas': 'with us', she says in Pound's translation, 'there is no deceit'.[70] Later in the canto, 'the nymph of the Hagoromo came to me, / as a corona of angels', the speaker exclaims; the plural here suggests the thirty celestial maidens of the moon of whom the 'nymph of the Hagoromo' is one.

Together with the 'Tennin' of *Hagoromo*, who shortly makes a more explicit appearance in the canto, 'Kuanon' also comes to offer the speaker consolation, at first in a passage that likewise appears in the canto's earliest typescript draft:

and this day was made open
    for Kuanon of all delights[71]

Ewick correctly points out that this 'Kuanon' is the one of *Tamura*.[72] Shioji puts forward a rather intricate argument that Pound spells it this way because its 'first part is identical with the Chinese reading. Thus, the Japanese Kwannon and the Chinese Kuanyin merge into one figure who acts as a mediator between the world of Noh and the world of Chinese mythology.'[73] However, Pound's spelling of 'Kuanon' is, as we have seen, simply the one he took from Fenollosa's notebooks and used in periodical publications of his nō translations and the drafts of the 'Three Cantos' he sent to Monroe. It is possibly from Binyon, though, that Pound derives the following aspect of 'Kuanon':

Kuanon, this stone bringeth sleep[74]

Her 'stone' that 'bringeth sleep' may, as Arrowsmith speculates, be that of what Fenollosa calls the 'Yumedono Kwannon' at Hōryūji in Nara Prefecture: although an illustration is not included in Fenollosa's *Epochs*, one does appear

---

[68] *PC*, 24.
[69] *NA*, 176.
[70] Ibid., 171.
[71] *PC*, 6.
[72] Ewick, 'Strange Attractors', 21.
[73] Shioji, *Ezra Pound's Pisan Cantos and the Noh*, 121.
[74] *PC*, 13.

in Binyon's slides for his 1909 lecture series on 'Art and Thought in East and West', of which we know Pound attended some.[75] 'Kwannon' holds a 'jewel or casket of medicine'; this is a *kaen hōju* (from the Sanskrit *cintāmaṇi*), a Buddhist 'wish-fulfilling jewel' not otherwise associated with Kannon.[76] Pound must have yearned for this stone that 'giveth sleep' in his cage as the searchlights glared into it through the night.

As 'Kuanon's' role in *Tamura* indicates, however, she is not only a representation of 'mercy' and 'wisdom'; the 'favour of Kuanon' is bestowed upon benevolent imperial rule, with her 'light' pouring on the 'banner' of Tamuramaro's troops against the 'evil spirits' in Ise. This political dimension of Pound's nō translations is especially apparent in the passage of Canto LXXIV that describes the Japanese soldiers following their defeat:

> Says the Japanese sentry: Paaak yu djeep over there,
> some of the best soldiers we have said the captain
>   Dai Nippon Banzai in the Philippines
> remembering Kagekiyo: 'how stiff the shaft of your neck is.'
>   and they went off each their own way
> 'a better fencer than I was,' said Kumasaka, a shade,
> 'I believe in the resurrection of Italy   quia impossibile est[77]

Pound here makes absolutely explicit the implication of his 4 March 1940 *Japan Times and Mail* article that the 'gist of what three or more races have meant by chivalry, Ritterschaft and bushido finds concentration in that Noh drama', *Kumasaka*, and that *Kagekiyo* is connected to the 'classic epos' of Greece and the 'nordics': that is to say, that the Japanese imperialist and wider Axis war effort continued the 'old Bushido spirit' in these two plays. The Japanese soldier telling an Allied one to 'Paak yu djeep over there' is as able to rise above conflict as Kagekiyo praising his enemy's strength, and as honourable in defeat as Kumasaka admitting Ushiwaka was 'a better fencer than I was'. Just as Kagekiyo and Kumasaka live on through their nō plays, charging the present with their 'Bushido spirit', the fascist dream remains for Pound, 'now in the mind indestructible'.[78]

---

[75] Arrowsmith, *Modernism and the Museum*, 210–11.
[76] As Arrowsmith notes, William Watson observed in 1959 that 'The position of the hands and of the sacred jewel they hold is not repeated in any other image: neither is characteristic of Kannon', thus providing further reasons for doubting it to have originally been a 'Kannon' at all. Ibid., 211.
[77] *PC*, 20.
[78] Ibid.

As in the 'Three Cantos', Kuanon is associated with Venus as depicted in Botticelli's *Nascita di Venere*. Even in the 'pit' of 'hell' in which the speaker finds himself, she appears nonetheless to console him, 'forgetting the times and seasons':

> in this air as of Kuanon
> enigma forgetting the times and seasons
> but this air brought her ashore a la marina
> with the great shell borne on the seawaves
>   nautilis biancastra[79]

Because of Kuanon and the Botticelli Venus's association with the coming of the spring in 'Three Cantos – I', it can be said that the speaker thus recalls the spring in which these lines first appeared, that of 1917, in his own spring now spent in exile. This leads into the reference to the Genji of *Suma Genji*, who also grew his 'young cherry tree' and, looking at it, thinks of the spring cherries blossoming at the imperial palace from which he is exiled at Suma:

>   By no means an orderly Dantescan rising
> but as the winds veer
>   tira libeccio
> now Genji at Suma   ,   tira libeccio[80]

Pound thus remembers his translation of the play broadcast on television just over eight years earlier in London. He not only recalls Genji because of their shared exile: he also shares Genji's solitude, 'knowing all sorrow of sea-fare, having none to attend to my dreams, no one to hear the old stories'.[81] When Pound was first incarcerated at Pisa, the medical staff were so concerned that he had 'no one to talk to' that they feared for his mental health.[82] During the months he composed the *Pisan Cantos*, 'he was not permitted to communicate with anyone, not with his wife, nor with legal counsel'.[83] Genji's separation from his lovers in the capital adds to the parallels between him and Pound. In his striving for a vision of paradise, though, Pound also imagines a return to 'heaven' out of the 'hell' of his exile to which 'Genji the gleaming' ascends in the nō play.

While Pound returns to his nō translations of 1914–16, he also remembers his 'handful of "very much over-civilized"' Japanese friends from whom he had

---

[79] *PC*, 27 and 21.
[80] Ibid., 21.
[81] *NA*, 40.
[82] Moody, *Ezra Pound: Poet*, vol. 3, 120.
[83] Ibid., 123.

learned so much about nō. As he thinks back on Venice in Canto LXXVI, he recalls 'Tami's dream' in his Paris apartment:

> the hidden nest, Tami's dream, the great Ovid[84]

This refers, as Terrell and, more recently, Tateo Imamura have observed, to a lost painting by Kume currently only known by Pound's name for it in this canto.[85] In *L'asse che non vacilla*, Pound's 1945 Italian translation of Confucius's *Zhongyong*, Pound had included an epigraph of Kume which stated that 'We are at the crisis point of the world'.[86] A photograph taken in Pound's Paris apartment, however, includes part of it. The vigorous, swirling lines suggest the Vorticist influence Mizusawa Tsutomu detects in his other work.[87] Following Pound's incarceration, the painting itself has never been seen again. Itō is also remembered, in Canto LXXVII, for his dancing at the most prestigious London residences in 1914 despite his poverty:

> So Miscio sat in the dark lacking the gasometer penny
>   but then said: 'Do you speak German?'
>
>   to Asquith, 1914[88]

Itō's account ten years later, at a lecture given at Tokyo Woman's Christian University, corroborates Pound's memory. Itō was so poor that he had to pawn his twenty ties, for which he received sixpence, spending 'two of the six pence to turn on the gas and water'.[89] When dancing at Lady Cunard's, however, Itō 'was asked about Japanese art' by 'an extremely distinguished elderly gentleman'; unable to express himself well in English, though, Itō said to him, 'If I may speak in German, I can answer your questions more intelligently'.[90] At Pound's moment of greatest personal crisis, he thus remembered with fondness two of his Japanese friends who taught him about nō.

The *Pisan Cantos*, though, is of course not 'an orderly Dantescan rising' to Pound's visions of paradise. Despite his attempt to be as honourable in defeat as Kumasaka, the speaker struggles with his anger at his situation and the causes of the 'wreckage of Europe'.[91] At first, the following allusion to *Aoi no ue*, which

[84] Ibid., 40.
[85] *CCP*, 400–1; Imamura, 'Hemingway', 37–47.
[86] Bacigalupo, *The Forméd Trace*, 184.
[87] Imamura, 'Hemingway', 42.
[88] *PC*, 47.
[89] Itō, *Reminiscences*, 23.
[90] Ibid., 27.
[91] *PC*, 36.

Pound had seen in *Atarashiki tsuchi* and in Washington, DC, six years earlier, in Canto LXXVII seems to suggest the possessive envy felt by another inmate:

> As Arcturus passes over my smoke-hole
> > the excess electricity illumination
> > is now focussed
> on the bloke who stole a safe he cdn't open
> > > (interlude entitled: periplum by camion)
> > and Awoi's *hennia*   plays hob in the tent-flaps[92]

Many other interpretations of this allusion are possible: it anticipates Pound's identification of 'Awoi' with Dorothy and Olga in Canto CX; it could also represent the malevolence of the 'war profiteers' he criticizes later in the canto. The canto's context also suggests, though, that it refers to Pound himself. That it is 'Awoi's' *hennia* rather than Rokujō's corresponds with Pound's earlier interpretation of the latter as 'a phantom or image of Awoi no Uye's own jealousy' and the play as a 'combat with the phantoms of the mind'.[93] The canto's speaker rages against the perceived injustice of 'the bombardment at Frascati after the armistice / had been signed' and at those 'who live by debt and war profiteering'.[94] Pound thus sees himself as the Cassandra who foresaw the conflict manufactured by such 'war profiteering': like the *hennia* 'play[ing] hob in the tent-flaps', 'the wind' is 'mad as Cassandra / who was as sane as the lot of 'em'.[95] Pound's identification with Cassandra and 'Awoi' indicates his resentment at not being listened to as he tried to prevent the United States from entering the war and again when he offered to negotiate a peace with the Japanese.

Time and again, though, Pound returns in the *Pisan Cantos* to 'Kuanon' to lift him out of such resentment. In the same canto, he remembers his friend and patron, Margaret Cravens, who had committed suicide in Paris on 1 June 1912: 'O Margaret of the seven griefs / who hast entered the lotus.'[96] In contrast with the 'doom of Atreus', who, like Procne and Raymond of Roussillon, illustrates his barbarity by cooking three of his brother's sons and serving them to him, and the 'american army', whose 'caduceus' of 'Mercury god of thieves' is used on its 'packing case', Kuanon rises, as she does above the evil of Procne and Raymond

---

[92] Ibid., 43.
[93] *NA*, 194.
[94] *PC*, 52.
[95] Ibid., 53.
[96] Ibid., 49.

of Roussillon in Canto IV, over such states of mind through her 'mercy' and 'wisdom':

> above which, the lotus, white nenuphar
> Kuanon, the mythologies[97]

In this passage, Pound recalls 'Kuanon's' association with the lotus that had appeared in 'Three Cantos – I', in which Kuanon foots 'a boat that's but one lotus petal', and the 'forked branch-tips flaming as if with lotus' of the 'pines of Ise' lighted by Kuanon in Canto IV.[98] As well as 'mercy' and 'wisdom', Pound connects 'Kuanon's' 'forked tips flaming as if with lotus' with the 'Divine Love' that 'runs in the branches' in an early manuscript draft of Canto IV.[99] An instance of such divine love occurs in Canto LXXXI when a soldier brings Pound a 'packing box' for him to write:

> What counts as the cultural level,
> > thank Benin for this table ex packing box
> 'doan yu tell no one I made it'
> > > from a mask fine as any in Frankfurt
> 'It'll get you offn th' groun'
> > > Light as the branch of Kuanon[100]

The 'branch of Kuanon' here is the 'arborem vitae' whose 'forked tips flam[e] as if with lotus'. The 'light' that governs such loving actions is a state of mind, brought about through the development of a sufficient 'cultural level'. It is through such love that Pound can also 'get [. . .] offn th' groun' towards the 'Divine Love' of Kuanon.

Just as he compares 'Kuanon' with Aphrodite, throughout Pound's engagement with nō, Pound emphasized its ability to stand as equal with Greek literature: *Kagekiyo*, in particular, is repeatedly described as 'Homeric'. In Canto LXXIX, Pound returns to the contrast he made in the earliest drafts of *The Cantos* between a peaceful, unchanging East and a West once more in turmoil:

> Greek rascality against Hagoromo
> > Kumasaka vs/ vulgarity
> > > no sooner out of Troas
> than the damn fools attacked Ismarus of the Cicones[101]

---

[97] Ibid., 49 and 50.
[98] Pound, 'Three Cantos – I', 129.
[99] *EPP*, 3115.
[100] *PC*, 96–7.
[101] Ibid., 63.

The example of 'Greek rascality' is given in the last two lines: after leaving Troy, Odysseus 'sacked the city' of Ismarus 'and killed their men / But from the city took wives and much treasure', for which Zeus punishes him.[102] Pound therefore goes further than his earlier comparison of *Kagekiyo* and Homer: the sincerity of the celestial maiden in *Hagoromo* and Kumasaka's honour in declaring that the young boy who killed him was 'a better fencer' demonstrate that these nō possess for him a higher refinement of emotion than that presented in Homer.[103] Indeed, the celestial maiden's sincerity is contrasted with the 'fog' that 'rose from the marshland' when 'bad government prevailed':

'With us there is no deceit'
    said the moon nymph   immacolata
    Give back my cloak, *hagoromo*.
    had I the clouds of heaven
        as the nautile borne ashore[104]

The celestial maiden's reassurance to Hakuryō that she will dance for him if he returns her 'cloak' because 'Doubt is fitting for mortals; with us there is no deceit' would reappear on multiple occasions in Pound's drafts of his later cantos as a contrast with the deception of usury and the 'war profiteers'. While Pound connects the 'moon nymph' with Botticelli's Venus, 'the nautile borne ashore', as he had done with Kuanon as well, it is her quality of sincerity that makes the maiden stand out for Pound. The maiden's 'strange sorrow' at missing her home in the 'wonder of clouds that fade along the sky that was our accustomed dwelling' transforms into Pound's own desire in the *Pisan Cantos* to rise up out of his confinement towards his vision of paradise.[105]

Pound's personal identification with the celestial maiden of *Hagoromo*, and previously with Kagekiyo, Kumasaka, Genji and even Awoi, at his moment of greatest crisis, having almost no one to communicate with and the possibility of execution for treason hanging over him, demonstrates that his rekindled enthusiasm for nō was not merely motivated by an opportunistic attempt to gain favour with his new-found Japanese correspondent, Kitasono, or with a political ally of fascist Italy. Pound's incorporation of nō in the *Pisan Cantos* was the culmination of a decade of profound engagement with nō in which he praised it in the highest terms. Most of the nō plays he had translated that reappear in the

---

[102] Homer, *Odyssea ad verbum*, trans. Andrea Divo di Iustinopolitano (Salingiaci, 1540), 73.
[103] *PC*, 20.
[104] Ibid., 78.
[105] *NA*, 170.

Pisan Cantos were those performed in London, such as *Suma Genji*; those he saw on film, such as *Awoi no Uye*; or those he discussed in his *Japan Times* articles and radio broadcasts. His appreciation of nō was political as well as aesthetic: in both his *Japan Times and Mail* articles before the outbreak of the Pacific War and in the *Pisan Cantos*, *Kagekiyo* and *Kumasaka* are models for the 'old Bushido spirit' of the Japanese soldiers in the war. It is through the benevolent imperial rule supported by military strength, as in *Tamura* and *Atarashiki tsuchi*, that Pound thought the causes of wars could be prevented; in this way, too, he believed the world could ascend, like the celestial maiden, towards paradise. As Ewick notes, this ascent is imagined through Pound's readoption of nō as a structural model for *The Cantos*: once more, the '"ghosts move about me" "patched with histories"', fragments of luminous detail gathered across vast spatial and temporal distances and comprehensible only 'for the few', as Pound wrote of nō, 'for those trained to catch the allusion'.[106]

---

[106] Ewick, 'Strange Attractors', 21–2; *NA*, 5.

12

'The light sings eternal'
Nō's place in the *Paradiso* of Pound's later cantos

During Pound's awaiting trial for treason because of his wartime Rome Radio broadcasts, Japan continued to be a place to which he imagined escaping from his ordeal: the poet and Pound adept Charles Olson, visiting Pound on 29 January 1946, reported that Pound told him, 'I understand they think to send me to Japan'.[1] Dr Marion King, one of the psychiatrists whose report led to Pound being sent to St. Elizabeths Hospital, explained testifying at the court hearing: 'He believes he could be useful to this country if he were designated as a diplomat, or agent, and sent to Japan [. . .] with the idea now of maintaining the peace of the world.'[2] Like his proposal made before the dropping of the atomic bombs on Hiroshima and Nagasaki, Pound's idea remains consistent with his view expressed in 1919 that 'the Americo-Japanese negotiations' ought to be conducted by 'someone who had read "Nishikig" and "Hogoromo" [*sic*]'.[3] Yet again, though, Pound's plea was ignored, and he was deemed too insane to stand trial and sent to St. Elizabeths Hospital. There he translated two Greek plays not only inspired by nō but which he wished to 'add to the repertoire' of nō plays acted by the Umewaka family of nō actors, and composed two further sections of *The Cantos*, *Section: Rock-drill 85-95 de los cantares* and *Thrones 96-109 de los cantares*, in which nō continues to play an important and thus far underexplored role. In the final cantos, written after his release in 1958, nō features prominently in the poem's culminating paradisal vision.

By January 1949, Pound had embarked on the first of what he intended to be a series of translations of Greek plays.[4] He wished to bring about a 'revival' of Greek

---

[1] Catherine Seelye (ed.), *Charles Olson & Ezra Pound: An Encounter at St Elizabeths* (New York: Grossman Publishers, 1975), 61.
[2] Quoted in Moody, *Ezra Pound: Poet*, vol. 3, 211.
[3] Pound, 'Pastiche: Regional – XVIII', 48.
[4] Liebregts, *Translations of Greek Tragedy in the Work of Ezra Pound* (London: Bloomsbury, 2019), 57.

drama, in which appeared, in his view, the 'rise of [a] sense of civic responsibility'.[5] The first translation he and Rudd Fleming, a University of Maryland professor, produced was of Sophocles' *Elektra*. Pound had felt an admiration for the 'hard Sophoclean light' as one of the models for his Imagist poetics at least since this phrase was used in his poetic sequence 'Xenia', published in *Poetry*'s November 1913 issue.[6] Fenollosa's comparisons of nō and Greek drama, however, may also have played a part in Pound's turn to the latter. *Elektra*'s tale of vengeance differs from the conclusions of nō demon plays, in which the evil spirit is pacified by Buddhist prayer; in his stage directions, though, Pound explicitly incorporates nō elements. When Elektra, who seeks revenge for her father Agamemnon's death at the hands of her mother, Klytemnestra, is told by her sister Chrysothemis that her brother Orestes is still alive, Pound indicates that '*Elektra masked, at first not even looking at Chrysothemis but boredly into distance, gradually grows attentive*'.[7] There is then a '*Slowness in turning of head, as per Noh*'.[8] This turn from despair to elation marks a pivotal moment in the play. Pound's familiarity with nō staging through seeing Itō, Kōri and Kume perform nō for him in London and Paris, and a film of *Aoi no ue* allowed him to develop an understanding not just of nō texts but also of nō costumes and dramatic gestures.

This seeing of Greek drama through nō becomes more apparent in Pound's translation of Sophocles's *Women of Trachis*. He later recalled that 'The *Trachiniae* came from reading the Fenollosa Noh plays for the new edition', a reference either to the reprint of the entirety of 'Noh' or Accomplishment in *The Translations of Ezra Pound*, published in 1953, or of *The Classic Noh Theatre of Japan* in 1959.[9] Pound and Fleming were translating *Women of Trachis* by June 1949.[10] It was published in the Winter 1953–4 issue of the *Hudson Review*. Pound's prefatory note to the play makes his connection of the play with nō explicit:

> *A version for KITASONO KATUE, hoping he will use it on my dear old friend Miscio Ito, or take it to the Minoru if they can be persuaded to add it to their repertoire.*[11]

Kitasono told Pound in his 12 November letter that Michael Reck would 'take it to Mr. Ito Michio', whom Pound had fondly remembered in the *Pisan Cantos*,

---

[5] Pound, 'Hellenists', quoted in Pound and Fleming (trans.), *Elektra*, xii.
[6] Pound, 'Xenia I-VII', *Poetry* 3, no. 2 (November 1913): 60.
[7] Pound and Fleming (trans.), *Elektra*, 48.
[8] Ibid.
[9] Hall, 'E. P.: An Interview', 40.
[10] Liebregts, *Translations of Greek Plays*, 165.
[11] *WT*, 487.

though there is no evidence that it reached Itō or 'the Minoru'. Pound's proposal for the 'Minoru' to 'add' *Women of Trachis* 'to their repertoire' suggests that Pound even saw *Women of Trachis* as being itself a nō play. Pound's reference to 'the Minoru' is to Umewaka Minoru and his second son, Umewaka Rokurō (1878–1959), who inherited the name 'Umewaka Minoru'. Pound knew of the continuation of 'the Minoru' because on 7 December 1949 Kitasono had sent Dorothy 'stills' of plays which 'were acted by Umewaka Minoru Junior'.[12] Though it may appear at first as a mistaking of a Japanese surname ('Umewaka') for a first name ('Minoru'), the entire name has been passed on down the Umewaka family to the present day, so that Pound was partially correct in referring to 'the Minoru' as an hereditary line of nō actors.

Pound also states in his prefatory note:

> The Trachiniae *presents the highest point of Greek sensibility registered in any of the plays that have come down to us, and is, at the same time, nearest to the original form of the God-dance.*[13]

His description of the *Trachiniae* as 'nearest to the original form of the God-dance' resembles his remarks that the nō play *Hagoromo* 'shows the relation of the early Noh to the God-dance' and that *Suma Genji* is 'very near to the original, or early form, of the God-dance'.[14] Pound explains this 'God-dance' as 'The first legendary dance [which] took place when the light-goddess', the sun goddess Amaterasu, 'hid herself in a cave and the other gods danced on a tub [. . .] [to] lure her out'.[15] Both *Hagoromo* and *Suma Genji* commemorate the arrival of the spring's new growth fed by the sun: in *Hagoromo*, 'Nippon' is 'the sun's field' blessed by the gods as 'Miwo puts on the colour of spring'; *Suma Genji* depicts the blossoming of Genji's cherry tree and the manifestation of 'Genji the gleaming' in the 'springtime'.[16] This is not just the 'Shinto god dance', as Miho Takahashi claims, but rather the 'God-dance' in cultures around the world according to Frazer's *The Golden Bough* – the dance of the sun's warmth bringing spring's fecundity – to which Pound wishes to refer.[17]

---

[12] Kitasono, letter to Dorothy Pound (7 December 1949), in *EPJ*, 122.
[13] *WT*, 487.
[14] Pound, 'The Classical Stage of Japan', 223.
[15] Ibid.
[16] Pound, 'The Classical Drama of Japan', 475; Pound, 'The Classical Stage of Japan', 222.
[17] Miho Takahashi, 'Kasōdaijō no Herakuresu: Ezura Paundo han "Torakisu no onnatachi" wo meguru ichikōsatsu' ('Heracles on the Blazing Pyre: A Reading of *Women of Trachis*, a Version by Ezra Pound'), *Ezra Pound Review* 10–11 (2008): 3–4.

This interpretation of Pound's *Women of Trachis* assists in making sense of several passages. Its hero is 'Herakles Zeuson', 'the Solar vitality'.[18] His death at the end marks that of the old year, as it does in the countless festivals in *The Golden Bough*. As in 'Three Cantos – I', the death of the old year and the coming of the spring is heralded by Venus. In 'Three Cantos – I', she corresponds with 'Kwannon', who tells the 'gardens of the nymphs' to 'put forth your flowers'.[19] In *Women of Trachis*, 'Kupris' appears, 'lit up strongly so that the gauze is transparent'.[20] In his instructions to Reck about translating the play into Japanese, Pound keeps this correspondence in mind: as well as telling Reck to 'drag in phrases from Noh itself' in the 'sung parts', Pound suggests placing a 'willow bough' in the goddess's hand, like 'Kuanon'.[21] When Herakles realizes that he must die and Pound inserts the invented line, 'SPLENDOUR, / IT ALL COHERES', which Pound defines as 'the key phrase, for which the play exists', it not only indicates 'how snugly each segment of the work fits into its box', thus also demonstrating Pound's emphasis on aesthetic unity previously formulated in the 'Unity of Image' he discovered in nō; it also signals the completion of the annual cycle. Herakles's death marks the destruction of the old year and the start of the new.[22]

That Pound held nō, and more specifically his translations of nō, in high regard at this time is also demonstrated by the inclusion of the entirety of *'Noh' or Accomplishment*, excluding only the musical score for *Hagoromo*, in *The Translations of Ezra Pound*, published on 1 January 1953. Despite this inclusion – which takes up 149 of the 408 pages in the New Directions edition – Hugh Kenner's introduction to the book is strongly dismissive of nō's importance for Pound:

> In the *Cathay* poems, made from Ernest Fenollosa's notes and cribs to the ideograms of Rihaku (Li Po), Pound is at his best as poet and as translator; he is amazingly convincing at making the Chinese poet's world his own. If the series of *Noh* dramas is somehow less successful, it is because there is less of Pound in them.[23]

---

[18] WT, 487.
[19] Pound, 'Three Cantos – I', 119–20.
[20] WT, 510.
[21] Pound, letter to Michael Reck (12 March 1954), in *EPJ*, 236. Fenollosa describes the eighth-century Tang-dynasty painter Wu Daozi's 'Standing Kwannon' as 'sway[ing] a wisp of willow'. *ECJA*, vol. 1, 132–3. In his translation of *Yōrō*, Pound describes 'Yorin (willow) Kuanon' blessing the prosperous imperial reign. Fenollosa and Pound (trans.), *Yoro*, ed. Richard Taylor, *Paideuma* 6, no. 1 (Spring 1975): 353.
[22] WT, 520.
[23] T, 13.

Kenner concludes that in Pound's nō translations there is 'a remoteness, a sense on Pound's part that he is doing something exotic, thin, appreciated rather than lived, that just prevents the *Noh* sequence from standing, as *Cathay* does, with his finest original work'.[24] Kenner's conclusion recalls Eliot's view in *Ezra Pound His Metric and Poetry* of 1917 that 'The Noh are not so important as the Chinese poems (certainly not so important for English); [. . .] the work is not so solid, so firm. "Cathay" will, I believe, rank with the "Sea-Farer" in the future among Pound's original work: the Noh will rank among his translations'.[25]

The development of such a critical misunderstanding of Pound's view of nō at this time can also be detected in reviews of Pound's *Translations*. In John Edwards's review in *Poetry*, the book is criticised for giving 'over one-third of the book to the *Nōh* [sic] plays'. Edwards quotes Pound's 1918 letter to Quinn to argue that Pound 'never really liked the *Nōh* [sic] plays himself, calling them "unsatisfactory" and "too damn soft"'.[26] Edwards would have been led in this direction by the appearance of these words describing nō in Pound's letter to John Quinn of 4 June 1918 in D. D. Paige's *The Letters of Ezra Pound 1907-1941*, published in 1951.[27] Edwards claims that the translations of the nō plays 'were done during a winter with Yeats', whereas in fact they were done not only over three winters with Yeats but throughout the intervening periods, as Chapters 6 to 8 demonstrate.[28] He then uses the Quinn letter to conclude that the nō plays 'meant very little to Pound, and they stand apart from the central line of Pound's studies with language'.[29] From Kenner's introduction to Pound's *Translations* and its reviews, this misunderstanding of nō's importance for Pound has since been accepted without sufficient scrutiny and widely replicated in Pound studies.

Crucially, however, Kenner and Edwards would not have had access to Pound's then as yet unpublished letter to Kitasono of 3 March 1939 in which he expresses his 'nostalgia for Japan, induced by the fragment of Noh in *Mitsuco*', demands that 'ALL of the Noh ought to be filmed', and that 'It is a music like no other'; nor to Pound's article in the *Japan Times and Mail* of 15 May 1939, in which he described nō as 'a treasure like nothing in the Occident', a 'masterwork' on a par with 'Mozart, Purcell, Janequin, Dowland'.[30] Nor, evidently, did they read Pound's next *Japan Times and Mail* piece describing Kume's dancing

---

[24] Ibid., 13–14.
[25] Eliot, *Ezra Pound His Metric and Poetry*, 27.
[26] Edwards, 'Pound's Translations', 235.
[27] Pound, letter to Kitasono (3 March 1939), in *EPJ*, 73.
[28] Ibid.
[29] Ibid.
[30] Pound, 'Tri-lingual System', 4.

of the 'movement of the tennin's wings' in *Hagoromo* as 'the most beautiful movements I have seen on or off any stage'.[31] Pound's proposal that Guam should be exchanged for films of 300 nō plays was one he still held at this time: on 12 March 1954, he wrote to Reck that 'the last message I got thru to U. S. press <1940> was: We shd/ GIVE Guam to the Japs, but INSist on having 300 sound films of Noh in exchange. (And how much better THAT wd/ have been.) Don't lie down on the fight to get sound films of actual Noh.'[32] This does not, of course, take away from Kenner and Edwards their right to prefer *Cathay* over Pound's nō translations; what it does show, however, is that their view of Pound's nō translations at this time was not Pound's at this time, and that this explains the inclusion of all of *'Noh' or Accomplishment* in *The Translations of Ezra Pound* despite Kenner's criticisms in the book's introduction.

The composition of further cantos probably 'began soon after Pound's incarceration at St. Elizabeths'.[33] Nineteen notebooks for the next section of *The Cantos, Section: Rock-drill 85-95 de los cantares*, are dated from August 1951 to October 1954; three earlier ones are undated.[34] Within these first three, Pound's return to the 'Fenollosa Noh plays' evidently made Pound remember Kume. Pound had sketched out a plan for 'CANTOS 85-100 in brief' as an exploration of the 'Bellum [. . .] perenne' fought 'between the usurer & the man who wd do a good job' and the rising to the Dantescan 'Thrones'.[35] He then draws a line across the page and marks out in red pencil the beginning of a possible 'Canto':

> Canto
>
> 'with us there is
>   no deceit'
>
>   Tami Kumé
> Hagoromo[36]

'Doubt is fitting for mortals', the celestial maiden in *Hagoromo* tells Hakuryō when he suspects her of lying about whether she will dance as she had promised; 'with us there is no deceit'.[37] Pound had associated 'sinceritas' with the 'nymph of the Hagoromo' in the *Pisan Cantos*; now her 'sinceritas' reappears in the

---

[31] Pound, 'Study of Noh Continues in West', 8.
[32] Pound, letter to Reck (12 March 1954), in *EPJ*, 237.
[33] Michael Kindellan, *The Late Cantos of Ezra Pound* (London: Bloomsbury, 2017), 58.
[34] Notebooks 68–89, *EPP*.
[35] Notebook 68, *EPP*.
[36] Ibid.
[37] *NA*, 171.

schema of the next section of *The Cantos* as a contrast with the 'usurer' fighting the eternal war with 'the man who wd do a good job'. In thinking of *Hagoromo*, Pound cannot help also remembering Kume dancing 'the movement of the tennin's wings'. On the following page of the notebook, Pound also records how 'the young dimio [sic] noted it / a time / of translation / Tami [...] Kumé', which recalls Pound's influential claim in 1917 that 'A great age of literature is perhaps always a great age of translations'.[38]

The most important nō play in *Section: Rock-drill*, however, was *Takasago*. After Kenner claims in *The Pound Era* that Pound 'never got round' to translating '*Takasago*', he subsequently states that 'Instead after 40 years its hymn to vegetal powers became the whole of *Rock-Drill*.[39] 'The story of Baucis and Philemon' in Ovid's *Metamorphoses* 'is cognate; so is the heaven-tree', in Norse mythology Yggdrasil.[40] This book is the first to explore this proposition in detail. In the earliest dated notebook, of August 1951, the 'pine trees' are contrasted with Roosevelt's 'pack[ing] the Supreme court':

under the larches
        of paradise
seated firmly on their
        thrones
@height of the pine trees –

    Kung & the Bhuddists [sic]

—

'He has packed the Supreme court
so that they will
declare anything he does
        constitutional'
Senator Wheeler   1939[41]

The political corruption Pound identified in Roosevelt's actions, and which thus enabled him, as Pound saw it, to engage in war, would eventually appear as the opening of Canto C and echoes Pound's similar contrast in 'MS Ur 1' with a West that had descended into the barbarity of the First World War and an idealized East governed by benevolent imperial rule, as in *Takasago*. Furthermore, the draft

---

[38] Notebook 68, *EPP*; Pound, 'Elizabethan Classicists – II', *The Egoist* 4, no. 9 (October 1917): 136.
[39] *PE*, 283–4.
[40] Ibid., 529.
[41] Notebook 5, *EPP*.

crucially identifies the 'thrones' of his 'paradise', the supreme destination of *The Cantos*, with the 'height of the pine trees', the key structural motif of *Takasago* and of Cantos IV, XXI and XXIX.

The association of vegetal regeneration with love is introduced in Notebook 8, dated May to July 1953, after Pound had encountered Sheri Martinelli. In 'a splendour', 'Cythera', the goddess of love invoked in 'Three Cantos – I' where she brings the 'clear-outlined blossoms' of the spring and in Canto I, here 'descends thru and / above pine' to the heavens above, an ascent to paradise that also recalls the ending of Canto XXIX as the 'Pine [. . .] trees melted in air'.[42] The pine trees thus function in *The Cantos* as a repeated motif of a natural increase that leads to paradise. Trees continually recur in the drafts of *Section: Rock-Drill*, representing not only vegetal, sexual and literary regeneration but also that of the 'mind'. The notebook dated July–October 1953 includes the following passage:

> thought is a vegetable
>   木   (mu$^{4\text{-}5}$)!
>   sd Wm. Yeats
> & later denied it.
>
> Kultur has trunks
> 4546   &   branches.
> 7114   末   未   wei^4
>   mo$^{4\text{-}5}$ [43]

The first character, 木, means 'wood' or 'tree'; both 未 and 末 are pictographic in origin and represent, respectively, 'end', from the apex of a tree's branches, and 'not yet', from a tree's branches having not yet fully grown. The mind's cultivation is what achieves 'Dioce': 'mind is / phylotaxis [sic]', the arrangement of leaves on a tree springing from its trunk.[44] The leaves of the pine, the 'inexhaustible words' of literary tradition sustained by a 'country well-governed' through imperial rule, are likewise perpetually gathered by the old couple in *Takasago*.

This imperial underpinning of such natural increase is evident in the published cantos of *Section: Rock-Drill*. Canto LXXXV, which first appeared in the *Hudson Review*'s Winter 1953–4 issue, opens with the Chinese character 靈 and, underneath it, 'Our dynasty came in because of a great sensibility', a reference to King Tang's overthrow of the Xia dynasty and founding of the

---

[42] Notebook 8, *EPP*.
[43] Notebook 10, *EPP*.
[44] Ibid.

Shang dynasty with the assistance of his adviser, 'Y Yin' (Yi Yin).[45] Underlying this action were 'the roots' of this virtuous 'sensibility' out of which 'Kultur' would spread its branches.[46] It is 'Not led of lusting, not of contriving / but is as the grass and tree'.[47] The 'roots' of Y Yin's actions thus give rise to 'the tree of heaven', 'Ygdrasail'.[48] Such imperial rule is typified by its emphasis on unity. Whereas 'the pivot' of 'Justice, d'urbanité, prudence' had been 'perceived by Y Yin / quam simplex animus Imperatoris', in post-war America Pound saw 'No classics, / no American history, / no centre, no general root'.[49] In Canto LXXXVI, Pound returns by way of contrast with such imperial 'Justice' to the conflict that had animated the earliest drafts of *The Cantos*. The conflict broke out because of 'Dummheit, nicht Bösheit'; it was led by a 'Mind (the Kaiser's) like loose dice in a box'.[50] Those actually doing the fighting 'don't hate anybody' but merely 'fight when the Emperor says so'; it is no righteous war but rather part of what Pound saw as the 'Bellum [. . .] perenne' in the interests of usura.[51]

Canto LXXXVII continues the contrast of enlightened imperial rule according to Confucian principles with the modern-day West:

And after the year 1600 Nakae Toji
    carried Wai' Ya'
        (name worn out in some dialects)
            Min's lamp in Nippon.
The total dirt that was Roosevelt,
    and the farce that was Churchill[52]

Terrell notes that 'Pound got the name and the association from Carsun Chang, who visited him at St. Elizabeths' but does not give the right name: the Japanese Confucian was in fact Nakae Tōju (1608–48).[53] As Canto LXXXVII suggests, Tōju was influential in introducing the thought of the Ming dynasty ('Min', the dynasty's Japanese reading) Confucian Wang Yangming ('Wai' Ya") into Japan. Indeed, Takayanagi Toshiya observes that he is known as 'the founder of Yangming studies in Japan'.[54] The metaphor of tradition as a 'lamp' is transmitted

---

[45] Pound, 'Canto LXXXV', *Hudson Review* 7, no. 4 (Winter 1954): 487.
[46] Ibid.
[47] Ibid., 488.
[48] Ibid.
[49] Ibid., 487–92.
[50] Pound, 'Cantos 86-7', *Hudson Review* 8, no. 1 (Spring 1955): 13.
[51] Ibid., 15 and 17.
[52] Pound, 'Cantos 86-7', 20.
[53] *CCP*, 491.
[54] Takayanagi Toshiya, *Nakae Tōju no shōgai to shisō* ('The Life and Thought of Nakae Tōju') (Tokyo: Kōjinsha, 2004), 52.

throughout *The Cantos* in opposition to what Pound considered the 'dirt' of Roosevelt and Churchill.

Pound contrasts this encounter with the West's descent into the 'bellum [. . .] perenne' waged by usury. Canto LXXXVIII explores the motivations underlying the 'opening' of Japan to trade through the arrival of Commodore Matthew Perry in Edo Bay in 1853, about which Pound read in Brooks Adams's *The New Empire*.[55] As the Americans had 'bust the abundance' of their own territory instead of ensuring a harmonious co-prosperity with natural increase, they needed 'to make war' in order to 'export':

So that Perry 'opened' Japan.[56]

Pound's moral condemnation of the motives for 'opening' Japan is more explicitly apparent in the drafts for the canto, in which Pound gives the above line as 'so that snot Perry "opened" Japan'.[57] Perry's actions, as Adams notes, 'caused an economic disturbance, which brought on a revolution. In 1868, the Shogun fell'; the 'immediate effect' on Japan, therefore, 'was war'.[58] Pound would not only have lamented the overthrow of the government led by the military 'Shogun' because of its patronage of nō and the cessation of that patronage with the fall of the shōgunate in 1868, as he had discovered through reading Umewaka Minoru's account in *'Noh' or Accomplishment*; it also led to the destruction of a form of rule founded on the Confucian values that Nakae Tōju had transmitted from China. Pound's criticism of the 'opening' of Japan in this way is consistent with his regret expressed in 'MS Ur 2' of Canto IV at how 'Japan turns european'; in the 'daimio' faces of Itō and Kume, as opposed to the Westernized Kōri, Pound felt he had encountered this pre-Meiji Japan.

Against this destruction of Confucian government Pound places adventurous men like the explorer John Charles Frémont (1813–90), who 'climbed the loftiest peak of the Rocky Mountains, until then untrodden by any human being' in 'the summer of 1842', and Michael Reck, who when he first met Pound was a student at the Institute of Contemporary Arts in Washington in 1951.[59] When, in June 1954, Reck was posted with the army to Japan, he visited Fenollosa's grave

---

[55] *CCP*, 506.
[56] Pound, 'Cantos 88-9', *Hudson Review* 8, no. 2 (Summer 1955): 187.
[57] *EPP*, 3422.
[58] Brooks Adams, *The New Empire* (London: Macmillan, 1902), 188–9.
[59] Thomas Hart Benton, *Thirty Years' View: Or, A History of the Working of the American Government for Thirty Years, from 1820 to 1850*, vol. 2 (New York: D. Appleton, 1856), 478–9; Michael Reck, *Ezra Pound: A Close-Up* (New York: McGraw-Hill, 1967), 108.

at Miidera, a temple overlooking Lake Biwa, a moment that concludes Canto LXXXVIII:

> I want Frémont looking at mountains
>   or, if you like, Reck, at Lake Biwa,[60]

Reck later recalls that 'I described my visit in a letter to Pound'; this letter is not among their extant correspondence, but Reck does give an account of it in his biography of Pound, in which he describes visiting 'Fenollosa's grave' with the poet Fujitomi Yasuo, with whom he was translating *Women of Trachis* into Japanese, and seeing the 'immense vista of Lake Biwa' below.[61] As Reck puts it, 'Frémont was of course the American explorer of the West; and I suppose that for Pound I was another such explorer. He may have seen in my visit to Fenollosa's grave that meeting of East and West which was his dream.'[62] The comma at the canto's end leads into the central paradisal canto of *Section: Rock-drill*, Canto XC, which Reck interprets as the point at which 'East and West are joined'.[63]

The opening – and central – image of Canto XC, the start of Pound's 'Paradiso proper', as Moody observes, continues the earlier *Section: Rock-drill* drafts' emphasis on 'thought' and 'Kultur' being 'a vegetable' with 'trunks' and 'branches':

> Beatific spirits welding together
>   as in one ash-tree in Ygdrasail.
>   Baucis, Philemon.[64]

'Ygdrasail', alluded to in Canto LXXXV, recalls the 'arborem vitae' in the drafts of Canto IV. The Ovidian tale of Baucis and Philemon, meanwhile, is 'cognate' with that of *Takasago*, as Kenner notes; just as the old couple in the *Metamorphoses* could, in Ovid's day, be seen 'growing yit together' in Golding's translation, the old couple in *Takasago* are the spirits of the paired pines at Takasago and Suminoe, who are said to be *aioi*, 'growing together'. As in Cantos IV, XXI and XXIX, *Takasago*'s theme is thus not only an instance of the correspondences between such disparate cultures as medieval Japan and the Mediterranean classical world; its paired pines function as the structural model for such correspondences across great distances in space and time throughout *The Cantos*. From the Chinese 'San Ku' to 'the room in Poitiers where one can stand / casting no shadow', the canto

---

[60] *SRD*, 64.
[61] Reck, *Ezra Pound*, 174.
[62] Ibid., 175.
[63] Ibid.
[64] Moody, *Ezra Pound: Poet*, vol. 3, 357; *SRD*, 65.

continues, 'That is Sagetrieb, / that is tradition', just as the 'inexhaustible words' of the 'pine-needles' represent the evergreen literary tradition in *Takasago*. Such fusions of the 'primal and valid donations' of the East and the West, of which *The Cantos* and Canto XC in particular constitute an example, light the way to a *paradiso terrestre*.

The scene then shifts to the 'Moon's barge over milk-blue water' and 'Kuthera sempiterna'; as in the 'Three Cantos', Canto IV and Canto LXXIV, Venus ('Kuthera') is associated with 'Kuanon', who comes on a 'small boat', a 'Bright flame upon the river', in 'Three Cantos – I', a metaphor that anticipates the 'Moon's barge'. In Pound's translation of *Tamura*, 'Kuanon' appears as a 'golden light floating on the Kotsu river'; she is also associated with the moon, which 'lights the cherry flowers' before she 'pours lights' on the 'banner' of Tamuramaro's troops.[65] As in Pisa, Kuanon comes to console the speaker:

> from the dulled air and the dust,
>
> m'elevasti
>
> by the great flight,
>
> m'elevasti,
>
> Isis Kuanon
>
> from the cusp of the moon,
>
> m'elevasti[66]

Kannon's 'blessing', 'mercy' and 'wisdom', as in Canto IV, are equated with the divine love that 'runs in the branches' of *Takasago*'s paired pines. The comparison of 'Kuanon' with 'Isis' likewise echoes Canto XXI's 'Grow with the pines of Isé / as the Nile swells with Inopos'; the latter two, Frazer's *Golden Bough* claims, are associated with festivals for Isis. In Canto XXIX, this divine love commemorates Pound's and H. D.'s relationship; the 'Isis Kuanon' in Canto XC is likewise the result of 'the effect upon his own mind of being in love with Martinelli'.[67]

Many of the associations with the *Takasago* and *Tamura* motifs in Canto IV are also repeated in Canto XC: the 'light' that 'rains, thus pours' in the former is now 'the light perpendicular, upward'; the 'liquid, and rushing crystal' that 'whirls up the bright brown sand' reoccurs in the 'water' that 'jets from the rock' in 'Castalia', the fountain of literary inspiration on Mount Parnassus; the 'Nymphs, white-gathered about' Diana by the 'pool' are reduced to 'a lone nymph by the pool', 'the flat pool as Arethusa's', one of Diana's nymphs; and the

---

[65] *NA*, 84–5 and 90.
[66] *SRD*, 66.
[67] Moody, *Ezra Pound: Poet*, vol. 3, 313.

'Brook film bearing white petals' turns into 'Wei and Han rushing together / two rivers together'.[68] As in Canto IV and their previous repetitions in Cantos XXI and XXIX, these associations weld with *Takasago*'s foregrounding of vegetal, sexual and literary regeneration. That the trees in the canto allude specifically to *Takasago* rather than just to Baucis and Philemon is first suggested by the following passage:

> the trees rise
> and there is a wide sward between them[69]

These lines' emphasis on the distance between the 'trees' has no equivalent in the Ovidian tale, but does recall the old woman in *Takasago*'s expression of her love for the old man: 'Though the mountain and river lie between us we are near in the ways of love.' The 'wide sward between them' serves as the model for the resonances between the classical world and the Far East.

That these trees are those of *Takasago* is further implied in the lines that follow those mentioned earlier. After 'myrrh and olibanum' are offered on the 'altar stone' for the *chthonoi*, the 'spirits of the underworld', the spirits, represented as butterflies' wings, emerge:

> and where was nothing
> now is furry assemblage
> and in the boughs now are voices
> grey wing, black wing, black wing shot with crimson
> and the umbrella pines
> as in Palatine,
> as in pineta.[70]

The 'furry assemblage' indicates the new growth of spring. That 'in the boughs now are voices' refers back to 'Three Cantos – I' and Canto III's 'leaves' that are 'full of voices', which parallels *Takasago*'s 'pine-needles' of the literary tradition's 'inexhaustible words'. Rather than the 'elm-oak' of Baucis and Philemon, these trees in Canto XC are 'umbrella pines' like the 'paired pines' of *Takasago* that grow in Cantos IV and XXI before they are 'melted in air' at the close of Canto XXIX. At the conclusion of Canto XC, these pines similarly 'rise' as the spirits of 'Tyro, Alcmene' and the 'cavalieri' are 'free now, ascending'. At the heart of

---

[68] *SRD*, 67.
[69] Ibid., 68.
[70] Ibid.

Canto XC, then, is *Takasago*'s 'welding together' of vegetal, sexual and literary regeneration through the image of paired pines.

Takasago, Tamura and *Hagoromo* also return in Pound's next collection, *Thrones 96-109 de los cantares*, published by New Directions in 1959. After the 'coil of Geryon' has, in the words of the nineteenth-century Kentucky senator John Griffin Carlyle, wrapped itself in the West, the speaker of Canto XCVII seeks 'novelle piante 新 / what ax for clearing?' Pound thus draws out the 'ax' element (斤) in the character for 'new' or 'renewal' (新). 'Kuanon' also reappears in a line Pound first composed between 24 and 27 June 1954:

> Kuanon, by the golden rail,
>   Nile διϊπετέος the flames gleam in the air[71]

The 'golden rail' and the flowing of the 'Nile' suggest the 'golden light floating on the Kotsu river' signalling the appearance of 'Kuanon' in *Tamura*; the 'flames' that 'gleam in the air', meanwhile, recall her 'forked branch-tips flaming as if with lotus' in Canto IV. The subject rhyme with the Nile, likewise, continues the pairing of 'Kuanon' with Isis made in Cantos XXI and XC. Just as her appearance coincides with the spring's blossoms in *Tamura*, too, 'under Kuanon's eye there is oak-wood' in Canto CI.[72] *Tamura*'s 'Kuanon' thus brings the renewal that the speaker of *The Cantos* seeks.

The trees of *Takasago*, meanwhile, rise further towards Pound's *paradiso* in *Thrones*. Canto CVI marks a return to the paradisal motif in Cantos IV, XXI, XXIX and XC. The spring's growth that brings autumn's harvest is represented in the form of Persephone, Demeter's 'daughter', after which the canto cites the pre-Confucian Chinese philosopher Guanzi's saying that 'The strength of men is in grain', the natural increase provided by the spring's regeneration reaped in the autumn. Moody notes that the 24-year-old Marcella Spann, who had begun visiting Pound in April that year and was in daily contact with him at the time of the canto's composition, is its 'Persephone'.[73] It draws a parallel between the importance of this regeneration in the West and the East, as do the paradisal cantos listed earlier. All are rooted in the 'grain rite':

>   this is grain rite
>   near Enna, at Nyssa:
>   Circe, Persephone
> so different is sea from glen that

---

[71] Pound, 'Canto 97', *Hudson Review* 9, no. 3 (Autumn 1956): 393.
[72] *TDLC*, 77.
[73] Moody, *Ezra Pound: Poet*, vol. 3, 393 and 397.

>   the juniper is her holy bush
> between the two pine trees, not Circe
>   but Circe was like that[74]

The pairing of 'Circe, Persephone' is that of sexual and vegetal renewal. This pairing, in turn, is made to correspond with 'the two pine trees' of *Takasago*. Terrell notes the correspondence with the 'pines of Ise' in Canto IV, in which *Takasago*'s two pine trees are compared with Kannon's wisdom; here, though, the reference is specifically to *Takasago*'s two pines, not the *Tamura* pines in Ise.[75] The love between the couple in *Takasago* is 'like' Circe; as in the previous allusions to *Takasago* in *The Cantos*, the 'single Image' of *Takasago*'s paired pine trees provides the model for these cross-cultural correspondences.

At the conclusion of Canto CVI, the theme of renewal depicted in the allusions to *Tamura* and *Takasago* is extended to the appearance of 'Arsinoe Kupris', Queen Arsinoe II of Egypt, who was worshipped as such at Zephyrium.[76] A temple was built:

> TO APHRODITE EUPLOIA
>   'an Aeolian gave it. ex voto
>   Arsinoe Kupris.
>   At Miwo the moon's axe is renewed[77]

The scene thus shifts, as in Canto XXI, towards a shore to the east, 'Miwo', the setting of *Hagoromo*. The comparison of Arsinoe with the celestial maiden of the play lies in Pound's association of both with renewal and the moon ('Selena Arsinoe').[78] Ōwada notes the 'jewelled axe's construction [*shūri*]' of her home, the 'palace of the moon', which the chorus describes as she performs the 'dance of the rainbow-feathered garment', emphasizing its stability and longevity. Due to the Hirata-Fenollosa translation, however, Pound reads the passage as 'The jewelled axe takes up the eternal renewing'.[79] This line thus encapsulates Pound's well-known dictum, 'make it new'.[80] Central to Pound's thinking was this conception from *Hagoromo* of 'eternal renewing', just as the maiden's dance coincides with the recurrence of the spring and the phases of the moon.

---

[74] *TDLC*, 105–6.
[75] *CCP*, 691.
[76] Ibid.
[77] *TDLC*, 107.
[78] Ibid.
[79] *NA*, 172.
[80] Pound, 'Canto 98', *L'Illustrazione Italiana* 85, no. 9 (September 1958): 36.

In *Drafts and Fragments*, the final part of *The Cantos*, nō returns to play a pivotal role in Pound's culminating paradisal vision. Canto CX, the collection's first canto, commemorates his visit to Venice with Marcella from 10 to 13 November 1958, some seven months after his release from St. Elizabeths.[81] On 12 November, he drafted its opening passage, in which the speaker remembers 'Thy quiet house', Marcella's at Torcello, and marvels at the 'exultant [. . .] boat's wake on sea-wall' and how it 'crests'.[82] By the following month, a typescript version included the 'paw-flap, wave-tap' of the 'boat's wake': 'that is gaiety'. Immediately afterwards, we read:

> Toba Sojo,
>   toward limpidity,
>   that is exultance,
>   here the crest runs on wall[83]

Bacigalupo and Stoicheff explain that Toba Sōjō was a Buddhist priest named Kakuyū (1053–1140), who painted the *Chōjū jinbutsu giga* ('Comic Pictures of Animals and People'). What neither Bacigalupo nor Stoicheff mentions, however, is that 'Toba Sojo' is discussed in Fenollosa's *Epochs*, in which the *Chōjū jinbutsu giga* is described as containing 'humorous sketches, largely of animals', thus corresponding with the 'gaiety' of the 'boat's wake' and commended for its 'simplicity of line' and depiction of 'motion' in 'The Battle of the Bulls', which is reproduced in the book. This explains the 'limpidity' Pound identified in Toba Sōjō's pictures.[84]

After the 'exultance' of the opening lines, Canto CX turns to remembrance of love lost. The 'wave-tap' of the 'boat's wake on sea-wall' reappears but the speaker turns from exultation to dejection. In addition to the Naxi rites for a couple who have committed suicide, the canto returns to the 'single Image' of the nō play *Kakitsubata* ('Iris'):

> Yellow iris in that river bed
>   yüeh$^{4\text{-}5}$
>   ming^{2}
>   mo$^{4\text{-}5}$
>   hsien^{1}
>   p'eng^{2} [85]

---

[81] Moody, *Ezra Pound: Poet*, vol. 3, 451.
[82] Ronald Bush, '"Unstill, Ever Turning": The Composition of Ezra Pound's *Drafts & Fragments*', in *Ezra Pound and Europe* (Amsterdam: Rodopi, 1993), 227; *DF*, 7.
[83] Ibid.
[84] *ECJA*, vol. 1, 174–5.
[85] *DF*, 8.

The 'Yellow iris in that river bed' recalls Pound's translation of *Kakitsubata*: 'By the eight bridges, by the web of the crossing waters in Kumode, the iris come to the full, they flaunt there and scatter their petals.'[86] When Narihira arrives there, he composes an acrostic *waka* on the iris that expresses his longing for his lover, Fujiwara no Takaiko. Narihira weeps for the loss of his past: 'The waves, the breakers return, / But my glory comes not again.'[87] The waves of the canto's opening can therefore be read as the speaker's lament for a lost time. The 'past friends' ('hsien^1 / p'eng^2') are now no longer there ('mo$^{4\text{-}5}$'). In this way, the opening's 'exultance' is tinged with disappointment that his 'glory comes not again'. Pound thus re-enacts what he saw as nō's bringing back of 'the shadow of the past in bright form'.

Pound's journeys to places redolent with memories continued into the winter: on 11 January 1959, he visited Lake Garda with Dorothy and Marcella.[88] They stayed at the Albergo Le Palme in Limone; on the back of one of its brochures, Pound wrote out these lines of Canto CX:

> And in thy mind beauty, O Artemis
> > as of mountain lakes in the dawn
> Foam and silk are thy fingers,
> > > Kuanon,
> and the long suavity of her moving,
> > willow and olive reflected[89]

The association of 'Kuanon' with water leads back to her first appearance in Pound's translation of *Tamura* as 'a golden light on the Kotsu river'. Her more specific connection with 'Foam' is suggested by Fenollosa's comments on the illustration of Wu Daozi's 'Standing Kwannon' in *Epochs*, in which Kannon 'descends from Heaven upon a cloud-like mass that breaks into the actual foam of water as it pierces space', an exhibition of 'water as the pure elementary symbol of Kwannon'.[90] In Kannon's left hand, Fenollosa observes, is a 'wisp of willow', a feature of Kannon's depiction Pound recommended including to Reck in his Japanese translation of *Women of Trachis*; as *Yōrō*'s depiction of 'Yorin (willow) Kuanon' suggests, her water is life-giving.[91] Pound's return to Lake Garda also

---

[86] Bacigalupo, *The Forméd Trace*, 468; Wendy Flory, *The American Ezra Pound* (New Haven: Yale University Press, 1989), 194; Stoicheff, *The Hall of Mirrors*, 96; Ewick, *Japonisme, Orientalism, Modernism*; NA, 209.
[87] NA, 216.
[88] Moody, *Ezra Pound: Poet*, vol. 3, 451.
[89] Ibid.; DF, 8; Moody, *Ezra Pound: Poet*, vol. 3, 612.
[90] ECJA, vol. 1, 132.
[91] Ibid., 133; Fenollosa and Pound (trans.), *Yoro*, 353.

takes him back to the 'Three Cantos', in which 'Gods float in the azure air', among whom 'Kwannon' on the water. Pound's phrasing here echoes Fenollosa's description of the seventh-century Chinese bronze 'Kwannon of Contemplation' as having 'perfect suavity of contour'.[92] Just as 'Kuanon' is Sheri Martinelli in Canto XC, now she is Marcella at Limone in Canto CX.[93]

Because Pound was 'pledged with many a lady', as Narihira had been, this led to resentment between the women involved.[94] Pound began a new notebook on 5 February 1959 when back in Brunnenburg with the first lines of Canto CX's close:

> That love be the cause of hate,
> > something is twisted,
> Awoi[95]

This refers to Princess Rokujō's jealousy of Genji's wife, 'Awoi', in Pound's translation. 'Awoi' is the one who expresses jealousy in Pound's version of the play, though Pound felt 'diffident' about whether 'Awoi' or 'Rokujo' is jealous. It is similarly ambiguous whether the 'type of envy' in Pound's own family drama at this time is Marcella or Dorothy. In the canto's final lines, deliverance from such jealousy is sought:

> Lux enim –
> > versus the tempest.
> The marble form in the pine wood,
> > The shrine seen and not seen,
> From the roots of sequoias
> > > > ching⁴
> > > pray 敬 pray
>
> > > There is power
> Awoi or Komachi,
> > the oval moon.[96]

'Awoi' could be any of them, while Komachi, the old woman who has lost the 'pride' of her youth, could be read as Dorothy, Olga or Pound himself, as the earlier allusion to Narihira would suggest. Stoicheff reads the reference to the

---

[92] *ECJA*, 43.
[93] Moody, *Ezra Pound: Poet*, vol. 3, 451.
[94] *NA*, 217.
[95] *DF*, 10.
[96] Ibid.

moon as the salvation for which the speaker prays 'beneath the Noh moon'.[97] Indeed, for the exorcism of Rokujō's 'evil spirit' out of 'Awoi', the 'holy man' asks if there is a 'clear moon' for it to take place; in *Kayoi Komachi*, likewise, Komachi offers a 'cup of moonlight' to Shōshō, after which 'Both their sins vanished'.[98] This canto thus demonstrates the shift from Pound's earlier distaste for many nō as 'romantic', a quality he associated with femininity, and 'too damn soft', compared with the 'rugged' masculine classicism of 'Li Po'. Pound's turn in *Drafts and Fragments* to the 'Noh moon', as Stoicheff puts it, is an ultimate embrace of the feminine as worthy of 'respect' (Pound's translation in Canto XC of 敬) and offering the 'power' of consolation.

In the 'long draft for 115', written between 23 July and 16 August 1959, Pound returns once more to *Kakitsubata*:

> A blown husk that is finish'd
> but the light sings eternal
> a pale flare over marshes[99]

The temporary nature of human life, which the earlier references to Narihira and Komachi in Canto CX indicate was in Pound's thoughts as he approached the end of his life, is suggested in *Kakitsubata* by 'the cracked husk of the locust', a contrast with the 'permanence' of the iris's 'spirit'.[100] Pound's additions to the play emphasize the association of Narihira and Takaiko's love with light: she was 'his light in her youth'; and Pound adds the verbs in the description of 'the flowers Kakitsubata / That flaunt and flare in their marsh', the latter reappearing in the canto.[101] The choice of verb in the second quoted line, too, is crucial: the 'light' that 'sings eternal' is that of song, the literary tradition also foregrounded in the 'inexhaustible words' of the 'pine-needles' in Pound's *Takasago*; the 'spirit' of the 'iris' is the 'Bosatsu' of song and dance Narihira's 'remembrance' of his love, first in his acrostic poem, then in the nō and now at the close of *The Cantos*. Such music, as Pound says when introducing the play, 'will lift a man's soul into paradise'; it is thus fitting that these lines should come towards the end of his forty-four-year quest to reach his *paradiso*.[102]

---

[97] Stoicheff, *The Hall of Mirrors*, 99.
[98] *NA*, 202 and 35–6.
[99] Ibid., 458–9.
[100] *NA*, 219.
[101] Ibid., 213 and 216.
[102] Ibid., 207.

And yet, as Stoicheff points out, Pound is unable to arrive at the 'foreseen paradisal culmination' to which *The Cantos* builds: the poem is, of course, 'a tangle of works unfinished', with the final lines having been composed in August 1959, more than thirteen years before Pound's death.[103] It fails to achieve this because, in the words of the speaker in Canto CXVI,

> I am not a demigod,
> I cannot make it cohere.[104]

Since the beginning of *The Cantos*' composition, Pound strove to achieve the 'Unity of Image' inspired by Fenollosa's interpretation in his notebooks of the nō plays Pound edited and published from them. This 'Unity of Image' referred to a political as well as an aesthetic unity: the 'single Image' of Pound's translation of *Takasago*, the 'paired pines' that formed 'the theme' of *The Cantos* at the outset, represent the harmony of a 'country well-governed' by a single ruler, the emperor. This politicized 'Unity of Image' was deployed in Pound's reading of 'the great Roman vortex' which, in his view, led to the cultural prosperity of the Roman Empire under the rule of one 'outstanding personality'. Like Mussolini, Pound developed this emphasis on Roman political unity into a fascist one, as the Roman origin of the 'fasces' indicates: his proposition in Mosley's fascist magazine that 'THE STATE SHOULD MOVE LIKE A DANCE' encapsulates this fusion of Pound's aesthetics and his politics. Like Mussolini, too, Pound also failed to realize such a unity in his life's work, *The Cantos*, though he never gives up on his dream: 'it coheres all right / even if my notes do not cohere.'[105]

Nō's importance for Pound right to the end of *The Cantos* is underscored by the appearance in the same year as the composition of the last cantos of *The Classic Noh Theatre of Japan* by New Directions, a new edition of *'Noh' or Accomplishment*. Pound's love of nō also persisted to the end not just of *The Cantos* but also of his life. He entered his 'silent period' soon after completing the final cantos. Nevertheless, when the Kanze school toured Europe performing nō in the summer of 1970 for the first time in its 600-year history, Pound made sure not to miss the opportunity finally to see nō being performed by a true nō school in the flesh and to meet 'the Minoru', whose 'Pride of descent, pride of having served dynasties now extinct' Pound had praised in 1915 and to whom he had wanted to give Reck's and Fujitomi's Japanese translation of *Women*

---

[103] *DF*, 25.
[104] Ibid., 26.
[105] Ibid., 27.

of *Trachis* to 'add' to their 'repertoire'. On 10 June 1970, Pound attended the second night of their performances at the Teatro Eliseo in Rome. Umewaka Makio, Umewaka Minoru's great-grandson, performed the lead role in *Aoi no ue*, followed by Umewaka Manzaburō II, Minoru's grandson, as the *shite* in the *shimai* dance of *Takasago*.[106] Pound thus not only saw the play whose film he had seen in 1939 and which had inspired him to demand that 'The whole of the Noh could be filmed' and that nō was 'a treasure like nothing in the Occident'; he also witnessed the performance of part of the play, *Takasago*, that formed 'the theme' of *The Cantos* at its outset and continued to function as an important model in the paradisal cantos towards the poem's close. While Pound never managed to visit Japan, he did see nō performed live by a professional nō school just before his death.

The importance of Pound's attendance, in turn, was not lost on the Japanese accompanying the tour: Pound's appearance at the Teatro Eliseo was even reported in the *Asahi Shimbun*, one of Japan's biggest national newspapers, as the most important event of the Teatro Eliseo performances in an article by the Ōsaka University of Arts professor Kitagishi Yūkichi, who had come with the Kanze School on their European tour: his *Asahi Shimbun* article on them was titled, 'Meeting Ezra Pound: A Sudden Visit of Manzaburō by the "Silent Man" Who Transmitted the True Value of Nō'.[107] After the final curtain call, when the nō actors were told backstage that 'Ezra Pound has come', Kitagishi relates that he 'could not believe [his] ears'.[108] Pound was known for his 'co-edition of *'Noh' or Accomplishment: A Study of the Classical Stage of Japan* with the benefactor of Japanese art, Ernest Fenollosa'. Pound also 'understood the truth of Japanese literature and taught the true value of nō to westerners'.[109] Because of his exile from his 'motherland' and his confinement in St. Elizabeths, however, 'he no longer seemed like someone of this world'; it seemed as if Pound had become one of the spirits in the *mugen* nō plays.[110] He had come 'to see Umewaka Minoru's grandson', Umewaka Manzaburō II. Pound and Minoru's grandson shook hands, and the 'silent man' looked intensely at Manzaburō, perhaps seeing in his face that of his grandfather, whose photo appeared in *'Noh' or Accomplishment*; then Pound left for the

---

[106] Kitagishi Yūkichi, 'Ezura Paundo ni au: totsuzen, Manzaburō ni hōmon: nō no shinka tsutaeta "chinmoku no hito"' ('Meeting Ezra Pound: A Sudden Visit of Manzaburō by the "Silent Man" Who Transmitted the True Value of Nō'), *Asahi Shimbun*, Ōsaka evening edition (22 June 1970): 7.
[107] Ibid.
[108] Ibid.
[109] Ibid.
[110] Ibid.

exit without another word. As Kitagishi explained in a later piece in *Kanze*, 'Pound's "oath of silence" could not be broken; but even just meeting the face of this benefactor of nō was a bountiful harvest'.[111] Hori Masato, whose nō teacher had also taken part in the tour, rightly concluded that 'Pound's interest in and love of nō lasted his whole life'.[112]

---

[111] Kitagishi, 'Doō wo oete' ('Completing the European Tour'), *Kanze* 37, no. 9 (September 1970): 31.
[112] Hori, 'Ezura Paundo to nōgaku', 8.

Bibliography

Works and translations by Pound

'Affirmations VI: The "Image" and the Classical Japanese Stage'. *Princeton University Library Chronicle* 53, no. 1 (Autumn 1991): 17–22.
'Canto LXXXV'. *Hudson Review* 7, no. 4 (Winter 1954): 487–501.
'Canto 97'. *Hudson Review* 9, no. 3 (Autumn 1956): 387–98.
'Canto 98'. *L'Illustrazione Italiana* 85, no. 9 (September 1958): 34–9.
The Cantos. London: Faber & Faber, 1975.
'Cantos 86–7'. *Hudson Review* 8, no. 1 (Spring 1955): 13–27.
'Cantos 88–9'. *Hudson Review* 8, no. 2 (Summer 1955): 183–204.
'Chronicles'. *BLAST* 2 (July 1915): 85–6.
'The Classical Drama of Japan'. *Quarterly Review* 221, no. 441 (October 1914): 450–77.
'The Classical Stage of Japan: Ernest Fenollosa's Work on the Japanese "Noh"'. *The Drama* 18 (May 1915): 199–247.
'The Coming of War: Actaeon'. *Poetry* 5, no. 6 (March 1915): 255–6.
'The Condolence'. *Poetry* 2, no. 1 (April 1913): 2.
'D'Artagnan Twenty Years After'. *The Criterion* 16, no. 5 (July 1937): 606–17.
A Draft of the Cantos 17-27. London: John Rodker, 1928.
A Draft of XVI Cantos for the Beginning of a Poem of Some Length. Paris: Three Mountains Press, 1925.
A Draft of XXX Cantos. Paris: Hours Press, 1930.
Drafts and Fragments. New York: New Directions, 1968.
'Early Translators of Homer'. *The Egoist* 5, no. 7 (August 1918): 95–7.
'Edward Wadsworth – Vorticist'. *The Egoist* 1, no. 16 (15 August 1914): 306.
'Elizabethan Classicists – II'. *The Egoist* 4, no. 9 (October 1917): 135–6.
'Epitaph'. *The Smart Set* 41, no. 4 (December 1913): 47.
'Ezra Pound Asks Scholars Here to Solve Issues'. *Japan Times and Mail* (4 March 1940): 6.
Ezra Pound to His Parents: Letters 1895-1929. Edited by A. David Moody, Joanna Moody and Mary de Rachewiltz. Oxford: Oxford University Press, 2010.
'Ezra Pound Speaking': Radio Speeches of World War II. Edited by Leonard W. Doob. Westport: Greenwood Press, 1978.
'Fan Piece for Her Imperial Lord'. *The Glebe* 1, no. 5 (February 1914): 45.
'A Few Don'ts by an Imagiste'. *Poetry* 1, no. 6 (March 1913): 199–206.
The Fourth Canto. Paris: Ovid Press, 1919.
'From Rapallo: An Ezra Pound Letter'. *The Japan Times and Mail* (26 August 1940): 8.
'The Garden'. *Poetry* 2, no. 1 (April 1913): 3–4.

Guide to Kulchur. New York: New Directions, 1968.

'Histrion'. *Evening Standard and St James's Gazette* (26 October 1908): 3.

'How I Began'. *T. P.'s Weekly* (6 June 1913): 707.

How to Read. London: Desmond Harmsworth, 1931.

'In a Station of the Metro'. *Poetry* 2, no. 1 (April 1913): 12.

'In a Station of the Metro'. In *Modern American Poetry: An Introduction*, edited by Louis Untermeyer, 137. New York: Harcourt, Brace and Howe, 1919.

'In a Station of the Metro'. In *Education Manual 131*. Edited by the United States Armed Forces Institute, 345. Washington, DC: War Department, 1942.

'Itarii tsūshin'. Translated by Kitasono Katué. *Shin gijutsu* 32 (March 1941): 22–4.

The Letters of Ezra Pound 1907–1941. Edited by D. D. Paige. London: Faber & Faber, 1951.

The Letters of Ezra Pound to Alice Corbin Henderson. Edited by Ira Nadel. Austin: University of Texas Press, 1993.

A Lume Spento and Other Early Poems. New York: New Directions, 1965.

'Music: Le Mariage de Figaro'. *The New Age* n. s. 4, no. 7 (6 December 1917): 113–15.

'Pastiche: Regional – XVIII'. *The New Age* n. s. 26, no. 3 (20 November 1919): 48.

'Patria Mia: VIII'. *The New Age* n. s. 9, no. 26 (24 October 1912): 611–12.

Personae. London: Elkin Mathews, 1909.

The Pisan Cantos of Ezra Pound. Norfolk: New Directions, 1948.

Plays Modelled on the Noh (1916). Edited by Donald C. Gallup. Toledo: The Friends of the University of Toledo Libraries, 1987.

Pound/The Little Review: The Letters of Ezra Pound to Margaret Anderson. Edited by Thomas L. Scott, Jackson R. Myer and Melvin J. Friedman. New York: New Directions, 1988.

'Remy de Gourmont'. *The Fortnightly Review* n. s. 98, no. 588 (1 December 1915): 1159–66.

'The Renaissance – II'. *Poetry* 5, no. 6 (March 1915): 283–7.

'The Renaissance – III'. *Poetry* 6, no. 2 (May 1915): 84–91.

Review of *Certain Noble Plays of Japan* and '*Noh' or Accomplishment*. *The Little Review* 4, no. 4 (August 1917): 8–10.

Section: Rock-drill de los cantares 85–95. New York: New Directions, 1956.

The Selected Letters of Ezra Pound to John Quinn. Edited by Timothy Materer. Durham: Duke University Press, 1991.

'The Serious Artist'. *The New Freewoman* 1, no. 10 (1 November 1913): 194–5.

The Spirit of Romance. London: J. M. Dent, 1910.

'The State Should Move Like a Dance'. *British Union Quarterly* 11, no. 4 (October–December 1938): 43–51.

'Study of Noh Continues in West'. *The Japan Times and Mail* (10 December 1939): 8.

'Sword-Dance and Spear-Dance'. *Future* 1, no. 2 (December 1916): 54–5.

'Three Cantos – I'. *Poetry* 10, no. 3 (June 1917): 113–21.

'Three Cantos – II'. *Poetry* 10, no. 4 (July 1917): 180–8.

Thrones 96–109 de los cantares. New York: New Directions, 1959.

'To Whistler, American'. *Poetry* 1, no. 1 (October 1912): 7.
'Totalitarian Scholarship and the New Paideuma'. *Germany and You* 7, no. 4/5 (25 April 1937): 95–6 and 123–4.
The Translations of Ezra Pound. Norfolk: New Directions, 1953.
'Tri-lingual System Proposed for World Communications: Noted Scholar of Noh Suggests Bilingual or Trilingual Edition of Hundred Best Books of Japanese Literature'. *Japan Times and Mail* (15 May 1939): 4.
'Ts'ai Chih'. *The Glebe* 1, no. 5 (February 1914): 46.
'Usury and Humanity Do Battle While China is Heavily Engaged'. *Japan Times and Advertiser* (14 December 1940): 4.
'Vortex'. *BLAST* 1 (20 June 1914): 153–4.
'Vorticism'. *The Fortnightly Review* n. s. 102, no. 573 (1 September 1914): 461–71.
'VOU Club'. *Townsman* 1, no. 1 (January 1938): 4.
Women of Trachis. *Hudson Review* 6, no. 4 (Winter 1954): 487–523.
'Xenia I-VII'. *Poetry* 3, no. 2 (November 1913): 58–60.

Co-authored Works

Fenollosa, Ernest and Ezra Pound, trans. *Awoi no Uye*. *Quarterly Notebook* 1, no. 1 (June 1916): 9–16.
Fenollosa, Ernest and Ezra Pound, eds. *Certain Noble Plays of Japan*. Dundrum: Cuala Press, 1916.
Fenollosa, Ernest and Ezra Pound, trans. *Kakitsuhata*: *The Drama* 23 (August 1916): 428–35.
Fenollosa, Ernest and Ezra Pound, eds. *'Noh' or Accomplishment: A Study of the Classical Stage of Japan*. London: Macmillan, 1916 [1917].
Fenollosa, Ernest and Ezra Pound, trans. *Yoro*. Edited by Richard Taylor. *Paideuma* 6, no. 1 (Spring 1975): 349–53.
Pound, Ezra and Dorothy Shakespear. *Ezra Pound and Dorothy Shakespear: Their Letters, 1909–1914*. Edited by Omar Pound and A. Walton Litz. London: Faber & Faber, 1984.
Pound, Ezra and Rudd Fleming, trans. *Elektra*. Edited by Richard Reid. Princeton, NJ: Princeton University Press, 1987.

Secondary Sources

Adams, Brooks. *The New Empire*. London: Macmillan, 1902.
Advertisement for *BLAST*. *The Egoist* 1, no. 7 (1 April 1914): 140.
Advertisement for Ōwada Takeki. *Gunka*. *Nōgaku* 2, no. 5 (May 1904): 68.

Alexander, Neal. *Regional Modernisms*. Edinburgh: Edinburgh University Press, 2013.

Anderson, William. *Descriptive Catalogue of the Collection of Japanese and Chinese Paintings at the British Museum*. London: Longmans, 1886.

Arrowsmith, Rupert Richard. *Modernism and the Museum: Asian, African and Pacific Art and the London Avant-Garde*. Oxford: Oxford University Press, 2011.

Aston, W. G. *A Grammar of the Japanese Written Language*. 2nd edn. Yokohama: Lane, Crawford, 1887.

Aston, W. G., ed. *A History of Japanese Literature*. London: William Heinemann, 1899.

Atarashiki tsuchi. Directed by Arnold Franck and Itami Mansaku. J. O. Studios, 1937.

Bacigalupo, Massimo. *The Forméd Trace: The Later Poetry of Ezra Pound*. New York: Columbia University Press, 1980.

Bédier, Joseph. *Le Roman du Tristan*. 2 vols. Paris: Librairie de Firmin Didot, 1905.

Bénard, Charles. 'Analytical and Critical Essay upon the Aesthetics of Hegel'. Translated by J. A. Martling. *The Journal of Speculative Philosophy* 1 (1867): 36–52.

Bénard, Charles. 'Benard's [sic] Essay on Hegel's Aesthetics'. Translated by J. A. Martling. *The Journal of Speculative Philosophy* 2 (1868): 39–52.

Benton, Thomas Hart. *Thirty Years' View: or, A History of the Working of the American Government for Thirty Years, from 1820 to 1850*. 2 vols. New York: D. Appleton, 1856.

Béroul. *Roman de Tristan*. Paris: Librairie de Firmin Didot, 1903.

Berryman, Jo Brantley. 'Ezra Pound and James McNeill Whistler: Modernism and Conceptual Art'. In *Ezra Pound and the Arts*, edited by Roxana Preda, 157–76. Edinburgh: Edinburgh University Press, 2019.

Binyon, Laurence. *The Flight of the Dragon*. London: John Murray, 1911.

Binyon, Laurence. *Painting in the Far East*. London: Edward Arnold, 1908.

Brinkley, Francis. *Japan: Its History, Art and Literature*. 8 vols. Boston: J. B. Millet Company, 1901–2.

Britten, Benjamin. *Letters from a Life: Selected Letters and Diaries of Benjamin Britten*. Edited by Donald Mitchell and Philip Reed. 4 vols. London: Faber & Faber, 1991–2008.

Brooks, Van Wyck. *Fenollosa and His Circle: With Other Essays in Biography*. New York: E. P. Dutton & Co., 1962.

Browning, Robert. *Sordello*. London: Edward Moxon, 1840.

Bush, Christopher. '"I Am All for the Triangle": The Geopolitical Aesthetic of Pound's Japan'. In *Ezra Pound in the Present: Essays on Pound's Contemporaneity*, edited by Paul Stasi and Josephine Park, 75–106. London: Bloomsbury, 2016.

Bush, Ronald. *The Genesis of the Cantos*. Princeton: Princeton University Press, 1976.

Bush, Ronald. '"Unstill, Ever Turning": The Composition of Ezra Pound's *Drafts & Fragments*'. In *Ezra Pound and Europe*, edited by Richard A. Taylor and Claus Melchior, 223–42. Amsterdam: Rodopi, 1993.

Byron, Mark. 'In a Station of the *Cantos*: Ezra Pound's "Seven Lakes" Canto and the *Shō-Shō Hakkei* Tekagami'. *Literature and Aesthetics* 22, no. 2 (December 2012): 138–52.

Caldwell, Helen. *Michio Ito: The Dancer and His Dances*. Berkeley: University of California Press, 1977.

Callimachus. *The Works of Callimachus*. Translated by H. W. Tytler. London: T. Davison, 1793.
Carr, Helen. *The Verse Revolutionaries: Ezra Pound, H. D. & the Imagists*. London: Jonathan Cape, 2009.
Chamberlain, Basil Hall. 'Bashō and the Japanese Poetical Epigram'. *The Transactions of the Asiatic Society of Japan* 30 (1902): 244–362.
Chamberlain, Basil Hall, ed. *The Classical Poetry of the Japanese*. London: Trübner, 1880.
Chamberlain, Basil Hall. 'The Death-Stone: A Lyric Drama from the Japanese'. *Cornhill Magazine* 34 (July–December 1876): 479–88.
Chamberlain, Basil Hall. *A Handbook of Colloquial Japanese*. London: Trübner, 1889.
Chamberlain, Basil Hall. *Japanese Poetry*. London: John Murray, 1910.
Chamberlain, Basil Hall. 'Preface'. In Konakamura Kiyonori. *Kabu ongaku ryakushi*. 2 vols. Tokyo: privately printed, 1888.
Chamberlain, Basil Hall. *Things Japanese*. 4th edn. London: Kegan Paul, Trench, Trübner & Co, 1902.
Chisolm, Lawrence. *Fenollosa: The Far East and American Culture*. New Haven: Yale University Press, 1963.
Chūinbon Heike monogatari. Edited by Imai Shōnosuke and Chigira Mamoru. 2 vols. Tokyo: Miyai shoten, 2011.
Coffman, Stanley. *Imagism: A Chapter in the History of American Poetry*. Norman: University of Oklahoma Press, 1951.
Couchoud, Paul-Louis. 'Les haïkaï (Épigrammes poétiques du Japon)'. *Les Lettres* 3 (April 1906): 189–98.
Dante Alighieri. *The Paradiso*. Translated by Philip Wicksteed. London: J. M. Dent, 1910.
Dickins, F. V. *Chiushingura; or, The Loyal League: A Japanese Romance*. Yokohama: The Japan Gazette, 1875.
Dickins, F. V., ed. *Primitive & Medieval Japanese Texts*. Oxford: Clarendon, 1906.
Dōgen. *Shōbōgenzō zenyaku dokkai*. Edited by Masutani Fumio. 8 vols. Tokyo: Kōdansha, 2004.
Edwards, John. 'Pound's Translations'. *Poetry* 83, no. 4 (January 1954): 233–8.
Edwards, Osman. *Japanese Plays and Playfellows*. London: John Lane, 1901.
Eliot, T. S. *Ezra Pound His Metric and Poetry*. New York: Knopf, 1917.
'Enzetsu'. *Nōgaku* 2, no. 2 (February 1904): 1–4.
Ewick, David. 'Ezra Pound and the Invention of Japan, I'. *Eibei bungaku hyōron* 63 (2017): 13–39.
Ewick, David. 'Imagism Status Rerum and a Note on Haiku'. *Make It New* 2, no. 1 (2015): 42–57.
Ewick, David. *Japonisme, Orientalism, Modernism: A Critical Bibliography of Japan in English-Language Verse*. Online.
Ewick, David. 'A Little History of Ezra Pound and Arthur Waley'. Conference paper given at Ezra Pound and Japan, Tokyo Woman's Christian University. 12 March 2018.

Ewick, David. 'Notes Toward a Cultural History of Japanese Modernism in Modernist Europe, 1910–1920: With Special Reference to Kōri Torahiko'. *The Hemingway Review of Japan* 13 (June 2012): 19–36.

Ewick, David. 'Strange Attractors: Ezra Pound and the Invention of Japan, II'. *Eibei bungaku hyōron* 64 (2018): 1–40.

Fenollosa, Ernest. *Bijutsu shinsetsu*. Translated by Ōmori Ichii. Tokyo: Ryūchikai, 1882.

Fenollosa, Ernest. 'The Chinese Written Character as a Medium for Poetry [I]'. *The Little Review* 6, no. 5 (September 1919): 62–4.

Fenollosa, Ernest. 'The Chinese Written Character as a Medium for Poetry [II]'. *The Little Review* 6, no. 6 (October 1919): 57–64.

Fenollosa, Ernest. *Epochs of Chinese and Japanese Art*. 2 vols. New York: Frederick A. Stokes, 1912.

Fenollosa, Ernest. 'Imagination in Art: Introductory Remarks'. *The Annual Report of the Boston Art Students' Association* 15 (June 1894): 3–11.

Fenollosa, Ernest. 'Lecture V. *No*'. In *The Ernest F. Fenollosa Papers: The Houghton Library, Harvard University*. Edited by Akiko Murakata, 274–92. Vol. 3. Tokyo: Museum Press, 1987.

Fenollosa, Ernest. *Nishikigi*. In *Poetry* 4, no. 2 (May 1914): 35–48.

Fenollosa, Ernest. 'Notes on the Japanese Lyric Drama'. *Journal of the American Oriental Society* 22, no. 1 (1901): 129–57.

Fenollosa, Ernest. *Published Writings in English*. Edited by Yamaguchi Seiichi. 3 vols. Tokyo: Edition Synapse, 2009.

Fenollosa, Mary McNeil. 'Preface'. In Ernest Fenollosa. *Epochs of Chinese and Japanese Art*. 2 vols. Vol. 1, vii–xxii. New York: Frederick A. Stokes, 1912.

Ferguson, Robert. *The Short Sharp Life of T. E. Hulme*. London: Allen Lane, 2002.

Fisher, Margaret. *Ezra Pound's Radio Operas: The BBC Experiments, 1931–33*. Cambridge, MA: MIT Press, 2002.

Flint, F. S. 'Belated Romanticism'. *The New Age* n. s. 4, no. 18 (25 February 1909): 371.

Flint, F. S. 'Book of the Week: Recent Verse'. *The New Age* n. s. 3, no. 11 (11 July 1908): 212–13.

Flint, F. S. 'Book of the Week: Recent Verse'. *The New Age* n. s. 3, no. 16 (15 August 1908): 312–13.

Flint, F. S. 'Book of the Week: Recent Verse'. *The New Age* n. s. 3, no. 18 (29 August 1908): 352–3.

Flint, F. S. 'Book of the Week: Recent Verse'. *The New Age* n. s. 4, no. 16 (11 February 1909): 327–8.

Flint, F. S. 'Contemporary French Poetry'. *The Poetry Review* 1, no. 8 (August 1912): 355–414.

Flint, F. S. 'The History of Imagism'. *The Egoist* 5, no. 11 (1 May 1915): 70–1.

Flint, F. S. 'Imagisme'. *Poetry* 1, no. 6 (March 1913): 198–200.

Flint, F. S. 'Palinode'. *The New Age* n. s. 2, no. 12 (18 January 1908): 232.

Flory, Wendy. *The American Ezra Pound*. New Haven: Yale University Press, 1989.

Frazer, James. *The Golden Bough*. 3rd edn. 12 vols. London: Macmillan, 1906–15.
Froula, Christine. *To Write Paradise: Style and Error in Pound's Cantos*. New Haven: Yale University Press, 1984.
Fujisawa Morihiko. *Nihon densetsu kenkyū*. Tokyo: Subaru shobō, 1978.
Fujita Fujio. *Itō Michio: sekai wo mau: taiyō no gekijō wo mezashite*. Tokyo: Musashino, 1992.
Furukawa Hisashi. *Meiji nōgakushi josetsu*. Tokyo: Wanya shoten, 1969.
Furukawa Hisashi. *Ōbeijin no nōgaku kenkyū*. Tokyo: Tokyo Woman's Christian University Academic Society, 1962.
Fusetsu. 'Meiji shonen no seiyōga'. *Bijutsu shashin gahō* 1, no. 4 (April 1920): 81.
Fusetsu. 'Shukyaku'. In *Gadō ippan*, 57. Tokyo: Hakubunkan, 1906.
Gabō Sanjin. Introduction to *Haika kijin dan*. Edited by Takenouchi Gengenichi. Osaka, 1816.
Garthorne-Hardy, Robert, ed. *Ottoline: The Early Memoirs of Lady Ottoline Morrell*. London: Faber & Faber, 1963.
Gikeiki. Edited by Kajihara Masa'aki. Tokyo: Shōgakukan, 1999.
Giles, Herbert, ed. *A History of Chinese Literature*. London: William Heinemann, 1901.
'Hagoromo sōdan'. *Nōgaku* 1, no. 5 (November 1902): 19–22.
Hakutani, Yoshinobu. *Haiku and Modernist Poetics*. Basingstoke: Palgrave Macmillan, 2009.
Hall, Donald. 'E. P.: An Interview'. In *Writers at Work: The Paris Review Interviews, Second Series*, edited by George Plimpton, 25–59. New York: Viking, 1963.
Hanada Ryōun. *Yōkyoku ni arawaretaru bukkyō*. Kyoto: Kōgyō shoin, 1938.
Hardacre, Helen. *Shinto: A History*. Oxford: Oxford University Press, 2016.
Harmer, J. B. *Victory in Limbo: Imagism 1908–1917*. London: Secker & Warburg, 1975.
Hartmann, Sadakichi. *Collected Poems, 1886–1944*. Edited by Floyd Cheung. Stroud: Little Island Press, 2016.
Hartmann, Sadakichi. *Japanese Art*. Boston: L. C. Page & Company, 1904.
Hartmann, Sadakichi. 'The Japanese Conception of Poetry'. *The Reader* 3, no. 2 (January 1904): 185–91.
Hartmann, Sadakichi. *White Chrysanthemums: Literary Fragments and Pronouncements*. Edited by George Knox and Harry W. Lawton. New York: Herder and Herder, 1971.
Hatcher, John. *Laurence Binyon: Poet, Scholar of East and West*. Oxford: Clarendon, 1995.
H. D. *HERmione*. New York: New Directions, 1981.
Hearn, Lafcadio. *Exotics and Retrospectives*. Boston: Little, Brown & Co., 1898.
Hearn, Lafcadio. *In Ghostly Japan*. Boston: Little, Brown & Co., 1899.
Heike monogatari. Edited by Nagai Kazutaka. Tokyo: Yūhōdō, 1912.
Heike monogatari. Edited by Ichiko Teiji. 2 vols. Tokyo: Shōgakukan, 1994.
Hofmann, Reto. *The Fascist Effect: Japan and Italy, 1915–1952*. Ithaca: Cornell University Press, 2015.
Homer. *Odyssea ad verbum*. Translated by Andrea Divo di Iustinopolitano. Salingiaci, 1540.

Hori Masato. 'Ezura Paundo to nōgaku'. *Tōzai gakujutsu kenkyūsho kiyō* 4 (March 1971): 1–12.

Houwen, Andrew. 'Ezra Pound's Early Cantos and His Translation of *Takasago*'. *The Review of English Studies* 65, no. 269 (April 2014): 321–41.

Hulme, T. E. 'Belated Romanticism'. *The New Age* n. s. 4, no. 17 (18 February 1909): 350.

Hulme, T. E. 'A Lecture on Modern Poetry'. In *The Collected Writings of T. E. Hulme*, edited by Karen Csengeri, 49–56. Oxford: Clarendon, 1994.

Hulme, T. E. 'Romanticism and Classicism'. In *Speculation: Essays on Humanism and the Philosophy of Art*. Edited by Herbert Read, 111–39. London: Kegan Paul, Trench, Trübner, 1924.

Ibsen, Henrik. *The Pillars of Society and Other Plays*. Translated by Havelock Ellis. London: Walter Scott, 1888.

Iei Michiko. 'Nishikizuka no kōsatsu'. *Artes Liberales* 44 (June 1989): 173–90.

Ikenouchi Nobuyoshi. 'Shiba nōgakudō no yurai oyobi ryakureki'. *Nōgaku* 1, no. 2 (August 1902): 11–15.

Imamura, Tateo. 'Hemingway, Pound, and the Japanese Artist, Tamijuro Kume'. *The Hemingway Review of Japan* 13 (June 2012): 37–47.

Ise monogatari. Edited by Katagiri Yōichi and Tanaka Maki. Osaka: Izumi shoin, 2016.

Ishibashi, Hiro. 'Marie C. Stopes to nō (2)'. *Eigo seinen* 124, no. 4 (1 July 1978): 36–7.

Itō Masayoshi, ed. *Yōkyokushū*. 2nd edn. 3 vols. Tokyo: Shinchōsha, 2015.

Itō Michio. *Reminiscences*. Translated and edited by David Ewick and Dorsey Kleitz. New York: Edwin Mellen, 2018.

Itsumin Koji, ed. *Kembushū*. Tokyo: Shūmeisha, 1890.

Iwakami, Haruko and Peter F. Kornicki, eds. *F. V. Dickins' Letters to Ernest M. Satow, Kumagasu Minakata and Others: A Collection of Transcriptions and Japanese Translations*. Tokyo: Edition Synapse, 2011.

Josui Ikiru. 'Ishin tōji no nōgaku'. *Nōgaku* 1, no. 1 (July 1902): 21–5.

Kaneko Kentarō. 'Ware to Fenorosa'. *Kōyūkai gappō* 19, no. 6 (November 1920): 165–6.

Kanze Katsuko. 'Kaikyūdan'. *Nōgaku* 9, no. 8 (August 1911): 34–9.

Katagiri Yōichi and Takaoka Masao, eds. *Kokinshū zenhyōshaku*. 3 vols. Tokyo: Yūbun shoin, 1976.

Kayano Hatakazu [Kōri Torahiko]. 'Dōjōji'. *Mita bungaku* 3, no. 4 (April 1912): 1–27.

Kayano Hatakazu [Kōri Torahiko]. 'Erekutora kōgai'. *Shirakaba* 1, no. 1 (April 1910): 38–51.

Kayano Hatakazu [Kōri Torahiko]. 'Kiyohime moshiku wa Dōjōji'. *Subaru* 4, no. 6 (June 1911): 1–14.

Keene, Donald. *Emperor of Japan: Meiji and His World*. Tokyo: Yushodo, 2004.

Keene, Donald. *The Winter Sun Shines In: A Life of Masaoka Shiki*. New York: Columbia University Press, 2013.

Kenner, Hugh. *The Poetry of Ezra Pound*. Norfolk: New Directions, 1951.

Kenner, Hugh. *The Pound Era*. Berkeley: University of California Press, 1971.

Kindellan, Michael. *The Late Cantos of Ezra Pound*. London: Bloomsbury, 2017.

Kitagishi, 'Doō wo oete'. *Kanze* 37, no. 9 (September 1970): 28–31.
Kitagishi Yūkichi, 'Ezura Paundo ni au: totsuzen, Manzaburō ni hōmon: nō no shinka tsutaeta "chinmonku no hito"'. *Asahi Shimbun*, Ōsaka evening edition (22 June 1970): 7.
Kitasono, Katué. 'Eikoku ni okeru "Suma Genji" no jōen'. *VOU* 17 (March 1937): 29–30.
Kiuchi Toru. 'Noguchi Yonejirō – haiku wo sekai ni hirometa hito'. *Kadokawa haiku* 66, no. 10 (September 2016): 118–29.
Kleitz, Dorsey. 'Michio Ito and the Modernist Vortex'. *The Hemingway Review of Japan* 13 (June 2012): 49–57.
Kodama, Sanehide, ed. *Ezra Pound & Japan: Letters & Essays*. Redding Ridge: Black Swan, 1987.
Kōri Torahiko. *Zenshū*. Edited by Yamauchi Hideo. 3 vols. Tokyo: Sōgensha, 1936.
Kornicki, P. F. 'William George Aston (1841–1911)'. In *Britain and Japan 1859–1991*, edited by Hugh Cortazzi and Gordon Daniels, 64–75. London: Routledge, 1991.
Kōson. *Sōrinshi hyōshaku haikai ron hakkenden shohyōtōshū*. Tokyo: privately printed, 1893.
Kōyō. *Haikai meikasen*. Tokyo: Shunyōdō, 1897.
Kōyō. *Ozaki Kōyō zenshū*. Tokyo: Iwanami shoten, 1994.
Kumamoto Kenjirō. *Meiji shoki raichō Itaria bijutsuka no kenkyū*. Tokyo: Sanseidō, 1940.
Kumārajīva. *The Lotus Sutra*. Translated by Burton Watson. New York: Columbia University Press, 1993.
Kume Kunitake. *The Iwakura Embassy 1871-3: A True Account of the Ambassador Extraordinary & Plenipotentiary's Journey of Observation through the United States of America*. Translated by Graham Healey and Chūshichi Tsuzuki. 4 vols. Princeton: Princeton University Press, 2002.
Kume Kunitake. 'Nōgaku no kako to shōrai'. *Nōgaku* 9, no. 7 (July 1911): 1–7.
Kurata Yoshihiro. 'Meiji nōgakukai no hikari to kage'. *Nōgaku kenkyū* 25 (2000): 1–20.
Liebregts, Peter. *Ezra Pound and Neo-Platonism*. Teaneck: Fairleigh Dickinson University Press, 2004.
Liebregts, Peter. *Translations of Greek Tragedy in the Work of Ezra Pound*. London: Bloomsbury, 2019.
Longenbach, James. *Stone Cottage: Pound, Yeats & Modernism*. Oxford: Oxford University Press, 1988.
Maeda Kyōji. *E no yō ni: Meiji bungaku to bijutsu*. Tokyo: Hakusuisha, 2014.
Mailla, Joseph Anne-Marie de Moyriac de. *Histoire générale de la Chine, ou Annales de cet empire*. 13 vols. Paris: Pierres et Clousier, 1777–85.
Maitre, Claude Eugène. 'Japon'. *Bulletin de l'École française d'Extrême-Orient* 3, no. 1 (1903): 723–9.
Makin, Peter. *Pound's Cantos*. Baltimore: Johns Hopkins University Press, 1985.
Mallarmé, Stéphane. 'Crise de vers'. In *Divagations*, 233–49. Paris: Bibliothèque Charpentier, 1897.

Matsui Takako. *Shasei no henyō: Fontaneeji kara Shiki, soshite Naoya e*. Tokyo: Meiji Shoin, 2002.

Matsumoto Kintarō. 'Ishingo no keireki dan'. *Nōgaku* 1, no. 7 (January 1903): 29–31.

Miner, Earl. *The Japanese Tradition in British and American Literature*. Princeton: Princeton University Press, 1958.

Miner, Earl. 'Pound and Fenollosa Papers Relating to Nō'. *Princeton University Library Chronicle* 53, no. 1 (Autumn 1991): 12–16.

Mitford, Algernon. *Tales of Old Japan*. London: Macmillan, 1871.

Moody, A. David. *Ezra Pound: Poet: A Portrait of the Man & His Work*. 3 vols. Oxford: Oxford University Press, 2007–15.

Morita, Norimasa. 'The Toils of Kōri Torahiko'. In *Britain and Japan: Biographical Portraits*. Edited by Hugh Cortazzi, 296–310. 9 vols, vol. 7. Folkestone: Global Oriental, 2010.

Morse, Edward S. *Japan Day by Day*. 2 vols. Boston: Houghton Mifflin, 1917.

Miyake, Akiko, Sanehide Kodama and Nicholas Teele, eds. *A Guide to Ezra Pound and Ernest Fenollosa's Classic Noh Theater of Japan*. Orono: National Poetry Foundation, 1994.

Murakata, Akiko, ed. *The Ernest F. Fenollosa Papers: The Houghton Library, Harvard University*. 3 vols. Tokyo: Museum Press, 1987.

Murasaki Shikibu. *Genji monogatari*. Edited by Ishida Jōji and Shimizu Yoshiko. 8 vols. Tokyo: Dai Nippon, 2014.

Murasaki Shikibu. *The Tale of Genji*. Translated by Arthur Waley. London: G. Allen & Unwin, 1925.

Musset, Alfred de. *Oeuvres posthumes*. Paris: Charpentier, 1860.

Nicholls, Peter. 'An Experiment with Time: Ezra Pound and the Example of Japanese Noh'. *Modern Language Review* 90, no. 1 (January 1995): 1–13.

Noguchi, Yone. *The American Diary of a Japanese Girl*. New York: Frederick A. Stokes, 1902.

Noguchi, Yone. 'Hokku'. *The Academy* (13 July 1912): 57–8.

Noguchi, Yone. *Lafcadio Hearn in Japan*. London: Elkin Mathews, 1910.

Noguchi, Yone. *The Pilgrimage*. 2nd edn. 2 vols. London: Elkin Mathews, 1909.

Noguchi, Yone. 'A Proposal to American Poets'. *The Reader* 3, no. 3 (February 1904): 248.

Noguchi, Yone. *The Story of Yone Noguchi as Told by Himself*. London: Chatto & Windus, 1914.

Noguchi, Yone. 'What Is a Hokku Poem?' *Rhythm* 4 (January 1913): 354–9.

'Notes'. *Poetry* 4, no. 2 (May 1915): 71–2.

Okimori Takuya, Satō Makoto and Yajima Izumi, eds. *Kojiki: shinkō*. Tokyo: Ōfū, 2015.

Ōkura Hanjirō. 'Komparu ryū no kokiroku'. *Nōgaku* 9, no. 12 (December 1911): 46–8.

Ono, Ayako. *Japonisme*. London: Routledge, 2003.

Oshukov, Mikhail. *Representation of Otherness in Literary Avant-Garde of Early Twentieth Century: David Burliuk's and Ezra Pound's Japan [sic]*. PhD Thesis: University of Turku, 2017.

Ota, Yuzo. *Basil Hall Chamberlain: Portrait of a Japanologist*. Richmond: Japan Library, 1998.
Ovid. *Heroïdes, with the Greek Translation of the Planudes*. Edited and translated by Arthur Palmer. Oxford: Clarendon, 1898.
Ōwada Takeki. 'Nikki bansui'. *Nōgaku* 9, no. 2 (February 1911): 80–4.
Ōwada Takeki. 'Nikki bansui'. *Nōgaku* 9, no. 4 (April 1911): 69–73.
Ōwada Takeki. 'Nikki bansui'. *Nōgaku* 9, no. 5 (May 1911): 64–8.
Ōwada Takeki. 'Nikki bansui'. *Nōgaku* 12, no. 5 (May 1913): 110–15.
Ōwada Takeki. *Seiro gunka*. Tokyo: Ikueisha, 1904.
Ōwada Takeki. *Shijin no haru: shinchō shōka*. Tokyo: Bunseidō, 1887.
Ōwada Takeki. *Utai to nō*. Tokyo: Hakubunkan, 1900.
Ōwada Takeki. 'Yōkyoku kōgi: Takasago'. *Nōgaku* 1, no. 1 (July 1902): 2–14.
Ōwada Takeki, ed. *Yōkyoku tsūkai*. 8 vols. Tokyo: Hakubunkan, 1892.
Ōwada Takeki, ed. *Yōkyoku tsūkai*. 2nd edn. 8 vols. Tokyo: Hakubunkan, 1896.
Pater, Walter. 'The School of Giorgone'. *The Fortnightly Review* 28 (1877): 526–31.
Pellecchia, Diego. 'Ezra Pound and the Politics of Noh Film'. *Philological Quarterly* 92, no. 4 (Fall 2013): 499–516.
Poorter, Erika de. *Zeami's Talks on Sarugaku*. Amsterdam: J. C. Giebens, 1986.
Preda, Roxana. 'Three Cantos I-III: Calendar of Composition'. In *The Cantos Project*. Online.
Preston, Carrie J. *Learning to Kneel: Noh, Modernism, and Journeys in Teaching*. New York: Columbia University Press, 2016.
Reck, Michael. *Ezra Pound: A Close-Up*. New York: McGraw-Hill, 1967.
Redman, Tim. *Ezra Pound and Italian Fascism*. Cambridge: Cambridge University Press, 2009.
Régnier, Henri de. 'Odelette IV'. In *Jeux Rustiques et Divins*, 228–9. Paris: Société du Mercure de France, 1897.
Rodman, Tara. *Altered Belonging: The Transnational Modern Dance of Itō Michio*. PhD Thesis: Northwestern University, 2017.
Roseki. 'Hechimabutsu'. *Takarabune* 3, no. 1 (November 1902): 4–7.
Roseki, ed. *Keichū kushū*. 2 vols. Ōsaka, 1896–7.
Roseki. *Kushū*. Edited by Tsubouchi Nenten. Tokyo: Furansudō, 2009.
Ruthven, K. K. *Ezra Pound as Literary Critic*. London: Routledge, 2013.
Sakanishi Shio. 'Manukarezaru kyaku: Ezura Paundo (ichi)'. *Eigo bungaku sekai* 7, no. 8 (November 1972): 2–4.
Sakanishi, Shio. 'Manukarezaru kyaku: Ezura Paundo (ni)'. *Eigo bungaku sekai* 7, no. 9 (December 1972): 10–12.
Salel, Hugues. *Les dix premiers livres de l'Iliade d'Homère, prince des poètes*. Paris: Jehan Loys, 1545.
Sasaki Suguru. *Iwakura Tomomi*. Tokyo: Yoshikawa, 2006.
Satow, Ernest. *A Diplomat in Japan*. London: Seeley, Service & Co., 1921.
Sawai Taizō. *Muromachi monogatari to kohaikai: Muromachi no 'chi' no yukue*. Tokyo: Miyai Shoten, 2014.

Seelye, Catherine, ed. *Charles Olson & Ezra Pound: An Encounter at St Elizabeths.* New York: Grossman Publishers, 1975.
Senda Koreya. 'Atogaki – Yume to Genjitsu'. In Helen Caldwell, *Itō Michio: hito to geijutsu.* Translated by Nakagawa Einosuke, 157–89. Tokyo: Hayakawa shobō, 1985.
Shiki. *Bokujū itteki.* Tokyo: Iwanami shoten, 1994.
Shiki. *Fudemakase.* Edited by Kanai Keiko, Munakata Kazushige and Katsuhara Haruki. Tokyo: Iwanami shoten, 2003.
Shiki. *Haikai taiyō.* Tokyo: Iwanami shoten, 2016.
Shiki. 'Keichū kushū jo'. In *Keichū kushū,* edited by Roseki, n. p. Vol. 1. Ōsaka, 1896.
Shiki. *Kushū.* Edited by Takahama Kyoshi. Tokyo: Iwanami shoten, 2013.
Shiki. *Shiki zenshū.* Edited by Masaoka Chūsaburō. 22 vols. Tokyo: Kōdansha, 1975–8.
Shiki, Meisetsu, Kyoshi and Hekigotō, eds. *Buson kushū kōgi.* 4 vols. Tokyo: Hototogisu, 1911.
Shioji, Ursula. *Ezra Pound's* Pisan Cantos *and the Noh.* Frankfurt am Main: Peter Lang, 1998.
Sima Qian. *The First Emperor: Selections from the* Historical Records. Edited and translated by Raymond Dawson. Oxford: Oxford University Press, 2007.
Slatin, Myles. 'A History of Pound's Cantos I-XVI, 1915–1925'. *American Literature* 35 (March 1963): 183–95.
Spencer, Herbert. *The Philosophy of Style.* New York: Appleton & Co., 1872.
Spencer, Herbert. *Philosophy of Style: An Essay.* Tokyo: Kimura & Sons, 1887.
Stock, Noel. *The Life of Ezra Pound.* Harmondsworth: Penguin, 1974.
Stoicheff, Peter. *The Hall of Mirrors: Drafts and Fragments and the End of Ezra Pound's Cantos.* Ann Arbor: University of Michigan Press, 1995.
Sugiyama Seiju. *Kōri Torahiko: Sono yume to shōgai.* Tokyo: Iwanami shoten, 1987.
Surette, Leon. *A Light for Eleusis: A Study of Ezra Pound's Cantos.* Oxford: Clarendon, 1979.
Suzuki Hideo, ed. *Ise monogatari hyōkai.* Tokyo: Chikuma Shobō, 2013.
Synge, J. M. *The Playboy of the Western World: A Comedy in Three Acts.* Dublin: Maunsel and Company, 1911.
Takahashi, Miho. 'Kasōdaijō no Herakuresu: Ezura Paundo han "Torakisu no onnatachi" wo meguru ichikōsatsu'. *Ezra Pound Review* 10–11 (2008): 1–16.
Takayanagi Toshiya, *Nakae Tōju no shōgai to shisō.* Tokyo: Kōjinsha, 2004.
Takeishi, Midori. *Japanese Elements in Michio Ito's Early Period (1915–1924): Meetings of East and West in the Collaborative Works.* Edited and revised by David Pacun. Tokyo: Gendaitosho, 2006.
Tanaka Heiji, ed. *Kembu no shishū.* Kyoto: Kōyūsha, 1893.
Terrell, Carroll F. *A Companion to* The Cantos *of Ezra Pound.* 2 vols. Berkeley: University of California Press, 1980.
Terrell, Carroll F. *A Companion to* The Cantos *of Ezra Pound.* 2nd edn. Berkeley: University of California Press, 1993.
Tharp, Louise Hall. *Mrs. Jack: A Biography of Isabella Stewart Gardner.* Boston: Little, Brown and Company, 1965.

Tsunoda Shirō. 'Paundo to Kume Tamijūrō no kōyū'. In *Ezura Paundo kenkyū*, edited by Fukuda Rikutarō and Yasukawa Akira, 11–15. Kyoto: Yamaguchi shoten, 1986.
Tyler, Royall, ed. *Japanese Nō Dramas*. Harmondsworth: Penguin, 1992.
Ueda Masa'aki. *Sumiyoshi to Munakata no kami*. Tokyo: Chikuma Shobō, 1988.
Umehara Takeshi and Kanze Kiyokazu, eds. *Nō wo yomu*. 4 vols. Tokyo: Kadokawa gakugei shuppan, 2013.
Umewaka Minoru. *Nikki*. Edited by Umewaka Rokurō and Torigoe Bunzō. 7 vols. Tokyo: Yagi shoten, 2003.
Umewaka Minoru and Josui Ikiru. 'Ishin tōji no nōgaku'. *Nōgaku* 1, no. 1 (July 1902): 21–5.
Umewaka Rokurō. 'Bōfu no kushin'. *Nōgaku* 7, no. 2 (February 1909): 48–56.
Wada Katsushi. *Shiki no isshō*. Mishima: Zōshin, 2003.
Waley, Arthur, ed. *The Nō Plays of Japan*. London: George Allen & Unwin, 1921.
Wallace, Emily Mitchell. 'Interior of 166 Fernbrook Avenue and Other Matters'. Conference paper given at *The Ezra Pound International Conference*, Wyncote. 22 June 2017.
Whistler, James McNeill. *The Gentle Art of Making Enemies*, 2nd edn. New York: G. P. Putnam's Sons, 1892.
Wright, Adrian. *The Innumerable Dance: The Life and Work of William Alwyn*. Woodbridge: Baydell Press, 2008.
Yamaguchi Seiichi. *Fenorosa: Nihon bunka no senyō ni sasageta isshō*. 2 vols. Tokyo: Sanseidō, 1982.
Yamazaki Kagotarō, *Haikaishi dan*. Tokyo: Hakubunkan, 1893.
Yanagida Izumi. 'Meiji bungaku ni okeru haikai seishin'. In *Zuihitsu: Meiji bungaku*, 160–77. 3 vols. Tokyo: Heibonsha, 2005.
Yano Hōjin. *Eibungaku yawa*. Tokyo: Kenkyūsha, 1955.
Yeats, W. B. 'A People's Theatre: A Letter to Lady Gregory'. *Irish Statesman* 1, no. 23 (29 November 1919): 572–3.
Yoshida Sachiko. '*Hagoromo* to *The Cantos*: Paundo no Paradise no ichidanpen'. In *Ezura Paundo kenkyū*, edited by Fukuda Rikutarō and Yasukawa Akira, 169–88. Kyoto: Yamaguchi shoten, 1986.
Zhao Jianhong, 'Chūnichi hagoromo setsuwa kō'. *Chūgokugaku ronshū* 40 (July 2005): 52–70.

Index of Published Works by Pound

'Affirmations VI: The "Image" and the
    Classical Japanese Stage'   134
Awoi no Uye   8, 15, 16, 163, 165–6, 191,
    192, 205, 213, 216

The Cantos
    'Cantos 86-7'   225–6
    'Cantos 88-9'   226–7
    'Canto 97'   230
    'Canto 98'   231
    'Canto LXXVII'   225–6
    'Canto LXXXV'   224–5
    'Canto LXXXVI'   225
    Drafts and Fragments   232–6
    A Draft of the Cantos 17-27   17,
        187–90
    A Draft of XVI Cantos   14, 185–6
    A Draft of XXX Cantos   17–18, 192–5
    The Fourth Canto   184–6
    The Pisan Cantos of Ezra Pound   3, 16,
        18, 204, 208–16, 218, 222
    'Three Cantos–I'   17, 176–8, 189–91,
        194, 208–11, 214, 220, 224, 228–9
    'Three Cantos–II'   178–9
    Thrones 96-109 de los cantares   217,
        230–1
Certain Noble Plays of Japan   8, 157, 163,
    168–70, 180
'Chronicles'   119
'The Classical Drama of Japan'   7, 69,
    120–2, 155, 219
'The Classical Stage of Japan: Ernest
    Fenollosa's Work on the Japanese
    "Noh"'   11–12, 126–8, 130, 132–4,
    142, 144, 152, 155–6, 168, 199, 219,
    237
'The Coming of War: Actaeon'   160
'The Condolence'   67

'D'Artagnan Twenty Years After'   77

'Early Translators of Homer'   170
'Edward Wadsworth–Vorticist'   66, 75

Elektra   15, 218
'Elizabethan Classicists–II'   223
'Epitaph'   73
*Ezra Pound and Dorothy Shakespear: Their
    Letters, 1909-1914*   21, 65, 119
'Ezra Pound Asks Scholars Here to Solve
    Issues'   206
Ezra Pound's Letters to His Parents   8,
    11, 13, 17, 64–6, 117, 119, 126, 136,
    139–41, 147, 149–50, 153–4, 156–8,
    168, 170, 175, 185–7, 191
*'Ezra Pound Speaking': Radio Speeches of
    World War II*   207

'Fan Piece for Her Imperial Lord'   73
'A Few Don'ts by an Imagiste'   1, 24–5,
    37, 70–1
'From Rapallo: An Ezra Pound Letter'
    140

'The Garden'   67–8
Guide to Kulchur   14, 18, 199–200

'Histrion'   124
'How I Began'   1–2, 6, 71–2, 74, 78, 145
How to Read   188

'In a Station of the Metro'   1–4, 41–2,
    68–75, 77, 119
'In Durance'   2
'Itarii tsūshin'   206–7

Kakitsuhata   163, 166, 168, 170

The Letters of Ezra Pound 1907-1941   1,
    7–8, 13, 67–8, 122, 175, 185, 192,
    221
*The Letters of Ezra Pound to Alice Corbin
    Henderson*   12, 142–5, 150, 175,
    177
'Liu Ch'e'   119
A Lume Spento and Other Early Poems
    160

'Music: Le Mariage de Figaro'   159

'Noh' or Accomplishment   8, 110, 139, 141–2, 169–71, 175, 178, 180, 192, 202, 204, 218, 220, 222, 226, 236–7

'Pastiche: Regional–XVIII'   182, 207, 217
'Patria Mia: VIII'   66
Personae   2, 160
Plays Modelled on the Noh (1916)   8, 11, 13, 135, 154–63, 171
Pound/The Little Review: The Letters of Ezra Pound to Margaret Anderson   65, 181, 188
'Praise of Ysolt'   160

'Remy de Gourmont'   76
'The Renaissance–II'   17, 188, 236
'The Renaissance–III'   188
Review of Certain Noble Plays of Japan and 'Noh' or Accomplishment   169–70

Section: Rock-drill de los cantares   85–95, 217, 222–30
The Selected Letters of Ezra Pound to John Quinn   126, 147, 149, 157, 179, 181
'The Serious Artist'   146, 185
'Sestina for Ysolt'   160
The Spirit of Romance   152, 159, 198
'The State Should Move Like a Dance'   18, 201, 236

'Study of Noh Continues in West'   140–1, 205, 222
'Sword-Dance and Spear-Dance'   148–9, 154

Le Testament de Villon   16, 18, 186
The Translations of Ezra Pound   8, 218, 220, 222
'Totalitarian Scholarship and the New Paideuma'   18, 197, 205
'To Whistler, American'   66–7
'To Ysolt. For Pardon'   160
'Tri-lingual System Proposed for World Communications: Noted Scholar of Noh Suggests Bilingual or Trilingual Edition of Hundred Best Books of Japanese Literature'   14, 205, 221
'Ts'ai Chih'   73–4

'Usury and Humanity Do Battle While China is Heavily Engaged'   206

'Vortex'   11–12, 125, 130, 143, 158–9, 163
'Vorticism'   2, 6–7, 9–11, 27, 75, 77–8, 124–6, 131, 144, 147, 171
'VOU Club'   198

Women of Trachis   15, 18, 218–20, 227, 233

'Xenia I-VII'   73, 218

Yoro   220, 233

Index of Names

Actaeon 14, 17, 160, 183–4, 188, 194
Adams, Brooks 226
Agamemnon 218
Akemi 35
Aldington, Richard 122
Alexander, Neal 155–6
Alfred, Prince 97–8
Al-Kamil, Sultan 182
Alwyn, William 197
Amaterasu 119, 121, 129–30, 145, 204, 219
Anderson, Margaret 180–1, 188
Anderson, William 107, 115
Aoi no ue 163–6, 213, 215, 234–5
Aoi no ue 8, 15–16, 18–19, 109, 139, 163–6, 191–2, 202–3, 205, 212–13, 215–16, 218, 234–5, 237
Aphrodite, *see* Venus
Apollo 167–8
Arrowsmith, Rupert Richard 3–4, 67, 69, 74, 117, 209–10, 210 n.76
Arsinoe 231
Asai Chū 31–3
Ashikaga Yoshimasa 105, 118
Ashikaga Yoshimitsu 81, 105, 118
Ashikaga Yoshimochi 179
Asquith, Herbert 137, 212
Aston, W. G. 5–6, 41–6, 56, 58, 61, 65, 68, 104–7, 114–15, 119, 142, 168–9, 189
Atarashiki tsuchi 14, 17–18, 202–3, 205, 213, 216
Auden, W. H. 200
Awoi no Uye, *see* Aoi no ue

Bacigalupo, Massimo 16, 212, 232–3
Barrie, J. M 181
Bashō 4–6, 23–4, 26–7, 29, 34–9, 42–7, 49–59, 64, 70, 72, 74, 167
Baucis 19, 223, 227, 229
Bédier, Joseph 160, 162–3
Bénard, Charles 100
Benton, Thomas Hart 226

Béroul 159, 162
Binyon, Laurence 64, 115, 117–19, 121, 126–7, 130, 133, 141, 150, 187, 209–10
Bird, William 185
Blair, Hugh 25
Botticelli, Sandro 178, 211
Brinkley, Francis 41, 112–13, 115, 118–20, 127, 155, 170, 199, 204
Brinkley, John 186
Britten, Benjamin 200
Brooks, Van Wyck 24, 104
Browning, Robert 150, 176, 178
Buddha 128–9
Buddha 136
Buddhism 34, 37, 46, 48, 50, 62, 123, 127, 132, 164, 168, 202–4, 210
Bush, Christopher 17, 198, 202
Bush, Ronald 9, 181 n.28, 184, 232
Buson 37–9, 44, 49, 51–2, 54, 56–9, 61–3
Byron, Lord 138
Byron, Mark 68

Cabestanh, Guillems de 14, 183–4
Caldwell, Helen 136–7
Callimachus 190
Campbell, Joseph 63
Cao Zhi 74
Carr, Helen 3, 10, 63, 65, 124
Catullus 73, 146–7, 183
Chamberlain, Basil Hall 3, 5–6, 43–51, 53–9, 61, 64–5, 68–70, 73–4, 86, 99, 105–6, 111, 113, 115, 119
Chang, Carsun 225
Chisolm, Lawrence 101, 104, 108, 115
Chiyo 43, 48, 56
Chōryō 111, 142
Christianity 204
Chrysothemis 218
Chūinbon Heike monogatari 170
Cid, El 14, 152, 179
Circe 230–1
Coffman, Stanley 3, 9

Index of Names

Colvin, Sidney   115
Confucianism   144, 188, 195, 204, 225–6, 230
Confucius   212, 223
Corot, Jean-Baptiste Camille   32
Couchoud, Paul-Louis   56–9, 61–2, 73
Cunard, Maud   137, 156
Cunard, Nancy   192
Cunizza   192–3
Cythera, *see* Venus

Daigo, Emperor   82, 89
Danaë   188, 192–3
Dante Alighieri   121–2, 126, 130, 135, 145, 150, 152, 166–7, 171, 179–80, 191–2
Daphne   168
Date Munenari   84
Débussy, Claude   136
Demeter   189–90, 230
Diana   121, 183, 188, 192, 228
Dickins, F. V.   6, 41, 58–9, 67–9, 98–9, 106, 114–15, 120, 142, 199
Dōgen   30
Dōjōji   111, 138–9
Dōsen   148
Dowland, John   205, 221
Duncan, Ronald   198, 200

Eboshiori   131
Eder, David   60
Edwards, John   8, 15, 221–2
Edwards, Osman   109, 112, 119
Eiki   52
Eishō, Empress Dowager   10, 85, 94–5, 105, 111
Elektra   218
Elektra (by Richard Strauss)   138, 149
Eliot, T. S.   8, 119, 200, 221
Ewick, David   3, 8–9, 13, 18, 55, 78, 116, 124, 136–8, 140–1, 149, 208–9, 216, 233

Farr, Florence   63
Félix, Rachel   159
Fenollosa, Ernest   7–12, 15–16, 24, 54, 99–124, 126–7, 130–2, 134–5, 139–41, 144–5, 150–2, 155, 163–71, 178–9, 191–2, 199, 204, 209, 218, 220, 222, 226–7, 231–4, 236–7

Fenollosa, Mary McNeil   7, 108–10, 119–20, 122, 139, 164
Ferguson, Robert   62
Fisher, Margaret   16, 186
Fleming, Rudd   18, 218
Flint, F. S.   2, 6, 59–69, 71–3, 76
Florian-Parmentier, Ernest   66
Flory, Wendy   233
Fontanesi, Antonio   32–3, 48, 101–2
Foujita, Léonard, *see* Fujita Tsuguharu
Franck, Arnold   202
Frazer, James   188–90, 219, 228
Frederic II, Emperor   182, 207
Frémont, John Charles   226–7
Froula, Christine   13, 146, 149, 183
Fudō-Myō-ō   164
Fujisawa no Nyūdō   131–2
Fujita Fujio   136–7
Fujita Tsuguharu   137, 140, 157
Fujitomi Yasuo   227, 236
Fujiwara no Takaiko   15, 166–8, 233, 235
Furukawa Hisashi   81, 83–4, 94, 97, 110
Fusetsu   5, 31–4, 36–9

Gabō Sanjin   5, 42
Gakkai   84
Gardner, Isabella Stewart   104
Gart, Hermione   147, 193–4
Garthorne-Hardy, Robert   137, 140
Gaudier-Brezska, Henri   2, 12, 145, 147, 149, 153–4, 161, 165, 171, 182–3, 194, 198, 201
Gengenichi   5, 42
Genji   15, 129, 134, 161–5, 171, 197, 204, 211, 215, 219, 234
Genjō   142
Gikeiki   131–2
Giles, Herbert   73–4
Golding, Arthur   168, 227
Go-Tsuchimikado, Emperor   83
Grant, Ulysses S.   85, 103
Guanzi   230

Hachinoki   97
Hagoromo   7–8, 11, 14–18, 31, 69, 98–9, 109–10, 120–2, 128, 130–5, 141, 145, 150–1, 157, 166, 169–70, 177–8, 180–2, 194, 198, 204–5, 207
Hajitomi   109, 134, 163
Hakuryō   120–1, 170, 215, 222

Hakutani, Yoshinobu 3, 6, 68, 70
Hall, Donald 135
Hanada Ryōun 133
Hara Setsuko 202
Hardacre, Helen 92–3
Harmer, J. B. 3, 6, 119
Hartmann, Sadakichi 53–6, 59, 61, 73, 78
Hashitomi, see Hajitomi
Hatcher, John 115, 117
Hayashi Gahō 204
H. D. 125, 147, 160, 165, 193, 228
Hearn, Lafcadio 5–6, 43–5, 48, 50, 52, 56, 59, 61, 64, 68, 72–3, 146
Hegel, G. W. F. 10, 99–103, 115
Heijō 94
Heike monogatari 169–70
Heizei, Emperor 133
Hekigotō 58
Henderson, Alice Corbin 12–13, 141–2, 145–6, 150, 175
Hera 170
Hirata Kiichi 109–12, 120–2, 124, 127, 131, 135, 143–4, 151, 155, 164–6, 169
Hirosada 107
Hiroshige 49
Hitomaru 169
Hofmann, Reto 200
Hofmannsthal, Hugo von 138, 149
Hokusai 1, 3–4, 67, 69, 76
Homer 132, 135, 150, 152, 170–1, 175, 179, 180, 199, 206, 214–15
Honda Kinkichirō 31
Hori Masato 238
Hōshō Arata 206
Hōshō Kurō 83–5, 94, 97
Houwen, Andrew 142
Hughes, Glenn 191–2
Hulme, T. E. 2, 36, 62–4, 67–8, 71, 75, 180–1

Ibsen, Henrik 165
Iei Michiko 123
Ikenouchi Nobuyoshi 85
Imamura, Tateo 140, 186, 212
Inada Hogitarō 3–4
Ise monogatari 91–2, 166–7
Iseult, *see* Yseult
Ishibashi Hiro 135

Isis 190, 228, 230
Isolt, *see* Yseult
Itami Mansaku 202
Itō Masayoshi 167
Itō Michio 7, 135–41, 148–51, 153–7, 178, 196, 212, 218–19, 226
Itsumin Koji 148
Itys 183–4
Iwakami, Haruko 114
Iwakura Tomomi 10, 41, 84–5, 101, 103, 106
Iwasaki, Yozan T. 191
Iwasaki Ryōzō 140–1, 186
Izen 50
Jacques, Henri 182
Jefferson, Thomas 17, 187–8, 190–1, 193
Jimmu, Emperor 204
Jingū, Empress 87–8, 93
John, Augustus 137
Jōsō 50, 74
Josui Ikiru 83–4, 96

Kagekiyo 15, 169–70, 179–80, 182, 192, 199, 204, 210, 215
Kagekiyo 8, 15, 18, 112, 157, 163, 169–70, 179–82, 191–2, 197–9, 204, 206–7, 210, 214–16
Kakitsubata 8, 15–16, 112, 163, 166–7, 169–70, 181, 191, 232–3, 235
Kakuyū, *see* Toba Sōjō
Kanami 81, 118, 127
Kanawa 110, 138–9
Kandinsky, Wassily 75
Kaneko Kentarō 101–2
Kannon 11–12, 14–15, 17, 19, 132–4, 145, 151–2, 160, 170, 178, 181, 184–5, 189–90, 195, 201, 209–11, 213–15, 220, 228, 230–1, 233–4
Kant, Immanuel 108
Kantan 99, 104
Kanze Katsuko 81
Kanze Kiyokado 137
Kanze Kiyokazu 87, 120, 132, 167
Kanze Kiyotaka 81, 83–5
Kanze Kokusetsu 95
Kanze no Ujinobu, *see* Komparu Zenchiku
Kanze Tetsunojō 84
Katagiri Yōichi 88, 166
Kayano Hatakazu, *see* Kōri Torahiko

Index of Names 257

Kayoi Komachi 7, 110, 127–30, 133–5, 161, 180, 191, 235
Keene, Donald 31, 34, 85
Kenner, Hugh 3, 8–9, 15–16, 19, 142, 175
Kenshin 133, 151, 170
Kenshu, *see* Kenshin
Kikaku 42, 54
Kimura Shotarō 60
Kindellan, Michael 222
King, Marion 217
Kinuta 7, 69, 109, 119–20
Kitagishi Yūkichi 237–8
Kitasono, Katué 14, 18, 77–8, 141, 186, 191, 196–201, 203–5, 207, 215, 218–19, 221
Kiuchi Toru 3, 6, 68, 72
Kiyotsugu, *see* Kanami
Klaproth, M. J. 204
Kleitz, Dorsey 136–7, 139–41, 155, 212
Klytemnestra 218
Kodama, Sanehide 1, 14, 16, 18, 64, 77, 120, 122, 140–1, 186–7, 191, 196–9, 201, 203–5, 219–22
Kokinshū 60, 88–9, 92, 105, 143, 162
Komachi 3, 15–16, 67, 69–70, 127–9, 145, 162, 234–5
Komparu Zenchiku 132, 167
Konakamura Kiyonori 86, 92, 97
Kongō Tadaichi 85
Kōri Torahiko 7, 13, 110, 137–41, 149–50, 153, 155, 157, 186, 218, 226
Kornicki, P. F. 41, 114
Kōson 29–30, 35, 46, 49–51
Koyama Shōtarō 32–3
Kōyō 35, 46, 49–51
Kuanon, *see* Kannon
Kumamoto Kenjirō 32
Kumārajīva 166
Kumasaka 14–15, 131–2, 148, 152, 169, 179, 199, 210, 212, 214–15
Kumasaka 7–8, 14–15, 112, 131–2, 135, 148, 150, 152–5, 157–8, 169, 171, 177, 179, 181, 191, 199, 206–7, 210, 212, 214–15
Kume Kunitake 85, 94, 106
Kume Tamijūrō 7, 13–15, 139–41, 151, 153, 155, 157–8, 186–7, 192, 196, 201–2, 205, 212, 218, 221–3, 226
Kume Taminosuke 140

Kung, *see* Confucius
Kurata Yoshihiro 83–5, 95, 97, 103
Kuroda Nagahiro 101–2
Kuthera, *see* Venus
Kwannon, *see* Kannon
Kyoshi 27, 44, 52, 58

La Farge, John 101
Lehmann, Elisabeth Maria 136
Leona, Margaret 18, 197, 200
Lewis, Wyndham 2, 74, 124, 147, 198, 200–1
Li Bai 12, 18, 180–1, 197, 200, 220, 235
Li Bo, *see* Li Bai
Li Po, *see* Li Bai
Liebregts, Peter 180, 217–18
Loba 183
Longenbach, James 9, 12–13, 126–7, 155, 157
Lotus Sūtra 165–6
Lowndes, George 147, 193

MacCauley, Clay 67
MacLeod, Fiona 181
Maeda Kyōji 31, 36, 39
Maeterlinck, Maurice 136, 138, 149
Maihime Daria 136
Mailla, Joseph Anne-Marie de Moyriac de 204
Maitre, Claude Eugène 56–7, 59, 61, 73
Makin, Peter 184
Malatesta, Sigismondo 185, 188
Malek-Comel, *see* Al-Kamil, Sultan
Mallarmé, Stéphane 61–2
Manyōshū 12, 89, 105–6, 143, 162, 177
Martinelli, Sheri 224, 228, 234
Mathews, Elkin 64
Matsui Takako 24, 32, 39
Matsumoto Kintarō 83–4
Maximilian I, Emperor 117–18
Medici, Lorenzo de' 17, 64, 117–18, 187–8, 190–1, 193
Meiji, Emperor 85, 94
Meisetsu 51, 58
Metastasio, Pietro 177
Minamoto no Toshiyori 123
Minamoto no Yoritomo 204
Minamoto no Yoshitsune, *see* Ushiwaka
Miner, Earl 9, 15–16
Mionoya 169–70, 192

Mitford, Algernon 97–9, 105, 114–15, 119
Miyake, Akiko 16, 167
Mizusawa Tsutomu 212
Monro, Harold 65
Monroe, Harriet 1, 7, 9–10, 12–13, 66–8, 70, 73, 122, 142, 175, 178, 182, 194, 209
Moody, A. David 63, 168, 186, 200, 205–8, 211
Mōri Yasotarō 205
Morita, Norimasa 140
Moritake 6, 29–30, 35–6, 39, 42, 46, 48, 50–2, 57, 61–3, 68, 73–6, 78
Morrell, Ottoline 137, 139
Morris, Margaret 154
Morris, William 168
Morse, Edward S. 101, 103–4
Mosley, Oswald 201, 236
Motokiyo, *see* Zeami
Mozart, Wolfgang Amadeus 77, 205, 221
Murakata, Akiko 10, 108–13, 122, 155
Murasaki Shikibu 129–30, 163, 171
Musset, Alfred de 158–9
Mussolini, Benito 207, 236

Nabeshima Naomasa 84
Nagata Mikihiko 136
Narihira 15, 166–9, 233–5
Nevinson, Christopher 124
Nicholls, Peter 143
Nietzsche, Friedrich 149
Nishikigi 7–8, 10–11, 13, 112, 122–5, 127, 129–32, 135, 143, 154, 157–9, 161–2, 169, 171, 180, 182, 191, 205
Nishio Tada'atsu 84
Noguchi, Yone 1, 3–4, 6, 44, 44 n.20, 52–3, 55–6, 64–5, 68–72, 74, 138
Nōin 123
Norton, Charles Eliot 101

Okakura Kakuzō 108–9
Okikaze 88–9
Okimori Takuya 93
Okinori 129, 161
Ōkura Hanjirō 81–2
Ōmi fudoki 159
Onitsura 35, 50–1, 69–70
Ono, Ayako 49
Orestes 218
Oshukov, Mikhail 159, 161–2

Ota, Yuzo 43
Ōtani Masanobu 5, 44, 44 n.20
Ovid 161, 167–8, 171, 183, 212, 223, 227, 229
Ōwada Takeki 81–2, 86–9, 91–5, 98, 105–6, 112, 121, 124, 127–8, 130, 133, 142–4, 155, 164, 167–8, 170, 184 n.36, 231

Pater, Walter 103, 181
Peake, Charlotte 60
Pellecchia, Diego 16–18, 202
Perry, Matthew 226
Persephone 230–1
Phèdre 159
Philemon 19, 223, 227, 229
Phoebus, *see* Apollo
Poorter, Erika de 93
Porter, William N. 65, 67, 146
Pound, Homer 8, 11, 13, 66, 117, 119, 126, 136, 139, 141, 147, 149–50, 153–4, 156–7, 168, 170, 175, 186–7, 191
Pound, Isabel Weston 17, 64–5, 117, 126, 140, 150, 156, 158, 168, 185–7
Preda, Roxana 1, 13, 175
Preston, Carrie J. 13, 142 n.52, 149
Procne 183, 213
Purcell, Henry 205, 221

Quinn, John 8, 15, 126, 147, 149, 157, 179–81, 183, 221

Racine, Jean 159
Ransetsu 58–9
Raphael 100–1
Reck, Michael 218, 220, 222, 226–7, 233, 236
Redman, Tim 201
Régnier, Henri de 65–6
Rembrandt 118
Ridgeway, Peter 197
Rihaku, *see* Li Bai
Rodin, Auguste 136–7
Rodker, John 184–5, 187, 189
Rodman, Tara 13
Rokujō 163–6, 180, 206, 213, 234–5
Roseki 5, 44–5, 50, 59
Rousseau, Théodore 32
Ruthven, K. K. 160

Index of Names

Sachs, Leonard 197
Sadanaru, Prince 94
Saigō Takamori 148
Sainsbury, Hester 140, 157
Sakanishi, Shio 205
Sakanoue no Tamuramaro 11, 133, 184, 201, 228
Sakurama Kintarō 206
Salel, Hugues 170
Salmacis 183
Sampū 50
Sanyō 148
Sasaki Suguru 84
Satow, Ernest 97
Sawai Taizō 29
Seelye, Catherine 217
Senda Koreya 136
Sesshōseki 99
Sesshū 31, 33, 38–9, 102, 118
Shakespear, Dorothy 7, 65, 119–20, 200, 208, 213, 219, 233–4
Shakespear, Olivia 200
Shelley, Percy Bysshe 138
Shi Huangdi 90–1, 145, 180
Shiki 4–6, 23–52, 54, 56, 58–9, 62, 73, 78, 86, 97, 102–3, 118, 166
Shinkei 27
Shintō 92–3, 97, 114, 164, 189, 203, 219
Shioji, Ursula 208–9
Shōjō 7, 111, 132, 148
Shōshō 128–9, 180, 235
Shūbun 102
Shūishū 122
Sima Qian 91
Sinbu, *see* Jimmu, Emperor
Slatin, Myles 15
Sōgi 29, 36
Sōkan 6, 48–9, 57, 69, 73
Sōkyū 37
Soremonda 183
Sotoba Komachi 7, 15–16, 127
Soushenji 120
Souza, Robert de 66
Spann, Marcella 230
Spencer, Herbert 4–6, 23–9, 36–9, 43, 78, 101, 108
Stock, Noel 200
Stoicheff, Peter 16, 232–6
Stopes, Marie C. 126, 135, 141
Storer, Edward 63

Storm, Gerda 202
Strater, Henry 185
Strauss, Richard 138, 149
Sugiyama Seiju 137–9
Suma Genji 7, 15, 18, 110, 129–31, 134, 161, 163, 191, 196–7, 200–1, 211, 216, 219
Surette, Leon 193–4
Suruga fudoki 120
Suzuki Hideo 91
Synge, J. M. 155–6

Taigi 35, 50
Takahashi, Miho 219
Takaoka Masao 88
Takasago 7, 12–17, 19, 82–3, 86–95, 98, 104–7, 112, 114–15, 124, 127, 131, 137, 142–8, 152–3, 161–3, 167, 169, 171, 175–7, 179–85, 187, 189–92, 194–5, 199–201, 203, 207, 223–4, 227–31, 235–7
Takayanagi Toshiya 225
Takeishi, Midori 148, 154
Tamura 7, 11–12, 14, 17, 110, 132–5, 144–6, 148, 151–2, 160–1, 170, 177–8, 181, 184–5, 187, 190–2, 194–5, 199, 201, 203, 209–10, 216, 228, 230–1, 233
Tanaka Heiji 148
Tanaka Maki 166
Tanaka Uson 138
Tancred, F. W. 63
Tancrède 159
Tang, King 224
Tango fudoki 120
Terrell, Carroll F. 15–17, 184, 184 n.36, 212, 225–6, 231
Tharp, Louise Hall 104
Toba Sōjō 232
Tokuboku, *see* Hirata Kiichi
Tokugawa Iemochi 82
Tokugawa Iesada 84
Tokugawa Iesato 85
Tokugawa Yoshinobu 83
Tomonari 87–9, 91, 93, 98, 106, 143–4
Toyotomi Hideyoshi 81–2, 105
Tristan 8, 158–63, 165
Trivia, *see* Diana
Ts'ao Chih, *see* Cao Zhi
Tsukida Mōsai 148
Tsunemasa 7, 98
Tsunoda Shirō 140, 186

Tsurayuki 88–9
Tyler, Royall 87
Tytler, H. W. 190

Uchiyama Masami 8, 13, 148, 153
Ueda Masa'aki 87, 93–4
Umehara Takeshi 87, 120, 132, 167
Umewaka Manzaburō 110
Umewaka Manzaburō II 237
Umewaka Minoru 10, 18–19, 36, 83–6, 94–6, 104–5, 108–14, 127, 139, 140, 164, 170, 199, 217–19, 226, 237
Umewaka Rokurō 83, 219
Untermeyer, Louis 2–3
Upward, Allen 74
Ushiwaka 14, 131–2, 152, 169, 179, 210
Utchiyama Masirni, *see* Uchiyama Masami

Ventadorn, Bernart de 161–2
Venus 161, 178, 192, 211, 214–15, 220, 224, 228, 231
Vidal, Peire 14, 17, 183–4
Voltaire 159

Wada Katsushi 31
Wadsworth, Edward 66, 75
Wagner, Richard 159
Waley, Arthur 3–4, 141, 170–1, 178, 192
Wallace, Emily Mitchell 147, 193
Wang Yangming, *see* Yangming
Watson, William 210 n.76
Werkmeister, Heinrich 136
Whately, Richard 26
Whistler, James McNeill 1–2, 6, 48–9, 66–7, 73, 75, 77, 125, 147, 199

Wilde, Oscar 138
Wright, Adrian 197
Wu Daozi 220, 233

Xuanzhongji 120
Xuanzong, Emperor 12

Yamaguchi Seiichi 24, 99, 101, 103–4, 115, 140
Yamato Mitsuko 202–3
Yamato Rieko 202–3
Yamato Teruo 202–3
Yamazaki Kagotarō 30, 38–9, 42, 46–7
Yanagida Izumi 29
Yangming 225
Yano Hōjin 109
Yashima 50, 169
Yeats, Elizabeth 156
Yeats, W. B. 7–9, 119, 127, 137, 139–40, 153–4, 156–7, 168–9, 181, 221, 224
Yi Yin 225
Yōkō 107
Yōrō 220, 233
Yoshida Sachiko 121, 182
Yseult 159–63, 165
Yūgao 134, 163–4
Yumiyawata 98
Yuri no Tarō 131–2

Zeami 81, 86, 88–9, 93, 98, 109, 118, 122, 129–30, 169
Zeus 170, 189, 194, 215
Zhao Jianhong 120
Zhu Xi 204

www.ingramcontent.com/pod-product-compliance
Lightning Source LLC
Chambersburg PA
CBHW072131290426
44111CB00012B/1858